D1086824

Contexts for
Early English Drama

Contexts for Early English Drama

EDITED BY
Marianne G. Briscoe
AND
John C. Coldewey

INDIANA UNIVERSITY PRESS
Bloomington and Indianapolis

© 1989 by Indiana University Press

All rights reserved

No part of this book may be reproduced or utilized in any form or by
any means, electronic or mechanical, including photocopying and
recording, or by any information storage and retrieval system, without
permission in writing from the publisher. The Association of American
University Presses' Resolution on Permissions constitutes the only
exception to this prohibition.

Manufactured in the United States of America

Library of Congress Cataloging-in-Publication Data
Contexts for early English drama.
Includes index.
1. English drama—Middle English, 1100-1500—History
and criticism.   2. Mysteries and miracle-plays, English—
History and criticism.   3. Theater—England—History-
Medieval, 500-1500.   I. Briscoe, Marianne G.
II. Coldewey, John C.
PR641.C68   1989   822'.1'09   88-45099

ISBN 0-253-31413-5

1 2 3 4 5 93 92 91 90 89

Contents

Acknowledgments

From the time these essays were first discussed until their publication here we have accumulated many debts of thanks, and we are pleased indeed to acknowledge them now. The largest of these debts belongs to our contributors, who patiently and punctually followed our editorial instructions, and who bore our sometimes strident demands with good grace. The essays began their lives in relatively primitive form as part of a 1982 symposium sponsored by the Medieval Academy of America and hosted by the Medieval Institute at Western Michigan University; to Luke Wenger at the Academy and to Otto Gründler at Western Michigan we owe special thanks for their help at this early phase of Contexts. Thanks are also due to the British Academy, which made it possible for English participants to travel to the Seventeenth International Congress on Medieval Studies, where the symposium was conducted. Our gratitude, too, goes to individual Session Commentators, who we hope will be pleased at the effects their comments had. These were: David Bevington, Leonard Boyle, Clifford Davidson, Barbara Hanawalt, Alan E. Knight, William Mahrt, Christina von Nolcken, Barbara Palmer, Martin Stevens, and John Wasson.

Grants generously provided by the University of Washington supported travel during every phase of this book's preparation, and secretarial help in its final stages. Of all our contributors, we are indebted most to Larry Clopper, who selflessly acted as our on-site liaison with Indiana University Press. At the Press itself we benefited from the careful attention and the professional expertise of Janet Rabinowitch, who has ushered our manuscript with gratifying efficiency. Carey Hendron and Roberta Diehl saved us a wide range of awkward errors in form and style—although we must of course claim those that have survived their diligent pencillings.

In sum, our thanks go to more than a score of people who have shared our conviction that "context" is an important dimension of the study of early English drama; their continuing encouragement made this volume possible.

Abbreviations

CBEL	*Cambridge Bibliography of English Literature*
CFMA	Classiques Français du Moyen Age
CHEL	*Cambridge History of English Literature*
EDAM	*Early Drama, Art and Music*
EETS	Early English Text Society
ELN	*English Language Notes*
HMC	Historical Manuscripts Commission
MS	E. K. Chambers, *The Mediaeval Stage*
MLQ	*Modern Language Quarterly*
N&Q	*Notes and Queries*
PLS	*Poculi Ludique Societas*
PMLA	*Publication of the Modern Language Association*
REED	Records of Early English Drama
RES	*Review of English Studies*
RILA	*International Repertory of the Literature of Art*
RMA	Royal Musical Association
RORD	*Research Opportunities in Renaissance Drama*
SATF	Société des Anciens Textes Français
TLF	Textes Littéraires Français
VT	*Viel Testament*
WP	A. C. Cawley, *Wakefield Pageants in the Towneley Cycle*

Introduction

In the original essays presented in this volume, twelve distinguished English, American, and Canadian scholars have appraised old and new contexts, or cultural settings, for early English drama. They have written these essays in response to several recent developments in the study of English culture including a revival in social history studies, especially local and community history studies, which has given us a new understanding of the life of the communities that produced these plays. In addition, the past decade has seen the Records of Early English Drama project bring forward much detailed information about dramatic and musical production and performance in Great Britain in the period before 1642. Finally, some dramatic contexts, like art, music, and preaching, have long been recognized but can now benefit from a reevaluation of suitable approaches and premises. The contributors to *Contexts for Early English Drama* have only begun the work of integrating our understanding of the early English plays as literary works with these growing insights into the cultural, religious, and artistic environments that produced them. We hope this collection stimulates much further study.

To assist in such further study, the essays define pathways through an amalgam of familiar and unfamiliar territories, offering extensive bibliographies and surveys of earlier writings. They also address important questions of methodology and source materials, and they explore, sometimes speculatively, characteristic problems and special challenges that accompany research in these domains. They are written for students wishing to take up serious study of early English drama, and for scholars and teachers looking for guides and introductions to several of the various contexts through which the plays can be approached.

The title of this collection reflects the historical realities of the English vernacular drama, which flourished from the time of Chaucer to the time of Shakespeare. Both "medieval" and "renaissance" patterns of thought, social and aesthetic structures, are implicated in its composition and performance over these two centuries. While some of the essays here concentrate on earlier, hence "medieval" topics, it should be understood that in all cases the theatrical and dramatic traditions they address are traditions that bridge the cultural watershed usually considered to divide medieval and renaissance sensibilities.

This drama has, of course, far more than twelve contexts. The ones selected for this volume represent fields in which the contributors are specially expert and which provide a sense of the spectrum, ranging from the textual to the economic, in which early English drama can be studied. Broadly speaking, the essays fall into two divisions, the sociological and the literary. This reflects the essential distinction that drama enjoys: more than any other genre, it is a social as well as a literary endeavor, dependent upon both a text and a performance of that text before a certain audience.

The essays concerning sociological contexts focus on political, religious, and economic forces affecting this drama, on considerations of the auspices and circumstances under which plays were performed, and on the importance of the allied arts, visual and musical. Those concerning literary contexts include considerations tied more specifically to texts and performance: the historical records showing patterns of early productions; the evidence provided by codicology and textual histories; the actual staging of plays and the acting in them; the sharing of materials and methods in the related genre of sermons; and the continuing influence of continental dramatic and theatrical traditions. Taken together, these various contexts offer a fuller, more coherent and detailed picture than has been available before of how integral early English plays were to the culture that first produced them and that still echoes so powerfully in them.

Alexandra F. Johnston's "What if No Texts Survived?" opens the collection with a far-ranging survey of evidence found in historical records of dramatic activity. Johnston voices the growing uncertainty among scholars about what early English dramatic practices *were*. Records tell a rather different story regarding the popularity and production of dramatic activities of all kinds than do currently available histories of drama based on surviving dramatic texts.

Taking the opposite and complementary tack in "When Is a Text a Play? Reflections upon What Certain Late Medieval Dramatic Texts Can Tell Us," Donald C. Baker examines closely some texts that *have* survived. Baker demonstrates how the physical evidence of manuscripts and the histories of texts can be used, first, to construct a probable history of performances and, second, to make larger, sometimes surprising inferences about the writing–and rewriting–of early English plays.

Robert Potter, in "The Unity of Medieval Drama: European Contexts for Early English Dramatic Traditions," turns to questions posed by the existence of dramatic and theatrical traditions abroad. Potter points out that it is increasingly plausible to assume that the playscripts and dramatic events in medieval European vernaculars were part of a single complex tradition. He looks with special interest at how the English mystery cycles are in fact related variants of continental Passion plays, and how the study of English morality plays can benefit from attention paid to German and Dutch traditions.

In counterpoint to Potter's broad view, Lynette Muir provides, in "Medieval English Drama: The French Connection," a detailed survey of French language in English plays, of parallel passages in English and French biblical plays, and of similar methods of production to be found in the civic dramas of medieval and Renaissance England and France. Although the connections Muir examines are rarely direct, they suggest a practical, ongoing exchange between two distinct traditions of theatre.

The next three essays cross the Channel again, exploring particular English contexts: first, to consider the dramatic possibilities and theatrical limitations dictated by changing circumstances in the English economy; second, to view in some detail the changing political, religious, and economic fortunes of a single town, Chester, and observe what this can tell us about civic plays in general; and third, to characterize the plays presented in the universities.

John C. Coldewey, in "Some Economic Aspects of the Late Medieval Drama," explores how the rise of English guilds as economic units within English towns made possible the rise of great civic productions, and how small rural dramatic enterprises followed. Coldewey suggests that the willingness of guilds to mount the cycle plays had an economic motive, and that many of the smaller plays put on by towns and parishes across the land were produced for profit. When profits ceased and guilds weakened in the sixteenth century, the plays were abandoned.

In "Lay and Clerical Impact on Civic Religious Drama and Ceremony," Lawrence M. Clopper explains that the city of Chester produced its plays for a variety of reasons—economic, political, religious—all associated with its civic identity and with its leaders' sense of responsibility and moral purpose. Clopper argues that some of the revisions apparent in the Chester banns and plays can be traced to shifting Protestant factions within the town, and he offers new evidence to explain the secularization of the vernacular biblical drama in other towns around the country.

Alan H. Nelson, in "Contexts for Early English Drama: The Universities," provides a history of academic theatrical entertainments stretching from the fifteenth to the seventeenth century. Nelson distinguishes the plays produced by the universities from plays produced elsewhere, citing differences ranging from staging–the use of portable stages–to essential philosophy–the increasing importance of humanism.

Perhaps the most often cited but least studied genre related to medieval drama is the sermon. In "Preaching and Medieval English Drama," Marianne G. Briscoe examines how the two are related in themes, subject matter, and technique, and the extent to which preachers were involved in writing and producing plays. Briscoe shows how medieval drama, like sermons, uses rhetorical and argumentative structures to develop its themes.

Pamela Sheingorn's "The Visual Language of Drama: Principles of Composition" moves from consideration of rhetorical and theatrical argument to a study of the theatrical language of visual images. Sheingorn argues that the study of art and drama can go well beyond an appreciation of iconography; that understanding perception theory, which attends to artistic form and convention, can allow a modern audience new insights and help us to see what a medieval audience saw. By contrast, in "Music in the Cycle Plays," Richard Rastall examines what a medieval audience *heard*. Rastall surveys the philosophical and social aspects of music in the Middle Ages along with scholarship devoted to it, and he defines four musical traditions necessary to an understanding of the plays. He continues with a study of music surviving in the plays and concludes with a discussion of technical, stylistic, symbolic, and theatrical questions needing further investigation.

The last two essays turn specifically to the performance of medieval plays. Stanley J. Kahrl, in "Medieval Staging and Performance," reviews the profound changes in scholarly opinion over many years as the evidence from local records has come to light. Focusing in particular on the concept of theatrical space, Kahrl observes that critical notions of performance have been shaped in large part by limited, or wrongheaded, understanding of what constituted the "stage" for a medieval play. John R. Elliott, Jr., in "Medieval Acting," gathers evidence from England and the Continent to counter the belief that medieval acting was stylized or formal. Elliott argues that in virtually all eyewitness reports of medieval plays the same qualities are praised: naturalness and appropriateness of speech and gesture, and the ability to move the audience's emotions. The affective quality of medieval plays, he concludes, does not differ from that of great plays in any era.

Twelve essays can only begin to suggest the opportunities for greater study that await the student of early English drama. We hope this collection will set forth some provocative and interesting pathways and serve as a model for others to follow.

Marianne G. Briscoe
John C. Coldewey

ALEXANDRA F. JOHNSTON

What if No Texts Survived?

External Evidence for Early English Drama

I

Over the past two decades an increasing number of scholars have turned their attention to the surviving external evidence of dramatic activity in Great Britain in the late Middle Ages and early Renaissance. Earlier scholars led the way. In the nineteenth century J. O. Halliwell-Phillipps toured the provincial towns in search of Shakespeare.[1] J. Tucker Murray, less particular in his search, gathered evidence of the Elizabethan and later Stuart dramatic companies. Local antiquarians (such as the three generations of the Raine family in York), more interested in local activities than in the visits of strangers, toiled over editions and collections of local records published by local antiquarian societies. E. K. Chambers used many of these works to compile his still important general studies of the early English theatre.

The year 1955 was a seminal year in the study of medieval drama, for in that year two very different books appeared. The one, *English Religious Drama* by Hardin Craig, came at the culmination of a lifetime of study and marked the end of the old-style scholarship that tended to generalize, homogenize, and patronize the religious drama of the late Middle Ages. The other, *Medieval Drama in Chester* by F. M. Salter, was also written by a man at the end of a long and distinguished career. Salter presented his material first as one of the prestigious series of lectures, the Alexander lectures, at the University of Toronto in 1954. He reexamined the surviving external evidence related to the formation of the Chester Cycle, exploding most of the existing theories, and then went on to proclaim boldly, not the theological significance of the play, but its commercial importance to the city that sponsored it.

Within ten years younger scholars, coming fresh to the plays and excited by their dramatic power, began to turn, as Salter had, to the surviving evidence. In their quest they were greatly aided by the increased support provided by the British government for the care and housing of local documents. Salter's generation had been frequently at the mercy of volunteer archivists. Anna J. Mill, the pioneer collector of evidence for Scottish drama, was dependent on the judgment of Angelo Raine while she was working on the York records in the 1930s and 1940s. Mr. Raine let her examine those documents, and only those documents, that he felt were relevant. The documents were then housed in the damp cellars of the Guild Hall with few facilities for readers. Since the Second World War trained county archivists have been appointed with supporting personnel; documents have been catalogued and repaired; and reading space has been provided. The kind of research that was pursued by eccentric gentlemen in the nineteenth century and that became the crusading effort of a few determined academics in the early twentieth century is now possible for anyone with the necessary interest and expertise to seek out and decipher the documents.

Paralleling this improvement in the preservation and availability of original documents has been a renewed interest in local history in Great Britain. A researcher setting out on a quest for dramatic material now often has, besides the invaluable and voluminous Reports of the Historical Manuscript Commission, new editions of the Victoria County History replacing the less scholarly work of earlier contributors. Under the leadership of such historians as Peter Clark and Charles Phythian-Adams new detailed works on popular culture and local history undertaken at the universities are beginning to be published, and much valuable material is appearing in pamphlet form as a result of the energy of competent amateur researchers working in local record offices. All such offerings can be grist for our mill. They should be used, however, as guides to the manuscript sources. Other scholars whose interests are not those of a theater historian will sometimes fail to transcribe important details or inadvertently misconstrue the evidence.

In the twenty years following 1954, the quest for dramatic evidence intensified. Giles Dawson went to Kent. Stanley Kahrl turned his attention to Lincolnshire. Lawrence Clopper followed Salter to Chester, while R. W. Ingram returned to his native Coventry, and David Galloway returned to work in Norwich where he had grown up. Galloway was joined in East Anglia by John Wasson who turned his attention to the county records of Norfolk and Suffolk. John Coldewey undertook research in Essex for his doctoral dissertation under the direction of Donald Baker, while JoAnna Dutka, under the direction of John Leyerle at Toronto, used external evidence extensively in her dissertation (now published) on music in the cycle plays. Meanwhile, Arthur Cawley of Leeds, the dean of British scholars in medieval drama, had suggested that J. J. Anderson investigate Newcastle and had set a young Australian research student, Margaret Dorrell (now Margaret Rogerson), to work in York. It was there that I met her when I went to York myself in pursuit of some answers to the tantalizing questions raised by the York Cycle.

Meanwhile, Ian Lancashire, another student of Leyerle, had begun the same search on a different level. He began to assemble a supplement to Stratman's *Bibliography of Medieval Drama*, but once he moved into the publications of local antiquarian and record societies it was clear that what he was collecting went far beyond a mere supplement. The first collected result of his work has now been published as *Dramatic Texts and Records of Britain: A Chronological Topography to 1558.*

In 1974, two decades after Salter had delivered his lectures on the Chester Cycle at the University of Toronto, the first steps were taken to coordinate the work of all the scholars in the field of records research and to take it a step beyond the Malone Society Collections. The very large collections that were being gathered for York, Chester, Coventry, and Norwich seemed unsuitable for Malone format. Thus Records of Early English Drama (REED) was founded in Toronto in February 1975. REED combines two different approaches to external evidence: the search through original manuscripts and the collection of bibliographical references.[2] Today it has over forty scholars associated with its ongoing work. As General Editor of REED, I have been privileged to follow the progress of research all over Great Britain, and I want here to draw some preliminary conclusions regarding what the external evidence is telling us about English drama before Shakespeare. These conclusions, of course, are based upon incomplete data. Until the REED project is completed (and even thereafter), new evidence will continue to be uncovered. I launch myself upon sometimes controversial seas in this essay, hoping to make clear that we should all expect to reconsider our long-cherished ideas about medieval drama.

II

The three hundred years of dramatic activity in Great Britain from the thirteenth to the sixteenth century are bounded on either end by prohibitions—prohibitions so alike that one feels one is moving into the world beyond the mirror. Although there are a few incidental allusions to drama during the thirteenth and early fourteenth centuries, such as the important reference to a miracle at a Resurrection play in Beverley (Chambers, *MS*, II, pp. 238–39), almost all indications of the existence of plays in England before the last quarter of the fourteenth century are couched in terms of prohibitions. Bishop after bishop, following first Innocent III in his answer to a problem in Poland in 1207 and then the decretals of Gregory IX, issued prohibitions against "ludos inhonestos." In England these became particularly directed toward activities in churchyards and involving the adult minor clergy. Such prohibitions appear in the records surviving from Canterbury in 1213,[3] Lincoln in 1235 (p. 274), Worcester in 1240 (pp. 297, 313, 321), York (p. 486) and Durham in 1241 (pp. 440, 432), Chichester in 1245 (p. 461), and many more. What these prohibitions mean is less easily discovered. The activities that were being frowned upon do not appear to be what we would call plays. Rather the prohibitions seem to be addressing the kind of game recorded by Robert

Manning of Brun in *Handling Sin*. In that very early fourteenth-century poem, we have evidence from the story of the sacrilegious carolers that the "ludi inhonesti" were simply rowdy, and perhaps bawdy, singing and dancing (Furnivall, pp. 283–89). Indeed, the gloss to the decretals of Gregory IX explicitly excludes from the prohibition involvement by clergy in representations of the Nativity, Herod, the Magi, Rachel, and various Easter ceremonies (*Decretales*). What seemed of most concern to the bishops was the abuse of the priestly office and the desecration of hallowed ground. The same instinct to preserve decorum seems to be behind this late sixteenth-century prohibition of Archbishop Grindal of York:

> Item that the minister and churchewardens shall not suffer anye lordes of misrule or sommerr Lordes or ladyes or anye disguised persons or others in christmasse or at may games or anye minstrels morrie dauncers or others at Ryshebearinges or at any other tymes to come vnreverently into anye churche or chappell or churchyard and there daunce or playe anye vnseemelye partes with scoffes ieastes wanton gestures or rybaulde talke namely in the tyme of divine service or of anye sermon. (*REED: York*, I, p. 258)

This and similar edicts from other bishops—and, indeed, from secular courts influenced by such edicts—effectively brought to an end the community play-making that had been such a feature of British life for three hundred years.

The life of early English drama, rather than being "rounded with a sleep," then, is rounded with ecclesiastical bad temper. Yet though these pageants have indeed faded, they have, unlike Prospero's pageant, left considerably more than a "rack behind." What has been left is enigmatic and infuriating: a payment here, a complaint there, a property list, a fine, a list of pageants, a transfer of responsibility—all written for and by men who knew exactly what they were referring to (they had just seen it, after all) and who were anxious to satisfy not our curiosity but, in the main, the sharp eyes of the auditors.

Financial accounts provide the most valuable and frequent source of evidence. Whether a city or great household was supporting local drama or paying traveling players, the amounts paid out would be recorded. Similarly, any profit made would be recorded. It is from such accounts that we can reconstruct costumes and props from the ells of canvas, damask, or velvet that were bought or the amount of gold or silver foil that was paid for. We also learn the amount of lumber that was purchased for wagons or sets or other similar construction details. In some accounts we find records of payment to specific characters that allow us, in such cities as Chester, to compare the text and the banns with the actual performance practice in a given year. In some cities where the local plays were integral to the social fabric of the community—York, Chester, Coventry, Beverley, and Newcastle, for example—considerable evidence is found in city council minutes, memoranda, or guild ordinances. Sometimes, depending on local conditions, manuscripts from the offices of sheriffs, bailiffs, bridgemasters, and harbor masters provide evidence. In York, for example, the masters of Ousebridge rented the land on which most of the pageant houses stood, and so, from their accounts, we learn what guilds stored their pageants where. Occasionally, personal account books or diaries kept by priors, abbots, or other monastic officials survive and yield valuable insights into the activities in the religious houses that can supplement the few official accounts that have survived the dissolution. Churchwardens' accounts, supplemented by wills and inventories, provide much of the evidence for parish drama.

Records of the secular and ecclesiastical courts provide the other major source of evidence. Players, playmaking, or other revelry is sometimes the subject of a case before the justices of the court of quarter session or the archdeacon's or the bishop's courts. Sometimes they are the occasion of a libel suit. More often, however, references are incidental to a brawl, a seduction, a robbery, or a murder. These are the hardest to find since there is no logic to their survival; but they are often our most detailed accounts of actual playing conditions, especially if the verbatim depositions survive. Parish customs or other folk activity are frequently mentioned in the archdeacon's court records toward the end of the sixteenth century when the Sabbatarian laws were being enforced.

Other classes of documents, such as civil or ecclesiastical edicts, wills, documents concerned with the transfer of property, and letters, sometimes contain valuable evidence. REED editors necessarily read through much material that contains no relevant entries at all as they seek the evidence that will be gathered together into REED editions. These editions will form the basis upon which the history of public performance in Britain before 1642 can be rewritten.

In any work with records it is particularly important to appreciate the linguistic context of the evidence. It is very easy, for example, to be misled by a reference to a "ludi magister" in a Latin account. *Ludi magister* was the term used for an ordinary schoolmaster. Monks often had permission to withdraw for "ludi" in what, from the context, is clearly a form of rest and recreation away from the rigors of monastic life. The word *pagina* means (besides "page") an episode in a cycle play, a pageant wagon, and, we are discovering in some accounts, simply statues of parish patron saints (*REED: Devon*, pp. xxxi, xxii). A more fundamental problem exists in the words used to denote performers. A Receivers' Account from Exeter in 1568 refers to a group of performers as "lusoribus musicis" (*REED: Devon*, p. 152). Such refinements are virtually unknown elsewhere in the records. It is often impossible to distinguish whether a record is referring to actors or musicians when the reference is simply to "lusores," "histriones," "mimi," or "players." Conclusions drawn from records evidence, therefore, must always take into account the possible ambiguity of the linguistic context. We have found at the REED project that, as our glossarians work through more and more material, we can define usage more precisely, and we anticipate a useful collected glossary of terms. But until such a glossary is generally available we must always keep in mind that in the more laconic entries we may not be dealing with actors at all.[4]

III

The external evidence makes it clear that community drama, as it emerged in the fifteenth century, falls into three major categories: biblical drama, saints' plays, and folk drama, particularly Robin Hood plays. Biblical drama includes the large episodic narratives that have come down to us, but it was by no means confined to them. Evidence of plays at Christmas and Easter is plentiful. How many of these were what we would now categorize as liturgical it is impossible to say, but many, such as the ones at Lichfield, Staffordshire, undoubtedly were (Young, pp. 514–23). Other feast days had plays that may have dramatized the biblical basis of the feast, such as an apparent Assumption play at Leicester (Chambers, *MS*, II, pp. 376–77) and a Pentecost play at Lincoln, as well as the complex Marian Play in that city on St. Anne's Day (Kahrl, *Records*, pp. 27, 43–65). Other biblical episodes seem to have had lives of their own, unhampered by the liturgical year. Kingston upon Hull, in the East Riding of Yorkshire, produced a Noah play on Plough Day for nearly sixty years (Mill, "Hull Noah Play," pp. 489–505), and Pontefract, in the West Riding of Yorkshire, seems also to have had an independent Noah play (Homes, pp. 371–74). Churchwardens' accounts show that in the early sixteenth century the parish of St. Laurence Reading, Berkshire, did a play involving Adam and Eve one year, a Cain play another, and, to the confusion of all those who wish to identify plays with the liturgical year, apparently mounted a play of the Kings of Cologne on May Day, 1498.[5] From only a few towns—York, Chester, Coventry, Newcastle upon Tyne, Beverley, Norwich, and Lincoln—comes hard evidence that the plays were large, lavish, annual, and integral to the social fabric of a metropolitan community.[6] Some of the evidence, such as that from Essex, East Anglia, and Cornwall, indicates dramatic activity on a large scale, but mounted infrequently, for special occasions at the impetus of individual entrepreneurs such as Thomas Massey who, as R. W. Ingram has shown, single-handedly kept "medieval drama" alive in Coventry well into the seventeenth century (*REED: Coventry*, pp. 495–502). More often the evidence is of a small-scale, parish-based production, as integral to the life of the parish as the York Cycle was to York, but on a much more modest scale.

Saints' plays, though less frequent in the records than liturgical or narrative drama based on the scriptures, were performed all over the kingdom. Plays on Christina, Christian, Feliciana, Meriasek, Swithin,

Andrew, Eustace, Katherine, Nicholas, Thomas the Apostle, Lawrence, Thomas à Becket, James, George,[7] Dennis, and Mary Magdalen were performed, many in several places, as well as plays on less well known "saints" such as Tobias, Susannah, and Robert of Sicily.[8] Whether these were celebrating the saint for which a parish was named, were part of confraternal celebrations, or were demonstrating a miracle is hard to decide. There is early twelfth-century evidence, from the record concerning a St. Katherine play at Dunstable in Bedfordshire, that the common way to refer to saints' plays was as miracle plays. The record reads "ubi quendam ludum de S. Katerina (quem Miracula vulgariter appellamus)" (Riley, *Gesta*, p. 73). It is probable that the "ludum miraculum" that was the occasion of a brawl in Carlisle in 1345 was a saints' play (*REED: Cumberland, Westmoreland, Gloucestershire*, pp. 63–64). Yet the fourteenth-century *Treatise against Miracle Playing* (Davidson) casts its condemning net widely. Perhaps here again we should draw back from attempting dogmatic definitions and allow ourselves to see Jankin and the Wife of Bath attending more than saints' plays as they attend the "pleyes of Myracles."

The popularity of Robin Hood in the south and west of England and in Scotland is truly astounding. Exactly what is meant by a Robin Hood play or game is again unclear.[9] They were largely parish-based, associated with May Ales and other May Day activities such as morris dancing. There is some evidence that they represented a secular manifestation of the boy/bishop role reversal. In Wing, Buckinghamshire, for a few years in the sixteenth century, we have evidence that the Lord and Lady of the May, elsewhere identified as Robin Hood and Marian, were servants of a local landowner who explicitly granted permission allowing them to become the rulers of the festival.[10] On the other hand, Robin Hood, with his traditional cronies Little John and Maid Marian, may more normally have performed formulaic farces, versions of which have survived.[11] Hard evidence for Robin Hood activities is now available from over fifty locations (from such counties as Berkshire, Buckinghamshire, Cambridgeshire, Devon, Dorset, Herefordshire, Shropshire, Surrey, Wiltshire, and Worcestershire), and more is being found each year as we cull through the surviving churchwardens' accounts. The likelihood of parish references to a play at midsummer being on anything other than Robin Hood is seeming increasingly slim.

It was Robin Hood and other parish or folk games, rather than the great narrative episodic drama of such cities as York, that provoked the wrath of the Puritan bishops displayed in Grindal's injunction. The three great plays of York, for example, had been dealt with more directly, more ruthlessly, and far less openly several years before the general prohibition was issued (*REED: York*, I, pp. 352–70). City councils could be reached politically. The eradication of widespread peasant custom was far more difficult. The central authorities had to contend not only with long-held custom, but also with the indisputable fact that such activities were often the main source of income for a country parish. It was from the proceeds from their play, their ale, or their gatherings that the churchwardens of southern and western England repaired the fabric of their ancient buildings. Like their modern counterparts they had to struggle to repair the roof, mend the gate, shore up the pillars, or replace the rood screen. Indeed, one of the fascinating differences between civic drama of the midlands and the north and parish drama of the south is that in civic accounts one looks for dramatic entries primarily in the expense column, while in parish accounts one checks the receipt entries first.

Many small parishes were not satisfied to collect money from the local inhabitants. Like many a modern group, once they had their play "up," they took it on tour. In the late fourteenth and early fifteenth centuries, the town council of Reading, itself apparently uninterested in mounting plays, paid to see the plays of such surrounding villages as Henley on Thames in Oxfordshire, Sonning, Wokingham, Sindlesham, Aldermaston, and Yately in Hampshire.[12] In 1535 the Exeter Receivers' Accounts record payments to four "playing laddys" from the village of Towton (REED: Devon, p. 134). We do not know what the plays performed were. Indeed the largest body of the evidence cannot be tabulated by type because the type is simply not revealed. Again and again we have evidence of a "play" or payment to "players of enterludes," but no real evidence of the content of the plays.

Traveling groups were plentiful all over the kingdom from the mid-fifteenth century, making J. T. Murray's starting date of 1558 more than one hundred years too late. Evidence for their existence comes from payments made by city councils from general funds, from the mayor's special allowance, or from the privy purse allowances of priors or bishops. An outstanding example of their number and variety can be found in the York Chamberlains' Books from the 1440s (REED: York, pp. 65–77). Many of the named troupes are clearly musicians, but some are traveling players. Wherever these payments occur it is clear that we have not only troupes carrying warrants from the king or major magnates of the realm, but also groups that can be localized by villages or by the name of a member of the local gentry. Traveling players is a term, then, that applies not only to groups touring the provinces from London but also to more local groups on a more restricted circuit. Such a circuit is best demonstrated by evidence from the Carlisle accounts where the waits of such northern towns as Leeds, Wakefield, Richmond, Durham, and York are paid by the Carlisle Chamberlains (REED: Cumberland, Westmoreland, Gloucestershire, pp. 65–72). The acting troupe of "Mr. Smith of Coventry" (REED: Coventry, p. 251) is an example of players who toured locally, as they appear in the accounts of Abingdon, Berkshire.[13] The banns of the N-Town Cycle and the Castle of Perseverance show that these large plays did move from town to town. Whether each began as a town play and moved around the neighboring towns in East Anglia, where the flat terrain makes traveling with large wagons loaded with props and costumes feasible, or whether each was performed by local professional or semi-professional actors, it is impossible to tell. Indeed, the difference between "town players" and "local professional or semi-professional actors" may be a distinction without a difference.

Although records rarely tell us what play was being performed, they often do tell us where the players performed. New and substantial evidence from Shrewsbury indicates that the old quarry just outside the town was the location for all kinds of shows, including stage plays (Somerset, "Scenes"). This quarry still exists and is now part of the civic swimming pool. Here we have a known and measurable outdoor playing site. We also have new evidence from indoor sites. Alan H. Nelson has found interesting details concerning the occasional conversion of a Cambridge dining hall into a theatre. Most frequently the local guildhall was the location of at least one performance by a visiting troupe. Many of these guildhalls still stand, such as the tiny one in Leicester. These halls (often complete with great pillars to offend our modern obsession with sight lines) were so popular for playing in that when, as late as 1592, the village of Blandford Forum in Dorset built a new guildhall the companies came and hired the hall for several years thereafter (Blandford MS). There is some evidence that inn-yards were used by the players. The affray at the Red Lion in Norwich makes it clear that the inn-yard was being used by the King's Men at the time of the disturbance (Galloway, pp. 82–110). However, the overwhelming evidence for the location of performances points to rather small meeting halls without provision for elaborate staging devices.

IV

The broad pattern that emerges from the external evidence is of widespread folk drama throughout the countryside responding to the seasonal needs of a basically rural community. To catch a sense of what those customs were we would be wise to go beyond the corrupt surviving Robin Hood texts and first look more particularly at Robert Herrick's bucolic poems such as "Corinna Goes A-Maying" and the pastoral underpinnings of *A Midsummer Night's Dream* and *Love's Labours Lost*. Shakespeare was a country lad, and we should listen to the rhythms of the countryside under the mocking sophistication of his courtiers.

Second, there were many small-scale plays from parishes, villages, or small towns. These could be on almost any subject: biblical narratives, saints' lives, or secular farces bearing relationships both to Chaucer's Miller's Tale and to the plays of John Heywood. Some of these small plays were, like the York Cycle, both to the glory of God and to the honor and profit of the city, but many, it seems, were primarily for profit.

Third, there were the large occasional plays. These suddenly appeared in places like Chelmsford in Essex (Coldewey, *Essex*, pp. 294–322) or Boxford in Suffolk (Wasson, pp. 136–38) under the direction of a hired "property player," and galvanized the towns into a season of excitement. It has been argued, particularly by Coldewey, that such special enterprises needed the imported expertise of a professional to accomplish the lavish effects ("Player," pp. 5–12).

Finally, there is evidence for a few larger annual events sponsored by certain large towns for close to two hundred years. Many of these were the collective efforts of the craft guilds that formed the corporations of the cities. Some were the collective efforts of religious guilds. Many seem not to have been plays in a way we would define them, but rather a series of dumbshows or unrelated actions. For example, the Corpus Christi event in Dublin was made up of the following pageants in 1498: Expulsion from the Garden, Noah, Abraham and Isaac, Pharaoh, a combination of Moses and the people of Israel with Mary and Joseph and the Flight into Egypt, the Three Kings of Cologne, the Shepherds, the Crucifixion, Pilate, Anna and Caiphas, King Arthur, the Twelve Apostles, the Prophets, the Tormentors, the Nine Worthies, and St. George (Chambers, *MS*, II, pp. 363–64). All the processional events bear some relationship, in their origins, to the religious processions of the fourteenth century and, in their curtailments, to the military displays of the sixteenth century. They seem to grow from a ceremony marking community religious devotion and fold back into a ceremony marking community nationalistic fervor. All are in some way reflected in the surviving evidence of royal entries or other pageantry, recorded particularly in London but also in York and Coventry, and in such documents as the account of the royal progress of Henry VII throughout England in 1486.[14] I doubt that many beyond the surviving texts were much more than ceremonial displays or "ridings" such as the many ridings of St. George, Gog and Magog in London, or Yule and Yule's wife in York (*REED: York*, pp. 356–62). Such ridings were iconic statements, not dramatic narratives and, as such, bear as much relationship to the Jacobean masque as they do to the contemporary drama.

It is my belief that the few dramatic texts that have survived are the special ones. It is, for example, fascinating that the only places that have surviving evidence of large single productions are in East Anglia and Cornwall. This fits with the linguistic origin of the surviving lavish plays we have come to call moralities. Similarly, the mixture of short liturgical and nonliturgical Biblical plays is reflected in the survival of the so-called Shrewsbury fragments and the two noncyclic *Abraham and Isaac* plays, as well as others. What we are learning, however, is that for every *Castle of Perseverance* there were a dozen *Abraham and Isaacs* throughout the kingdom. We are learning that *Mankind*, with its small cast and deliberately inserted begging sequence, is more likely to represent the generality of moral interlude than *Wisdom*, with its need for lavish costuming and music. The normal payment in the surviving accounts is sufficient to pay the "five men and a boy" needed for *Mankind*, but is not sufficient to pay for the costumes, properties, and supernumeraries needed for *Wisdom*. Except for the large-scale productions of *Mary Magdalen* and the *Conversion of Paul* we have lost the genre of saints' plays. Indeed, we have lost the truly local saints' plays with the possible exception of *Meriasek* (Stokes). Similarly, the medieval and Tudor folk plays by their very nature are largely lost to us, paradoxically because some survived into the eighteenth century to become patronized by the antiquarians as folklore. What interests me here is that while the proportional survival of texts is unrepresentative, we still have examples of most of the types of plays named in the records. All we need to do is to find one of the three *Pater Noster* plays[15] and a complete *Creed* play and the set will be complete.

However, I want to end with a caveat. It has become very clear to me that we must disabuse our minds of the idea that a "Corpus Christi Play" is a generic term. The evidence makes it plain that, although Corpus Christi Day was a favorite day for playmaking, any play was possible. The churchwardens' accounts of the parish of Ashburton in Devon make this abundantly evident. In one year the offering at Corpus Christi seems clearly to involve King Herod, in another to involve devils, in another to include God Almighty and St. Rosmont, while in another year the production was of Robin Hood (*REED: Devon*, pp. 24–28). Similar evidence exists from all over the country. It is clear that the reference in the *Paston Letters* to playing Herod on Corpus Christi is not *prima facie* evidence for a cyclic narrative drama (Davis, pp. 113–14). The only demonstrably biblical cycle that was performed on Corpus Christi is the York Cycle. The Coventry plays were performed on Corpus Christi, but a careful reading of the evidence from Coventry suggests that the play there may have been a Creed Play. Because this play was mounted on Corpus Christi it has always been assumed that the remaining texts were fragments of a structure similar to York and Chester. It is this assumption that I feel we should question. First, the apparent absence of any Old Testament episodes in this play immediately sets it apart from the four complete cycles. Second, the allegorical figures, such as the Worm of Conscience in the Drapers' Pageant and the Mother of Death in the Cappers' Pageant, suggest a different kind of structure from the surviving texts (*REED: Coventry*, pp. 115–290). Third, the preacher in Rastell's *A Hundred Mery Tales* (1526) enjoins the reader, if he wishes to know about the Creed, to "go your way to Coventre, and there ye shall se them all played in Corpus Christi playe."[16] In Coventry the term "Corpus Christi Play" may have meant a Creed Play. This should not surprise us since every ten years in York the Creed Play was substituted for the regular cycle play on Corpus Christi.[17] The Chester Cycle, as we have it, is a Whitsun Play, and there is no evidence to state definitely either where or when the N-Town and Towneley plays were performed. The only certain evidence of playmaking activity in Wakefield comes from the prohibition of a performance there "on Whitsun or thereabouts" (Cawley, p. 125). The other external evidence normally cited connecting the Towneley Plays with Wakefield has recently been seriously challenged (Forrester and Cawley, pp. 108–16). A second possibility for a biblical cycle on Corpus Christi Day is the play at Beverley, but the only definitive list of episodes for that play comes from 1520, the year in which the newly rewritten play had its first and apparently last performance (Leach, pp. 218–19). Newcastle upon Tyne had a coherent series of biblical episodes for their event on Corpus Christi, but the nature of that event seems to have been different from York. At Newcastle the pageants were carried. This may only reflect the nature of the terrain, but it may also indicate that at Newcastle, as at places such as Aberdeen, Dublin, Hereford, Bury St. Edmunds, Ipswich, and Boston,[18] the Corpus Christi event was a procession of dumb shows or of spectacles rather than a coherent dramatic unit. There is strong evidence from several towns supporting the idea that corporate episodic presentations occurred on Corpus Christi Day, but we must be constantly alert to the three possible varieties of presentation: Biblical narrative drama, other episodic configurations such as Creed Plays, and processional pageantry. It has become clear that we cannot base an interpretation of any surviving text other than the York Cycle on the offices of the feast of Corpus Christi.

We have all been concerned during the last two decades to establish medieval drama as a literary mode worthy of critical attention. In our fascination with the richly complex texts that have been preserved for us, we have sought to find literary and religious contexts for the plays. The search has been exhilarating and, as the increasing number of good productions has shown, medieval drama has proved itself as a dramatic literature of rigorous vitality. Yet we have all been too quick to generalize, too anxious to assume that the surviving texts are all we need to consider, too content to spin our literary, critical, and theological webs independent of the factual context of the drama. We must begin to look at each text and each piece of evidence as the survival of a unique event similar to, but never identical with, any other. The players and playwrights of the period were marvelously flexible, responding to the situation that was presented to them. As Quince says to Bottom in *A Midsummer Night's Dream*, "and here's a marvelous convenient place for our rehearsal. This green plot shall be our stage; this hawthornbrake our tiring house" (III, i, 2–3). Such inventiveness is the hallmark of the community drama of England in the late Middle Ages and Renaissance. We must be sensitive to the evidence both of the texts and of the records. If we strip our minds of presuppositions and confront the evidence as it has survived to us, we will truly come to understand the literary, religious, and social context of what, for perhaps too long, we have persisted in calling medieval drama. Far from being merely a precursor to the Elizabethan stage, the dramatic literature and history of this period is the linchpin binding together the medieval world of Chaucer and the Tudor world of Wyatt, Sidney, Spenser, and Marlowe—as Tudor as it is Plantagenet. To seek to understand this dramatic form as a literary and social phenomenon is to seek to understand English society during a period of political, social, and religious change. It is the glass through which we can glimpse, however darkly, a vanished yet vital world.

NOTES

1. Halliwell-Phillipps collected his evidence in scrapbooks now mainly deposited in the Folger Shakespeare Library in Washington, D.C. The evidence has been indexed by J. A. B. Somerset.

2. The printed material collected and brought to REED by Professor Ian Lancashire (now supplemented by the work of REED bibliographers), as well as a specialized library of reference works and the collected records used in compiling REED volumes, is available for consultation in Toronto.

3. Powicke and Cheney, pp. 26, 35. The subsequent five citations are from this work.

4. Preliminary findings have been published by the REED Latinist, Abigail Young, in "Plays and Players: The Latin Terms for Performance," *REED: Newsletter*, pt.1, vol. 9, no. 2 (1984); pt. 2, vol. 10, no. 1 (1985), pp. 9–16.

5. St. Laurence MS PR DP/97 5/2, pp. 31, 103, 1 (from research in progress by A. F. Johnston).

6. For York, Chester, Coventry, and Newcastle, see the appropriate REED volumes; for Beverley, see Leach, pp. 218–19; for Norwich, see Chambers, *MS*, II, 386–89; for Lincoln, see Kahrl, *Records*, pp. 32–65.

7. St. George was often part of larger processions. Ridings in his honor were more common than plays: see Kelly, pp. 60–61, 191; Thomas and Thornley, pp. 251–52; Grace, pp. 6–149; Fripp, pp. xix-xx; *REED: York*, pp. 289–327; and *REED: Devon*, pp. 208–12.

8. For documentation of plays on Christina, see Mercer, pp. 3–5, 9–12, 79–80; on Christian, see *REED: Coventry*, pp. 100, 128; on Feliciana, see Shropshire Record Office MS 3365–438, #f31 (research in progress by J. A. B. Somerset); on Meriasek, see Stokes, p. 6; on Swithin, Andrew, and Eustace, see Coldewey, *Essex*, p. 226; on Katherine, see Legge, pp. 311–12, Thomas, pp. 337–44, and Tyrell and Nicholas, pp. 80, 154; on Nicholas, see Greenfield, pp. 83–93, and Brown, *passim*; on Thomas the Apostle and Lawrence, see Kahrl, *Records*, pp. 24–25, 30; on Thomas à Becket, see Dawson, pp. 191–98, and Wasson, p. 190; on James, see *REED: York*, p. 68, and Kahrl, *Records*, p. 32; on Dennis, see *REED: York*, pp. 77, 88; on Mary Magdalen, see Furnivall's EETS edition of the play; on Tobias, see Kahrl, *Records*, pp. 67–68; on Susannah, see Bakere, pp. 18–19; on Robert of Sicily, see *REED: Chester*, pp. 26, 484.

9. A. F. Johnston, "Folk-drama in Berkshire," *Etudes d'Histoire du Théâtre Médiéval*, I (1982), forthcoming.

10. Wing MS PR 234 5/1, ff. 66v–81v (1565–79) and f. 174v (research in progress by A. F. Johnston).

11. One that has recently been revived with great success is *A Mery Geste of Robyn Hood and of Hys Lyfe* (c. 1560). It is available in an acting text edited by Mary Blackstone.

12. Reading MS R/FAa 14, 16 and 20. See also Historical Manuscript Commis-

sion 11th Report, Appendix I, p. 172 for several references from manuscripts destroyed by enemy action (research in progress by A. F. Johnston).

13. Abingdon MS A/FAc 1 f. 114v (research in progress by A. F. Johnston).

14. British Library: Cotton Julius B XII. See *REED: York*, pp. 146–52.

15. *REED: York*, pp. 6–378; Leach, *Report*, p. 128, 142–43; Kahrl, *Records*, pp. 27–50.

16. Sigs. Dii-Diiv. See *REED: Coventry*, pp. xvii and lxii.

17. *REED: York*, pp. 68–353. See also Johnston, "Plays," pp. 55–90.

18. For Aberdeen, see Mill, pp. 116–23; for Dublin, see Gilbert, pp. 242, 476; for Bury St. Edmunds, see Chambers, *MS*, II, pp. 343–44; for Ipswich, see Wasson, p. 170: for Boston, see Kahrl, *Records*, pp. 3–4.

BIBLIOGRAPHICAL NOTE

Since so much work on the external evidence is in progress, it is particularly difficult to provide precise and useful guidance to students. The three specialized journals *Research Opportunities in Renaissance Drama, Medieval Theatre,* and *REED Newsletter* (particularly the biannual annotated bibliographies by Ian Lancashire) are major sources of new material. The REED volumes, as they are published, provide the raw data for a new theatre history. Students should consult the Select Bibliographies for each volume where the articles written by the editors interpreting the material are listed. An older source for primary evidence is the Malone Society *Collections* volumes listed in the general bibliography. The *Proceedings of the First Colloquium of Records of Early English Drama, 1978,* edited by JoAnna Dutka, contains several articles that exemplify how record evidence can be interpreted. Two recent bibliographical guides are J. A. B. Somerset's *Halliwell-Phillipps Scrapbooks: An Index* and Ian Lancashire's *Dramatic Texts and Records of Britain.* Still useful for listing occurrences of drama is Appendix W of E. K. Chambers's *Mediaeval Stage,* II, pp. 329–406. J. T. Murray's *English Dramatic Companies,* though now incomplete and often inaccurate, remains a starting point for later sixteenth-century information. Three recent books are particularly useful. These are *Aspects of English Drama,* edited by Paula Neuss, volume one of the *Revels History of Drama in England,* edited by A. C. Cawley et al., and Peter Meredith and John Tailby's *The Staging of Religious Drama in Europe in the Later Middle Ages.* Useful as an introduction only are the various volumes by Glynne Wickham. Wickham's general outlines are challenging to the imagination but his detailed information is based on now outdated printed material.

WORKS CITED AND SUGGESTED READING

MANUSCRIPTS

Abingdon Chamberlains' Accounts. Berkshire Record Office, A/FAc 1 f. 114v.
Blandford Forum Chamberlains' Accounts, 1554–1750. Dorset Record Office, ff. 11–16v.
British Library: Cotton Julius B XII.
Public Record Office, C 49/46/8.
Reading Chamberlains' Accounts. Berkshire Record Office, R/FAa 14, 16 and 20.

Shropshire Record Office, MS 3365–438, f31.

St. Laurence Reading Churchwardens' Accounts. Berkshire Record Office, PR DP/97 5/2 pp. 31, 103, 1.

Wing Churchwardens' Accounts. Buckinghamshire Record Office, PR 234 5/1, ff. 66v–81v (1565–1579) and f. 174v.

PRINTED WORKS

Alton, R. E., ed. "The Academic Drama in Oxford: Extracts from the Records of Four Colleges." Malone Society *Collections* 5 (1960).

Anderson, J. J., ed. *Records of Early English Drama: Newcastle upon Tyne.* Toronto, 1982.

Anglo, Sydney. *Spectacle, Pageantry and Early Tudor Poetry.* Oxford, 1968.

Axton, Richard. *European Drama of the Early Middle Ages.* London, 1974.

Bakere, June A. *The Cornish Ordinalia: A Critical Study.* Cardiff, 1980.

Baskerville, C. R. "Dramatic Aspects of Medieval Folk Festivals in England." *Studies in Philology* 17 (1920): 79–87.

Blackstone, Mary, ed. *Robin Hood and the Friar.* PLS Performance Texts. Toronto, 1981.

Blair, Lawrence. *English Church Ales.* Ann Arbor, Mich., 1940.

Boas, Frederick S. *University Drama in the Tudor Age.* Oxford, 1914.

Brown, Carlton. "An Early Mention of a St. Nicholas Play in England." *Studies in Philology* 28 (1931): 594–601.

Cawley, A. C., ed. *The Wakefield Pageants in the Towneley Cycle.* Manchester, 1958.

Cawley, A. C., Marion Jones, Peter F. McDonald, and David Mills. *The Revels History of Drama in English,* vol. 1, *Medieval Drama.* London, 1983.

Cawte, E. C., Alex Helm, and N. Peacock. *English Ritual Drama: A Geographical Index.* Publications of the Folk-Lore Society. Vol. 127. London, 1967.

Chambers, E. K. *The Elizabethan Stage.* 4 vols. Oxford, 1923.

———. *The Mediaeval Stage.* 2 vols. London, 1903.

Chambers, R., ed. *The Book of Days: a Miscellany of Popular Antiquities in Connection with the Calendar Including Anecdote, Biography and History, Curiosities of Literature and Oddities of Human Life and Character.* 2 vols. London, 1863.

Clark, Peter. *English Provincial Society from the Reformation to the Revoluion: Religion, Politics and Society in Kent, 1500–1640.* Hassocks, England, 1977.

Clark, Peter, and Peter Slack, eds. *Crisis and Order in English Towns 1500–1700: Essays in Urban History.* London, 1972.

Clark, W. S. *The Early Irish Stage: The Beginnings to 1720.* Oxford, 1955.

Clopper, Lawrence M., ed. *Records of Early English Drama: Chester.* Toronto, 1979.

Coldewey, John C. "Early Essex Drama: A History of Its Rise and Fall, and a Theory Concerning the Digby Plays." Ph.D. Dissertation, University of Colorado, 1972.

———. "That Enterprising Property Player: Semi-Professional Drama in Sixteenth Century England." *Theatre Notebook* 31 (1977): 5–12.

Cox, J. C. *Churchwardens' Accounts from the Fourteenth Century to the Close of the Seventeenth Century.* London, 1913.

Craig, Hardin. *English Religious Drama of the Middle Ages.* Oxford, 1955.

Davidson, Clifford, ed. *A Middle English Treatise on the Playing of Miracles.* Washington, D.C., 1981.

Davis, Norman, ed. *Paston Letters.* Oxford, 1958.

Dawson, Giles, ed. *The Records of Plays and Players in Kent 1450–1642. Malone Society Collections* 7 (1965).

Decretales Domini Gregorii Papae Noni. Leon, 1583.

Douglas, Audrey, and Peter Greenfield, eds. *Records of Early English Drama: Cumberland, Westmorland, Oxfordshire.* Toronto, 1986.

Dutka, JoAnna. *Music in the English Mystery Plays.* Early Drama Art and Music Reference Series 2. Kalamazoo, Mich., 1980.

———. "Mystery Plays at Norwich: Their Formation and Development." *Leeds Studies in English.* New Series 10 (1978): 107–20.

———, ed. *Records of Early English Drama: Proceedings of the First Colloquium at Erindale College, University of Toronto, 31 August–3 September 1978.* Toronto, 1979.

Feuillerat, Albert, ed. *Documents Relating to the Revels at Court in the Time of King Edward VI and Queen Mary. Materialen zur Kunde des alteren Englischen Dramas* (1914).

———, ed. *Documents Relating to the Office of the Revels in the Time of Queen Elizabeth. Materialen zur Kunde des alteren Englischen Dramas* 21 (1908).

Forester, Jean, and A. C. Cawley. "The Corpus Christi Play of Wakefield: A New Look at the Wakefield Burgers Court Records." *Leeds Studies in English.* New Series 7 (1974): 108–116.

Fripp, Edgar I., ed. *Minutes and Accounts of the Corporation of Stratford-upon-Avon and Other Records 1553–1620.* Dugdale Society Publications 1 (1921).

Furnivall, F. J., ed. *The Digby Plays,* EETS, ES 70 (1896).

———, ed. *Robert of Brunne's Handlyng Syne.*

Galloway, David R., ed. *Records of Early English Drama: Norwich 1540–1642.* Toronto, 1984.

———. "Records of Early English Drama and What They Tell Us about the Elizabethan Theatre." *The Elizabethan Theatre VII.* University of Waterloo, 1980.

Gilbert, J. T. *Calendar of Ancient Records of Dublin,* I. Dublin, 1889.

Gibson, Gail McMurray. "Bury St. Edmunds, Lydgate, and the *N–Town Cycle,*" *Speculum* 56 (1981): 56–90.

Grace, Mary, ed. *Records of the Guild of St. George in Norwich, 1399–1547.* Norfolk Records Society 9 (1937).

Greenfield, Peter. "Medieval and Renaissance Drama in Gloucestershire." Ph.D. Dissertation, University of Washington, 1981.

Harbage, Alfred. *Annals of English Drama 975–1700.* 2d ed., rev. by S. Schoenbaum. Philadelphia, 1964. Supplements by S. Schoenbaum (1966, 1970).

Hazlitt, W. Carew. *Faiths and Folklore.* 2 vols. London, 1905; rpt. New York, 1965.

Historical Manuscript Commission 11th Report. Appendix I.

Holmes, Richard H., ed. *The Book of Entries of the Pontefract Corporation 1653–1726.* Pontefract: R. Holmes, 1882.

Ingram, R. W., ed. *Records of Early English Drama: Coventry.* Toronto, 1981.

Johnson, Richard. *The Ancient Custom of the City of Hereford.* 2d ed. London, 1882.

Johnston, A. F. "Folk-drama in Berkshire." *Etudes d'Histoire du Théâtre Médiéval,* I (1982), forthcoming.

———. "The Plays of the Religious Guilds of York: the Creed Play and Pater Noster Play." *Speculum* 50 (1975): 55–90.

———. "Wisdom: Is There a Moral?" in Milla Cozart Riggio, ed. *The Wisdom Symposium.* New York, 1986, pp. 87–101.

———, ed. *Editing Early English Drama: Special Problems and New Directions.*

Proceedings of the Nineteenth Conference on Editorial Problems, Toronto, 1984. New York, 1987.

Johnston, A. F., and Margaret Rogerson, eds. *Records of Early English Drama: York.* 2 vols. Toronto, 1979.

Kahrl, Stanley J., ed. *Records of Plays and Players in Lincolnshire 1300–1585.* Malone Society *Collection* 8 (1974).

———. *Traditions of Medieval English Drama.* London, 1974.

Kelly, William. *Notices Illustrative of the Drama and Other Popular Amusements, Chiefly in the Sixteenth and Seventeenth Centuries, Incidentally Illustrating Shakespeare and his Contemporaries: Extracted from the Chamberlains' Accounts and Other Manuscripts of the Borough of Leicester.* London, 1865.

Lancashire, Ian. *Dramatic Texts and Records of Britain: A Chronological Topography to 1558.* Toronto, 1984.

Laroque, Francois. "A Comparative Calendar of Folk Customs and Festivities in Elizabethan England." *Cahiers Elisabéthains* 8 (1975): 513.

Leach, A. F. *Report of the Manuscripts of the Corporation of Beverley.* HMC (1900).

———. "Some English Plays and Players, 1220–1548." *An English Miscellany Presented to Dr. Furnivall.* Ed. W. P. Ker, A. S. Napier, and W. W. Sheat. London, 1901.

Legge, M. D. "The Anglo-Norman Drama." *Anglo-Norman Literature and its Background.* Oxford, 1963.

Lumiansky, R. M., and David Mills. *The Chester Mystery Cycle: Essays and Documents.* Chapel Hill, 1983.

Mercer, Francis R. *Churchwardens' Accounts at Betrysden 1515–1573.* Kent Records 5 (1928).

Meredith, Peter, and John Tailby, eds. *The Staging of Religious Drama in Europe in the Later Middle Ages: Texts and Documents in English Translation.* Kalamazoo, 1983.

Mill, Anna J. "The Hull Noah Play." *Modern Language Review* 33 (1938).

———. *Medieval Plays in Scotland.* St. Andrew's University Publications 24 (1927).

Mill, Anna J., and E. K. Chambers, eds. "Dramatic Records of the City of London: The Repertories, Journals, and Letter Books." Malone Society *Collections* 2, part 3 (1931): 285–320.

Mills, A. D. "A Corpus Christi Play and Other Dramatic Activities in Sixteenth Century, Sherborne, Dorset." Malone Society *Collections* 9 (1977).

Mills, David, ed. *Staging the Chester Cycle.* Leeds, 1985.

Motter, T. H. Vail. *The School Drama in England.* London, 1929.

Murray, John Tucker. *English Dramatic Companies 1558–1642.* 2 vols. London, 1910.

Needham, Joseph. "The Geographical Distribution of English Ceremonial Dance Traditions." *Journal of the English Folk Dance and Song Society* 3 (1931): 1–45.

Nelson, Alan H. *The Medieval English Stage: Corpus Christi Pageants and Plays.* Chicago, 1974.

Neuss, Paula, ed. *Aspects of Early English Drama.* Cambridge, 1983.

Nichols, John. *The Progresses and Public Processions of Queen Elizabeth.* 3 vols. London, 1823.

Nungezer, Edwin. *A Dictionary of Actors and of Other Persons Associated with Public Representation of Plays in England before 1642.* New Haven, 1929.

Parker, Roscoe E. "Some Records of the 'Somyr Play.'" *Studies in Honor of John*

C. Hodges and Alwin Thaler. Ed. Richard Beale Davis and John Leon Lievsay. Knoxville, 1961.

Phythian-Adams, Charles. *Desolation of a City: Coventry and the Urban Crisis of the Late Middle Ages.* Cambridge, 1979.

Powicke, F. M., and C. R. Cheney. *Councils and Synods.* Oxford, 1964.

Rastall, Richard. "The Minstrels of the English Royal Households, 25 Edward I–1 Henry VIII: An Inventory." *R.M.A. Research Chronicle* 4 (1964): 1–41.

———. "The Minstrel Court in Medieval England," in R. L. Thomson, ed., *A Medieval Miscellany in Honour of Professor John le Patourel.* Leeds, 1982.

Rastell, John. *A Hundred Mery Talys.* 1526.

Records of Early English Drama: Newsletter, 1976–

Riley, H. T. *Gesta Abbatum Monasterii Sancti Albani a Thoma Walsingham.* 3 vols. London, 1867–1869.

———. *Memorials of London and London Life . . . : A.D. 1276–1419.* London, 1868.

Robertson, Jean, and Gordon, D. G., eds. *A Calendar of Dramatic Records in the Books of the Livery Companies of London, 1485–1640.* Malone Society Collections 3 (1954).

Salter, F. M. *Medieval Drama in Chester.* Toronto, 1955.

Smith, G. C. More. "Academic Drama at Cambridge: Extracts from College Records." Malone Society *Collections* 2, part 2 (1923).

Somerset, J. A. B. *Halliwell-Phillipps Scrapbooks: An Index.* Toronto, 1979.

———. "Scenes, Machines and Stages at Shrewsbury: New Evidence," in M. Chiabo, F. Doglio, and M. Maymone, eds., *Atti Del IV Colloquio della Société Internationale pour l'Etude du Théâtre Médiéval.* Viterbo, 1984.

Stokes, W., ed. *The Life of Saint Meriasek, Bishop and Confessor.* London, 1878.

———, ed. *The Life of St. Meriasek, Bishop and Confessor* (London, 1812); trans. Markham Harris, *The Life of Meriasek: A Medieval Cornish Miracle Play.* Washington, D.C., 1977.

Strutt, Joseph. *The Sports and Pastimes of the People of England . . . from the Earliest Period to the Present Time.* Edited with index by William Hone. London, 1838.

Thomas, A. H., and I. D. Thornley, eds. *The Great Chronicle of London.* London, 1938.

Thomas, C. B. C. "The Miracle Play at Dunstable." *Modern Language Notes* 32 (1917): 337–44.

Thomas, Charles, ed. *The Medieval Cornish Drama.* Cornwall Archaeological Society, Special Bibliography, no. 3 (1969).

Tydeman, William. *English Medieval Theatre, 1400–1500.* London, 1986.

Tyner, John Walton. *Historical Survey of Holy Week: Its Services and Ceremonial.* Alcuin Club Collections, no. 29. London, 1932.

Tyrell, E., and N. H. Nicholas. *A Chronicle of London from 1089–1483.* London, 1827.

Underdown, David. *Revel, Riot and Rebellion: Popular Politics and Culture in England, 1603–1660.* Oxford, 1985.

Wasson, John, ed. (with David Galloway). *Records of Plays and Players in Norfolk and Suffolk.* Malone Society *Collections* 11 (1980–1981).

———, ed. *Records of Early English Drama: Devon.* Toronto, 1986.

Wickham, Glynne. *Early English Stages: 1300 to 1600.* 2 vols. in 3 pts. London, 1959–1972; 2d ed., vol. 1: London, 1980.

Withington, Robert. *English Pageantry: an Historical Outline.* 2 vols. Cambridge, Mass., 1918–1920.

Woodfill, Walter L. *Musicians in English Society from Elizabeth to Charles I.* Princeton, 1953.

Wright, A. R., comp., and T. E. Lones, ed. *British Calendar Customs: England.* Publications of the Folk-Lore Society. Vols. 97, 102, 106. London, 1937, 1939, 1941.

Young, Karl. *The Drama of the Medieval Church.* 2 vols. Oxford, 1933.

DONALD C. BAKER

When Is a Text a Play?

Reflections upon What Certain Late Medieval Dramatic Texts Can Tell Us

The textual problems in late medieval English drama are in many ways not so very different from those in Elizabethan drama. But from the late sixteenth century until recently, the medieval drama has not been a living drama, and the surviving texts have thus been seen largely as dead records. We know, for instance, from the quartos and folios, that Shakespeare's plays existed in various forms; any decision to perform or edit one of his plays today necessarily involves making a choice between two or possibly more versions of the play in many cases. Nearly all performances and editions of *King Lear* are amalgams, as are those of *Hamlet*. Much speculation has been lavished upon the whys and wherefores of these versions: did they represent political or religious censorship, special performances, or accretions by the author for various reasons over the years? Or were they additions by one or more of that stable of "bad authors" who were kept around for the purpose of writing the "bad" scenes in Shakespeare?

In the case of the medieval English drama, scholars have been grateful that *any* texts have survived. Considerable learning has been devoted to the evolutions of the individual play books or registers, but relatively little to what the form of the surviving texts tells us about a play's nature and development, or about the relations of the plays to one another. What the surviving texts tell us about the plays, their history of performance, and the people who created and altered them, is perhaps much greater than we, still nourished in the myth of medieval anonymity, have been willing to allow.

I wish to direct my attention in this chapter to a small group of plays, some of which I have recently edited (Baker, Murphy, and Hall). My comments will be largely about materials and considerations for which the policies of the publishers of my edition, as well as the exigencies of space, did not permit full discussion; I shall, in addition, allow myself speculation which did not then seem permissible or perhaps even warranted.

My subjects are the so-called Digby Plays: *The Conversion of St. Paul*, *The Killing of the Children*, the partial text of *Wisdom*, and some aspects of the *Mary Magdalen*. I will also touch upon two of the plays of the Macro MS in relation to these, and one other play of the East Anglian area, *The Play of the Sacrament*. In addition, I will survey the textual problems of the two religious plays of Bodleian MS e Museo 160, which were for so long considered a part of the Digby group. I have chosen these because each presents particular and reasonably well-defined problems and possible solutions, and because each is short enough—excepting the *Mary Magdalen*—to allow of fairly extensive treatment even in a short essay. The much more challenging problems of the cycles and of the *N-Town Plays* are obviously too extensive to allow for detailed treatment; in any case, the later plays are being studied anew by Professor Stephen Spector, and I would not wish to rush in before his conclusions are fully presented.

I have another reason for selecting these particular plays. All are, excepting the e Museo 160 plays, from one geographical area, East Anglia, perhaps with the extension of that traditional description to include all of Cambridgeshire and, moving below Suffolk, to include at least part of Essex. Three of the plays have an association with Myles Blomefylde[1] and one exists in another copy, which gives an excellent opportunity for textual comparisons and for some conclusions about the ways in which scribes and writers went about their work in the drama. Some of the conclusions that I draw will, I hope, be applicable to the other drama of the area, as well as to some of the late medieval drama elsewhere.

The Conversion of St. Paul has drawn a great deal of attention, primarily because of the peculiarity of staging suggested by a direction and other implications in the text, rather than for any inherent qualities of the play. The MS is in two hands, as Furnivall noted, with the addition of some marginal directions by a third. Or, rather, it should be said, the *text* of *The Conversion of St. Paul* is in one hand throughout, a hand of about 1500. To this manuscript, about thirty or forty years later, a gathering of four leaves (only three leaves bear writing; the fourth is cut to a stub) was added, in which a second hand has marked out St. Paul's sermon after his conversion (f. 44ᵛ) and has inserted an interesting scene in which Belial receives news from Mercury about the conversion of St. Paul, their special agent. After this scene (ff. 45–7, ll. 412–515), the new scribe, or, more probably the author of the scene, has carefully again written St. Paul's sermon on the Seven Deadly Sins; then the play continues as before. Whether or not the third hand's stage directions ("Daunce":) were added still later, or were in the manuscript before the Belial scene was attached, is not certain. I incline to the opinion that they were added between the original writing of this text and the composition of the Belial scene. The manuscript, in quarto, has been carefully folded in two places and the depth of the creases would seem to indicate that the folding had been done quite a number of times.

Though one line seems to be missing from the main text (from a stanza between ll. 496 and 501), the text is very competently written, with stage directions and speakers' names clearly and neatly lettered with plenty of space, as a look at the Leeds facsimile will reveal (Baker and Murphy, *Digby Plays*). We need not conclude that the main hand is that of the author of the play, although our fear of suggesting such a possibility is at times laughable. An error or two of anticipation clearly suggests copying, but the possibility that the copying was done by the author himself cannot and should not be dismissed. The play is a whole and is coherent and easy to follow. The only real confusions are geographical, where the princes or priests seem to be in both Jerusalem and Damascus. There is also a confused reference to "Liba"; but these Biblical place-names were very much in the air, and should not be taken as implying too certain a geographical place in the writer's mind. In short, nothing in the text indicates that we are eons away from the original author. The evidence of use of the manuscript would seem to indicate that we are dealing with a play which had a vigorous life over a period of years. We must assume, from the apparently missing line ("apparently" because no real sense is lost), and from the errors of anticipation, that there had existed at least one other copy. But there is no compelling reason to assume that there were many copies. Families of manuscripts are the legitimate concerns of scholars studying the productions of the professional and monastic scribes and scriptoria over a period of years. In most of the texts of the late medieval English drama, what we see is what we get. (The Chester manuscripts are a special case.) The careful insertion of the Belial scene by the later writer and the re-connection with the original play suggest that the later writer felt he was dealing with a fairly precious commodity, one which still had use in itself and which must be treated with respect.[2] Paper was not otherwise really so expensive that another copy of the new, extended play could not have been made. Perhaps it was made, but we have no way of knowing this.

Though some of the surviving texts may well have been written in monastic institutions, it would not seem that they were copied extensively. A play text would have been a valuable commodity to the players, as were the Elizabethan texts to the companies of Shakespeare's time. A group of players would want enough texts—and one may have been enough—but probably no more than enough. There was certainly, in any case, not the reading public that existed in Shakespeare's day to form a clientele for many copies of play texts. There would have been, on the other hand, powerful reasons why a group of players, of whatever origin and composition, would not have wanted many texts of their plays around. For one thing, there was the ever-present danger of ecclesiastical and political interference; and, as the century moved on, that danger became much more real.

The Conversion of St. Paul without the Belial scene is quite an interesting play, even with Paul's sermon. The obligatory buffoonery with the stabulerius is nicely done, the ranting is of a reasonably high quality, and the light on the road to Damascus offers impressive possibilities. We must not take the addition of "Daunce" notations by the third hand to mean necessarily that the play was found to be, or in time became, a dull play which needed enlivening. This may indeed have been the case. But when examining the evidence of a surviving text in order to understand as best we can what the play was like as a living thing, we must take into consideration matters other than our own tastes. The "Daunces" may have been added because a small dancing group became attached to whatever company may have had *The Conversion* in its repertoire. Likewise, the later Belial scene may have been added because, quite some years later, whatever group had *The Conversion* (and we cannot assume that it remained the same group) had a member particularly known for his good deviling whose talents it seemed a shame to waste. But the Belial scene is not a mere thoughtless attachment to tart up the play; it takes its cue from the prayers of the two priests, Caiphas and Anna, to their pagan gods. It does, in fact, make a good addition to the new play, attributing further motives to the scheming of the priests, providing satire on manners and morals, and illustrating the sins against which the converted Paul is to preach. That the scene does enliven the play is incontrovertible; that this effect was the only reason for its being added, in line with the traditional view that the religious plays became more decadent as the players strove to keep up with the times, by no means follows.

The Conversion of St. Paul, in the earliest form that we have it, without the additions, was already a rather flexible play. This is clearly indicated by the introduction, with the phrase "si placet," of the Poeta's "conclusyon" speech at the end of the first action. In fact the speech, which contains the famous requirement that the audience move on to a second station, might or might not have been delivered. It is true that "si placet" is inserted in the right margin of f. 39ᵛ—as is the name of the speaker, Poeta—so that this instruction may have been an afterthought. But it is in the same hand and ink as those of the bulk of the play—excluding "Daunce" and the Belial scene—and seems to be of the same time. Here, at this point, the second "Daunce" notation occurs (the first is in the right margin after the Poeta's introductory speech). This raises an interesting question: was the "Daunce" designed later to take the place of the Poeta's "conclusyon?" Or was it intended as a brief interval before the Poeta's speech? We cannot know for certain, but a very plausible guess is that the practice of the players changed from time to time under varying conditions of playing.

Much has been made of *The Conversion of St. Paul*'s being the sole survivor of a type of play which was "processional" in its nature, although Wickham disputes this interpretation (Wickham, "Staging"). It seems to be a matter very little susceptible to dogmatic and theoretic argument. The evidence would seem to indicate that the play could have been performed under a variety of conditions. It could well have been, and probably was, originally designed to be played at two stations: one, the Jerusalem station, and the other, where the audience was invited by Poeta to succeed, the Damascus station. Added to this was the road to Damascus where the fervent conversion occurred, and which was equipped with some sort of stage or device from which God could speak. At one point, it was clearly a play designed for street performance, or performance of a processional nature of some sort, rather than performed in the round or with stage and scaffolds. For one thing, it is a rather short play to have been mounted elaborately—only 552 lines without Belial. But the writer of the main text clearly indicates that the instructions to the audience to move on to the next station need not always be given. This seems to indicate that the writer anticipated, or an early copier anticipated, that the play might be performed, let us say, in the round. The intrusion later of the "Daunce" notations suggests the latter kind of performance, though the dances would not have been impossible in a processional performance. But by the time the Belial scene was added, I would guess the play was being acted more often in the round. There is no question of further audience movement, and a definite third, very important station had been added to the play. I would conclude that we have a text which gives indication of a fairly long period of use—and for performances under whatever conditions may have prevailed—in short, a very professional little play which could easily be adapted to circumstances.

The language of the play, both in the main play and in the Belial scene, is essentially that of East Anglia, i.e., Norfolk and Suffolk with east Cambridgeshire thrown in. Richard Beadle (*Medieval Drama of East Anglia*, II, pp. 119–21) has recently emphasized the scantiness of the linguistic evidence for this assertion, but in view of the lateness of the texts, I believe that the case is a sound one (see Baker, Murphy, and Hall, pp. xix-xxii). The text gives no hint of where the play may have been acted at various times, but it seems unlikely that, at least for the first part of its life, it would have been performed outside this area. It seems to me fruitless to speculate on specific towns; everything about the play would suggest traveling drama which might have been acted at the many game places of the area or in the squares or streets of small villages. John Coldewey has argued, partly on the basis of Myles Blomefylde's signature on the first leaf, that it was one of the plays acted in the 1560s at Chelmsford in the pyghtle of the church there (Coldewey, "Digby Plays"). I am not as convinced as he that the Chelmsford churchwardens' accounts book bears this out; but there can be no doubt that the play was at Chelmsford, at least later, in the possession of Myles, who was himself a churchwarden in the 1580s. Richard Beadle has questioned the likelihood of *The Conversion of St. Paul*'s being played at Chelmsford so late because the language would have seemed strange to the audience (*Medi-*

eval Drama, II, p. 67). This does not seem to me to be a strong argument; the pronunciation of the later players would, in any case, have naturally varied from that of those who had played it originally; but it seems improbable that fifty or sixty years in the late fifteenth and early sixteenth centuries would have made the play difficult to understand—and, after all, the difficult words in the ranting speeches were surely intended to be wondered at from the beginning.

The evidence of the manuscript thus leaves us with a short history of the play. It originated around 1500 or a bit earlier as a play designed for a brief street performance in which the audience, not the players, were the procession, at least from the first station to the second. Even in its earliest form it gives evidence of adaptability to other playing conditions. The subsequent additions reveal the play's being made more flexible, and the addition of the Belial scene might suggest that the Poeta's speech at the end of the first action was no longer in use at all. (Why it was not crossed out might seem a puzzle; but we have seen that the care taken with the MS by subsequent users and revisers would indicate a certain reverence for it.) The playwright clearly indicated "station" to mean both a part of the action and a location of that action. By "pagent" the playwright meant the players themselves and their limited properties, together with the location. "At this pagent" cannot readily admit of another interpretation. The word "place" seems to have meant in general the acting area, as in Saul's riding around the place. The language clearly identifies the area of playing as East Anglia and, by the end of the sixteenth century, it and two other East Anglian plays—*Mary Magdalen* and the partial text of *Wisdom*—are in Essex as the property of Myles Blomefylde, who also owned a copy (now the unique copy) of Henry Medwall's *Fulgens and Lucres*. How Myles acquired the texts is not known, though I have speculated elsewhere (Baker and Murphy, "Late Medieval Plays"). In one play, then, we have the evidence of three possibly rather different plays, each one laid upon the preceding, and the original Norfolk-Suffolk career possibly followed by a second in Essex (see Coldewey, "Digby Plays"). Future discussion of staging, in particular, should take rather more note of these facts than previous discussion has done.

The manuscript of *The Killing of the Children* is a most interesting one. The introduction by the Poeta gives, as everyone has noticed, the two little plays, the Candelmes play and *The Killing of the Children* itself, in the reverse order from that in which they appear in the following text. What should be made of this is far from clear; what can be adduced is that the order may not have been terribly important to the players, that the Poeta's speech caught the plays in an order, perhaps for a particular performance, which was generally speaking of no great significance. It is perhaps important that the speech of the Poeta is on the first of two leaves which clearly had been at one time detached from the rest of the manuscript (Baker, Murphy, and Hall, pp. lii-lvi). They may well be part of the quarto, but pasted on to the first leaf of the integral quarto, they likely had separate lives and uses, only being reattached from time to time. They seem to be from the stock of paper of the rest of the manuscript. What can be seen of the watermark is the same; and, with the first leaves originally attached, the manuscript would have been composed of three folio sheets with three complete watermarks. It is worth noting also that, whatever the intentions of the original author and players, a later hand has noted "vacat ab hinc" immediately after the death of Herod, indicating that at least on one occasion the play of Candelmes was not performed.

The two plays are largely in the one hand, supplemented by a second in the Candelmes play (ll. 465–550). The fact of the two hands, together with some errors of anticipation here and there, suggests that we are not dealing with the original manuscript. But the acceptance of this does not necessarily bring the conclusion that the principal writer of the text may not have indeed been the author. At any rate, the sweeping confidence of the scribe suggests that he was far more than a hired penman. After Herod's speech of f. 147^r, all of f. 147^v is canceled in ink like that used by the principal writer throughout. Here, in this canceled portion, Herod has finished his ranting to the audience and now addresses his "messenger" whom he charges to scour the countryside and find if there are any who disobey Herod's commands or flout his religion. The messenger, named here in the margin as "Watkyn, Messanger," says that he has already fulfilled Herod's request and tells him about the three kings who have deceived him. Originally, Watkyn was made to say "Your commaundement I shall fulfill," but, as the following speech clearly indicates that he has already brought news, the writer changed the wording to "have fulfilled," then crossed out the scene altogether, recommencing with another Herod speech on f. 148^r in which Herod announces that the three kings have deceived him. Watkyn's appearance, or speaking, is thus delayed until f. 149^r when Watkyn asks Herod to make him a knight. Clearly, a rather curious state of affairs exists in the text. One may also notice that, while the vast bulk of the verse of the two plays is in Chester eights, most of the lines of the canceled passage are in rhyme royal stanzas (three stanzas, with a quatrain left over). In the remainder of *both* plays, there are only three rhyme royal stanzas, all between ll. 315 and 364. There is an additional speech on a bit of paper inserted between folios 152 and 153—the speech of Watkyn, who announces the mothers' curse upon Herod, a speech which may have been skipped by the writer-copier, but which very possibly may have been added. This speech, inserted by the writer between ll. 353 and 365, is, curiously enough, a rhyme royal stanza. It is certainly in the hand of the main scribe. He attached it to the preceding eight-line stanza by an insertion mark in the margin and wrote on the tipped-in sheet the first few words of the following speech, so that its place in the order of lines is secure. There is also an insertion mark in the margin (after l. 7 of the canceled passage of f.147ᵛ), but the paper on which the added speech was tipped in has been lost, or probably detached by the writer when he later canceled the whole passage. The treatment of Watkyn thus suggests a change in plan during the revision; on the first four occasions when Watkyn is mentioned, either by Herod or by the writer, as the speaker of lines, he is designated simply by "Messanger." On the second occasion, the name "Watkyn" is inserted before "Messanger" as the name of the speaker. Thereafter, "Watkyn" is "Watkyn"; and his name is given the honor of being placed in the center at the top of f. 149ʳ. His domination of the first play is thus seemingly belatedly recognized.

This wholesale alteration, added to the mysterious fact that almost all the initial canceled passage is in a stanza form different from that of almost all the rest of the play, provides food for thought. The manuscript is dated 1512, once in a later hand, but once at the end, with the list of players, in the hand of the main scribe. For various reasons, there are grounds to think that the play is, in one form or another, slightly older than this date. I will dash into a speculation: that we have in this manuscript (of the first play, at least) a play which was extensively reworked by the man whose hand is the principal one. He has also elsewhere added many other touches, changing phrases and rhymes here and there in ways that make clear that he is revising to suit his preferences. We may say that the principal hand is that of the author of the play, at least the first one, as it stands. He is clearly to some extent copying and using older material, perhaps for *The Killing of the Children* even using material from two older plays, one of which may have been largely in the rhyme royal stanza. That he *is* using older material is strongly suggested by the extent to which he can turn over a part of the second play to be copied by a second hand, though he returns to write the final couplet, the conclusion, and the list of players. Whether or not I have gone too far in stating that, in a sense, we are dealing here with the author of the plays as they stand, we are certainly dealing with someone who is far more than the hired scribe. The sense of movement and characterization in the play, revealed in the alterations, suggests that the writer was, at least, the man in charge of preparing the texts for whatever group of players he was working with. Whether or not he was the "Jhon Parfre" who "did write this book" we cannot know. But if it were possible to know, I would not bet against it.

What do we have? In one "book," we have two plays, fronted by Poeta's introduction, in the eights form of most of the play text. It is apparently a pair of plays, closely joined in subject matter, and in the correct chronological and festial order, in spite of the reversal in the Poeta's introduction. The plays could be performed separately, as the "vacat ab hinc" suggests; and apparently on one occasion, for St. Anne's Day, for at least one particular playing place, the plays were given in reverse order. This strongly suggests, as in the case of *The Conversion of St. Paul*, great flexibility in the material and in the manner of playing. Apparently, everything points to a customary playing in a central place while Joseph and Mary are conveyed into Egypt (f. 151ᵛ). It would seem suitable for the sort of game place that K. M. Dodd describes at Walsham le Willows in Suffolk. The last stage direction, that the dance should include "as many virgins as a man will," suggests dancers drawn from among village maidens. Everything about the texts points to little plays that were a part of the repertoire of a traveling group or groups. It is also, clearly, an East Anglian text: its language is quite conclusive, particularly considering an important word like "sharme" (l. 142), which is pure Norfolk.

This play is the only play text in Digby 133 which does not have the name or initials of Myles Blomefylde. But there are two matters, which I have commented on elsewhere, that suggest a link of some kind between *The Killing of the Children* and two other of the *Digby Plays*—the first half text of *Wisdom* and the *Mary Magdalen* (see Baker, Murphy, and Hall, pp. xlii, liv, lxiv-lxvii).

The first can easily be dealt with. Although I once thought differently (Baker and Murphy, "The Late Medieval Plays," p. 158), I am now absolutely convinced that the main scribe of *The Killing of the Children* and the scribe of the Digby *Wisdom* were the same man. At the beginning of the texts, the hands do not look the same—the *Wisdom* hand appearing much more formal and considerably older—and I was fooled. But the longer I looked at the hands and the further I looked into the manuscript, the more the superficial dissimilarities wore away. By the time the scribes were in the midst of their texts, I could no longer doubt. M. B. Parkes, Ian Doyle, and Neil Ker kindly confirmed my second opinion. This identity of hands raises a number of questions. I think that the Digby *Wisdom* was copied from the exemplar of the Macro *Wisdom* (see Baker, Murphy, and Hall, pp. lxiv-lxvii), which we know to have been at some time at Bury St. Edmunds, though it may not have originated there. If the Digby *Wisdom* did have its origin at Bury, too, then clearly it is not beyond the bounds of possibility that the scribe was a member of that monastic community. That he also wrote *The Killing of the Children* (or copied, or revised it) would suggest the community was interested in a somewhat greater variety of drama than the *Wisdom*, which strikes modern readers as a quite different kind of play, would indicate. Pursuing this view, Gail Gibson has recently (1981) published a long article making a provocative, if circumstantial, case for the monastery at Bury's being a center of dramatic activity.

The other connection between *The Killing of the Children* and one play of Digby 133 is a short passage of eight lines which appears in slightly different forms in both *The Killing of the Children* and *Mary*

Magdalen. In *The Killing of the Children* this is ll. 97–104 and in *Mary Magdalen*, ll. 217–24:

The Killing of the Children

PRIMUS MILES. My lord, ye may be sure that I
shalle not spare,
    For to fulfille your noble commaundement,
With sharpe sword to perse them alle bare,
    In all cuntrees that be to you adiacent!
SECUNDUS MILES. And for your sake, to obserue your
commaundment!
TERCIUS MILES. Not on of them all oure handes shalle
astert!
QUARTUS MILES. For we wole cruelly execute youre
judgement,
With swerde and spere to perse them thurgh the hert!

Mary Magdalen

HERAWDES. Be he sekyr I woll natt spare
    For [to] complyshe hys cummavnddment,
With sharp swerddys to perce the[m] bare
    In all covntres wythin thys regent,
    For hys love to fulfyll hys intentt.
Non swych xall from ower handys stertt,
    For we woll fulfyll hys ryall juggement
Wyth swerd and spere to perce [them] thorow the hartt!

The speeches are not identical, but they are very, very close. The lines are assigned to the knights in *The Killing of the Children* and, in *Mary Magdalen*, to Herod. The speech, which boasts of intended achievement against the enemies of their religion and sovereignty, etc., is, in its tone of eagerness, much more suitable to the knights desirous of pleasing Herod, who is in their presence, than it is suitable to Herod, speaking of a faraway emperor. Further, the *Mary Magdalen* lines are cruder and are lacking certain words. If one borrowed from the other, clearly the writer of *Mary Magdalen* borrowed from *The Killing of the Children*. It is perhaps as likely, if not more so, that the two writers borrowed, for their own purposes, from a common source. Wickham's suggestion ("Staging," p. 117) of a common set of scenes from which the longer plays were constructed is too pat, though it must be taken seriously. In any case, the texts bear evidence of a common body of drama and a general association of players. It is possible that all the Digby manuscript plays were indeed at one time part of a common playbook, in the form of the surviving manuscripts or of their originals or copies. The commonalty of these plays, and of those of the Macro MS, of *The Play of the Sacra-*

ment, the *N-Town Plays*, and others, is further borne out by a large body of common rhetoric and rhetorical patterns (Pfleiderer). In closing, neither in the manuscript nor in the text of the play is there anything that would in itself support the suggestion made long ago by H. R. Patch that this play was once a part of what is now the *N-Town Plays*.

The moral play *Wisdom* has caused much confusion as scholars have attempted to guess for what kind of audience it was intended. It has been urged as a play by and for ecclesiastics, and also as a part of the repertoire of a professional or semiprofessional group (see Smart; Molloy; Fifield). Theological arguments have certainly arrived at no convincing conclusion. *Wisdom* would *appear* to be such a different kind of play from the others discussed that one would not ordinarily associate it with the bulk of surviving East Anglian drama if it were not, alas, present in two of the principal collections. The manuscripts of the play, the full Macro text and the partial Digby text, do shed some light on its history. The Macro text, as is generally acknowledged, spent at least some of its early years at the monastery at Bury St. Edmunds, or in any case, in the town itself. It is, as Professor Eccles and I agree, a somewhat earlier copy of the play than that preserved in the Digby manuscript. Professor Eccles and I, however, disagree on the relation between the two texts; I insist that the two were copied from the same exemplar, some years apart, whereas Professor Eccles regards this as unproven and unlikely (see Baker, Murphy, and Hall, pp. lxv-lxvii; Eccles, p. 262).

One thing both texts reveal clearly is that the play was not closet drama: it was played, and apparently played over a considerable period, perhaps thirty or forty years. That the Digby copy of *Wisdom* was written some time in the last two decades of the fifteenth century by a man responsible for the major part of the writing of *The Killing of the Children* is clearly an indication of an active theatrical life for *Wisdom*. Why else would an apparently currently engaged writer or copier of plays for performances have copied it? That both surviving texts of *Wisdom* reveal an original intended for real performance is made clear not only by the extremely elaborate stage directions but also by the fact that in both texts the note "Va" ("Va-cat" or "it may be omitted") is written after l. 684. The Digby manuscript is defective after l. 752, but the Macro text reveals that this omitted section was the scene of the three "Sutes" illustrating with words, dance, and mime the debauchery of Mind, Will, and Understanding. It concludes in the Macro text at l. 785 with the "cat" of "vacat." Clearly the scene was written for playing, but just as clearly the two surviving texts indicate that it was at one time omitted. This proves, as nearly as such things can be said to be proven, that we have texts intended for, and probably reflecting, performance. The interesting question is why the exemplar, apparently containing this note of omission, should have been followed by both writers who copied it. Was *Wisdom*, in all its performances, if any, truncated after the first text or texts? We have no answer, but there finally can be no doubt that *Wisdom*, cloistered as it seems to us, was very much connected with live drama. For not only is the Digby text in the hand of the main writer of *The Killing of the Children*, which certainly speaks to a popular, probably outdoor audience, but the Macro text of *Wisdom* is apparently in the hand of the man who wrote the major part of the text of *Mankind*. This last play was a popular one, and one which was also performed at Bury St. Edmunds, if Monk Hyngham was there, for he (whoever he was) has inscribed it with his ownership tag, as he did *Wisdom*.

The identification of the scribe of the Macro *Wisdom* with that of the main scribe of *Mankind* was asserted by Eccles against the earlier opinion of Pollard who said there was no community of hands among the three plays of the Macro manuscript (Eccles, p. xxvii; Pollard, p. xxvii). The argument has supporters on both sides.[3] The latest case, made by Richard Beadle, marshals the arguments of paleography, philology, and orthography, and argues convincingly that the two hands are the same.[4] Beadle, however, has added another ingredient to the stew: he asserts that the two plays are in the same hand as the inscription identifying Monk Hyngham as the owner of the two manuscripts! It is, of course, difficult to speak with confidence from such small scraps of writing as the inscriptions afford, but the argument certainly does not seem weak. One may be led to conclude, as did Bevington in his facsimile of the Macro, that the very difference in *nature* between *Wisdom* and *Mankind* makes it seem unlikely to us that the same man could have written or would wish to have copied both. But perhaps the difficulty is in our perception. A single individual was certainly at pains to tell us that he *owned* both! Perhaps our categories stand in the way of our understanding.

Although there is no room to examine the matter in detail, I wish here, quite briefly, to consider an aspect of the manuscript of *Mary Magdalen*, which is unique among those of the late medieval English drama in its hurriedness and its general sloppiness. I argue in my edition that at least thirty, and perhaps many more, lines are missing as deduced from stanzaic and syntactic forms. Not only are many lines missing, but the scribe has confused speeches and speakers on at least four occasions, got lines out of order twice at the very least, repeated a speech once, copied directions out of place, made many, many verbal errors and got many rhyme words wrong, and skipped a leaf in his copying (see Baker, Murphy, and Hall, pp. xxxi–xxxiv). One rather amusing piece of evidence of the scribe's incompetence has resulted in an extra line being added to the text. At the bottom of f. 129^v there appears, after the speaker's name (Mary) the phrase "Jhesu Mercy." This has been printed by all previous editors as the first line of Mary's speech. But in fact it has nothing to do with Mary's speech. It is not written at the left margin, as are the ordinary speeches, but is placed in the middle, at the bottom of the page, as the last words on the page. Two of the previous three pages have found the scribe hurrying along, paying little attention to what he was doing, ending a page by writing the speaker's name as the last words, and leaving no room for the first line of the speech. On this leaf, at the third occurrence of such short-sightedness, I maintain he has rather plaintively written "Jhesu Mercy." After this, he is a bit more careful in such matters.

There is no text of late medieval English drama which is quite like that of *Mary Magdalen* in its physical details. We cannot compare it with the various types of Elizabethan "bad quartos," for we do not have a second text. But it does not look to me at all like the other texts, each with its own peculiarities. Yet it attempts to remain faithful to the exemplar in various touching ways, as in the concluding quatrain begging the "redars" to blame cunning and not the writer if anything be amiss. (I suspect that the quatrain in which this appears should really not be numbered as lines in the play, as it may well have been added in exculpation by our worried scribe.) Although we cannot assume that the scribe's exemplar was appreciably better than our present text, I think Schmidt's conclusion long ago that much of the imperfection of stanza and rhyme was due to bad copying is correct. Our manuscript does not appear to have been copied in the leisurely conditions of a monastic scriptorum (and it was not copied by Myles Blomefylde, contrary to the opinion of scholars from Furnivall to Wickham [*Medieval Theatre*, p. 71]. It also does not appear to be a copy made by a person familiar with the forms of a dramatic text (the tagging of lines, etc.). There are many possible explanations: an exemplar almost as bad as the present text (though one cannot imagine why two bad texts of an obviously active play should have been required), drunkenness on the part of the scribe, and so on. But I hazard the guess, in spite of so much unfortunate Shakespearean analogy, that we may, with the manuscript of *Mary Magdalen*, be in possession of the earliest pirated copy of an English play. I am not speaking of whatever sort of borrowing went on between Wakefield and York, but the actual, surreptitious stealing of a dramatic text. The play can, of course, be acted from the manuscript, and has been several times, but I can attest from correspondence with those responsible for such performances that one is forced to take considerable liberty with the text.

To conclude my treatment of plays in the Digby 133 and in the Macro manuscripts, I would say that they reveal a community of drama—various, extremely flexible and adaptable, perhaps drawn from common sources, borrowing from one another, certainly reflecting and refracting one another in a common body of language and rhetoric. The texts reveal the reverence in which their owners and scribes held them. That manuscripts such as *The Conversion of St. Paul* and *The Killing of the Children* should have survived as they did, instead of having been completely recopied and the manuscripts themselves destroyed, is instructive. The texts reveal plays in various layers of existence—expanded, cut and re-cut. The scribal connections suggest much less concern for nicety of genre than we are accustomed to impose upon drama. For *Wisdom* was copied by the same hand responsible for most of *Mankind* and played, one may assume, in the same company as *The Killing of the Children* and *Mankind*. The two playbooks together (if we may so designate them), the Digby and the Macro, reveal a small but fascinating dramatic history from about 1440 to 1540. The community of language is reflected in the similarity of textual transmission; it is not impossible, perhaps, that they were one large playbook at one time, though I would not seriously pursue this notion. But if my guess about the manuscript of *Mary Magdalen* is even close to being right, there was at least as much competition as cooperation among the players!

Having taken leave of two of the principal groups of East Anglian plays, I wish to turn to a single play of the area. *The Play of the Sacrament* is, like all the East Anglian plays discussed, *sui generis*. It is the only surviving full-blown miracle play (though the *Mary Magdalen* has some aspects of this tradition). But for all its peculiarity, it shows many of the qualities seen in the other plays. It is unquestionably a traveling play which "nine may play at ease," and is equipped with an introduction of the ranting, polysyllabic sort so common. Although Waterhouse (*Non-Cycle Mystery Plays*, p. lvi) thought it had a number of Irish linguistic characteristics—no doubt, in part, because of its current location in Dublin—Davis, in his introduction to his EETS edition (pp. lxxix-lxxxv), effectively disposed of these assumptions, placing the language squarely in the East Anglian area, and showing that it shares many of the linguistic features of the other plays that we have looked at. The paper of the manuscript is very similar to that in *Mankind*, the *N-Town Plays*, *The Conversion of St. Paul*, and *The Killing of the Children*. Too much should not be made of this, for the hand watermark with the figure 3 is very common generally in the period and area. Many of the Paston letters, for example, bear it. Even though the last leaf but two of *The Play of the Sacrament* bears the date 1461, the date of the hands, plus the evidence of the watermark, cause Davis to posit a date of the second quarter of the sixteenth century. This makes the manuscript a late contemporary of those of *The Conversion of St. Paul*, *The Killing of the Children*, and *Mary Magdalen*. The date 1461 may have marked the beginning of the active life of the *Play of the Sacrament* in its original text. If this is the case, then we must presume that the play survived seventy or eighty years. Some linguistic evidence that Davis assembles indeed points to an earlier origin for the language than the approximate date of the manuscript. This in itself is a strong argument against Beadle's assumption that such a play as *The Conversion of St. Paul* or *Mary Magdalen* would not have been acted so late as the 1560s, so long after their "first" careers, because the language would have been hard to understand. Judging from the evidence of such long active lives, the language would not seem to have presented much of a problem.

The manuscript itself is very similar in appearance to those of *The Conversion of St. Paul*, *The Killing of the Children*, and the Digby fragment of *Wisdom*. All four have their first leaves well worn, indicating that though they may have been parts of a loose "playbook," their active lives were probably quite individual. A curiosity is that, in such a relatively short play (1,007 lines), Davis finds three distinct hands cooperating, occasionally even taking over from one another in the middle of a line (pp. lxxi-lxxii). Waterhouse (p. lvii) identified only two hands in the manuscript. In my review of the Davis edition (*ELN*, 9 [1972], p. 294), I argued, with, I think, considerable evidence, that there are in fact four hands in the manuscript (the second appearance of hand C of Davis, which finishes the work, is really hand D). This multiple copying presents quite a different situation from those in the other plays described: the text of *The Conversion of St. Paul* is in one hand except for the later addition of the Belial scene; *The Killing of the Children* has a second hand for a hundred lines in the Candelmes part of the play; all of *Mary Magdalen* is in the same poor hand; and the fragment of *Wisdom* is in one hand. The Macro plays are not noted for a proliferation of hands. Why are there so many hands in *The Play of the Sacrament*, even assuming only three, as Davis asserts? One possible, if not very probable, answer is that in its original state the play existed as separate partial manuscripts—not individual players' parts, but large sections—which were kept in this fragmentary condition for a period to guard against the sort of thing that may have happened to the text of *Mary Magdalen*. One copy was then created in the late 1520s or thereabouts by having the four custodians combine their booklets. If there *are* four hands, as against three, this proposal has more weight. Against it must be assessed the fact that hand B begins its part in the middle of a line (l. 10, f.338ᵛ). I am quite aware that I am arguing from one supposition to an even greater supposition, but where should theorizing take place if not in an essay like this? In any case, the multiplicity of hands would suggest, in the case of *The Play of the Sacrament*, that the players ("nine" or more) had perhaps more extensive roles in their company than are usually assumed, e.g., a "producer-Poeta-writer-copier" and his entourage of players. The copy of *The Play of the Sacrament* may have been made at an institution where many scribes were available, but in books of both monastic and professional secular scriptoria, several hands in such a small book was very uncommon. More likely by far would be the supposition that the players' company in this particular instance had at least three or four people quite capable of writing the play copy, revising it, and carrying it through performance.

The play was clearly one which was acted in and around Thetford because of such place names as Babwyll Mill and Croxton (l. 74). The Croxton may have been another Croxton than the one three miles north of Thetford, but Babwyll Mill could not have been as recognizable a place as the Croxton west of Cambridge, or as one of the several other Croxtons. The play may have had its headquarters at the Thetford priory or the priory at Babwyll Mill, but more than likely these place names are intended to pick up local allusion; there is nothing in the references that would denote these places as home.

I have, in discussing these plays, largely emphasized the similarities among them. To leave them without discussing, however briefly, their dissimilarities would be quite inappropriate. Each is quite a different kind of play from the others. Some are sprinkled with place references, others lack them completely. Some (*Mankind, The Killing of the Children*) have specific references to time of performance, others none. Some are short, two quite long and elaborate. All are, I believe, traveling plays whether we want to use the term professional or not. All are essentially East Anglian and all represent a type of East Anglian drama which differs radically from what we know of medieval drama elsewhere in England, though that may be simply the result of the luck of survival. All attest in their manuscripts to a living drama that lasted for well over a century, and to a drama which was easily adaptable to and responsive to changing requirements.

Leaving East Anglian drama, I wish to turn now to another manuscript, which is in many ways the most interesting example that we have of a playwriter at work. This is so despite the fact that our text is by no means outdoor drama, and far from professional, and almost certainly is one tied to a particular location. But, cloistered though it is, it may offer instruction as to the way in which medieval dramatists, or would-be dramatists, worked. I refer to the two plays of *The Burial and Resurrection of Christ*, contained in Bodleian manuscript e Museo 160. As has been shown, Furnivall was wrong in his assertion that these plays once belonged to Digby 133, for e Museo 160 is a fairly homogeneous manuscript of the early sixteenth century, for the most part in a single hand on paper with the appropriate continuation of watermarks.[5] Taking note that Jerome permits us to regard the early patriarchs as saints,[6] the writer proposed to create a kind of chronicle of the saints from Old Testament times to his own day so that they might be more easily addressed; in this undertaking he intended to include a picture of a principal saint at the top of each page. However, this plan did not work out, and beyond the first two lined spaces filled with crude drawings there is nothing but space occasionally doodled in by later readers; finally, the spaces are omitted altogether. The aid to prayer had become a historical chronicle, modeled, as the writer later acknowledges (f. 92ʳ), on Rolewinck's *Fasciculus Temporum*, with the saints of each century appended. As the centuries wear on, the writing becomes more and more lively, and the linked quatrains in which most of the chronicle is composed, more inventive. Though Christian matters are always to the fore, the meditative element gradually disappears as the writer becomes preoccupied with the events he is describing. Particularly is this true when he reaches the "modern" era and describes the founding and the fortunes of the Carthusian order, which, as he says (f. 103^v), Christ seems to favor more than he does the other orders. Finally, the chronicle runs out at Christmas 1518, where, as the writer sadly remarks, the "matter fails" (f. 108^r). There is a false start at a continuation to 1520, which was erroneously printed by Hazlitt (pp. 117–18) as a separate historical poem, and there is a fragmentary romance with a strong moral flavor (printed by M. C. Seymour), and some real meditative works (see further in Baker, Murphy, and Hall, pp. lxxvii–lxxxi). The plays themselves begin on f. 140^r.

I have rehearsed the matter of the first part of the book to draw a parallel between the writer's mode of operation there and later in the composition of the plays. The plays have been universally misunderstood. They begin, as the writer notes at the top of the first page, as a narrative aid to meditation, in somewhat the same way as the chronicle was begun. The play (plays) is called a meditation. But soon there is a change in plan, as had occurred with the chronicle. For the writer has gone over his lines in red ink, as opposed to the black that he normally used (highlighted with red in initial letters of lines), marking out the narrative elements ("said Holy Joseph," "answered Mary," etc.). A note is squeezed in at the bottom of f. 140^v saying that, if it is to be played, the first half is to be played on "gudfriday" and the second on Easter morn. This essential change of purpose is made clear by the fact that after f. 147^v there are no more narrative elements in the writing and nothing to be corrected or omitted. Therefore, although the two plays could still be read as meditations, clearly, their essential nature had become dramatic. The writer has turned narrative material from his sources, mostly meditative material such as the pseudo-Bernardine "Quis dabit," the narrative pseudo-Bonaventuran *Meditationes Vitae Christi*, and some others, into dramatic verse (Baker, Murphy, and Hall, pp. lxxv-xcv). Some of the longer speeches in the plays are lifted bodily from pre-existing *planctūs* for the Virgin Mary, Mary Magdalen, and Peter. These keep their original stanzaic structure, but the other material is turned into continuing six-line *rime couée* for the most part (Baker, Murphy, and Hall, pp. lxxxiii-lxxxv). Furnivall remarked when he noted a narrative element remaining in the text that "Our Poetaster has forgotten that he's writing a play" (p. 174). More correctly one could remark that our poetaster has forgotten that he had not been writing a play, and overlooked these bits of narrative in his alterations. Rosemary Woolf's two suggestions, first that a corrector has turned the meditative work into a play (*Lyric*, p. 243) and, second, that a corrector was restoring the dramatic text to its original, non-dramatic form (*Plays*, p. 422), are both off the mark when one looks at the manuscript and realizes that the corrector is the same man who wrote the rest of the text. The hands are identical, and are the same as that which wrote the chronicle, as I have demonstrated elsewhere (Baker, Murphy, and Hall, p. lxxxv-lxxxvii). The writer simply got as far as f. 147^v in his narrative meditation when he realized that, for whatever reason, he should make it into two plays. He went back and removed all the traces of narrative that he noticed, missing a few, and from f. 147^v on cast the narrative into an essentially dramatic form, including stage directions, speakers' names, etc. Then he put the note at the bottom of f. 140^v, suggesting hopefully that it might be played. The question of the role that religious drama had in religious houses is a complex one. We have evidence for a great deal in some orders, but almost none in others. The matter continues to be studied.

How the writer got the idea of the play as acted meditation we do not know; his house, if at Hull, was certainly close enough to Beverley for him to have seen the plays there, and perhaps he had seen the cycle at York. V. A. Kolve is almost certainly wrong when he claims (*Corpus Christi*, p. 35) that it was to such plays as these, i.e., *The Burial and Resurrection of Christ*, that medieval liturgical drama led. In the first place, we know of no other plays like these, and in the second, these bear even less resemblance to liturgical drama than do the cycles. What they have in common with the cycles is the inclusion of complaints and lyrics from meditative materials. They share with both secular religious drama and liturgical drama such elements as the "Victimae Paschali," "Dic nobis," "Scimus Christum," the race of Peter and John, and the dismissal at the end. The plays are almost accidents rather than developments of a traceable dramatic tradition.

What this one instance of dramatic composition reveals to us is that the author, who undoubtedly *was* the author, created plays out of poetic or prose narrative derived from a number of sources, and incorporated already existing poetic entities into his play. Although not too many parallels are to be drawn, perhaps, between these plays and other religious drama, one point is, I hope, instructive. The variation of stanzaic patterns and of length of lines does not in this case provide evidence for gradual development of any kind. The plays were written at one time, to serve two purposes, individual meditation and group dramatic meditation, of which the dramatic quickly becomes predominant. Though they may be unique, and perhaps no analogies should be drawn from them, we have here at least one instance in which nearly all the explanations of the growth and development of drama are beside the point. Is it not possible that this instance, cloistered and isolated and crude as its form may be, may actually be helpful in understanding the way that professional or secular ecclesiastical play-writers worked? To the question in this case, "When is a text a play?" the answer is, obviously, when the writer says it is, on "gudfriday" afternoon and Easter morning. The plays were performed in 1974 in Southwark Cathedral; one rather hopes that this was not their dramatic debut.

NOTES

1. The association is spelled out in full in Baker and Murphy, "Late Medieval Plays," and "The Books of Myles Blomefylde."

2. The care that was taken to preserve the "play-book" of communities is well documented; see especially Coldewey, "Digby Plays."

3. David Bevington, in his facsimile edition of *The Macro Plays*, agrees with Pollard; but Norman Davis, in a review of the facsimile, quite positively asserts the identity of the hands, supported by M. B. Parkes (*N&Q*, 220 [1975], p. 79). R. L. Alton in another review agrees with Bevington (*RES*, n.s. 28 [1977], p. 329), but his arguments seem less weighty than those of Davis. Ian Doyle has given me his opinion that the hands are the same, the only differences being the larger writing of the one and the use of a different final *s* between the two hands, easily accounted for by a lapse of time between the copyings.

4. See Beadle, "The Scribal Problem in the Macro Manuscripts."

5. See Baker, Murphy, and Hall, pp. lxxiv-lxxxiii. The writer of the plays, a Carthusian probably in Hull, had written a vast verse chronicle in the first half of the book, which has received very little attention. In fact, it is quite interesting. This chronicle begins as a help to meditation, as are so many of the Carthusian books, which often bear more than a passing resemblance to the later emblem books. See Holtgen, "*Arbor, Scala* und *Fons Vitae*."

6. See the second plate in Baker and Murphy, *The Digby Plays*.

WORKS CITED AND SUGGESTED READING

Baker, Donald C. Review of *Non-Cycle Plays and Fragments, ELN* 9 (1972), 294.

———, and John L. Murphy. "The Books of Myles Blomefylde," *The Library* 5, xxxi (1976) 377–80.

———, and John L. Murphy. *The Digby Plays* (MS 133 and e Museo 160). Leeds Texts and Monographs: Medieval Drama Facsimiles Series, 3. Leeds: University of Leeds, 1976.

———, and John L. Murphy. "The Late Medieval Plays of the MS Digby 133: Scribes, Dates and Early History," *Research Opportunities in Renaissance Drama* 10 (1967).

———, John L. Murphy, and Louis B. Hall, Jr., eds. *The Late Medieval Religious Plays of Bodleian MSS Digby 133 and e Museo 160*. EETS, o.s., 283. Oxford: Oxford University Press, 1982.

Bakere, Janet A. *The Cornish Ordinalia: A Critical Study*. Cardiff: University of Wales Press, 1980.

Beadle, Richard. "The Medieval Drama of East Anglia: Studies in Dialect, Documentary Records and Stagecraft." York University Ph.D. Dissertation, 1977.

———. "The Scribal Problem in the Macro Manuscript," *ELN* 21 (1984) 1–13.

———, ed. *The York Plays*. London: Edward Arnold, 1982.

———, and Peter Meredith, eds. *The York Plays* (BL MS Add 35290). Leeds Texts and Monographs: Medieval Drama Facsimiles Series, 7. Leeds: University of Leeds, 1983.

Bevington, David M. *From Mankind to Marlowe: Growth of Structure in the Popular Drama of Tudor England*. Cambridge, Mass.: Harvard University Press, 1962.

———, ed. *The Macro Plays: The Castle of Perseverance, Wisdom, Mankind*. The Folger Facsimiles Manuscript Series, I. New York: Johnson Reprint Corp., 1972.

Block, K. S., ed. *Ludus Coventriae, or The Plaie Called Corpus Christi, Cotton Ms Vespasian D.viii.* EETS, 120. London: Oxford University Press, 1922 (repr. 1960).

Cawley, A. C., and Martin Stevens, eds. *The Towneley Cycle (Ms Huntington HM1).* Leeds Texts and Monographs: Medieval Drama Facsimiles, 2. Leeds: University of Leeds, 1976.

Chambers, E. K. *The Elizabethan Stage.* 4 Vols. Oxford: Clarendon Press, 1923.

———. *The Mediaeval Stage.* 2 Vols. Oxford: Clarendon Press, 1903.

———. *The English Folk Play.* Oxford: Clarendon Press, 1933.

Coldewey, John C. "The Digby Plays and the Chelmsford Records," *Research Opportunities in Renaissance Drama,* 18 (1975) 103–21.

Craig, Hardin. *English Religious Drama of the Middle Ages.* Oxford: Clarendon Press, 1955.

Davis, Norman, ed. *Non-Cycle Plays and Fragments.* EETS, e.s. 87. London: Oxford University Press, 1970.

———, ed. *Non-Cycle Plays and the Winchester Dialogues: Facsimiles of Plays and Fragments in Various Manuscripts and the Dialogues in Winchester College Ms 33.* Leeds Texts and Monographs. Medieval Drama Facsimiles Series, 5. Leeds: University of Leeds, 1979.

Denny, Neville, ed. *Medieval Drama.* Stratford upon Avon Studies 16. London: Edward Arnold, 1973.

Dodd, K. M. "Another Elizabethan Theater in the Round." *Shakespeare Quarterly* 21 (1970), 125–54.

Eccles, Mark, ed. *The Macro Plays: The Castle of Perseverance, Wisdom, Mankind.* EETS, 262. Oxford: Oxford University Press, 1969.

England, George and A.W. Pollard, eds. *The Towneley Plays.* EETS, e.s. 71. London: Oxford University Press, 1897.

Feuillerat, Albert, ed. *Documents Relating to the Revels at Court in the Time of King Edward VII and Queen Mary. Materialen zur Kunde des alteren Englischen Dramas.* Louvain: A. Uystpruyst, 1914.

———, ed. *Documents Relating to the Office of the Revels in the Time of Queen Elizabeth. Materialen zur Kunde des alteren Englischen Dramas,* 21. Louvain: A. Uystpruyst, 1908.

Fifield, Merle. "The Use of Doubling and Extras in *Wisdom,*" *Ball State University Forum* 6 (1965) 65–68.

Flanigan, C. Clifford. "The Liturgical Drama and Its Tradition: A Review of Scholarship 1965–1975." *Research Opportunities in Renaissance Drama* 18 (1975) 81–102; 19 (1976) 109–36.

Furnivall, F. J., ed. *The Digby Plays,* EETS, e.s. 70. Oxford: Oxford University Press, 1896.

Gibson, Gail M. "Bury St. Edmunds, Lydgate, and the *N-Town Cycle,*" *Speculum* 56 (1981) 56–90.

Harbage, Alfred, and Samuel Schoenbaum. *Annals of English Drama 975–1700.* Philadelphia: University of Pennsylvania Press, 1940.

Hazlitt, W. C., ed. *Remains of the Early Popular Poetry of England.* (1864).

Holtgen, K. J. "*Arbor, Scala* und *Fons Vitae*: Vorformen devotionaler Embleme in einer mittelenglishen Handschrift (BM Add. MS 37049)," in *Chaucer und seine Zeit: Symposium für Walter F. Schirmer,* ed. by A. Esche (1968) 355–91.

Kahrl, Stanley. *Traditions of Medieval English Drama.* London: Hutchinson's University Library, 1974.

Kolve, V. A. *The Play Called Corpus Christi.* Palo Alto: Stanford University Press, 1966.

Lumiansky, Robert M., and David Mills, eds. *The Chester Mystery Cycle*. EETS S.S. 3. London: Oxford University Press, 1974.

———. *The Chester Mystery Cycle (Ms Bodley 175)*. Leeds Texts and Monographs, Medieval Drama Facsimiles, no. 1. Leeds: University of Leeds, 1973.

———. *The Chester Mystery Cycle: A Reduced Facsimile of Huntington Library MS 2*. Leeds Texts and Monographs, Medieval Drama Facsimiles, no. 6. Leeds: University of Leeds, 1980.

Meredith, Peter, and Stanley J. Kahrl, eds. *The N-Town Plays: A Facsimile of British Library MS Cotton Vespasian D.VIII*. Leeds Texts and Monographs, Medieval Drama Facsimiles, no. 4. Leeds: University of Leeds, 1977.

Molloy, J. J. *A Theological Interpretation of the Moral Play, Wisdom, Who Is Christ*. Washington, D.C.: Catholic University of America Press, 1952.

Murray, John Tucker. *English Dramatic Companies 1558–1642*. 2 Vols. London: Constable and Company, 1910.

Nelson, Alan H. *The Medieval English Stage: Corpus Christi Pageants and Plays*. Chicago: University of Chicago Press, 1974.

Nicholl, Allardyce. *Masks, Mimes, and Miracles: Studies in the Popular Theatre*. London: Harrap, 1931.

Nungezer, Edwin. *A Dictionary of Actors and of Other Persons Associated with Public Representation of Plays in England Before 1642*. New Haven: Yale University Press, 1929 (AMS rpt., 1971).

Patch, H. R. "*The Ludus Coventriae* and the Digby Massacre." *PMLA* 30 (1920) 324–43.

Pfleiderer, J. "The Community of Language in the Late Medieval Drama of East Anglia," Ph.D. Dissertation, University of Colorado, 1981.

Pollard, A. *The Macro Plays*. EETS, e.s. 91 (1904).

Salter, F. M. *Medieval Drama in Chester*. Toronto: University of Toronto Press, 1955.

Schmidt, K. "Die Digby-Spiele." *Anglia* 1 (1885) 387–90.

Seymour, M. C. "Mandeville and Marco Polo: A Stanzaic Fragment." *AUMLA* 20 (1964) 39–52.

Smart, W. K. *Some English and Latin Sources and Parallels for the Morality of Wisdom*. Menasha, Wis.: G. Banta, 1912.

Smith, Lucy Toulmin. *York Plays*. Oxford: Clarendon Press, 1885.

Southern, Richard. *The Medieval Theatre in the Round: A Study of the Staging of the Castel of Perseverance and Related Matters*. London: Faber and Faber, 1957.

Stratman, Carl J. *Bibliography of Medieval Drama*, 2d ed. 2 vols. New York: Frederick Ungar, 1972.

Waterhouse, O., ed. *The Non-Cycle Mystery Plays, together with the Croxton Play of the Sacrament and the Pride of Life*. EETS e.s. 104 (1909).

Wickham, Glynne. *Early English Stages: 1300–1600*. 2 vols. in 3 pts. London: Routledge and Kegan Paul, 1959–1972, 1980, 1981.

———. "The Staging of Saint Plays in England," in Sandro Sticca, *The Medieval Drama*. Albany: State University of New York Press, 1972.

———. *The Medieval Theatre*. London: Weidenfeld and Nicolson, 1974.

ROBERT POTTER

The Unity of Medieval Drama

European Contexts for Early English Dramatic Traditions

Two traditional literary biases have seriously impeded our understanding of English medieval drama. The first and most pernicious of these has been an unwillingness to accept and read its texts as playscripts—that is as documents (whether *prescriptive* or *descriptive*) of a theatrical performance. In the past thirty years this anti-theatrical bias has been steadily reduced from an orthodoxy to a heresy, by a succession of theatrically-aware critical studies and a directly related profusion of theatrical revivals. We are no longer seriously in danger of underestimating the theatrical viability and inherent performance dimensions of medieval dramatic texts.[1]

However, a second and equally strong literary bias continues to hinder our perception of medieval plays, and that is the habit of studying them as pieces of English or French or German literature, distinct products of national cultures and languages. This nationalistic-linguistic bias, which derives from academic departmentalization (and the nineteenth-century nationalism for which it stands) is now undergoing a healthy reevaluation. The old insular philological boundaries are melting away like customs barriers, together with the cultural urgencies of demonstrating the preeminence of any single national literature or drama. New ecumenical circumstances—academic programs in Drama, Medieval Studies or Comparative Literature—are compelling us to consider our English dramatic texts as part of a wider and more complex tradition, more truly representative of the international reality of late medieval European culture.

ANTHOLOGIES

A measure of how far we have come in this regard, but also of the distance we have yet to travel, may be seen in comparing the formerly dominant anthology of our field, J. Q. Adams's *Chief Pre-Shakespearean Dramas* (1924) with its widely adopted successor, David Bevington's *Medieval Drama* (1975). The difference of emphasis, implicit in the titles of these books, is made clear in the tables of contents. Adams's focus is on the development of English drama, and the sixteen selections representing liturgical drama (covering seventy pages, or about ten percent of the volume) are in the nature of a prologue. The book's emphasis is on tracing a process of evolution, on English soil and in texts of English origin wherever possible (or northern France where necessary, positing lost English analogues).

Bevington, by contrast, treats the liturgical drama as a pan-European phenomenon worthy of sustained attention in its own right. He prints (and translates) twenty-seven selections, occupying over two hundred pages, or roughly twenty percent of the volume, ranging from Patristic sources to a full representation of the great twelfth century Continental masterpieces, including the *Jeu d'Adam*, the Beauvais *Play of Daniel* and the Benediktbeuern Christmas and Passion plays—none of which appear in Adams.

When texts emerge in the vernacular, however, the differences in the anthologies disappear. Adams and Bevington both move firmly into English as soon as texts permit, and Bevington prints no further translations of Continental plays. The heavy emphasis in each is on plays from the English mystery cycles, though Bevington prints a fuller sample (twenty-eight selections, including the N-Town Passion Plays, to Adams's nineteen). Bevington's final segments of text, covering moralities, saints' plays, and "Humanist Drama" duplicate exactly plays anthologized previously in Adams, though admittedly in better and unexpurgated texts.

Given the paucity of extant English texts in such genres as the morality play, farce, saint's play, and "secular drama," any anthology with an English Literature orientation would be similarly structured. Nevertheless these selections provide a highly inadequate picture of the history of late medieval drama—no proper saint's play, as Bevington points out,[2] and no secular dramatist previous to the belated sixteenth century *farceur* John Heywood. The obvious enrichment which the inclusion of Continental texts might bring—from literary Latin comedies like *Babio* or *Pamphilus*, the lyric minstrel plays of Adam de la Halle, classic farces like *Maitre Pierre Pathelin*, to the ingenious Dutch play-within-a-play of *Mariken van Nieumeghen*—demonstrates the relative frugality of any single national diet. What we need, and as yet lack, are anthologies (and in some cases even the texts and translations) to match the state of our critical understanding, as embodied in such excellent studies as Richard Axton's *European Drama of the Early Middle Ages*.

THEATRE HISTORY

The study of medieval staging has, perhaps because of its frequently nonverbal subject matter, been less afflicted with cultural and linguistic bias than most other aspects of scholarship in medieval drama. An additional factor causing English scholars to look to the Continent is the dearth of visual evidence of staging in English documents. Aside from the famous ground plan for *The Castle of Perseverance*, we have few English depictions of stages or staging. In these circumstances, the voluminous Continental visual evidence—pictures of pageant cars, stage plans, paintings of apparent theatrical performances—has been tacitly accepted as at least analogically useful. However, it is interesting that far less has been made by English critics of the ample *written* evidence on Continental staging practices, such as Philippe de Mezieres's prompt book for the 1385 production of *The Presentation of the Virgin* at Avignon, or Renward Cysat's exhaustive and definitive records of the 1583 Lucerne Passion Play.[3]

An early and vivid example of the potentialities of theatre history in bettering our understanding of English medieval texts is Richard Southern's *The Medieval Theatre in the Round* (1957). Aiming at a reconstruction of the original performance of *The Castle of Perseverance*, Southern begins with its unique stage plan, and the implicit and explicit stage directions of the text. But the study also makes brilliant use of textual and physical evidence of round staging in the Cornish drama, and includes an illuminating analysis of the apparent theatre-in-the-round shown in the fifteenth-century Jean Fouquet miniature "The Martyrdom of Saint Apollonia," a piece of visual evidence previously considered relevant only to Continental drama. Southern's reconstruction of the staging of *The Castle* has been accepted as persuasive in many, though not all, of its ingenious details. A whole series of important theatrical revivals, from the Cornish Mystery Plays at Piran Round (1969) to the Toronto *Castle of Perseverance* (1979), owe their genesis to Southern's deductions.[4]

In the years since Southern's book appeared our comprehension of the breadth and depth of medieval theatre history, and its applicability to English texts, has increased markedly. Glynne Wickham's complex three part study *Early English Stages* (1959–1972) has taught us to widen our concepts of stagecraft to include royal and civic pageantry, as well as applicable Continental evidence, such as the pageant wagon stages of the Spanish *Autos Sacramentales*. Two interesting French works, Henri Rey-Flaud's *Le cercle magique* (1973) and Elie Konigson's *L'Espace théâtral médiéval* (1975) have pursued Southern's investigation of the wide evidence of theatre-in-the-round staging, and have explored its philosophical implications—for example, Konigson's provocative hypothesis that medieval theatre space replicates the sacred design of the cosmos.

"The study of the medieval theatre requires a universal point of view," observed Alois Nagler in publishing *The Medieval Religious Stage* in 1976—a summary of thirty years of his own, and his Yale doctoral students' attempts to sift facts from surmise. "We cannot afford to be students of German or English or Romance matters alone. The boundaries of language must fall" (p. xi-xii). For all of its catholicity and scrupulous scientific method, however, *The Medieval Religious Stage* is a disappointingly negative work of scholarship. So frequent and caustic are Nagler's dismissals of other scholars' work that the edifice of received opinion is obscured in smoke from the scholarly battlefield. When evidence is plentiful enough to admit of no real dispute, as in the case of the Lucerne Passion Play, Nagler seems genuinely uninterested and hardly even bothers to summarize the facts.

A more encouraging and representative indication of the state of the art in medieval theatre history may be found in William Tydeman's admirable survey *The Theatre in the Middle Ages* (1978). Subtitled "Western European Stage Conditions, c. 800–1576," Tydeman's book traces the common historical origins of our Western dramatic traditions, organizing evidence with respect to kinds of theatres (e.g., indoor, street, open air) rather than national boundaries, and adds detailed and comparative chapters on scenic effects, actors, and economics. The only significant limitations of Tydeman's work are its self-imposed concentrations on Britain, France, Germany, and Spain, to the exclusion of Italy, the Low Countries, and other theatrically active parts of Europe.

GENRES OF DRAMA

How can our understanding of medieval English plays and dramatic traditions be widened by the perception of a larger European context? I wish to devote the remainder of this essay to a consideration of two examples of how a more ecumenical scholarship may approach old materials with new and illuminating critical perspectives. The subjects I have chosen are two major genres of medieval English drama—the "Corpus Christi cycle" and the morality play.

> The medieval religious drama in England has been too narrowly conceived of because chance has given us four great Corpus Christi plays with a good deal of information about them and has left us little about the great contemporary rival of the Corpus Christi play, namely the Passion play of London and southern England. . . . We may conjecture with reasonable assurance that [the London plays] were in form somewhat like those of France and Germany. That is, they were plays [on stationary stages], with or without Old Testament subjects, centering in the Passion and Resurrection, probably lacking plays of the Nativity and possibly lacking plays of the final judgment. . . . The loss of these great Passion plays from the most populous and dominant region of England forces us to conclude that the greater religious drama of the English Middle Ages was, neither quantitatively nor qualitatively, what it is ordinarily thought to be. (Craig, pp. 152–53)

These words of Hardin Craig, arguing for a wider critical perspective, deserve more attention than they have received. Recent medieval drama scholarship, for all of its theatrical sophistication, has tended to focus on the indigenous locality of English forms, rather than their links to the larger European dramatic scene. The flourishing of Continental-style Passion plays in England is well documented; Chambers cites a string of references to the play extending over an extraordinary period of centuries from the twelfth to the seventeenth, not merely in the south of England, but as far north as Aberdeen (*The Mediaeval Stage*). As the REED project brings us a fuller account of dramatic records in southern county archives, we should have the material for a reappraisal of this rich tradition.

Short of recovering the lost texts, we cannot physically reconstruct the English Passion plays. But scholarship can help us to comprehend the abundant links, both direct and indirect, uniting the extant religious drama of England with the Continental genres of the Passion play. For example, the so-called Cornish Cycle or *Ordinalia* is in effect a three-day Passion play on the Continental model; its three parts—Creation, Passion, and Resurrection—culminate not in a Last Judgment, but rather in a superb dramatization of Christ's Ascension. These plays in the Cornish language were presented in fixed, multi-scaffolded theatres in the round; the evident dramaturgical and theatrical links to Continental practice are confirmed and reappraised by the *Ordinalia*'s recent critics and editors.[5] Yet English and American critics continue to refer to the "Cornish Cycle," as if the *Ordinalia* were a derivative of the York and Wakefield plays. A far less inaccurate term might be the "Cornish Passion Play."

The dramatic subject of the Continental Passion plays is primarily, of course, the events of Passion week—from Palm Sunday to Easter. But it is insufficiently appreciated, in English-speaking critical circles, that many events before and afterwards are also dramatized. For example, the two-day *Passion de Semur* devotes its first day to events from the Creation to Christ's temptation in the wilderness, and its second day to the remainder of the Passion story. Arnoul Greban's *Le Mystère de la Passion*, a four-day play, begins with a prologue staging events in Genesis from the Creation to Cain and Abel; its first day is devoted to the Nativity, its second to Christ's ministry and its third and fourth to the events of Passion week. The twenty-five-day Valenciennes Passion play begins with the Trial in Heaven and concludes, like the Cornish *Ordinalia*, with the Ascension.

Among German examples, the Vienna Passion play begins with the Falls of Lucifer and Adam, as do the plays of Eger and Kunzelsau. Even when Old Testament scenes are not directly staged, the major events are narrated and their participants emerge as characters in the obligatory Harrowing of Hell sequences. The presence of Adam and Eve and their descendents is, after all, theologically crucial, in the sense that the redemption is the result of (and solution to) man's fall (see Froning, *Das Drama* and Creizenach, *Geschichte*).

The practice of referring to the four extant English cycles as "Corpus Christi plays" will not bear very close examination. Of the four, one (Chester) was written as a three-day play for performance at Whitsun, and another (N-Town) cannot be securely linked to any feast day (despite its manuscript's annotation as "the plaie called Corpus Christi") and was probably never presented in its entirety anywhere. Moreover, the central portion of the "N-Town" plays is a two-part Passion play on Continental lines, firmly conceived for a fixed-stage multiple-loca performance. Direct links have been found between the characters and events of this play and those of several Continental Passion plays—Alsfeld, Friedberg, and Villingen —produced under the auspices of the Franciscans (see Cameron and Kahrl, "Staging").

This leaves only two "pure" Corpus Christi plays (York and Wakefield), and even these are less unlike Passion plays than standard terminology would suggest. The usual "cosmic" definition of the English Corpus Christi play—as the history of the world from Creation to Doomsday—can be distinctly misleading. Such a definition implies a relatively consistent chronological survey, as does Kolve's suggestion that the selection of events in the plays is a working-out of the medieval concept of the seven ages of the world—Adam, Noah, Abraham, Moses, Prophets, Christ, and Doomsday (Kolve, pp. 117–23).

In fact the central dramatic subject of the Corpus Christi cycles is the life of Christ. If we define this life broadly as extending from the Annunciation to the Ascension, it is demonstrable that nearly two-thirds of the component plays of the Corpus Christi cycles focus on this brief span of years. Such an emphasis might almost lead us to the heretical conclusion that there is relatively little to separate the dramatic concept of the English cycles from the Passion play tradition—indeed that we might profitably study them not as a separate genre but as a related variant.

In any event there is certainly much to be gained by considering the English cycles in the larger context of European tradition and experiment, in staging the events of Christ's Passion in Jerusalem in the streets of a medieval city. Whatever else they are, Corpus Christi cycles *are* Passion plays. One of the principal discoveries that has emerged in staging cycle plays in this century, from the streets of Toronto to the halls of the National Theatre, has been the overriding power of the Passion story as a dramatic experience. It is most likely that what a medieval audience would carry away from any performance of the cycles would be the miraculous actuality that Nicodemus discovers in the past, present, and future, over Christ's dead body:

> It shall be so with outten nay.
> He that dyed on gud fryday
>   And crownyd was with thorne,
> Saue you all that now here be
> That Lord that thus wold dee
>   And rose on pasche morne.
>   (England and Pollard, p. 278)

The morality play has been a misunderstood and often maligned genre of English medieval drama. Its old subterranean public image was, as Paula Neuss has pointed out, as "something one may be obliged to dig up, in order to see what kind of 'roots' underlay the drama that blossomed with the Elizabethans, but really rather brown and grubby and of no intrinsic interest" ("Active and Idle Language," p. 41). In recent years we have begun to take a fuller measure of the morality play as an ingenious and wide-ranging tradition of drama which flourished in many localities in late medieval Europe. Though best known for their exotic allegorical characters, morality plays are best understood as dramatic attempts to define the human condition. They view life as a process of discovery, focusing particularly on the inevitability of sin, and on the cure to be found in repentance and forgiveness.

As I observed in 1975, there is much to be learned from studying the relatively few extant plays of the English tradition in the context of the numerous surviving French *moralités*, and the equally interesting if less well-known allegorical vein of the Spanish *Autos Sacramentales* (*The English Morality Plays*, chap. VII). In the present circumstances I wish to argue for more attention to the German and Dutch traditions as well.

For an example, one need look no further than Hans Sachs's remarkable Shrovetide play of 1536, *Das Narrenschneiden*, recently translated and staged by Martin Walsh under the title *Fool Surgery*.[6] German Shrovetide plays (*Fastnachtsspiele*) celebrate the occasion of Carnival, and their staple commodities are farce and scatology; nevertheless, students of such English morality plays as *Mankind* might recognize the possibilities for moral drama which such circumstances afford, and in *Fool Surgery* they will not be disappointed.

The literary sources of the play are eclectic; the protagonist appears to be a prototypical quack doctor, and his foil—an enormously rotund sick man—comes straight off the boat from Sebastian Brandt's *Ship of Fools* (Walsh, "The Surgeon of Folly"). Sachs's plot, however, rejects the easy path of doctor-gulls-fool, and rather assays the more difficult task of curing. The doctor decides that his patient is suffering from an infestation of fools and proceeds to perform a harrowing surgical operation on the bloated belly. He extracts in due course a series of grotesque fools—none other than Pride, Greed, Envy, Unchasteness, Gluttony, Wrath, and Sloth. When these familiar medieval infestations have been removed, with much medical ado, the sick man is cured. He promises to reform his life, a counsel which he also recommends to those in the audience who may be suffering themselves from such hidden afflictions.

The affinity which a play such as *Fool Surgery* has to the English traditions extends beyond the earthiness of the dialogue to the persistent motif of disease and curing in such plays as *Mankind* and *Wisdom*. Obviously we need to look more closely at the considerable canon of German plays in this genre; Sachs's collected works alone include eighty-five *Fastnachtspiele*.

Until very recently English-speaking scholars have been unaware of the nature and full extent of the Dutch tradition of moral drama. W. M. H. Hummelen, the distinguished bibliographer of the Dutch *Rederijkers*, drew astonishment from an international audience of medievalists in 1979 when he estimated that the Dutch corpus included no less than 586 extant plays, "most of which could be called moralities, if we used that term in Dutch literary history" ("The Dutch Rhetoricians Drama"). That the existence of such a vast body of plays should have remained virtually a scholarly secret in the last quarter of the twentieth century is partly the fault of Dutch literary scholarship (preoccupied as it has been with the later Golden Age of Dutch writing) and partly the fault of a world uninterested in dramatic accomplishments, however major, which were enacted in a minor language.

All the same, we should not have been surprised. The existence of the Dutch masterpiece *Elckerlijc* has been acknowledged widely, as has the English *Everyman*'s derivation from it—a much-debated but well-established scholarly fact. I must here record my own error in perpetuating in print the old argument that the Dutch play could be a translation derived from *Everyman* (*The English Morality Play*, p. 17). The facts are otherwise; indeed the best explanation for the unique artistic qualities of *Everyman*, in comparison with other English plays, is the likelihood that *it* is a translation, deriving from a parallel but distinct literary and dramatic context—the theatre of the Dutch *Rederijkers*.

The *Rederijkerskamers*, or Chambers of Rhetoric, were civic guilds which flourished in the sixteenth century in cities throughout the low countries. Descended, apparently, from French and Burgundian confraternities, they performed plays on festive occasions and competed with one another for prizes. Their repertory covered a wide variety of subject matter—from Biblical plays to occasional pieces, farces and classical mythology—but the most numerous and characteristic plays were their *Spelen van sinnen*, didactic plays with representative characters demonstrating a given theme or subject (Hummelen, *Repertorium*).[7]

A particularly delightful example is *Het Esbatement van den Appelboom* (c. 1500), translated into English by Neville Denny under the title *The Blessed Apple Tree*.[8] It tells the tale of an unfortunate farmer and his wife who, after suffering various barnyard calamities, beg the Lord God to give them an apple tree which will bear fruit all year long. They also ask a further favor—that anyone who climbs up in the tree to steal fruit will be stuck there.

Their wishes are granted, and soon passers-by appear (a peddler named Insatiability and an amorous couple, Loose Wanton and Riotous Living) who climb the tree in search of apples and become stuck. The farmer and his wife gloatingly lecture the sinners on the wages of their sins, meanwhile appropriating the belongings they have left below. But Death arrives to strike down the proud farmer. The stricken farmer begs a last request, however, and Death climbs the tree to fetch him an apple —producing delight for the farmer, panic among the sinners in the tree, and frustration for Death, trapped up a tree with the others. Now the Devil arrives, angry that people have stopped dying, and he in turn is lured up the tree. The play ends with a truce, in which Death and the Devil agree to leave the farmer alone for his appointed days, and the sinners repent of their cupidity.

In the ten years since its translation *The Blessed Apple Tree* has been widely staged in the English-speaking world and is, I believe, on the way to becoming a classic of its kind. Another most interesting script, Jan van den Berghe's *De Wellustige Mensch*, a play of the 1550s, has been successfully revived in Holland and has recently been translated into English as *The Voluptuous Man*; it concerns a wayward hero Lustful Man, who takes up with a pair of Vice-like tempters (who later transform themselves into Death and a Devil) and after some dalliance with Lady Lechery, ends on his knees in repentance and with the forgiveness of God's Grace.[9] The play embodies fluent language and an elegant five-part structure, as Merle Fifield has pointed out ("The Community of Morality Plays").

Among the many interesting stage conventions of the Dutch tradition, two in particular seem significant with respect to the English moralities. The first of these is the pair of tempter-commentators (as in *The Voluptuous Man*), known to the Dutch as "Sinnekins." This pair of comedians became a fixture in the Dutch plays—brash, fast-talking, and more than a match for the malleable human figures they encounter and manipulate; the more so because they are usually two-against-one. In the play *Man's Desire and Fleeting Beauty* (*Van 's Menschen Sin en Verganckilicke Schoonheit*) the Sinnekins are called Custom and Fashion, and their first victim is a lustful would-be lover, Man's Desire. To whet his appetites, they procure a gorgeous young woman called Fleeting Beauty, and convince her in turn that Man's Desire is just what she is looking for. The lovers banquet, sing, and court one another ardently as the Sinnekins laugh and mock them unobserved; eventually Man's Desire and Fleeting Beauty grow passionate, and send the Sinnekins away so that they may be alone together. A curtain is drawn over their subsequent activities. The Sinnekins reappear to mock the sexual goings-on concealed by the curtain; ultimately they decide to interrupt the lovers by opening the curtain, but when they do a terrifying sight is revealed— Death with a spear, about to stab the embracing couple *in flagrante delicto*. Translated into English in 1984, this play has now been successfully revived in England, Canada, and the U.S.A.[10]

The power of the visual spectacle in the Dutch-Flemish plays is worthy of far more study than it has yet received. It is worth remembering that the centuries of the *Rederijkers* coincided with the great flourishing of Dutch and Flemish painting, and the set designers included men like Hieronymus Bosch who, as David Jeffrey has shown, worked as costume and set designer for his confraternity, and used stage symbolism in his greatest paintings ("Bosch's Haywain").

A second convention of the Dutch stage tradition applicable to the English moralities then, is the fondness for spectacular theatrical tableaux or discoveries, known to Dutch scholars as *toogs*. As a case in point, I believe that a knowledge of the Dutch tableau-discovery convention is vital to unlocking the ambiguities of a particularly uncertain moment in the text of *Everyman*.

Following *Everyman*'s last lines "*In manus tuas*, of myghtes moost/ For euer, *Commendo spiritum meum*" (Crawley, ed., ll. 886–87), he presumably enters the stage grave that awaits him, explicitly called for in the text ("For into this caue must I crepe" l. 792; "What, into this graue?" l. 794; "Loke in my graue ones pyteously" l. 838). Knowledge confirms that he has "made endynge" but then tells us that he hears angels singing "Where Euerymannes soule receyed shall be" (l. 893). The next lines are given to an angel, who has not spoken or appeared previously:

> Come excellent electe spouse, to Jesu!
> Here aboue thou shalte go. . . . (ll. 894–95)

Directors of *Everyman* have struggled with this moment much as their opposite numbers must struggle with a similar stage circumstance at the end of *King Lear*. What are we supposed to see, at this climactic moment of *Everyman*? In the absence of a stage direction, what is going on? The text of *Elckerlijc*, it seems, is more explicit. Knowledge says:

> Mi dunct, ic hore der enghelen gheshal
> Hier boven. den Hemel is seker ontdaen,
> Daer Elckerlijc binnen sal zijn ontfaen.
>
> (I think I hear the flourish of angels
> Here above; Heaven has certainly been opened,
> Wherein Everyman will be received.)

And the Angel says:

> Coemt, uutvercoren bruyt,
> Hier boven, ende hoort dat suete gheluyt
> Der engelen mits uwe goede virtuyt.
>
> (Come, chosen bride
> Here above, and hear the sweet sound

Of the angels, because of your good Virtue.)[11]
(Vos, *van Elckerlijc*, my translation)

What we have here, it would seem, is a climactic discovery or *toog* in which a visual emblem of heaven is unexpectedly unveiled, supplying *Everyman* (and *Elckerlijc*) with its surprising happy ending. Some representation of Everyman's soul must join the Angel in the heaven scaffold, magically refuting what our eyes have seemingly witnessed only moments before, the "endynge" of Everyman.

Such theatrical sophistication, wedded to rhetorical complexity, is certainly an important part of what lifts *Everyman* beyond and above the level of its English contemporaries. A better understanding of such conventions will help us to make better sense of the English moralities—certainly in the case of *Everyman*, and quite likely in other cases as the possibilities of Anglo-Dutch theatre borrowings, following the trade routes, are further explored. Can we, for example, trace the multiple tempters of several moralities (e.g., *Mankind, Hickscorner*) to the Dutch Sinnekins? Such questions are easily posed, but must await patient scholarly study of the emerging Dutch corpus.

The fragmentary nature of the English medieval drama—its uncertain sources, haphazardly preserved texts and inadequately documented stagecraft—has fascinated many generations of scholars, and will continue to do so. But assuredly we can no longer afford to ignore the evidence of Continental practice over many centuries and across national boundaries, particularly when it provides actualities to help us make greater sense of our own expanding subject. I have alluded in this essay to a number of potential sources of further insight, including the texts and staging evidence of French secular and literary comedy, Dutch and Flemish allegorical drama, and German Passion plays and Shrovetide farces. Further illumination may be found in the musical sophistication of the Italian *Laude* and the religious dramas of the great Iberian playwrights from Gil Vicente to Calderon de la Barca. And certainly the final chapter of the story—the spread of European dramatic practices to the New World—needs to be more carefully studied, in the wake of Marilyn Ekdahl Ravicz's pioneering work on the fusion of Christian and Aztec traditions.[12]

Nevertheless we will return, as we must, to what remains to us of our own native traditions. My belief is that further research and a wider awareness of what has happened elsewhere will only deepen our sense of the distinctive artistry of the English plays, as well as enhancing our understanding of their larger contexts in the drama of the Continent. It is already clear that both belong to a reality that is at once more complex and more unified than has been previously imagined.

NOTES

1. On the contribution of theatrical revivals to a better critical understanding of the plays, see particularly V. A. Kolve, *The Play Called Corpus Christi* (London: Arnold, 1966); Stanley Kahrl, *Traditions of Medieval English Drama* (London: Hutchinson, 1974); and John Elliott, *Playing God* (Toronto: University of Toronto Press, forthcoming).

2. ". . . we are left with only three fifteenth century dramas in English worthy of consideration as saints' plays or conversion plays. All of them are untypical of the genre to a greater or lesser degree." Bevington, *Medieval Drama*, p. 662.

3. A selection of such written evidence is now available in English translation in Peter Meredith and John E. Tailby, eds., *The Staging of Religious Drama in Europe in the later Middle Ages*.

4. Richard Southern, *The Medieval Theatre in the Round* (London: Faber, 1957) pp. 91–107 and plates 1–5. The Fouquet miniature has been identified as representing a theatrical performance since the time of Germaine Bapst, *Essai sur l'Histoire du Théâtre* (Paris: Hachette, 1893).

5. Markham Harris, trans. *The Cornish Ordinalia* (Washington, D.C.: Catholic University of America Press, 1969); Neville Denny, "Arena Staging and Dramatic Quality in the Cornish Passion Play," in N. Denny, ed., *Medieval Drama*, Stratford upon Avon Studies 16 (London: Arnold, 1973) pp. 125–153; Robert Longworth, *The Cornish Ordinalia: Religion and Dramaturgy* (Cambridge, Mass.: Harvard University Press, 1967); Jane Bakere, *The Cornish Ordinalia: A Critical Study* (Cardiff: University of Wales Press, 1980).

6. Martin Walsh and Margarete Orlik-Walsh, trans., *Fool Surgery: a Shrovetide Play by Hans Sachs*, unpublished Playscript. Produced at the 1978 Ann Arbor Medieval Festival.

7. For a useful introduction to the *Rederijkers*, see the proceedings of the Cambridge Colloquium on the Medieval Drama of the Low Countries, published in *Dutch Crossing* 22 (April 1984), including my article "Morality Play and *Spel van Sinne*: What are the Connections?" (5–16), and W. M. H. Hummelen's "The Dramatic Structure of the Dutch Morality" (17–26). See also Elsa Streitman, "Teach Yourself Art: The Literary Guilds in the Low Countries," *Dutch Crossing* 29 (August 1986) 75–94.

8. "The Blessed Apple Tree," trans. Neville Denny in N. Denny, *Medieval Interludes* (London: Ginn, 1972). For the original see P. J. Meertens, ed., *Het Esbatement van den Appelboom* (Zwolle: Tjeenk Willink, 1965).

9. "The Voluptuous Man," trans. Peter King, with an introduction, *Dutch Crossing* 28 (April 1986) 53–107.

10. *Een Esbattement van 's Menschen Sin en Verganckilicke Schoonheit*, ed. Nederlands Institut R. U. Groningen (Zwolle: Tjeenk Willink, 1967). In an English translation by the author and Elsa Streitman, published in *Dutch Crossing* 25 (April 1985) 29–84, "Man's Desire and Fleeting Beauty" was performed in 1984 at Homerton College, Cambridge. There have been subsequent productions at the University of Toronto and at the Huntington Library in California.

11. Original text and translation from John Conley, Guido de Beare, H. J. C. Schaap and W. H. Toppen, *The Mirror of Everyman's Salvation* (Amsterdam: Rodopi, 1985) pp. 58–59.

12. And see my article "Abraham and Human Sacrifice: The Exfoliation of Medieval Drama in Aztec Mexico," *New Theatre Quarterly* 8 (November 1986) 306–12.

WORKS CITED AND SUGGESTED READING

Adams, Joseph Quincy. *Chief Pre-Shakespearean Dramas.* Cambridge, Mass.: Houghton Mifflin, 1924.

Axton, Richard. *European Drama of the Early Middle Ages.* London: Hutchinson, 1974.

Bakere, Jane. *The Cornish Ordinalia: A Critical Study.* Cardiff: University of Wales Press, 1980.

Bapst, Germaine. *Essai sur l'Histoire du Théâtre.* Paris: Hachette, 1893.

Bevington, David. *Medieval Drama.* Boston: Houghton Mifflin, 1975.

Cameron, Kenneth and Stanley Kahrl. "Staging the N-Town Cycle." *Theatre Notebook* 21, 1967.

Cawley, A. C., ed. *Everyman.* Manchester: Manchester University Press, 1961.

Chambers, E. K. *The Mediaeval Stage.* Oxford: Oxford University Press, 1903.

Conley, John, Guido de Beare, H. J. C. Schaap, and W. H. Toppen.*The Mirror of Everyman's Salvation.* Amsterdam: Rodopi, 1985.

Craig, Hardin. *English Religious Drama of the Middle Ages.* Oxford: Clarendon Press, 1955.

Creizenach, Wilhelm. *Geschichte des Neueren Dramas* Vol. I. Halle: Niemeyer, 1893.

De Mezieres, Philippe. *Figurative Representation of the Presentation of the Virgin in the Temple,* trans. and ed. Robert Haller, intro. by M. Catherine Rupp. Lincoln: University of Nebraska Press, 1971.

Denny, Neville. "Arena Staging and Dramatic Quality in the Cornish Passion Play." *Medieval Drama,* Neville Denny, ed. Stratford upon Avon Studies 16. London: Arnold, 1973, pp. 125–53.

———. *Medieval Interludes.* London: Ginn, 1972.

Een Esbattement van 's Menschen Sin en Verganckilicke Schoonheit. ed. Nederlands Institut R.U. Gronigen. Zwolle: Tjeenk Willink, 1967.

Elliott, John. *Playing God.* Toronto: University of Toronto Press, forthcoming.

England, George, and A. W. Pollard, eds. *The Towneley Plays.* EETS e.s. 17. London: Early English Text Society, 1897.

Evans, M. Blakemore. *The Passion Play of Lucerne.* New York: MLA, 1943.

Fifield, Merle. "The Community of Morality Plays." *Comparative Drama* 9 (1976) 332–49.

Frank, Grace. *The Medieval French Drama.* Oxford: Clarendon Press, 1954.

Froning, R. *Das Drama des Mittelalters.* Stuttgart: Union Deutsch Verlagsgesellschaft, 1891.

Greban, Arnoul. *Le Mystère de la Passion,* ed. Omer Jodogne. Brussels: Palais des Academies, 1965.

Harris, Markham, trans. *The Cornish Ordinalia.* Washington, D.C.: Catholic University of America Press, 1969.

Hummelen, W. M. H. "The Dramatic Structure of the Dutch Morality." *Dutch Crossing* 22 (April 1984) 17–26.

———. "The Dutch Rhetoricians Drama." Unpublished paper delivered at the Fourteenth International Congress on Medieval Studies, Medieval Institute of America, Kalamazoo, Mich., May 1979.

———. *Repertorium van het Rederijkersdrama 1500-c. 1620.* Assen: Van Goroun, 1968.

Jeffrey, David. "Bosch's Haywain: Communion, Community and the Theatre of the World." *Viator* 4 (1973) 311–32.

Kahrl, Stanley. *Traditions of Medieval English Drama*. London: Hutchinson, 1974.

King, Peter. "The Voluptuous Man." Introduction and translation, *Dutch Crossing* 28 (April 1986) 53–107.

Kolve, V. A. *The Play Called Corpus Christi*. London: Arnold, 1966.

Konigson, Elie. *L'espace théâtral médiéval*. Paris: Editions du Centre de la Recherche Scientifique, 1975.

———. *La Représentation d'un mystère de la Passion à Valenciennes en 1547*. Paris: Editions du Centre de la Recherche Scientifique, 1969.

La Passion de Semur, text by P. T. Durbin, ed. by L. R. Muir. Leeds: Leeds Medieval Studies, 1981.

Longworth, Robert. *The Cornish Ordinalia: Religion and Dramaturgy*. Cambridge, Mass.: Harvard University Press, 1965.

Meertens, P. J., ed. *Het Esbatement van den Appelboom*. Zwolle: Tjeenk Willink, 1965.

Meredith, Peter, and John E. Tailby, eds. *The Staging of Religious Drama in Europe in the Later Middle Ages*. Kalamazoo, Mich.: Medieval Institute Publications, 1983.

Michael, Wolfgang F. *Das Deutsche Drama Des Mittelalters*. Berlin and New York: De Gruyter, 1971.

Nagler, Alois. *The Medieval Religious Stage*. New Haven and London: Yale University Press, 1976.

Neuss, Paula. "Active and Idle Language: Dramatic Images in *Mankind*." *Medieval Drama*, Neville Denny, ed. Stratford upon Avon Studies 16. London: Arnold, 1973, pp. 41–65.

Nicoll, Alardyce. *Masks, Mimes and Miracles: Studies in the Popular Theatre*. London: Harrap, 1931.

Potter, Robert. "Abraham and Human Sacrifice: The Exfoliation of Medieval Drama in Aztec Mexico." *New Theatre Quarterly* 8 (November 1986) 306–12.

———. *The English Morality Play*. London: Routledge and Kegan Paul, 1975.

———. "Morality Play and *Spel van Sin*: What Are the Connections." *Dutch Crossing* 22 (April 1984) 5–16.

Potter, Robert, and Elsa Streitman. "Man's Desire and Fleeting Beauty: A Sixteenth Century Comedy." *Dutch Crossing* 25 (April 1985) 29–84.

Ravicz, Marilyn Ekdahl. *Early Colonial Religious Drama in Mexico: From Tzompantli to Golgotha*. Washington, D.C.: Catholic University of America Press, 1970.

Rey-Flaud, Henri. *Le cercle magique*. Paris: Gallimard, 1973.

Shergold, N. D. *A History of the Spanish Stage from Medieval Times until the End of the Seventeenth Century*. Oxford: Clarendon Press, 1967.

Southern, Richard. *The Medieval Theatre in the Round*. London: Faber, 1957.

Stratman, Carl J. *Bibliography of Medieval Drama*. 2d ed., New York: Frederick Ungar, 1972.

Streitman, Elsa. "Teach Yourself Art: The Literary Guilds in the Low Countries." *Dutch Crossing* 29 (August 1986) 75–94.

Tydeman, William. *The Theatre in the Middle Ages*. Cambridge: Cambridge University Press, 1978.

van den Berghe, Jan. *De Wellustige Mensch* in *Dichten en Spelen van Jan van den Berghe*, ed. C. Kruyskamp. The Hague: Nijhoff, 1959, pp. xx-xxiv, 91–144.

Walsh, Martin. "The Surgeon of Folly: Sachs's *Narrenschneiden* and the Image of the Physician on the Early German Stage." Unpublished paper delivered to the Ohio Conference on Medieval and Renaissance Studies.

————, and Margarete Orlik. *Fool Surgery: A Shrovetide Play by Hans Sachs*, trans. M. Walsh. Unpublished playscript produced at the 1978 Ann Arbor Medieval Festival.
Wickham, Glynne. *Early English Stages* Vols. 1 and 2, Parts 1 and 2, London: Routledge and Kegan Paul, 1959–1972.

LYNETTE MUIR

Medieval English Drama
The French Connection

Although in many areas of medieval literature comparative studies have been carried out over a number of years, there has not until recently been any consistent attempt to consider religious vernacular drama on a truly European basis. However, in the last twenty years, there have been encouraging signs that this nationalist iron curtain is being lifted: the foundation of the International Society for the Medieval Theatre, with its regular colloquia; other inter-traditional meetings; the publication of books and papers that are deliberately European in scope; and the inclusion in this very collection of two chapters on the relationship of English and continental drama. This trend seems to me, together with the increased interest in the staging of plays, to be the most hopeful and important development in the field of medieval theatre studies this century.

One reason, I believe, why French and English vernacular biblical plays of the later Middle Ages have rarely been compared in detail is that at first sight they seem so inescapably different from one another. What is usually thought of as being the "typical" English play is cyclical in content, ranging from Creation to Doomsday; its structure is linear and episodic, made up of twenty to forty short scenes; its performance was financed and staged by groups of guildsmen on an annual, single-day basis; its stage was a pageant wagon and the surrounding street; and its audience, a few hundred people at most, stood around the small acting area. The "typical" French play, in contrast, had little or no Old Testament material and never included the Last Judgment; its action was synchronic, with alternating interlaced scenes; the production was organized, financed, and performed by a whole civic community including the clergy and the women; it was performed on an occasional basis in a fixed location and on a purpose-built platform; and it had a paying audience of several thousand, many of them seated in elaborate stands some distance from the large multiple stage. Truly, between the 10,000 lines of the Chester play, from Creation to Doomsday, and the 30,000 lines of Michel's *Passion*, from Baptism to Burial, there is a great gulf fixed.

This gulf has been emphasized by the lack of editions of many of the less typical French plays. It may be worth pointing out here that some fifty or more French biblical plays have survived, ranging in length from six hundred to more than 60,000 lines; there are another fifty saints plays. Altogether the surviving *religious* drama alone is of the order of one million lines. There are also several hundred plays which may be loosely classed as secular: farces, *soties*, moralities and so on. In these circumstances, the shortage of good critical editions or even of an edition of any kind, though regrettable, is not entirely surprising.[1]

In this paper, I am limiting myself to the consideration of religious, and especially biblical, plays on both sides of the Channel and I shall suggest some of the main areas in which, despite the apparent differences listed above, there may be seen to be connections between the two dramas. In a limited space it is not possible to do more than indicate, rather than explain, these factors, though I hope that some kind of pattern may emerge. The areas of investigation can be roughly classified under the headings of language, subject matter, staging, and organization.

FRENCH LANGUAGE AND ENGLISH DRAMA

Biblical plays written in French are already found in England in the twelfth century, earlier than on the Continent. The celebrated *Adam* play actually only slithers into Anglo-Norman drama on the basis of one rhyme; otherwise, the language is Norman but not specifically Anglo-Norman, while the MS was copied in southwest France. The rare scene of the prior temptation of Adam, of which the only other example in European medieval drama is from Bologna, may have been influenced by the equally unusual Old English *Genesis-B* redaction.

The apocryphal *Vita Adae*, in which Adam and Eve, doing penance after the Fall, are tempted by Satan disguised as an angel of light, is certainly the source of the Bologna play, and Rosemary Woolf suggested it might also be the basis of both the *Genesis-B* and *Adam* accounts. However, her argument for a direct influence of the *Vita Adae* on *Adam* is not very convincing, and I believe it is quite possible that the author of *Adam* had knowledge of *Genesis-B*.[2]

Even if *Adam* were originally composed in Anglo-Norman and influenced by an Old English version of the Bible, there is no evidence that it stayed in England or had any direct connection with the subsequent development of drama there. The *Seinte Résurrection*, on the other hand, like the Prodigal Son's elder brother, remained faithfully at home: it was written throughout in Anglo-Norman, and the main MS, copied at Canterbury, has always been in England. Despite its impeccably insular ancestry, this play has been largely ignored by students of English drama except for its staging prologue. The text is of high quality and worthy of close analysis; in its treatment of Longinus, for example, it is more nearly related to the N-Town play than to the Continental French versions, as

Jean G. Wright showed in her comparative analysis of the Resurrection in French drama.[3]

Perhaps the most baffling of the language connections is that represented by the two surviving bilingual fragments to which their modern editor has given the names of *The Cambridge Prologue* and the *Rickinghall Fragment*.[4] The *Cambridge Prologue* consists of twenty-two lines of Anglo-Norman in octosyllabic rhyming couplets followed by the same number of English couplets on a very similar subject but without being a literal translation. The text has been confidently dated as not later than 1300, which makes the English section by far the earliest dramatic text extant, and although there are a few French play-texts of the thirteenth century[5] (in addition to the twelfth-century *Adam* and *Seinte Resurrection* mentioned above), none of them has a biblical subject. Nevertheless, the Cambridge text opens with a speaker calling for silence on behalf of his emperor:

Oez seygnur, oez, oez!	Nu sittet stille and herkint alle,
Escoutez tant cum wus poez!	þat hur no mis þing ev bifalle;
Escutez ben, pur uostre honur,	And sittet rume and wel
Le ban de nostre emperrur.	þat men moȝt among ev go.

This has always been considered the opening of a biblical play, possibly a Nativity, with the emperor being Augustus. (Later in the prologue the speaker swears by Mahun [Mahomet] which establishes the pagan character of the emperor concerned.) There is no French nativity play before the fifteenth century except for the brief text included among the Cangé *Miracles of the Virgin* from the fourteenth century.[6] A much closer parallel can be found with the saints' plays, especially the *Jeu de S. Nicolas* by Jean Bodel (Warne, ed., *Le Jeu de S. Nicolas*), written in Arras in 1201. The opening prologue of this play, which is very like the Cambridge opening, begins: "Oiiés, oiiés, seigneur et dames" (Hearken, hearken, lords and ladies). There is also a plea for silence: "Or nous faites pais, si l'orrés" (Bodel, 114; Now give us silence and you'll hear it). Since far more saints' plays than biblical plays are extant in French before 1400, and since many of them also contain a role for the emperor, it seems quite likely that the Cambridge fragment belongs to that tradition.

There is a major distinction between the bilingual play and the French texts, however, for the speaker of the prologue in the Cambridge fragment is part of the play, referring constantly to "his" emperor. This is extremely rare in French where the prologue is normally spoken, as in the case of Bodel's play, by a preacher or expositor, not a character. The only exception I have found to that rule is the Biard fragment of the *Passion d'Autun* edited by Grace Frank, which begins:

Ouyés les bons, entendés moy,	(Hearken, good men, listen to me,
je vous commande de par le roy,	I command you in the king's name,

de part Pilate le prevost	in the name of Pilate the governor
que vous ne disiés un seul mot	that you speak not a single word.)

(Biard 1–4)

The *Passion d'Autun* was composed in Burgundy in the fifteenth century, but the Biard fragment is short and it is not certain that the speaker of the prologue is truly an actor in the play, as he does not speak in the following scene.[7]

Before considering the bilingual nature of the prologue, I want to consider first the content of the other piece, from Rickinghall in Suffolk. In this fragment, which is slightly later (probably about 1330), the Anglo-Norman part consists of two stanzas in tail-rhyme in which a king summons his barons and other vassals. This is followed by one and a half stanzas in English which translate the same amount of the French very closely. Then there are a Latin stage direction and three lines of Anglo-Norman, addressed by the king to his messenger. These last two elements are not translated. The opening speech is clearly the beginning of a scene or possibly of a play in the English cycle tradition. The "pomping" tone would fit Herod but could also be used equally appropriately for any other pagan king. Once again, a slight resemblance to the *Jeu de S. Nicolas* may be perceived; at several points in this play the King summons his barons or instructs his messenger to do so, but summoning of the feudal *ban*, or levy, by such means was a commonplace of medieval times and it would be dangerous to lay too much stress on these parallels.

Although it is possible to suggest various plays in French or English with which these fragments have some resemblance of style or subject matter, the fundamental question remains: are they fragments of bilingual plays? Such texts do exist, though they are rare. The fourteenth-century play from St. Gall, for example, has each speech sung in Latin and then spoken in German (Mone, ed., *Schauspiele*). Thus, in the scene of the woman taken in adultery, "Jesus cantet antiphonam: nemo te condempnavit? . . . et tunc dicat Jesus: Vrauwe, ist ieman hie der dich versteine?" (ed. Mone, I.8.: Then Jesus said: Woman is there anyone here who shall stone you?). A similar arrangement is found throughout the play.

One might postulate such a transitional situation in early thirteenth-century England when the linguistic duality of society was very marked, but the Rickinghall fragment is much later, at least a century, and by the mid-fourteenth century, although French was still an important literary language, there seems little logic in presenting a bilingual play when English texts were coming into general use. In addition, whereas both parts of the *Cambridge Prologue* are in the octosyllabic couplet which was one of the commonest verse forms for French literature, including drama, the Rickinghall fragment uses tail-rhyme stanzas for both languages, a form common in English but very rare in French drama except in lyrical or elegiac speeches. The fact that in both texts the French section is in Anglo-Norman dialect emphasizes the strongly British nature of the two pieces, so that it is hard to envisage either as a copy from a French original with an English translation. The relationship between the French and English verses in the two texts also supplies some interesting facts. In both cases the French is correct in scansion and rhyme while the English has faults, such as a false rhyme: *bind / swenge (Cambridge* 17/18) or the omission of half a stanza in Rickinghall. The latter also uses a French rhyme *barnage / parage* in the second English stanza which implies that the audience was expected to understand such terminology. Overall, Rickinghall is much more blatantly an attempt at a literal translation than *Cambridge*, where the English is a free but accurate rendering of the sense of the original rather than a precise, line by line translation.

In neither of the two texts is there real, convincing evidence that they were once part of a bilingual whole. It seems much more probable that they were never other than they now appear: fragments. Perhaps they represent attempts at translation or composition that were never continued. This seems especially true of Rickinghall where the second stanza is fully Englished but only half the first is. Exercises and glossaries to help those who needed to know both languages were quite numerous, a good example being Walter of Bibbesworth's rhyming French vocabulary of the late thirteenth century.[8] The fact that both these fragments have a court setting, either royal or imperial, may also be significant, especially if considered in conjunction with the French speeches used by Octavian, Herod, and the Magi in the Chester cycle. Baugh's suggestion that these speeches show a derivation from a French original for the Chester cycle has little evidence to support it; a more likely possibility, in view of the rank of the speakers, is that we have here an attempt to use different language registers to show class distinctions. This is supported by the presence of smaller amounts of French (and Latin) in similar *milieux* in other English cycles.[9] A. C. Baugh concluded his survey of the relationship of the Chester cycle to the French plays with the shrewd observation that: "If the Chester plays are the work of an educated cleric the language is just what we should expect" ("Chester Plays," p. 45). May these fragments not have a similar source, being perhaps the drafts of a writer trying out speeches in both languages before deciding which to use? This of course still leaves open the question of the very early date of the *Cambridge Prologue* from an English drama point of view.

Before leaving the question of language as a connecting link between French and English drama, there is a small but rather curious point to note. The Ashmole fragment of the late fifteenth century contains a speech by *Secundus Miles* in English in which he promises the Emperor to avenge him on any *frensche gedling* who grieves him. Davis suggests that it might be replaced by *fresche* but is there any need to do so? The speaker, as usual, refers to "Mahound" and is therefore serving a pagan king. It might be Octavian, but equally, as with the *Cambridge Prologue*, it might be any other of the pagan rulers who appear in saints' plays. Wherever the play is set, however, a fifteenth-century audience would have no difficulty with the term French for an enemy. Moreover, in the Chester cycle there are two equally anachronistic references to France. An audience that could swallow Herod and other biblical villains swearing by Mahomet are not going to strain at a passing reference to their traditional foe across the Channel.

The curious way in which the fragments of English plays so often seem to have French connections of some kind is also exemplified by a final example: the *Durham Prologue*. Although here the connection is more one of subject matter than language, there is enough vocabulary involved to justify mentioning it in this section. The *Durham Prologue*, from the late fourteenth or early fifteenth century, is conventional in form, with the speaker asking for peace and quiet so that they may present a *game* on the subject of a knight who, having fallen from riches to poverty, came into the devil's power but was redeemed (*boured*) by the intervention of Our Lady. There are obvious similarities here to the legend of Theophilus whose tale was dramatized in France in the thirteenth century by Rutebeuf, in *Le miracle de Théophile*. The only English version is in narrative form, of course, but it is still interesting to find in the opening speeches of the *Théophile*, where he first laments his poverty and then complains of it to Salatin (the devil's emissary), a number of words which fit more closely the idea of Théophile as a knight than as the priest he in fact was. For example, he wonders what his *mesnie* (household) will do now he has no money to feed them. He regrets that God is so high above that he cannot get at him to fight him and laments that he cannot take his place *entre gent* (among society) without being pointed at scornfully. When Théophile speaks to Salatin, he says he used to be known as *seignor et mestre* (lord and master), as Salatin well knows, and finally declares there is nothing he would not do to be restored to his honor (*qu'a m'onor revenisse*; the word "honor" usually means an estate or manor). It seems then not impossible that the *Durham Prologue*, if it ever had a play attached to it, had a *Play of Theophilus*, despite the use of the word "knight" in the English, which at first sight seems to preclude such a connection.

SUBJECT MATTER

Whereas the use of the French language in England is easily identifiable, if not always as easily explicable, connections in the other areas under consideration are often less tangible. In subject matter, for example, there is an obvious, clear-cut difference in the choice and development of incidents dramatized, especially between the "typical" plays from each of the two traditions. The English cycles normally run from Creation to

Doomsday, including in their Old Testament section, in addition to the Creation and Fall of the Angels and Man, episodes of the Flood, Abraham, and Moses; some kind of prophetic material then ushers in the New Testament plays, from the Annunciation through the Christmas sequence to the Baptism, Ministry, and Passion, then the Resurrection, Ascension, and finally the Last Judgment. The best known group of French plays, however, including the Ste. Geneviève and Arras-Greban-Michel versions, have little or no Old Testament material—at most a Fall of Man sequence. Then comes some form of prophetic preparation for the Incarnation leading to the New Testament plays, which may deal only with the adult life of Christ or may include a Christmas series. All of them peter out, as did the Gospels themselves, in a series of post-Resurrection appearances. Last Judgment plays only exist in French as independent texts. The bulk of the Old Testament material was gathered together in a separate collection known as the *Viel Testament*, printed (no MSS survive) as a series of individual plays which might be performed separately or as a sequence. The Creation and Fall of the Angels and Man sequence in the *Viel Testament* was probably originally one play, perhaps with a Cain and Abel scene. The other stories are clearly composed as separate, individual plays.

There do exist in French, however, plays which are closer in content to the English cycles. Four texts contain substantial Old Testament plays, including the episodes of Noah, Abraham, and Moses. One reason why these plays are rarely considered is that one is still unpublished, an edition of the second is in press, a third has only been reedited after being out of print for many years, and the fourth, the Mons play, has survived only as a producer's copy, with the first and last lines of each speech. This last text has been copiously mined for information on staging but virtually neglected as to content. It is, however, of considerable interest since it represents a conflation of the versions of Greban and Michel, interwoven with each other and including also some apparently original material, especially in the Old Testament section. The Noah play, for example, is not from the *Viel Testament* and was long thought to be unique. Recently it has been shown to be almost identical with the text of the Flood in the unpublished Valenciennes twenty-day play of 1549.[10]

Two other French plays may loosely be called cyclic; the *Passion de Troyes* is mainly from Greban, and its section of Old Testament material is said by Petit de Julleville to be based on the *Viel Testament*. The *Passion de Semur* is quite independent of all the other French versions. It is short, by French standards, only ten thousand lines divided into two days; therefore, approximately the same length as an English cycle. It is also remarkably "English" in its content, both in choice and treatment. The first day has scenes of the Creation and Fall of the Angels, then of Man, followed by episodes of the Flood, Abraham, and Moses. A short prophet play ushers in the New Testament Christmas sequence and the first day ends with the Baptism and Temptation. The second day includes the Ministry and Passion, Harrowing of Hell (not found in Greban), and Resurrection. It then concludes with the Appearance to Thomas. The play was copied in Semur, in Burgundy, in 1488 and may have been written for that town. The Semur play is Burgundian, and Mons was situated in Hainaut, which had been under Burgundian rule, while Valenciennes, though in French territory, is situated only a very few miles from Mons, so that a tenuous connection may be adduced between at least three of the so-called cyclic French plays.

While considering Old Testament connections, my attention was caught by the anomaly of the Isaac and Jacob plays in the Towneley cycle being in octosyllabic couplets rather than the usual tail-rhyme. (There are a few other passages in couplets in the cycle but no other whole plays.) These are the only plays on the subject in English and when compared to the only French version, in the *Viel Testament*, they yielded some interesting facts. A line by line source analysis is beyond the scope of the present paper, but some spot checks reveal at least one element common to the two plays which is not in the biblical source. When God blesses Jacob, he says: "God give thee the dew of heaven and of the fatness of the earth, abundance of corn and wine" (Genesis 27, 28, Douay translation of the Vulgate). Both the French and the English play add oil to the corn and wine of the biblical account: "of wine, of oyll and of whete." (Towneley, 9–10); "de fourment / De vin, d'uille pareillement" (*VT* II, 158). It is clearly also possible that the connection here is merely a common source in a biblical paraphrase.[11]

Elsewhere in the two plays there is another small similarity when both authors use the proper names Aran and Laban as rhyme words (Towneley 43–44; *VT* II, 131, 21–2). There are a number of other minor parallels between the two texts, such as the use of mnemonic rhyme. The major objection to a link between the French and English plays of Jacob is the very different scale of the texts: the *Viel Testament* version is three thousand lines and the extant English material—the *Isaac* is incomplete—less than three hundred. However, the newly discovered Lille plays (see note 1) include a short play of Jacob and Isaac, so further comparison must await the editing of this new and potentially revolutionary material.

A connection of a very different kind is to be found in another of the couplet sequences in Towneley, God's opening speech in the *Annunciation Play*. English tradition, both narrative and dramatic, regularly mentions a period of four thousand years or more, for the sojourn in Hell of the Fallen Protoplasts. In *Cursor Mundi*, for example, we are told that Adam spent four thousand three hundred and four years in Hell (CM 1443–44). The York Adam says he has been in Hell 4,600 years (XXXVII, 39) while *Contemplacio* in N-Town makes it 4,604 (XI, 1). In the French narrative *Passion des Jongleurs*, Seth in Limbo says St. Michael told him it would be 5,500 years before the coming of the Savior (l. 2565).[12] It seems possible that this apparent anomaly can be explained as a misreading of Bede's dating of the ages of the world, which is quoted in a fourteenth-century French Bible by Jean de Sy as follows: "Bede en sa Cronique que il a fait de son aage meisme devise ainsi les aages du monde. ... La somme de la commencement du monde jusques a Jhesucrist est v^m et iii^c ans ... " ("Bede in his chronicle of his own era sets out the ages of the world as follows ... the total from the beginning of the world unto Jesus Christ is 5,300 years") (see Berger, La Bible française, 239). Since Adam lived nine hundred years, the 5,300 from Creation would be 4,400 from his death and arrival in Hell. This is exactly how the Towneley author calculates it:

> Deus: ffor he has boght his syn full sore
> thise fyfe thousand yeris and more
> ffyrst in erthe and sythen in hell.
> (X, 10–12)

The reference God makes to the "oyll of mercy" in this same speech recalls the story of Seth which is dramatized in French, including the Viel Testament, but not in any English play though it has an important place in the Cornish Ordinalia as the beginning of the Holy Rood legend, which forms a unifying element in the First Day of the play.[13] The Chester cycle, which as we have seen shows other French connections, includes the character of Seth in the Harrowing of Hell where, following the Passion des Jongleurs, he quotes St. Michael as having said he might not have the Oil of Mercy: "tyll fyve thousand yeres have gone / and fyve hundred eke" (XVII, 87–88). The Passion des Jongleurs was an important source of the early French plays and has also been shown to be a source for the Northern Passion narrative, which has many points of similarity with the English plays. As in the case of the Isaac and Jacob plays considered above and some of the other apparent "connections" of subject matter, it seems likely therefore that there was not a direct dramatic link between the two traditions but an interesting use of common sources of a more specific nature than just, for example, the Bible or the Golden Legend.

This kind of narrative connection may also be behind the similarity of treatment of the Four Daughters of God episode in the N-Town plays and the French Valenciennes 20. In each case the play contains material not found elsewhere in their own tradition but which they also share with two other plays: the Eerste Bliscap or First Joy of Mary play associated with Brussels, and the Low German play of the Fall of Man, the Sündenfall, attributed to Arnold Immessen.[14]

The section of N-Town which I want to consider is part of the Contemplacio or Marian group of plays which dramatize the Conception and Birth of Mary, the Presentation in the Temple, Betrothal to Joseph, and the Annunciation and Visitation. Preceding the Annunciation in play XI is the celebrated Parlement of Heaven, which like all this Marian material is found in England only in the N-Town plays. Some pre-Annunciation Marian episodes are found in various French plays, though not in the Ste. Geneviève and Arras-Greban-Michel groups. Arras and Greban do, however, include a version of the scene in Heaven of the Four Daughters of God, like the English, German, and Dutch plays noted above, as well as the Italian *Le Passion di Revello*.

In France, there are two basic versions of the scene, the Trial and the Debate. Both may be prefaced by laments of the prophets and patriarchs in Limbo but thereafter the substance of the versions is markedly different. In the Trial, or *Procès*, we have a formal courtroom situation with Mercy and Justice putting the case for and against the redemption of man in strictly legalistic terms. Peace, Truth, and sometimes Wisdom all join in the protracted argument: the scene in Greban is thirteen hundred lines long (nearly two hours playing time). The only member of the Trinity who appears is God the Father and his role is strictly limited to that of appeal judge who ratifies the decision of the Virtues and reluctantly agrees that the Son should become incarnate to pay man's debt. The theological source here is the Anselmian doctrine of the atonement as laid down in the *Cur Deus Homo*, and the judicial style of disputation owes much to the writings of Thomas Aquinas.

Versions of the Debate, as distinct from the Trial, are also found in a number of French plays. In *Semur*, for example, it is merely a brief and friendly discussion between Hope, Charity, and God on how man can be redeemed without God's being false to his own truth (ll. 1725–91). In *Valenciennes 20*, however, there exists a Debate scene which is extremely close to the Parlement of Heaven play in N-Town. The second day of the French play opens in Limbo where the patriarchs and prophets lament the fallen state of man and determine to send delegates to God to beg for his intervention and mercy. After discussion, David, Job, Isaiah, and Jeremiah are chosen, as being especially beloved of God. It is stressed that they will go in spirit only, their bodies remaining in prison. In the *Sündenfall*, the chosen messengers are Isaiah, Jeremiah, and David. In the *Eerste Bliscap*, David, Job, Isaiah, and Another (i.e., *ander*) send Bitter Misery who seeks the aid of Fervent Prayer.

There is no scene in Limbo in the N-Town version since the prophets have already appeared in play II, but the prologue of *Contemplacio* includes an appeal to God to "have mind of the prayer said by Isaiah" (7), and later quotes Jeremiah's words, "I cry to thy sight gracious Lord" (31), adding "Patryarchys and prophetys han made supplication" (35). There is some similarity, then, in the beginning of the plays, both of which continue with the Debate in Heaven where God expresses a willingness to show Mercy but is opposed by Truth because he cannot in justice do this. The discussion now centers on a solution to this problem rather than on the legalistic arguments of the *Procès*; the Son of God intervenes and speaking as Wisdom declares the need for the good death which must be suffered by a willing innocent victim. Truth and Mercy are set to search for such a candidate on Earth or in Heaven respectively; both fail. At this point the French and English plays separate. N-Town and the *Eerste Bliscap* both have a council of the Trinity, the latter being much longer and more verbose than the neat three quatrains of the English play, which leads into the Annunciation. *Valenciennes 20*, like other French plays, does not put the Third Person of the Trinity on stage, and the debate is concluded with God's decision to choose the one who shall be the mother of the victim. The play then continues with the Conception of Mary.

The existence of these parallels between the English and Continental plays raises inevitably the question of sources. It has long been recognized that a major source of the discussions of the Four Daughters of God is the *Meditationes* attributed to St. Bonaventure, which derive much material, explicitly, from a *Sermon on the Annunciation* by St. Bernard. The French *Nativité* from Rouen has a debate which follows the *Meditationes* very closely and includes marginal notes of the Latin text. The N-Town play, on the other hand, has close links with a particular version of Nicholas Love's translation of the *Meditationes*, the so-called *Charter of the Abbey of the Holy Ghost*. It is therefore interesting to find in the three Continental plays details which are peculiar to the English *Charter* and are not found in either the Latin or any of the extant French redactions. For example, the *Meditationes* has no scene of the prophets' pleas from Limbo, important in the Continental plays and also found in the *Charter* (337–62), where they are Isaiah, Jeremiah, and David.

Considerably more work obviously needs to be done on the interrelationship of these plays and their sources. All that can be said so far is that a link of some kind does connect the texts discussed and it seems to be one of common source rather than of direct influence of one text on the others.

STAGING AND PERFORMANCE[15]

Although I have tried to show that the very wide gulf that apparently divides the French and English drama is bridged more frequently than might seem to be the case at first sight, it would be foolish to deny that certain fundamental differences do exist, one of the most clear-cut being the complete absence in France of the concept of plays as particularly a Corpus Christi activity. The Feast was of course celebrated in France, as all over Europe, with religious processions which might include tableaux of biblical scenes, as at Béthune in Picardy in the fifteenth century. These wagon-tableaux covered the same subjects as the English cycle, from Creation to Doomsday, but never developed into a play-form with text.

Processional plays are recorded for Italy and Spain, and several German plays explicitly linked with Corpus Christi are extant, such as those from Eger and Kunzelsau.[16] In France, however, which often stands aloof from other European countries, the only plays recorded as being performed on carts are those presented in some Northern towns. At St. Omer in Flanders, floats drawn by oxen were used as stages for plays by small groups of townsfolk organized on a district, possibly parochial, basis. The town council contributed a small sum toward the cost of each carting or *charriement*. The recent discovery of the Lille plays—a group of short scenes based on the Bible or on Roman history and performed annually, processionally, on the occasion of the *Grande Procession de Lille*—provides the exception that only serves to emphasize the rule.

But pageant wagon performances, though distinctively English, are certainly not the only form of staging recorded for religious plays, and many examples can be quoted of similarities between the fixed-staging techniques of France and England, though the latter never reached the enormous scale of the French productions, apparently, and therefore the huge purpose-built wooden stages of Mons or Romans have no counterpart. Performances in amphitheaters or arenas with mansions arranged among the audience around a central *platea*, such as are suggested by the sketch plans for the *Castle of Perseverance* or the Cornish *Ordinalia*, are paralleled by the French productions illustrated in the Fouquet miniature of the *Martyrdom of Ste. Appolline* or the *Life of St. Lazarus* specially written for and performed in a veritable Coliseum at Autun in 1516. The quarry at Wakefield comes to mind when we read of French towns staging plays in a cleaned up Roman amphitheater (the one at Bourges had been used as a rubbish tip!) or a filled-in defensive ditch as at Alencon.[17] The use of interlaced scenes, made possible (almost essential) by the multiple stage, is not unknown in England, nor are some of the favorite stage effects; the ship in the Digby play of *Mary Magdalen* has many Continental parallels such as the French *Marie-Magdaleine* play, the ship of the Magi at Revello (an Italian play on the French model), or the whole range of boats listed for the *Acts of the Apostles* at Bourges in 1536, including one for St. Paul's shipwreck on Miletus.

Staging techniques were very varied in medieval drama though each country seems to have had a "preferred" or common style which it favored over others but without exclusivity. However, as far as I can discover, France is unique in one aspect of its staging: the civic organizers regularly charged admission to the performance, a practice which inevitably influenced the construction of the playing area. Whether the audience sat around the stage, in front of the stage or even on the stage, the whole area containing performers and spectators was enclosed within a natural or purpose-built wall with access only through one or more gates where the money could be conveniently collected.

The fundamental difference here between French staging and other traditions is that in all big productions spectators *had* to pay to see the play. This dictated the forms of theatre used and precluded open street performance, whereas at York, for example, a spectator might *choose* to pay for a place on a scaffold outside a house at one of the stations, or in Essex he might *choose* to contribute to the collections made by the gatherers.

ORGANIZATION AND FINANCE

French drama was organized on a professional, commercial basis, probably earlier than in any other European country if we can trust the records so far available to us. Already in 1402, King Charles VI granted Letters Patent to the *Confrérie de la Passion* in Paris giving them, among other privileges, the monopoly in biblical plays within the metropolitan area subject to official approval of texts. Their charter also included a dispensation for men to wear women's clothes in public places during the period of the performances; only thirty years later Joan of Arc was to be condemned for wearing men's clothes. It would be interesting to know of any other records of official attitudes to this necessary concomitant of all-male performances. The king expressly states that he favors the company and that their rights and revenues (*droiz et revenues*) should be increased so that others might be moved by devotion to join them. Surely a classic case of managing to serve both God and Mammon?

The reference to revenue, coupled with a mention earlier in the Letters to the expenses of the company and the profit they would have from public performance, suggests that some kind of audience contribution to the plays was involved, probably in the form of admission charges, which were common in France later in the fifteenth century. Since the *Confrérie* flourished as an active part of Parisian theatrical life for a hundred and fifty years and dragged out a dwindling existence for another century after that before they were finally disbanded by royal warrant in 1676, they may surely rate as the earliest example of a professional or, at least, a semi-professional company: professional in that they made money by their performances, but semi-professional in that they held other jobs at the same time. Their status, for example, was different from that of the minstrels. They possessed also a permanent theater building, in the Hospice of La Trinité which they rented from the Premonstratensians who owned it. Here on Sundays and Feast days they gave performances which attracted large crowds; so successful were these performances that in the sixteenth and possibly even in the fifteenth century the time of vespers was altered in some churches to allow the clergy and congregation to attend the plays.

In 1539 they had to leave La Trinité and move to the Hôtel de Flandres, where in 1541 they performed the *Acts of the Apostles* with a cast of more than five hundred over a period of several months with enormous success. But by 1542 their day was nearly over. When they wanted to stage the *Viel Testament* that year, they were only granted permission on stringent conditions that included limiting the days and times when they could perform and fixing a maximum entrance charge of two *sous* per person per session, or thirty *sous* for a box for the whole duration of the *mistère*. To crown it all, since people would be distracted by the play from church-going and the alms for the poor would consequently suffer, they had to pay to the poor "la somme de mil livres, sauf à ordonner de plus grande somme" (the sum of one thousand pounds unless a larger sum is ordered). It says much for the financial success they anticipated that they accepted the conditions and went ahead with the production (*Les Mystères*, I, pp. 412–39).

This highly organized, commercialized drama, which is very different from the civic cycles of England, is far from being unique in fifteenth and sixteenth century France. The standard pattern for large civic plays was to finance them by grants from the city, the church, and wealthy individuals who then shared the profits from the "gate" in proportion to their original contribution. Sometimes individual actors would buy a share in the profits by a preliminary donation, as at Valenciennes in 1547. So normal was this practice of charging for the plays that it is specifically mentioned when there is no charge, as at Autun in 1516 when the *Life of St. Lazarus* was presented *vehentissime et gratis* (energetically and free).

In this connection, the nearest English parallel is, of course, the celebrated Essex property-player, details of whose methods and financial organization can nearly all be matched from French practice, especially of the early sixteenth century for which we have the most detailed records, though it is clear that many of the procedures had been in use for some years (Coldewey, "Property Player"). The only detail that I have not found matched is the English practice of uniting several towns to make a viable economic unit. The French towns seem to have been large enough and wealthy enough to go it alone.

A good example of this kind of arrangement may be seen in the records of the performance at Romans, near Lyons, in 1509, when the inhabitants decided to stage a play on the lives of their three otherwise virtually unknown patron saints, Severinus, Exuperius, and Felician, collectively known as the *Trois Doms* (*Le Mystère des Trois Doms*). The specially written text and full accounts for the performance have survived and from them we can follow the arrangements in great detail. A certain Canon Pra was brought in from Grenoble to prepare the text and was given twelve florins a month subsistence allowance for himself and his clerk for a period of six months, as well as a down payment of thirty florins. (A florin was 2/3 £.) Local carpenters were commissioned to make the scaffolds for the stage and audience while one Master Francis, a painter, was charged with constructing and painting the scenery and properties, and organizing the *feintes* or special effects, which had been a feature of French plays for a century. For his trouble he was paid a hundred florins from which were deducted three for the box which he reserved for his friends for the performance.

The Romans play suffered a loss, although the takings of 680 florins–at 1/2 *sou* per person, plus seventy-nine boxes holding probably an average of four people—meant that more than 13,000 people attended over the three days. (Even if many of them were present on more than one day, there must have been at least 5,000 different spectators.) The loss of some one thousand florins was borne equally by the Chapter and the civic authorities by prearrangement. Despite the loss, the town benefited from the trade brought in and from the kudos. At Mons in 1501, they also had a loss of almost £1,000 despite having advertised their eight-day play widely in the surrounding area and arranged "fringe" activities in the form of a rhetoric contest in the evenings.

We do not know if the Master Francis who did the Romans *feintes* was a local man but it seems probable, as no mention is made of his traveling expenses. Examples do exist, however, of a man being brought in from outside especially to organize the performance and being paid a fee as is recorded in the case of the property-player. Jean Bouchet in his verse epistles pays tribute to Maistre Thomas le Provost from Rouen who had been invited to Saumur as *facteur* (organizer) because he was well known in the Poitiers and Loire area. Bouchet himself was also apparently an expert in such matters, and from the epistles and from records we gather that at Poitiers he had been responsible for the text (though he only selected from the *Moule* [mold], and the play was probably based on the well-known versions of Greban and Michel), and for various aspects of the production including costumes, casting, and general staging. He was not a craftsman, however. In 1536 he was invited to go to Issoudun to produce a play for them but declined; his letter includes some good advice on casting actors who are appropriate to the role; not using borrowed costumes unless they are suitable to the character being portrayed; and making sure the machinery is in good working order: test your *secrets*, he says, using the term commonly employed for trap-doors and stage effects generally. His insistence on this last point is explained by an account elsewhere of a disaster at Poitiers one year, when all the effects misfired due to over-hasty construction and lack of rehearsal time (Bouchet, *Epistres* and Petit de Julleville, II, 123–30).

The fame of a civic play rested largely on these *secrets* or *feintes*, which were talked of for years afterwards and sometimes became almost legendary. Thus a paradise created at Saumur in 1534 passed into proverb and is also referred to in Rabelais's *Tiers Livre* where Panurge declares: "Il m'est advis, que je joue encores le Dieu de la passion de Saumur accompaigné de ses Anges et Chérubins" (ch. 3: I feel as if I were still playing God in the Saumur passion accompanied by his angels and cherubim).

Some idea of the range and number of these effects may be gathered from the list produced for the *Acts of the Apostles* in Bourges in 1536. This mammoth play (forty days and 62,000 lines) is the biggest production recorded during the whole period. The printed list of the *feintes* required is sixteen pages long. It includes machinery for clouds and flying, trap-doors, blood, limbs, heads, flames, water, smoke, falling idols, animals both real and factitious, boats, and so on. We do not know who constructed them nor what the Bourges performance cost. The town spent so lavishly that it went nearly bankrupt, however. A less extensive but still impressive list is preserved from Modane in Savoy, where the play of *Antichrist* was performed in 1588 and again in 1606 (Gros, *Etude*). On each occasion painters were especially commissioned and contracted to do the *secrets* for 200 florins, paid by Savoy. They were not responsible for the platform itself which was built by local carpenters, as was customary, but had to produce the props and especially the fireworks, gunpowder, flames, and other spectacular devices, finding a way "par engin et industrie, tirer les deux yeux de la teste du catholique avec brochettes poignantes et a ces fins feront les yeux et faux visages nécessaires ou autrement le plus dextrement qu'ils pourront" (By skill and ingenuity to pull out the catholic's eyes with pointed iron skewers and for this purpose they will make the necessary eyes and false faces or some alternative as efficiently as they can).

Many of these French performances were very large, but the next and last contract is more on the scale of the Essex records, as well as being similar in other ways. In 1542 two citizens of the village of Athis-sur-Orge, near Paris, the church clerk and the innkeeper, contracted with a painter from a nearby village:

> to furnish and hire three devils' costumes, masks for death and envy, four crowns, four sceptres for the kings, a wig, beard and mitre for God the Father, two angels' heads supplied with wings, and a device for the *Judgement of Solomon*. To equip and paint the cart to transport Joseph and, following his craft as painter, all the other devices necessary for the *Selling of Joseph*, the *Judgement of Solomon*, and the *Rich Sinner* (a morality play) which the said Vinot and Tamponnet are putting on this same year in the village of Athis for the period of eight days and one day for the parade. And also to provide the cannons, flaming fireworks necessary for the devil scene and to provide the materials necessary to make everything as above . . . and also to provide on the day of the parade two Swiss drums and on each of the other eight days of performance one Swiss drum for the said painter to play or have played at his expense.

All this was done for the sum of seven pounds tournois and the organizers undertook to "feed the said painter and his servant who will play the said drum during the said nine days."[18]

The parade mentioned here was a regular feature of the French productions, the French word, *monstre* (from *montrer* = to show) makes the term identical with the English "showday" or pre-performance parade, mentioned in the Chelmsford records of the property-player (Coldewey, "Property Player").

Diversity in unity is the hallmark of medieval European life, whether in Gothic architecture, Arthurian romance, or biblical drama. Within the framework of a common Christian courtly or civic culture, each country found its own versions, its own vernacular, many of them showing to some extent the influence of France, which lay at the heart of the network of trade, travel, and intellectual inquiry that stretched from the west of England to the Eastern Mediterranean.

Although the closest connection between the French and English traditions seems to date from the period when theater all over Europe was moving out of the era of the great amateur civic dramas and into the age of the troops of traveling players and professional actors, there do appear to be a few examples of earlier links, a few creepers spanning the great gulf; they link especially the plays of Northern France and the Low Countries with the drama of Eastern England. Direct influence is virtually impossible to prove and in any case seems unlikely, but traffic between the two kingdoms was well established in more normal commercial goods, and the areas of apparent dramatic association are also those which were most closely linked through that outstanding Anglo-French connection of the later Middle Ages: the wool trade.

From Semur to cycle-play, Essex to Athis, Arras to Cambridge, N-Town to Valenciennes: the threads pass across the North Sea to and fro like a weaver's shuttle. Is it a patterned tapestry they weave? Or merely a tangled web intended to deceive?

NOTES

1. A descriptive list of the major biblical plays of the fifteenth and sixteenth centuries in France is given at the beginning of the bibliography below. The last item on the list, the Lille plays, were recently discovered among the Wolfenbüttel MSS and I am grateful to Graham Runnalls for mentioning them to me in April 1984. They are now being edited by Professor Alan Knight. The best general introduction to the European medieval drama is the section in the *Cambridge Guide to World Theatre* (Cambridge: Cambridge University Press, 1988), edited by Martin Banham; the medieval section is edited by Peter Meredith. For France the most useful book on the religious plays remains the century-old *Les Mystères* by Petit de Julleville. Considerable attention to the French drama and its links with the English cycles is paid by Rosemary Woolf in *The English Mystery Plays*.

2. The most recent edition of *Adam* is Noomen's (1971); for further references, see Muir, *Liturgy and Drama*. A discussion of the relationship between *Adam*, *Genesis-B* and the *Vita Adae*, including R. Woolf's theory, is given on pp. 18–21.

3. See Jenkins, et al., *La Seinte Résurreccion*, and Wright, *A Study*.

4. All the fragments discussed in this section, both bilingual and English, are printed in Davis, *Non-cycle plays and fragments*.

5. The five thirteenth-century plays are printed in English in Axton and Stevens, *Medieval French Plays*.

6. The Cangé MS *Nativité* is printed in vol. I of the *Miracles de Nostre Dame*, SATF, Paris, 1876. The play includes scenes of the birth, with midwives, presentation of Christ in the Temple, and Christ with the doctors. The total of one thousand lines gives it a scale similar to the cycle plays but there are no other real parallels.

7. See Carnahan, *The Prologue*, which includes a wide range of extracts from French prologues; the Biard prologue is in *La Passion d'autun*.

8. See Clanchy, *From Memory to Written Record*, chapter 6 (pp. 151–74), where the question of bilingualism in thirteenth-century England is discussed and some texts quoted, including that by Walter of Bibbesworth.

9. See Baugh's "Chester Plays," an excellent study which contains a mass of bibliographical information and sensible comment on the occurence of bilingualism in these plays.

10. See Foley, "Two Versions." *Valenciennes 20* should not be confused with *Valenciennes 25* (performed in 1547), which does not contain any Old Testament material.

11. There are a large number of medieval versions of the Bible in French, both verse and prose. As with the plays most of these too, unfortunately, still await an editor. The problems encountered in trying to track down sources of variants can be well demonstrated if we look at the Jacob sequence in the English *Cursor Mundi*. Here, the blessing given to Jacob omits verse 28 completely, while the blessing subsequently given to Esau promises him "dew ahd gress" (3757) which the editor has transcribed in his running headline as "dew and grass"; "gress," however, is clearly the "fatness" of the Genesis text. *Cursor Mundi*, to compound the problem though, also uses the Aran/Laban rhyme and is written in rhyming couplets.

12. Another version of the *Passion des Jongleurs* is printed in the Introduction to *The Northern Passion*.

13. The Cornish *Ordinalia* has many of the characteristics of the French plays, being arranged in three days with an epilogue at the end of the first two inviting the audience to return next day for the continuation of the story. Moreover, it was performed in a multiple mansion and *platea* set in the round. The diagram of the setting is in the MS. Since the action is continuous and not broken up into separate pageants, the same actor plays a role throughout. The content of the play also shows some general French similarities, omitting the Christmas sequence and ending with the Ascension and Entry into Heaven, not the Last Judgment. The *Death of Pilate* play which completes the third day has a similar subject (Veronica) as the French play of *Ste. Venice* or the *Vengeance of Jesus Christ* plays in *Mystères II*.

14. The link between these plays and *Valenciennes 20* was first pointed out by Mary O'Sullivan in her MA thesis The Valenciennes Twenty-day Play. . . . A detailed chart of the interrelationships between the different Debate scenes in these plays is set out in Meredith and Muir, "Trial in Heaven."

15. A wide range of French staging texts are translated in Meredith and Tailby, *Staging*. Material quoted in the next two sections can be found in that volume unless otherwise stated. Regarding financing of plays, see also Tydeman, chapter 8.

16. The German *Fronleichnamsspiele* are discussed by W. F. Michael in *Das Deutsche Drama des Mittelalters*, Berlin and New York, 1971.

17. The cleaning of the *Fosse des Arenes* for the production of the *Acts of the Apostles* in 1536 is described in a contemporary journal, cited in Raymond

Lebègue. *Le Mystère des Actes des Apôtres*, Paris, 1929, p. 78. Lebègue also gives references to other plays in this sandquarry.

18. The Athis contract is quoted in S. W. Deierkauf-Holsboer, "Les représentations à Athis-sur-Orge en 1542." In *Mélanges Cohen*, pp. 199–203. It is interesting to note that the plays of the *Vente de Joseph (Selling of Joseph)* and *Décision de Salomon (Judgement of Solomon)* are among those listed in the newly discovered Lille plays (see n. 1 above).

WORKS CITED AND SUGGESTED READINGS

Axton, R., and J. Stevens, trans. *Medieval French Plays*. Oxford, 1971.

Baugh, A. C. "The Chester Plays and French Influence," *Schelling Anniversary Papers*. New York, 1923 (repr. 1967).

Berger, S. *La Bible française au moyen âge*. Paris, 1884.

Bouchet, Jean. *Epistres Morales et familieres du traverseur*, ed. M. A. Screech. S. R. Publishers, Ltd., Johnson Reprint Corp., Mouton, 1969.

Carnahan, D. H. *The Prologue in the Old French and Provençal Mystery*. New Haven, 1905.

The Charter of the Abbeye of a Holy Gost in Yorkshire Writers: Richard Rolle of Hampole and His Followers, ed. C. Horstman. London, 1895.

Clanchy, M. T. *From Memory to Written Record*. London, 1979.

Coldewey, John. "That Enterprising Property Player: Semi-Professional Drama in Sixteenth-Century England." *Theatre Notebook* 31 (1977), 5–12.

Cornish Ordinalia. The Ancient Cornish Drama, ed. and trans. Edwin Norris. Oxford, 1859.

Davidson, Clifford, ed. *The Saint Play in Medieval Europe*. Western Michigan University Press, 1986.

Davis, N., ed. *Non-cycle plays and fragments*. EETS, 1970.

de Paris, Geoffroi. *Bible des Sept Etats du Monde*, ed. Ann Parry. Beauchesne, Paris, 1981.

Deierkauf-Holsboer, S. W. "Les représentations à Athis-sur-Orge en 1542," *Mélanges Gustave Cohen*. Paris, 1950, pp. 199–203.

Die Eerste Bliscap, ed. W. H. Beuken. Culenborg, 1973.

Foley, Mary F. (née O'Sullivan), "Two Versions of the Flood: the Valenciennes Twenty-Day Play and the Mystère de la Passion of Mons." *Tréteaux* II 1, May 1979, pp. 21–39.

Gros, Louis. *Etude sur le mystère de l'antéchrist et du jugement de Dieu*. Chambéry, 1962.

Immessen, A. *Der Sündenfall*, ed. F. Krage. Heidelberg, 1913.

Jenkins, T. A. et al., eds. *La Seinte Résurreccion*, Anglo-Norman Text Society, iv, Oxford, 1943.

Lebègue, Raymond. *Le Mystère des Actes des Apôtres*. Paris, 1929, p. 78.

Meredith, Peter, and Lynette Muir. "The Trial in Heaven in the Eerste Bliscap and other European plays: a question of relationships" in *Proceedings of the First Colloquium on Medieval Dutch Drama. Dutch Crossings*, Bedford College, London, April, 1984.

Meredith, Peter, and J. Tailby, eds. *The Staging of Medieval Religious Drama in Europe*. Western Michigan University, 1983.

Meditations on the Life of Christ, ed. and trans. Isa Ragusa and Rosalie Green. Princeton, 1961.

Michael, W. F. *Das Deutsche Drama des Mittelalters*. Berlin and New York, 1971.

Morris, R., ed. *Cursor Mundi*. EETS, 1874, repr. 1961.

Muir, L. R. *Liturgy and Drama in the Anglo-Norman Adam.* Oxford, 1973.

Le Mystère des Trois Doms Joué à Romans en 1509, avec des documents relatifs aux représentations en Dauphiné de 1400 à 1535, ed. Ulysse Chevalier and A. Giraud. Romans, n.d.

The Northern Passion, ed. F. A. Foster. EETS, 1913.

Noomen, W., ed. *Le Jeu d'Adam.* CFMA, Paris, 1971.

O'Sullivan, Mary. *The Valenciennes Twenty-day Play with Special Reference to the Old Testament Section.* MA thesis, University of Leeds Centre for Medieval Studies, Leeds, 1978.

La Passion d'Autun, ed. Grace Frank. SATF, Paris, 1934.

La Passion des Jongleurs (from the *Bible des Sept Estats du Monde* by Geoffroi de Paris, ed. Ann Parry. Beauchesne, Paris, 1981.

La Passion di Revello, ed. Anna Cornagliotti. Turin, 1976.

La Passion de Troyes, ed. Jean-Claude Bibolet. Droz, Geneva, 1988.

Petit de Julleville, Lucien. *Les Mystères.* Paris, 1880 (repr. 1968).

Rutebeuf. *Le miracle de Théophile,* ed. Grace Frank. CFMA, Paris, 1925 (repr. 1975).

Ste. Venice, ed. G. Runnalls. Exeter, 1980.

Tydeman, William. *The Theatre in the Middle Ages.* Cambridge, 1978.

Warne, J. F., ed. *Le Jeu de S. Nicolas.* Oxford, 1963.

Woolf, Rosemary. *The English Mystery Plays.* London, 1972.

Wright, Jean G. *A Study of the Theme of the Resurrection in the Medieval French Drama.* Bryn Mawr, 1935.

DESCRIPTIVE LIST OF THE PRINCIPAL FRENCH BIBLICAL PLAYS OF THE FIFTEENTH AND SIXTEENTH CENTURIES (WITH ENGLISH REFERENCE NAMES)

THE GREBAN-MICHEL GROUP:

1. The Arras Passion. c. 1440. 1 MS. 30,000 lines.
   Four days: Annunciation to Pentecost.
   (*La Passion d'Arras,* ed. J. M. Richard. Arras, 1891; repr. 1976).
2. Greban's Passion. Mid-15th century. Numerous MSS. 35,000 lines. (Use no. 1 above).
   Prologue: The Fall. Three days: Annunciation to Pentecost.
   (*Le mystère de la Passion* par A. Greban, ed. O. Jodogne. Brussels, 1965).
3. Michel's Passion. 1486. Printed texts only. 30,000 lines. (30% Greban) Four days: Baptism to Burial.
   (*Le M. de las Passion d'Angers* par J. Michel, ed. O. Jodogne. Gembloux, 1959).
4. The Mons Passion. 1501. 2 MSS, Producer's Copy.
   (Mainly nos. 2, 3 and 8) Four days: Creation to Pentecost.
   (*Le livre de Conduite du Régisseur . . . ,* ed. G. Cohen. Paris, 1925).
5. The Troyes Passion. Late 15th century. 1 MS. (Mainly nos. 2 and 8).
   Four days (3rd missing): Creation to Resurrection.
6. Valenciennes 25. 1547. 2 MSS., unedited. 50,000 lines. (Mainly nos. 2 and 3)
   Twenty-five days: Conception of Virgin Mary to Pentecost. (Analysis in Elie Konigson, *La représentation d'un M. de la Passion à Valenciennes en 1547.* CNRS Paris, 1969).

7. Valenciennes 20. 1549. 1 MS., unedited except in unpublished theses. 40,000 lines. (Uses nos. 2, 3, and 8) Twenty days: Creation to Assumption.
8. The *Viel Testament*. 15th-16th centuries. Printed texts only. 50,000 lines. (*Le M. du Viel Testament*, ed. J. de Rothschild. SATF, 7 vols., 1878).
9. Acts of the Apostles. Mid-15th century; Simon Greban. 2 MSS., unedited. 62,000 lines.
   Forty days: Pentecost to death of Peter and Paul.

THE SAINTE GENEVIÈVE PLAYS.

(Early 15th century. 1 MS. and a fragment. May have been the early repertory of the Confrérie de la Passion in Paris).
  1. *La Nativité et les trois roys*, ed. J. Whittredge, Bryn Mawr, 1944.
  2. *The Passion*, ed. Graham Runnalls. TLF, Geneva, 1974. Ministry to Resurrection Appearances. 4500 lines.
  3. *The Resurrection*, ed. J. Burks. Ann Arbor, Mich.,1957. Fall of Man, Resurrection. 1800 lines.

THE SEMUR PASSION.

1484. 1 MS. 10,000 lines. Two days: Creation to doubting Thomas. (*La Passion de Semur*, ed. L. R. Muir. Leeds, 1981).

THE AUVERGNE PLAYS.

Several MSS. and fragments which appear to belong to the same group. Possibly linked with Montferrand records.
  1. *The Baptism of Christ*. MS. fragment. 1250 lines. Baptism and Temptation. (*The Baptism of Christ*, ed. John Elliott and Graham Runnalls. Yale University Press, 1978).
  2. The Passion. 4,500 lines.
     Death of John Baptist to Burial of Christ.
     (*La Passion d'Auvergne*, , ed. Graham Runnalls. TLF, Geneva, 1982).

THE ROUEN NATIVITY.

1474. 1 MS. 10,000 lines. Prophets, Birth, Shepherds, Octaviam and Sibyl. (*Le M. de l'Incarnation et Nativité de NS . . . représenté à Rouen en 1474*, ed. P. Le Verdier. 3 vols. Rouen, 1884–1886).

THE LILLE PLAYS.

Late 15th century. 1 MS. 73 short plays, with a variety of subjects from Old and New Testaments. Ed. Alan Knight, in preparation.

JOHN C. COLDEWEY

Some Economic Aspects of the Late Medieval Drama

Historians of English drama often refer to medieval plays as "educational," "didactic," "communal," "festive," and "inspirational," echoing the familiar Horatian dictum about instruction and delight. Then they stop short, as though it were not polite to talk about money. Yet the historical fortunes of medieval drama were inextricably linked with real fortunes, of nations, regions, towns, and individuals. Like modern drama—like any drama that is actually produced—medieval drama depended upon a variety of economic circumstances and expectations. It is no accident that the single most important source of records of the drama is accounts: Churchwardens' accounts, Chamberlains' accounts, Bailiff's, Mayoral, Guild, Bursar's accounts, and others. Nor should it be thought peculiar that most of the surviving information about English cycle plays appears in documents which record hardheaded agreements between towns and guilds. The sources themselves seem to argue that one consistent feature shared by virtually all vernacular medieval drama is an economic concern; that is, a more material interest than has ordinarily been ascribed to the playwrights and producers of these plays.

Anyone familiar with medieval accounts knows how carefully ordinary people, and indeed, towns and parishes, husbanded their resources at the time this drama flourished. If theatrical productions cost them money, made them money, or were produced as part of some economic understanding, this was presumably an important fact. How important? What other economic concerns and circumstances pertained to the productions of these plays? How can an understanding of the economic nature of medieval English drama add to our own understanding of its history and to our appreciation of its power? The present essay attempts to address such questions and to emphasize the importance economic matters had for the drama. There may be no final answers to these questions, but there is indeed a need to explore economic avenues of inquiry and to see what useful directions future studies might take.

The overriding assumption throughout this study may seem obvious, but it needs constant restatement: economic conditions affected medieval drama. This observation is neither an endorsement of medieval economic determinism nor an indictment of personal or corporate greed in the Middle Ages. It is simply a statement of fact. Drama itself, more than any other genre, is a sociological artifact that in medieval times was publicly produced and publicly witnessed. It is, and was, subject to economic forces at large in the communities where it is performed. While motives behind much medieval dramatic activity can be couched in other terms, the bottom line (I use the phrase deliberately) for it and for most cultural possibilities was economic. Using this assumption as a starting point, there follow quite naturally some general and particular topics about which many students of the drama are in the dark: first, the state of the national economy and of various regional and civic economies from the late fourteenth until the mid-to-late sixteenth centuries; second, the economic motive and value of the craft cycle plays; third, the costs and benefits of parish plays and smaller town plays; fourth, the ways in which plays were financed; and fifth, the amounts and value of money involved in different kinds of productions. These issues require exploration so that we can more fully understand how the economic circumstances of a town, village, or parish dictated the possibilities of dramatic entertainment and, sometimes, the purposes for which they were produced. With some idea of the economic circumstances surrounding medieval playwriting and production, we may begin to face the critical question of how theatrical accomplishment and commercial success converged in the Middle Ages.

In the past, few historians of medieval drama have concerned themselves with its economic aspects.[1] This is understandable, as precious little specific information has been available until recently, and what *was* available seemed scattered, unreliable, inconclusive, and subject to the conflicting theories of medieval economic historians. Today the situation is more difficult, but due to a wealth rather than a dearth of material. With the advent of local and urban history as highly visible areas of study, medieval economic history has become in the last decade a dauntingly congested arena of sometimes recondite and usually hotly-argued controversies—and these between contestants with a great deal of specialization and talent, although with little specific knowledge or apparent interest in drama. Through all this, however, one thing has become absolutely clear: the medieval English economy was exceedingly complex, based as it was on hundreds of years of custom and experience, and responsive to anything affecting supply and demand. During the late Middle Ages, a partial list of such forces would include changing technologies, rapidly shifting demographic patterns, the supply and specie count of money itself (and its increasing use as a basis of trade), the advent of instruments of credit, habits of thrift and the amassing of capital, political events, and manipulation by virtually everyone involved at every level of commerce, taxation, and reward. To speak of any single aspect of this subject is obviously to simplify, to obscure, to falsify, and to gamble. But some general observations can be made; and whatever the risk, the English economy ought first to be confronted if we are to take the measure of medieval plays in their own time and place, or ours.

We might profitably begin with one general observation about the economy in England during the fifteenth century—the century, that is, when medieval drama came into full flower. The times were, by and large, economically stable and relatively prosperous. The overriding cause of this good fortune was, ironically, the unprecedented, catastrophic, and continuing ravages of the Black Death, which had begun in 1348.[2] First had come the notorious epidemics, and by the fifteenth century the plague was endemic in much of the country. It broke out sporadically now, unpredictably, just often enough to keep the population numerically low. By this time the population was less than half, probably, of the estimated six million people who had been alive in England in 1300.[3] But during the course of the fifteenth century, the plague gradually assumed a less virulent form. As if God had decided to offer restitution for the terrible sufferings experienced by victims of the plague, blessings were now conferred upon the survivors, with the last made first in his economic benediction.[4]

At the bottom of the social scale were the peasants, whom we know as the spectators of rural plays; the plague had devastated their ranks in the greatest numbers. For them, lowered population meant an increased demand for their services, a significantly higher wage, a better chance to secure freedom and property, and, in general, prosperity that had not been possible for perhaps two hundred years. Further up the scale, for urban craftsmen, whom we know as the main participants in the great cycle plays, the century brought similar, though lesser, rewards. Lowered supply also meant increased demand for their work, and with the widespread formation and development of craft guilds they parlayed this advantage into a larger share of their towns' fortunes. For lay and ecclesiastical landlords near the top of the social scale, whom we know as the patrons of traveling players and domestic drama, the fifteenth century was not quite as generous. The greatly diminished population made a shambles of traditional manorial economy and spelled an end to villenage. Beginning in the last quarter of the fourteenth century, labor costs rose, rents fell, and vacancies increased. But all was not lost. Since high labor costs were offset by high agricultural prices, shrewder landlords shifted from demesne farming to wholesale leasing—and not only of the demesne, but of their mills, marshes, meadows, and parks. Still, for a hundred years or more after the Peasants' Revolt in 1381 the demand for land dropped drastically and there occurred widespread desertion of villages. Taken together, the number and severity of difficulties signaled lower revenues for all except the most cunning landlords who could administer their properties with luck and efficiency. Fortunes of course were still made, but for established landowners money was harder to get and easier to lose than in the thirteenth and fourteenth centuries. Meanwhile, half-way up the social scale a new class was coming of age. The middle class, whom we know as sponsors as well as participants in every kind of dramatic activity, was gaining vigor. Often the lessees of the demesne, entre-preneurs among them were in a position to use their own and their lord's capital to enclose, to invest in new arable farming methods, or to diversify into industrial operations. Their enterprising ways paid off, frequently allowing them to enlarge their holdings and to realize genuine advancement in material goods.

To a greater or lesser degree then, members of all classes enjoyed the economic fruits made possible in the fifteenth century by the demographic consequences of the plague, and all had a stake in the drama. The prosperity in countryside and town usually translated into a redistribution of power and wealth from the relatively few to the relatively many, and the arrival of better times for the many was widely accompanied by the will to celebrate it. More and more cities and parishes sponsored plays, music, games, and other entertainments, and the cultural level accordingly rose with good fortune. It should again perhaps be emphasized that the connection between drama, society, and economic motive (even in known local financial circumstances) is rarely direct except to say that it takes money to produce plays. Since my purpose here is merely to sketch the background, there is little space to explore the larger cultural matrix in which theatrical activity and economic change are but two components. We should note in passing, though, that economic conditions creating poverty and wealth, the relationship between power and wealth, the ethical deployment of money (generosity or meanness), sins associated with money or committed because of it (avarice, greed, covet-ousness), all are given special contemporary tooth and lie at the heart of many medieval play texts. The tithing issue in the Chester *Cain and Abel* springs immediately to mind, as do the complaints about poverty in the Wakefield *Second Shepherds Play*. The shifting medieval economy was related materially, thematically, and ideologically to theatrical practices. Drama was in fact both its child and its witness.

In any event, the rosy picture painted above of general prosperity among classes needs to be modified. To assert prosperity is not to say that every shire shared equally, or shared at all, in the apparent wealth. Just as *who* you were was important, so where you lived could make all the difference. There was in the fifteenth century no single English economy, but rather a whole series of regional economies. Some prospered, some suffered, and there was wide variation within the regions themselves. A redistribution of power and wealth was taking place not only among classes but among these regions. We should pause for a moment to remark on this fact, for it has profound implications for regional theatrical practices.

Between the mid-fourteenth and the early sixteenth centuries, as subsidy (tax) returns show, there occurred a startling shift in the geographical distribution of wealth from the rich midlands to the Southeast, including London, and (to a lesser degree) to the Southwest (Bolton, 229). People with estates or livelihoods in areas such as Essex, Kent, or Cornwall benefited accordingly; those who lived and worked in such areas as Shropshire, Nottinghamshire, or Lincolnshire had to cope as best they could with stagnating local economies. The shift itself reflected a number of important developments: land use changing from arable farming to sheep farming; land ownership, rental, and custom changing as villeinage disappeared; and the cloth industry expanding rapidly as it triumphed over raw wool as the major export product. At the same time, London began casting an increasingly long shadow over the foreign trade of many provincial ports, signaling a shift not only of wealth but of economic power from North to South. London's size and importance led to the development of a network of support towns nearby, while its continued growth and influence fostered the establishment of new internal trade routes and thriving commercial centers further away.

As we might expect, along with the geographical shift of wealth and power from the Midlands and the North to the Southeast came a similar geographical shift in the possibilities for new dramatic entertainment. From the late fourteenth to the mid-fifteenth centuries we find that the centers where drama was first established were the larger successful commercial centers in the North and in the old Midland grain belt—York, Chester, Beverley, Coventry, and Lincoln. But during the later fifteenth and early to mid-sixteenth centuries we find new forms of drama arising, most notably in East Anglia and the Southeast. The cycle plays thus ran their course mainly in the North and the Midlands, where, as far as we can tell, they originated. Towns with dramatic traditions already in place continued to enjoy them during the late fifteenth and early sixteenth centuries. But when hardship became more commonplace again, newer, more economical and manageable forms of drama were adopted in places where elaborate annual productions were simply not feasible or, perhaps, desirable.

This is not to deny the existence of cycle plays or something like them in places as far north as Aberdeen in Scotland or as far south as Canterbury; only to emphasize that the form seems to have sprung up in one region at one time, and that this region was the richest in the country at that time. Other times and other regions would produce other forms of drama. We shall return to these rural and regional considerations in due course; for the moment they must serve as background to the vexed question of *urban* prosperity and decline, a topic which bridges the fifteenth and sixteenth centuries and brings into focus the very centers of the great vernacular cycles.[5]

It would seem logical to suppose that when rural fortunes rose or fell in a region, so would those of the towns. This was not, however, the case—

or, worse yet for our purposes, it was sometimes the case and in other instances, not. Towns within regions could prosper or suffer despite the fortunes of the surrounding countryside, and the local capacity or inclination for ceremony might be spurred or deterred accordingly. Thus, while the location of a town in a thriving region was important, it was not decisive. And in any case, location was only one factor affecting the economic health of any given town. Besides, the commercial health of a town, in turn, did not *determine* the sponsorship of plays in general or cycle plays in particular; it simply made them possible. Location and economic vitality in a community, then, were necessary but not sufficient causes for cycle plays to begin. We should not forget, however, that these *were* necessary causes, that both location and local prosperity strongly affected the rise of drama. We should not forget that by the end of the first quarter of the fifteenth century it was the commercially successful centers of York, Chester, Beverley, Coventry, and Lincoln in the North and Midlands that had developed cycle plays in highly elaborated forms. Without the combination of prosperity and strategic location, such a proliferation of drama in these towns is highly unlikely.

In contrast to the first quarter of the fifteenth century, the last brought declining prosperity for any number of these same towns—towns like York, Lincoln, and Nottingham. Other places, like Gloucester or Coventry, seemed more capable of coping with difficult economic circumstances until the very end of the century, when they too became distressed. Yet, curiously it would seem, in York and Lincoln, as in Coventry, the large dramatic productions originally begun early on were continued on a regular basis and sometimes augmented. Dramatic fortunes, then, did not always ebb with the economic tides, although they seem to have risen with them initially.

What seems to have played as important a role in the cycle plays' fate in every instance was the remarkable growth, development, and increase in sheer number of guilds. This occurred in most towns of any size, irrespective of their fortunes, during the 1400s. York had fifty-seven guilds in 1415, for example, and Hereford, a smaller regional center, twenty by the late fifteenth century (Bolton, 263). In at least a dozen of these towns, and perhaps many more where records and texts have not survived, craft guilds put on plays.[6] Why?

We have long known from surviving accounts a good deal about *how* money was spent by guilds to support cycle plays. We know about fines that could be levied against members who refused to participate, or against those who acted in more than one performance (Johnston and Rogerson, *Records of Early English Drama: York* [hereafter *REED: York*], 109). It has never been clear, however, *why*, in hard economic terms, the guilds did it. That is, we do not know the answer to a very fundamental question: why did guilds become involved in expensive productions in the first place? Moreover, why did they persist in putting them on in the face of hardship? While it is no doubt true that piety, civic pride or honor, and the hope of inspiration played a part in the launching of these productions, cash for expenses had to come from somewhere; and as productions go, the cycle plays were indeed expensive to start up and maintain. Pageant wagons or scaffold staging had to be acquired, decorated, repaired, and stored; money had to be found for costumes, for copying parts for actors, for props, make up, food and drink for rehearsals, and for other incidentals. In addition, the income lost from workers' spent time was considerable. What financial arrangements existed or were brought into being between a town and its guilds to make possible the production of these plays? What could induce the craft guilds—and in such numbers—voluntarily to empty their coffers, and to put themselves and their members individually at risk? The financial risks run by successive generations of guildsmen seem all out of proportion to supposed motives of piety and instructive entertainment.

If the craft guilds had been founded principally as social or ceremonial organizations, regular expenditures for plays and processions might make sense. But these guilds had come into being for strong economic reasons, and economic considerations continued to guide them. This fact needs underlining. As professional associations with fraternal activities they dated back, in one guise or another, to the twelfth century. Although their interests always had a religious cast, the guilds acted as the foci of local craft endeavor and pride.[7] In the fourteenth century, beginning in London and rapidly spreading elsewhere, guilds were recognized in civic constitutions as self-governing groups. Their responsibilities were to police their own trades, maintaining the standards of their work and enforcing any regulations affecting the quality of that work. Under this general rubric of quality control fell the enforcement of apprenticeship, which is to say the control of entry into the craft. By the mid-to-late fourteenth century it was clear that full membership in a craft guild meant a formal path to the freedom of a town, bringing with it the right to carry on business there. The power of the guilds to decide admissions to the freedom of a town brought, in turn, the possibility of collective action to control the market. It was the means, that is, to establish a local monopoly, an item of considerable economic importance to its members. A "foreigner" or non-freeman could only buy goods in town from a freeman, and could only sell goods to one. In York, for example, if goods changed hands in any other way, they were confiscated (see Palliser, "The Trade Gilds of Tudor York," 87). By enforcing apprenticeship, a guild maintained not only the standards of work but the level of wages; by controlling entry into the craft or "mystery," a guild preserved its monopoly.

A town, then, had a reciprocal economic arrangement with its guilds; indeed, the relationship between the two was close and mutually beneficial. In return for the town's most valuable gift to the craft—protection from the competition of outsiders—the guilds policed themselves and were willing to do almost anything the town council might ask. And here of course is the answer to our question of why, in economic terms, the guilds agreed to sponsor the cycle plays: closed shop and monopoly. Guild benefits are rarely mentioned in the records of the drama, so we have tended to ignore them; besides, in surviving documents where guilds often receive directives, the towns appear always to have had the upper hand. In the records, guilds apparently give up substantial profits and often supervisory rights; but in the unrecorded day-to-day world they enjoyed considerable economic power and control. They did take on additional supervisory duties and ceremonial responsibilities in their towns, including the support and management of the cycle plays, but the quid pro quo trade-off worked in their favor as well as the town's.

Once this mutually beneficial economic arrangement is recognized, many records of cycle plays in any number of towns begin to make more sense. Agreement after agreement between guilds and the towns protecting them appear clearly as attempts to set down with some precision exactly what duties, fees, and responsibilities the guilds were willing to be saddled with. Among the records relating to drama at York, for example, are dozens of ordinances affecting individual guilds, specifying what infractions of regulations can be fined, how much the fine will be, and how that fine is to be divided between the guild and the town or how spent by either alone. To illustrate this, we can use one entry to represent many. In the York A/Y Memorandum Book, in an entry dated 13 December 1388, it was agreed

> . . . that no fletcher of this city will work henceforth any Sunday at any work belonging to their said guild, nor put any arrows, bolts, nor others of their darts in front to show for sale on any Sunday on pain of 40^d to pay, one half to the Chamber and the other to their pageant of Corpus Christi, and this each time that they or any of them shall be convicted, except for putting the heads on the shafts when need be, the aforesaid ordinances notwithstanding (*REED: York*, 692).

This entry does little to further our specific knowledge of the plays put on in York. The word "pageant" in fact is mentioned only incidentally. The entry tells us nothing about the Fletchers' dramatic talents, nor about the play they performed ("The Trial of Caiaphas"), but it *can* tell us a great deal about the financial arrangements that allowed the plays to thrive. Let us focus, for a moment, on the nature of the restriction and on the fine itself with the eyes of a fourteenth-century fletcher, for this entry demonstrates how the system of fines operated, what the rationale behind the system seems to have been, and how the dramatic tradition in the town benefited accordingly.

We should note initially that a guild rule like this one was generated by its membership and voted into ordinance by the town council, thus allowing fines to be imposed legally for infractions. The guild, importantly, policed itself. In this case, any Fletcher working—or even advertising—on Sunday was subject to a 40^d fine. Half of the collected money was to revert to the guild and half to the city; but the half that came to the guild was earmarked for their dramatic production. This arrangement had the added benefit of protecting the guild membership at large from any possible conflict of interest among overzealous leaders, who might otherwise be tempted to uphold stricter standards than necessary in order to build up guild funds. The fine, then, was one of many in a balanced and much larger economic mechanism in York. The mechanism provided, almost as a side effect, a great deal of support for dramatic entertainments.

The York entry quoted above has dozens of counterparts in the town's records, for the number and kind of both restrictions and fines multiplied during the next century and a half. Other ordinances which seem strange appearing among the records of the *drama* in York stipulate that the Bakers could be fined for too small a loaf (*REED: York*, 841), the Coopers for a bad bucket (*REED: York*, 843–44), the Glovers for keeping a shop open on Sunday (*REED: York*, 841–42), the Tapiters for working anytime outside of daylight hours (*REED: York*, 840), the Potters for petty theft (*REED: York*, 847), the Saddlers for simple rebelliousness (*REED: York*, 846), and so on through restriction after restriction, as guilds burgeoned, coming under closer scrutiny by the city, and as the bureaucracy that linked them together grew. Lest we begin to think of the city as a bully or the guilds as simple pawns, it is instructive to note that in 1417–18 the Saucemakers and sellers of Paris candles threatened to stop supporting their pageant ("The Hanging of Judas") unless they received not only assurances of a continued monopoly, but also a means of enforcing support from retailers selling candles in the suburbs without belonging to the guild. The corporation responded quickly and arranged that both complaints be resolved (*REED: York*, 715–17). Fines collected for breaking regulations were often substantial, as were the entry fees guilds charged for admissions to freedom, part of which also went to the town. The town—and its drama, as was so often specified—was the main beneficiary of these policies. It had much to gain, and it benefited in two ways: more elaborate civic ceremonies and more civic funds. At the same time, however, the guilds maintained de facto control of all restrictions, as they were in charge of enforcing them.

The point is not that guilds *were* regulated by city ordinances but rather that they were *willing* to be regulated, regulated in sometimes very troublesome ways; further, that one main reason they submitted to such regulation was economic—that is, to preserve their respective franchises and control of entry into the freedom of a town. It made no difference whether the regulations were incidental to a town's drama or ceremony, or whether the instructions had specifically to do with the conduct of the plays. As we have seen, the main thrust of the ordinances often had no bearing whatsoever on the plays themselves. Some ordinances naturally enough pertained directly to the care and repair of the wagons, the order of march, the assignment of pageants and parts, or any number of the myriad details attended to, changed, and recorded over 175 years of performance. But all directives had the same force, and the guilds' willingness to obey the directives, pertinent to the plays or not, derived from the same economic motives.

York guilds were not of course alone in this regard; other towns and guilds had come to similar arrangements. In Chester, for example, a special agreement was struck early on to insure financing of civic entertainment. The Portmote Court Rolls of 1429–1430 record a meeting of the City Council where the stewards of the Weavers, Walkers, Chaloners, and Shearmen consented to an ordinance requiring all members of their guilds to pay assessments in support of the three main civic ceremonies: the Lady Day and Corpus Christi torchlit processions and the play of Corpus Christi (Clopper, *Records of Early English Drama: Chester* [hereafter *REED:Chester*], 494). Heavy fines were set for noncompliance with the ordinance, to be split as at York between the city and the guilds. With this arrangement the town could not lose, and guild members either paid voluntarily for the upkeep of the plays or were saddled with heavy fines and the threat of prosecution. In Chester, as in York, the guilds cooperated with the city. Cooperation, however, does not necessarily mean enthusiasm. In fact the fines may have been necessary in the first place because guild members were not always prepared to spend time and money in support of these enterprises.

One indication of the spirit in which at least some guilds approached their duty appears in a memorandum dated 1421/22, eight years earlier than the ordinance referred to above. This memorandum—the earliest reference in the records, incidentally, to Corpus Christi plays in Chester—appears among loose papers in the Coopers' Records. It concerns squabbling between the Ironmongers' and Carpenters' guilds over who would help them put on their plays: "whether one side or the other should have all the Fletchers, Bowers, Stringers, Coopers, and Tanners of the same city to help them in the Corpus Christi Play of the same city" (*REED: Chester*, 493). The Fletchers, Bowers, Stringers, Coopers, and Tanners, for their part, claimed that they "ought not to play nor are they held to play nor to be participants with one side or the other," since they had their *own* pageant to support—as indeed they did ("The Trial and Flagellation"). Implicit here is the recognition by all the guilds concerned that supporting the Corpus Christi plays was an onerous chore. This sentiment finds an echo in the royal charter granted the Saddlers' Guild in 1471, where inconvenience and power are openly balanced: in return for the power to limit, for forty years, those who would "enter or set up or occupy the aforesaid art and trade of the Saddlers" (*REED: Chester*, 498–99), the guild agreed to support the "manifold burdens ordered annually" by the city, specifically including the pageant, light, and Corpus Christi play. The reluctant tone and the recognition of heavy responsibility are common not only in the records of York and Chester, but in Coventry, Wakefield, Beverley, Newcastle, and, one suspects, virtually every town that struck a bargain with its guilds to produce these plays.[8] If, as we have seen, a guild's willingness to participate in dramatic entertainment was economically motivated, this same willingness was *limited* for economic reasons as well.

For the towns themselves the plays were good business. They brought together not only their own citizens but those of villages from miles around, and in a few instances they attracted royalty (Williams, *Drama of Medieval England*, 95). Then, as now, there was money to be made from a crowd. In York, for example, sites near stations where the plays were shown could be rented for some kind of commercial exploitation (*REED: York*, 829). But the plays also were an advertisement for a town's wealth, power, status, and stability. These readily translated, as the Chester records tell us, into "profitte," "common welth and prosperitie" (*REED: Chester*, 33, 115). Along the same lines should be mentioned what has often been noticed before, that the plays could act as shop windows for a guild's wares and services; hence the peculiar, sometimes humorous, sometimes grotesque, pairing of guild and pageant: the Bakers with "The Last Supper" (York), the Shipwrights with "The Building of the Ark" (York), the Mercers and Spicers with "The Coming of the Magi" (Chester), the Ironmongers and Ropers with "The Crucifixion" (Chester). But whatever benefits accrued to a guild from such advertising and publicity, it should be clear by now that the willingness of its members to undertake the chores of supporting the plays, of self-imposed regulation, and any other duties required by the town, depended very much upon that guild's power to preserve its monopoly and to serve the welfare of its individual members. To be Pageant Master at York was a duty for a junior officer in the Merchants' Guild; it carried with it no status and the officer had to advance his own money whenever necessary,[9] clear evidence that guilds were willing but not overly keen to involve themselves in the civic theatrical enterprise.

Starting in the late fourteenth and continuing into the fifteenth centuries, the independent status of guilds became increasingly important as both their responsibilities and their expenses increased, and they sought protection and perpetuity for their growing endowments in the form of real estate.[10] The accumulation of properties, common among all the crafts and trade guilds, helped to stabilize their assets, to underline their status, and to set guild fortunes on a somewhat separate footing than before. In practical terms, it gave them a larger interest in the town's welfare, a greater reason to cooperate in civic activities, and in many cases it brought guild members into the company of the town's ruling elite. The merchant guilds in particular, which had always been associated with the ruling structures of the community, characteristically gathered status, power, and property locally. This closer relationship with towns and their corporate fortunes, however, would prove in time to be a very mixed blessing for the guilds.

During the later fifteenth and early sixteenth centuries, as noted above, a general economic decline set in which affected many urban centers. It was also to have dire consequences for civic drama. Several reasons have been put forward for the decline; here we ought remark on three. First of all, population was on the rise again—a fact which spelled bad news for peasants, laborers, and those whose livings depended on simple skills. Second, the production of cloth had taken over raw wool export as the dominant English industry. This new industry did not depend on the services, conveniences, transportation links, or labor pools of the cities; on the contrary, it found the countryside and the suburbs more congenial than the towns, which had become expensive to work in and highly restrictive. Third, a national market for goods of all kinds was growing rapidly. The larger market made the assumptions and the practice of local regulation and protection—the very bases upon which guilds had been founded—obsolescent, while at the same time increasing the need for such protection (Jones, *The Tudor Commonwealth 1529–1559*, 4). For a century or more in some places, towns had been able to guarantee monopolies to the guilds; now, as competition for goods and services rose from outside town boundaries and jurisdictions, these guarantees became worthless. Over the course of the fifteenth century many towns had grown oligarchic, bureaucratic, and top heavy. As decay of trade and industry spread, those guilds which had become such powerful shareholders in the towns were also clear losers (Bolton, 262). Some guilds, in frantic efforts to retain their privileged positions, tightened restrictions. Ironically, this seems actually to have accelerated their own decline (Jones, 169).

The towns still had the power to order that their plays, processions, and other civic ceremonies be carried on, and as we know they continued to do so for some time. It was in part an attempt to bring life back to their failing economies. Modern industries that find themselves undercapitalized and hope to buy time with massive advertising campaigns do precisely the same thing. The guilds, of course, continued to follow orders: their monopolies, though shrunken, were still monopolies. But by this time—the early sixteenth century—guild fortunes were bound inextricably to those of their own suffering towns, not only by tradition but by *property*. Their objections to the economic burdens placed upon them grew more numerous and plaintive about this time, as the records testify, but availed them little. Then, at this moment in history, with towns and guilds locked in such unhappy circumstances, the English Reformation began, bringing its own massive and unparalleled dislocations of land, wealth, trade, and custom, accompanied by rampant inflation, crude plunder of the public treasury, and bitter religious strife. It is no wonder that plays—religious plays—supported by craft and trade guilds in early to mid-sixteenth century English towns, which were themselves often experiencing perilous financial debility, fell easy prey to this powerful combination of economic and social forces.[11]

The situation was exacerbated by the fact that in many places urban population declined during the first half of the sixteenth century, following the cloth industry out of town.[12] Thus, while the costs of maintaining plays and other civic ceremonies increased, a larger financial burden fell on fewer and financially less capable guildsmen. If, as we have seen, their enthusiasm may already have been waning, now the expenses often simply proved too much for them. In 1539 in Coventry, for example, the Mayor wrote to Thomas Cromwell that

> at Corpus christi tide / the poore Comeners be at such charges with ther playes & pagyontes / that thei fare the worse all the yeire aftere / And on Mydsomer even & on seynt peters even the maisters & kepers of Craftes vse such excesse in expences in drynkyng / that some such as be not worthe v li. in goodes shalbe then at xl s charges to ther vndoyng. . . . (*REED: Coventry*, 149)

In 1523 in Coventry, to cite another example, more than a third of the annual expenses of the Weavers' Guild went to pay for the Corpus Christi pageant ("The Destruction of Jerusalem"?) and midsummer celebrations (Phythian Adams, *Desolation*, 265), while at Chester *ninety percent* of the annual expenditures of the Painters' Guild was used for plays.[13] In 1523 the Cappers' Guild in Chester asked to be excused from putting on their play ("Balaack and Balaam") because they were "but verrey pouer men" (*REED: Chester*, 25). Likewise in Norwich in 1544 it was felt that the financial burden of supporting the pageants was so great that the crafts should be excused altogether (Phythian-Adams, "Urban Decay in Late Medieval England," 177). Clearly, as expenses and difficulties multiplied for both towns and guilds, the production of the plays faltered. Finally they ceased altogether.

Ultimately, of course, many factors contributed to the demise of the cycle plays, and these varied widely in individual towns and cities. But it is fair to say, given the steady deterioration of their mutually beneficial arrangements, along with the widespread decline, side by side, of towns and guilds in the face of demographic and economic crises, that the demise of these plays might be forecast from a time well before the Reformation. In any case it must be stressed that an important and continuing element to be reckoned with in both the rise and the demise of these craft plays was economic. The mutual dependence of town and guild is one economic context for these plays which has here been traced only in broad outlines. More detailed studies will surely discover more immediate causes, economic and otherwise, of the rise and fall of particular cycle plays, and more peculiar twists in their local fortunes; but the economic forces outlined above do much to explain why these craft plays fared as they did in the urban cultures that first nourished them and finally let them die.

Another kind of guild associated with dramatic presentations in urban centers was the religious guild, and we should deal with them briefly here. They can in fact lead us from consideration of larger urban enterprises to smaller rural plays. In some towns—Ipswich, for example—a religious guild (The Corpus Christi Guild) took on virtually the entire job of sponsoring and controlling the town plays.[14] In other places such a guild might have its own play, like the Creed Play in York sponsored by the Corpus Christi Guild (*REED: York*, i, xxxii-xxxiii). In still other towns such as Lincoln, a religious guild (St. Anne's Guild) took over the main task of supervising and coordinating productions.[15] Finally, a religious guild or guilds might in some places quite simply have contributed a pageant, very much like a craft guild would have done. Whatever ways the religious guilds were involved in the dramatic productions, they provided opportunities for townsfolk other than craftsmen and merchants to participate. With their diverse memberships, religious guilds often numbered in their ranks a cross section of the most capable, dedicated, responsible, committed, or powerful people in a town (see Kahrl, "Learning about Local Control"). It may well be that in some cases the leaders of a community put on productions to act either as a model or a catalyst for other dramatic activities. Sometimes—it is hard to tell how often—religious guilds were involved, willingly or not, in local political struggles (see Coldewey, "Reply").

As with the trade guilds, the key to understanding how religious guilds came to undertake plays in the first place is to understand their original character and responsibilities.[16] They too had a long history in both rural and urban settings, and they too flourished as never before in the late fourteenth century. Indeed, they seem to have sprung up like mushrooms after the Black Death. Fully 63% of the parish guilds reporting to a country-wide inquiry in 1389 claimed to have been founded since 1360—that is, during the most recent thirty years (Westlake, 64–65, 145). The guilds numbered in the thousands in the fifteenth century—perhaps 9,000 or more; in 1547 when they were abolished, there remained nearly 2,400 to be dissolved (Heath, 8; Westlake, 135).

Unlike the trade guilds with which they are sometimes confused, religious guilds were originally founded without economic motive. In both town and country their main role—the one for which they were begun, the one for which they were best known on a daily basis to their members, and the one for which they were ultimately disbanded—was religious. They promoted veneration for their patron saints, arranged charity for the living, prayers for the dying, and funeral services and memorial masses for the dead. To say this, however, is not to say that they lacked wealth or were uninterested in power. In fact, it was not unusual for a large urban religious guild to number among its members the ruling oligarchy of the town. Guild holdings—lands, buildings, and furnishings amassed through legacy, investments, and endowments—grew into impressive assets over many generations of pious members. However endowed, religious guilds provided a variety of economic services to their communities, urban or rural. They were a source of poor relief and a kind of accident insurance; they offered short-terms loans and a means for mutual investment in breeding herds or plough teams. And everywhere the guilds concerned themselves with the upkeep and improvement of the parish church, with particular emphasis on their own chapel, its furnishings and lights. In the main, guilds supported their ceremonial and charitable activities with entrance fees, membership dues and gifts. But they supplemented their regular income by sponsoring church ales, feasts, and plays.[17]

Evidence of rural religious or parish guilds' involvement in plays is relatively rare, perhaps because so many of their records perished when the guilds were dissolved in the mid-sixteenth century. Still, the occasional reference survives and we can be certain that many parish guilds around the country took part in dramatic activities to help support themselves. In Sleaford, Lincolnshire, for example, we find payments made by the Holy Trinity Guild for expenses of plays on the feast of the Ascension in 1480, and for "the wrytyng of spechys & payntyng of a garment for God" (Malone Society *Collections VIII*, 86). Unhappily, no receipts from this play survive, but it is clear that the guild was the main sponsor, responsible at least for copying and parceling out the parts and arranging for costumes. In Abingdon, Berkshire, by the mid-fifteenth century, "pageantes and playes and May games" were put on by the Holy Cross Guild (Chambers, *MS*, II, 337); and there is some indication of very early involvement of the Corpus Christi Guild in Cambridge in a "ludo filiorum Israelis" about 1350 (Chambers, *MS*, II, 344).

In some towns where religious guilds were reasonably strong and active organizations, the responsibility for dramatic activities seems often to have fallen naturally to them. But religious guilds in rural towns remained at best secondary units of administration. They operated within the context of their parish, which was the most common unit of local administration in smaller towns and villages dotting the English countryside. Thus rural religious guild plays were usually parish plays. Guild subservience to the parish is well illustrated in the records of Mildenhall, Suffolk. There, on St. Thomas Day (29 December) 1505, the Guild of St. Thomas à Becket collected £7, which "the Cherchewardenes affor namyd Rec' off ye profites & gyftes yat warn gevyn ffor a play off Sent Thomas played ye same day & yer in the hall yard all Charges deductyed" (Malone Society *Collections XI*, 190). In a mirror image of the Sleaford guild example cited above, play *receipts* are given here but no expenses listed. Importantly, the receipts were earmarked for the parish coffers, not the guild's. The guild, then, ordinarily served the parish, which was expected to profit from the productions.

Once we enter the arena of parish drama we have entered a world remarkably different from that of the cycle plays, and not only because life in a village or small town had a slower pace or a rougher texture to it. Town or parish plays, whether or not they were sponsored by religious guilds, were ordinarily not put on as displays of civic pride or power or as part of a mutual economic dependency, but rather as means of income. They seem to have arisen as a common practice somewhat later than the cycle plays, appearing with increasing frequency from the mid- to late fifteenth century until well into the sixteenth. They arose more commonly in the Southeast and Southwest, following the national shift in wealth down from the North and Midlands, away from some of the older ports. Generally produced under the auspices of Churchwardens—or, if the community were more developed, the Chamberlains of the town—these plays were as small or large as the ambitions of the parish. Some parishes produced short annual ventures resembling May ales or parish feasts, where communal goods and talents were pooled and where the audiences were purely local. Other more ambitious parishes launched truly breathtaking enterprises requiring enormous preparation, organization, investment, and risk; these commonly attracted audiences from other towns as well as local crowds.

Large or small, the plays were produced to bring in profits, often to fund specific maintenance projects or capital expansions in the local church or chapel. In Kingston-on-Thames (Surrey) in 1505, and in Boxford (Suffolk) in 1535, for example, proceeds from plays were used to repair deteriorated parish church steeples.[18] Boxford made more than £17 from their play—a substantial sum. At Tewkesbury (Gloucestershire) in 1600, brand new battlements were added to the steeple of the church, with the costs being offset by the profits of three plays, amounting to over £12 (Greenfield, 10–13). In Braintree (Essex) in 1534 "A Play of Placy Dacy alias St. Ewe Stacy" brought in more than £8 toward the building of the upper part of the church and the South aisle (Coldewey, "Early Essex Drama," 226), while in Sandon (Essex), the profits of a play were used to rebuild a bridge in 1562 (Essex Record Office MS Q/SR 8/8). Other examples abound, and these few can be taken as a representative list.

The main point to note here is that in the late fifteenth and early sixteenth century, parishes began to count on money they could make from plays. That proceeds were often earmarked beforehand for specific projects indicates quite clearly that profit itself was now a motive and a conscious goal. Although the practice was local and at best semiprofessional, we should recognize its novelty at the time and its importance to the history of the drama. This staging of plays for profit marks the beginnings of drama as a commercial venture. The entertainments were produced to do more than instruct the ignorant or inspire the knowing, and they signal a departure from the immediate goals of the great cycle plays—which, so far as we can tell, were never put on to bring in money.

Perhaps these plays for profit have been neglected or largely underrated in our histories of medieval drama because the practice arose in such out-of-the-way places and at such a low level of society; perhaps it is because few identifiable texts of the plays have survived. For whatever reason, the cycle plays have commanded our attention in the past: their size and scope are a matter of record, their texts and the documents recording conditions of their performances the ongoing subjects of inquiry. But this situation is in some ways quite misleading. During the fifteenth century the cycle plays do indeed seem to have been the most popular kind of theater and the most frequently produced. But the lion's share of drama performed in England for the first three quarters of the sixteenth century was not that supported by craft guilds as part of large civic enterprises; rather it was the smaller local productions put on by a truly astonishing number of parishes and towns around the countryside. While individual productions by individual parishes may hardly seem worth noticing, the publication of dramatic records on the county level is beginning to show that *hundreds* of places put on such plays.[19] Parishes owned playbooks and copied others; they made costumes and props to use not only for their own productions but for others to rent out. Towns and parishes hired men to manage plays, and sometimes took their plays on tour to neighboring towns and villages. They paid waits, traveling musicians, and sometimes professional players to act in their plays and to accompany them. In short, local non-cycle productions had now entered the game for earnest in vast numbers, and stages in communities of every size bristled with life.

Parishes financed their theatrical enterprises in a number of ways, some of them surprisingly modern. We rarely think of parishes having to come up with capital for plays, but like any other producer, then or now, the cruel truths of accounts payable and receivable had to be sorted out before anything further could be done. There were three main ways the parishes solved the problem of capital expenses. First, they used a subscription basis; that is, they sent out collectors or gatherers into their own neighborhoods and to nearby towns to collect for the play in advance. This money was then used as "seed money" for the production. Sometimes extremely elaborate staging and costumes were paid for ahead of time this way, as well as many of the other items necessary to get a play on its feet.

Subscription financing made possible, for example, the lavish production of a St. George play, mounted by the parish in Bassingbourn (Cambridgeshire) on St. Margaret Day in 1511.[20] For capital, the churchwardens coordinated the collection of money from twenty-seven towns and villages, whose contributions to see the play ranged from 8d. to 14s. 5d. In addition, the parish priest and parishioners donated time and materials toward the occasion. Feasting and drinking were also planned, and many gifts consisted of donated baking and brewing time, of meat or malt. The cash that had been collected was reserved mainly for services, materials, or expertise that parishioners could not themselves provide. Payments were made to set up stages, to hire minstrels and waits, to paint props and rent a playing place, to do the final cooking and brewing and other last minute preparations. The biggest expense of all was for a property player (called a "garnement man" or "propyrter") named Pyke, who received 20s. 2d. "for garnements and proprytes and play books."[21] As an independent stage manager, he was being paid to provide necessary theatrical gear and to oversee the production. All the arrangements could be made only with capital available ahead of time; financing by advance subscription was one way to make that possible.

There are other examples of subscription financing: Boxford (Suffolk) in 1535 (cited above), where gatherers collected money from twenty-nine or thirty surrounding towns and villages (Malone Society *Collections XI*, 136–37); Great Dunmow (Essex), where twenty-five surrounding communities contributed annually for twenty-five years (1526–1551) to put on Corpus Christi feasts and plays (Coldewey, "Early Essex Drama," 235–60); Heybridge (Essex), where twenty-three towns supported plays in 1530 and in 1532 (Coldewey, "Early Essex Drama," 29). Parishes using this kind of financing for theatrical ventures in these towns and in others appear to have been universally successful; without exception they brought substantial profits to their sponsors. They illustrate a canny grasp of the economic problems that had to be faced by hopeful towns with theatrical schemes, and a practical means to solve them.

The second means of securing capital to produce parish plays was simply to borrow it from local men of substance. As with the advance subscription method of finance, this one provided funds for initial costs, but without the bothersome bookkeeping, and overseeing and coordination of gatherers. An instructive illustration of this method at work can be found in the records of Chelmsford (Essex), where the parishioners raised over £21 for an elaborate series of four plays in 1562.[22] The men who lent money were all substantial citizens, the man who lent the most (nearly £9) destined to be churchwarden the following year. But despite their great initial support the Chelmsford plays turned out to be a financial disaster, losing a total of over £11. To repay its loans the parish had to dip into other sources of revenue for *years* to come (Coldewey, "Early Essex Drama"). More successful examples of parishes borrowing money from their own parishioners to finance plays can be found in New Romney (Kent) in 1560 (Malone Society *Collections VII*, 206), in an early (1516) Heybridge production (Coldewey, "Enterprising Property Player," 9), and in Lydd (Kent) in 1531/32, 1532/33, and 1533/34 (Malone Society *Collections VII*, 199–200).

The third and perhaps most common means of financing parish plays was simply to charge admission. The costs of production were thus treated as ordinary parish expenses and the gate receipts as ordinary income. This method was popular because of its simplicity, and we find evidence of these local productions everywhere in rural England, though most frequently in the south and east. It was the easiest way to finance relatively small productions requiring minimal investment and carrying little risk. Plays thus could be added to other ongoing or annual parish fundraising events like church ales or May feasts. If a performance proved successful and troublefree, it could be kept, repeated, augmented, or, in some cases, carried to neighboring communities to be put on there. Given the proliferation of such practices, we can only conclude that success was virtually assured. Parish accounts in many places record payments for the plays and players of other towns and villages as well as receipts and payments associated with their own productions.

Whatever kind of financing was involved, the foregoing discussions of profits and losses have highlighted the phenomenon of plays put on for money itself, as opposed to economic give and take arrangements between towns and guilds—arrangements which netted financial advantage and leverage rather than specific sums. The amounts of money involved in the parish plays may not seem very large by today's standards, and it is perhaps time to remark on the value of money in early English society. The role that money played in a rural, urban, or indeed in the national economy, was different in these early times than it would be only a century or so later, and it varied from one level of society to the next. In a village, coin itself might prove a relatively rare commodity at the turn of the sixteenth century, and trade was often carried on through long-standing barter arrangements and in-kind payments. Entry fees for a religious guild, for example, were often specified as a certain number of bushels of barley; a fine for an infraction of a rule was often specified as a pound of wax. Churchwardens' accounts show townsfolk making payment in the form of beef, grain, or services in lieu of cash. So the value of a penny or a groat (the shilling was not coined until 1504) might thus be enhanced by its scarcity in out-of-the-way towns and villages. Meanwhile, in larger and more economically sophisticated communities where money was more plentiful, buying and selling could take place much as in modern times. As road conditions and transportation improved, as trade routes became more frequented, and as travel became more common, the circulation of money also speeded up. The supply of coins increased too, although the specie count may have suffered, and by the mid-sixteenth century money had become the standard exchange medium across the land. It is instructive to note that as late as 1524 in Coventry, municipal regulations were enacted to establish that weavers and clothiers be paid "in ready money and not in wares," indicating that old practices were not reformed easily even in bustling centers of trade (Clapp, 483).

Another more familiar process affected the value of money: inflation. Money seems always to have been worth more in the past, that much is clear; but it is difficult to tell how much more it was worth at any given time. Rules of thumb that offer multipliers to reach some approximation of money's worth in former times are unreliable, and by definition obsolete as soon as they are published. Moreover, the *rate* of inflation changed radically during the course of the fifteenth and sixteenth centuries. The best way to determine what money was worth is to take comparative values of wages and goods.[23] We might note that the price of mutton, for example, was a penny per pound, and the price of butter two pence per pound in 1544 (*Documents in English Economic History*, 483). A laborer working then could expect to make six or seven pence per day (Phelps Brown and Hopkins, "Building Wages," 205). Prices of consumables of course would fluctuate during a normal year, and both wages and the prices of goods varied from one part of the country to another. Still, these figures will indicate some general financial circumstances familiar to the workers who watched, participated in, and paid for late medieval plays.

We can return more realistically now to the subject of parish profits from dramatic activities. It should be clear that the income generated by these plays, even if only a few pounds, might be enormous in relation to the income a parish normally enjoyed. In Great Dunmow (Essex), for example, the yearly Corpus Christi celebration brought in more than the sum total of rent for church lands. Interestingly enough, the only other parish activity which regularly brought in nearly as much money was the collection at Christmas by the Lord of Misrule. In 1535 the average net annual income of parishes was ten to thirteen pounds,[24] and plays that could bring in a third or a half of this amount or more would make for very tempting prospects indeed.

Economic matters, then, played important roles in the origins, development, and eventual passing away of much of medieval drama. For cycle plays, a healthy economy combined with the mutual dependence between town and guild lies at the heart of how and why these plays were fostered. For other, non-cycle plays, the question of profit lies closer to the historical circumstances of production than has generally been admitted. If, as has been suggested here, economic circumstances made medieval drama possible, and indeed help to explain its profusion of forms and its ultimate demise, we may in future studies explore whether this drama, like the Elizabethan and Jacobean drama that followed it, like any theatrical venture today, might be judged in part by its financial success. If medieval plays were box office bonanzas during their own heyday, we should judge them to begin with as commercially viable ventures. Criticism of the texts, performances, and theatrical possibilities of medieval drama to date have often sounded very much like critical judgments afforded amateur productions in school basements. What we need to recognize is that many medieval plays were part of tremendous enterprises where civic or parish stakes were high. These enterprises drew pleasure, profit, and blessings upon their participants. The plays paid their own way, and in doing so they offered for nearly two hundred years a platform, a local habitation, and a name, for the best theatrical talent England had to offer.

NOTES

1. The main exceptions are Arnold Williams, who devotes a chapter in *The Drama of Medieval England* (Ann Arbor, 1961) to "Production, Staging and Dramatic Technique" of the cycle plays; Glynne Wickham, who likewise spends a chapter of *The Medieval Theatre* (London, 1974) on "Amateurs and Professionals"; and, more recently, William Tydeman, who provides a chapter on "Financing the Plays" in his *The Theatre in the Middle Ages* (Cambridge, 1978). Some relevant material can be found in E. K. Chambers, *The Mediaeval Stage*, vol. II, chap. XXI, "Guild Plays and Parish Plays," and in the many appendices of this work. The material he prints, however, is not always reliable, and Chambers's well-known evolutionary theory of the development of the drama colors his presentation of the evidence. The most notable recent attempt on the part of an historian to address the issue of the drama in medieval towns is Mervyn James, who characterizes the cycle or Corpus Christi plays as cultic expressions of corporate honor, with the corporate body analogous to Corpus Christi, in "Ritual, Drama and Social Body in the Late Medieval English Town," *Past and Present* 98 (1983), 3–29.

2. A useful source for information regarding the plague and its consequences is John Hatcher's *Plague, Population and the English Economy, 1348–1530* (London, 1977), which includes a select bibliography. Cf. also J. M. W. Bean, "Plague, Population and Economic Decline in England in the Later Middle Ages," *Economic History Review*, 25 (1963), 423–37.

3. Estimates of population loss range from 25 to 60%. 30 to 45% is the current estimate of the national death rate in 1348–49, while figures for later epidemics in 1361–62, 1369 and 1375 range from 13 to 23% *apiece*. Hatcher estimates the net decline between 1348 and 1377 to have been between 40–50% (*Plague, Population and the English Economy 1348–1530*, 68, 71).

4. I base the following general survey of economic conditions mainly on J. L. Bolton's excellent work, *The Medieval English Economy 1150–1500* (Totowa, N.J., 1980), especially the chapters "Crisis and Change in the Agrarian Economy" and "Freedom Versus Restriction: Town and Countryside in the Later Middle Ages."

5. For much helpful information and a survey of the problem of urban decline and decay I am indebted to Professor Robert Tittler's "Recent Research in English Urban History, c. 1450–1650" (originally read at the Medieval Institute, Western Michigan University, in May 1981) and to Dr. Theodore DeWelles's "The Social and Political Context of the Towneley Cycle" (Ph.D. dissertation: University of Toronto, 1980). Important sources are Peter Clark and Paul Slack, *Crisis and Order in English Towns 1500–1700* (Toronto, 1972) and *English Towns in Transition 1500–1700* (Oxford, 1976); Colin Platt, *The English Medieval Town* (New York, 1976); John Patten, *English Towns 1500–1700* (Archon Books, 1978); Philip

Adams and E. A. Wrigley, eds., *Towns in Societies: Essays in Economic History and Historical Sociology* (Cambridge, 1978); A. R. Bridbury, "English Provincial Towns in the Later Middle Ages," *Economic History Review*, 34 (1981), 1–24; D. M. Palliser, "A Crisis in English Towns? The Case of York 1460–1640," *Northern History*, 14 (1978), 108–25; Charles Phythian-Adams, *Desolation of a City* (Cambridge, 1979).

6. A partial list: Aberdeen, Beverley, Chester, Coventry, Canterbury, Hereford, Ipswich, Newcastle-upon-Tyne, York, Lincoln, Norwich.

7. See D. C. Coleman, *The Economy of England 1450–1750* (Oxford, 1977), 73–74, and Platt, *Medieval Town*, 112–14, for further details of craft guild foundations.

8. See further complaints referred to in *Records of Early English Drama: Coventry*, xviii, and in Ingram's essay "'Pleyng geire accustumed belongyng & necessarie': guild records and pageant production in Coventry" in *Records of Early English Drama: Proceedings of the First Colloquium* (Toronto, 1979), 60–92; Alan Nelson, *The Medieval English Stage* (Chicago, 1974), 84, 94, 206.

9. According to Eileen White, "Setting Forth the Pageants at York," a paper read at the 1987 Medieval English Theatre Meeting, Bretton Hall College, Wakefield, 28 March 1987.

10. Cf. further in Platt, *Medieval Town*, 115.

11. For an account of how these forces affected *non*-cycle drama in one county, see J. C. Coldewey, "The Last Rise and Final Demise of Essex Town Drama," *MLQ*, 36 (1975), 239–60.

12. See Charles Phythian-Adams, *Desolation of a City*, where the process is traced in Coventry. While Adams's conclusions are not universally accepted, his sources and data demonstrating the population decline remain undisputed.

13. According to Alex Hamilton, "The Painters' Play at Chester," a paper read at the 1987 Medieval English Theatre Meeting, Bretton Hall College, Wakefield, 28 March 1987.

14. This role is apparent everywhere in the records of Ipswich. See Vincent Redstone's transcriptions of the Ipswich records in Malone Society *Collections II, Part iii*, (Oxford, 1931), and David Galloway and John Wasson's additional material in *Records of Plays and Players in Norfolk and Suffolk 1330–1642*, Malone Society *Collections XI*, (Oxford, 1980/81), 169–84.

15. See the Lincoln records, *passim*, in Stanley J. Kahrl's *Records of Plays and Players in Lincolnshire*, Malone Society *Collections VIII*, (Oxford, 1969 [1974]).

16. The standard reference on religious guilds is still Herbert F. Westlake's *The Parish Guilds of Medieval England* (London, 1919). Additional important sources are: Toulmin Smith and Lucy Toulmin Smith, eds., *English Gilds: The Original Ordinances of More than 100 English Guilds*, EETS Orig. Ser. 40 (London, 1870); Cornelius Walford, *Gilds: Their Origin, Constitution, Objects, and Later History* (London, 1879); William R. Jones, "English Religious Brotherhoods and Medieval Lay Piety: The Inquiry of 1388–89," *The Historian*, 36 (1974), 646–59. I am grateful to Professor Barbara Hanawalt of Indiana University for her helpful comments on an earlier version of this essay and for her allowing me to see a draft of her study "Peasant Gilds and Rural Economy in Medieval English Parishes."

17. Interesting examples of guild statutes showing the extent of involvement in the everyday lives of parishioners can be found in Cardinal Gasquet's *Parish Life in Mediaeval England* (London: Methuen & Co., Ltd., 1906), 261, 270–72.

18. See Chambers, *MS*, ii, 374 for the Kingston-on-Thames reference; for Boxford, see J. Charles Cox, *Churchwardens' Accounts*, (London: Methuen, 1913), 276–67, and Malone Society *Collections XI*, 136–38.

19. Lists of towns that participated in dramatic activities are being compiled

on a county-by-county basis by REED as it turns from publishing the records of main English towns to the records of counties. The names of many such towns are already available in the various Malone Society *Collections*, in Chambers's appendices to *MS*, and in Wickham, *EES*. The final number of these places will be enormous and is still to be guessed at.

20. See Cox, *Churchwardens' Accounts*, 270–74 for a transcription of the Bassingbourn accounts.

21. For more on property players, see J. C. Coldewey, "That Enterprising Property Player: Semi-Professional Drama in Sixteenth-Century England," *Theatre Notebook*, 31 (1977), 5–12. Still another property player, Thomas Parker, shows up in the Wymondham (Suffolk) accounts; see Malone Society *Collections XI*, 129.

22. For a more detailed examination of the Chelmsford plays, see J. C. Coldewey, "The Digby Plays and the Chelmsford Records," *RORD*, 18 (1975), 103–21.

23. See E. H. Phelps Brown and Sheila V. Hopkins, "Seven Centuries of Building Wages," *Economica*, 22, Series 2 (1955) and "Seven Centuries of the Prices of Consumables, compared with Builders' Wage-rates," *Economica*, 23, Series 2 (1956), for the most widely-used sets of figures of this sort. Bolton, p. 69, provides a graph which relates the figures.

24. According to the 1535 survey of parish income known as the *Valor Ecclesiasticus*. See Felicity Heal, "Economic Problems of the Clergy," in *Church and Society in England: Henry VIII to James I*, ed. Felicity Heal and Rosemary O'Day (London: The Macmillan Press Ltd, 1977), 103.

WORKS CITED AND SUGGESTED READING

Adams, Philip, and E. A. Wrigley, eds. *Towns in Societies: Essays in Economic History and Historical Sociology*. Cambridge, 1978.

Baker, Donald C. "The Drama: Learning and Unlearning" in *Fifteenth-Century Studies*. Hamden, Conn.: Archon Books, 1984.

Bean, J. M. W. "Plague, Population and Economic Decline in England in the Later Middle Ages," *Economic History Review*, 25 (1963), 423–37.

Bolton, J. L. *The Medieval English Economy 1150–1500*. Totowa, N.J.: Rowman & Littlefield, 1980.

Bridbury, A. R. "English Provincial Towns in the Later Middle Ages," *Economic History Review*, 34 (1981), 1–24.

Brown, E. H. Phelps, and Sheila V. Hopkins. "Seven Centuries of Building Wages," *Economica*, 22, Series 2 (1955).

———. "Seven Centuries of the Prices of Consumables, Compared with Builders' Wage-rates," *Economica*, 23, Series 2 (1956).

Chambers, E. K. *The Mediaeval Stage*, 2 Vols. Oxford: Oxford University Press, 1903.

Clapp, B. W. et al., eds. *Documents in English Economic History: England from 1000 to 1760*. London: G. Bell & Sons, Ltd., 1977.

Clark, Peter, and Paul Slack. *Crisis and Order in English Towns 1500–1700*. Toronto: University of Toronto Press, 1972.

———. *English Towns in Transition 1500–1700*. Oxford: Oxford University Press, 1976; rpt. 1979.

Coldewey, J. C. "Early Essex Drama: A History of Its Rise and Fall and a Theory Concerning the Digby Plays." Ph.D. dissertation, University of Colorado, 1972.

———. "That Enterprising Property Player: Semi-Professional Drama in Sixteenth-Century England," *Theatre Notebook*, 31 (1977), 5–12.

———. "The Digby Plays and the Chelmsford Records," *RORD*, 18 (1975), 103–21.

———. "The Last Rise and Final Demise of Essex Town Drama," *MLQ*, 36 (1975), 239–60.

———. "Reply" to S. J. Kahrl's "Learning about Local Control," *Proceedings of the First Colloquium*, ed. JoAnna Dutka (REED, Toronto, 1979).

Coleman, D. C. *The Economy of England 1450–1750*. Oxford, 1977.

Cox, J. Charles. *Churchwardens' Accounts*. London: Methuen, 1913.

DeWelles, Theodore. "The Social and Political Context of the Towneley Cycle." Ph.D. dissertation: University of Toronto, 1980.

Galloway, David, and John Wasson, eds. *Records of Plays and Players in Norfolk and Suffolk 1330–1642*, Malone Society *Collections XI*. Oxford, 1980/81.

Gasquet, Cardinal. *Parish Life in Mediaeval England*. London: Methuen & Co., Ltd., 1906.

Greenfield, Peter H. "Medieval and Renaissance Drama in Gloucestershire." Ph.D. dissertation, University of Washington, 1981.

Hanawalt, Barbara. "Peasant Gilds and Rural Economy in Medieval English Parishes." Unpublished essay kindly provided by author.

Hatcher John. *Plague, Population and the English Economy, 1348–1530*. London: The Macmillan Press, Ltd., 1977.

Heal, Felicity, and Rosemary O'Day, eds. "Economic Problems of the Clergy," in *Church and Society in England: Henry VIII to James I*. London: The Macmillan Press Ltd., 1977.

Heath, Peter. *The English Parish Clergy on the Eve of the Reformation*. London, 1969.

Ingram, Reginald W. "'Pleyng geire accustumed belongyng & necessarie': guild records and pageant production in Coventry" in *Proceedings of the First Colloquium*, ed. JoAnna Dutka (REED, Toronto, 1979), 60–92.

James, Mervyn. "Ritual, Drama and Social Body in the Late Medieval English Town," *Past and Present* 98 (1983), 3–29.

Jones, Whitney R. D. *The Tudor Commonwealth 1529–1559*. London, 1970.

Jones, William R. "English Religious Brotherhoods and Medieval Lay Piety: The Inquiry of 1388–89," *The Historian*, 36 (1974), 646–59.

Kahrl, Stanley J. "Learning about Local Control," in *Proceedings of the First Colloquium*, ed. JoAnna Dutka (REED, Toronto, 1979).

———. *Records of Plays and Players in Lincolnshire*, Malone Society *Collections VIII*. Oxford, 1969 [1974].

Malone Society *Collections II, Part iii*. Oxford, 1931.

Nelson, Alan. *The Medieval English Stage*. Chicago: University of Chicago Press, 1974.

Palliser, D. M. "A Crisis in English Towns? The Case of York 1460–1640," *Northern History*, 14 (1978), 108–25.

Patten, John. *English Towns 1500–1700*. Hamden, Conn.: Archon Books, 1978.

Phythian-Adams, Charles. *Desolation of a City*. Cambridge, 1979.

———. "Urban Decay in Late Medieval England" in *Towns in Societies*, eds. P. Adams and E. A. Wrigley. Cambridge, 1978.

Platt, Colin. *The English Medieval Town*. New York: David McKay Co., Inc., 1976.

Records of Early English Drama: Chester, ed. Lawrence Clopper. Toronto: University of Toronto Press, 1979.

Records of Early English Drama: Coventry, ed. Reginald W. Ingram. Toronto: University of Toronto Press, 1981.

Records of Early English Drama: Proceedings of the First Colloquium, ed. JoAnna Dutka. Toronto: University of Toronto Press, 1979.

Records of Early English Drama: York, ed. Alexandra F. Johnston and Margaret Rogerson, 2 vols. Toronto: University of Toronto Press, 1979.

Smith, Toulmin, and Lucy Toulmin Smith, eds. *English Gilds: The Original Ordinances of More than 100 English Guilds*, *EETS*, Orig. Ser. 40. London, 1870.

Tittler, Robert. "Recent Research in English Urban History, c. 1450–1650." Paper originally read at the Medieval Institute, Western Michigan University, May 1981.

Tydeman, William. *The Theatre in the Middle Ages*. Cambridge, 1978.

Walford, Cornelius. *Gilds: Their Origin, Constitution, Objects, and Later History*. London, 1879.

Westlake, Herbert F. *The Parish Guilds of Medieval England*. London, 1919.

Wickham, Glynne. *Early English Stages, 1300–1600*. 3 vols. London: Routledge and Kegan Paul, 1959–1981.

———. *The Medieval Theatre*. London, 1974.

Williman, Daniel, ed. *The Black Death: The Impact of the Fourteenth-Century Plague*. Binghamton, N.Y.: Medieval and Renaissance Texts and Studies, Vol. 13, 1982.

Williams, Arnold. *The Drama of Medieval England*. Ann Arbor, 1961.

LAWRENCE M. CLOPPER

Lay and Clerical Impact on Civic Religious Drama and Ceremony

Late nineteenth and early twentieth century scholars typically imagined early English drama to have originated as pure essence uncontaminated by the world—and therefore in Latin. They mourned the mutilation of these creations at the hands of vernacular speaking civic officials and their cronies, Bottom and his rude mechanicals, in a process that was called "secularization" (Chambers, II, pp. 68–105). Finally, they understood that these once noble creations fell to the axe in the hands of the Protestant reformers (Gardiner). In our more enlightened and secular age we have discovered that the plays were actually the occasion for considerable drinking and feasting, and we link their performance on market days with the city fathers' desire for greater revenues and tariffs. We even allow that the audience who came to see the plays did not have to watch them but could wander off at will.[1]

In the process of readjusting theories that we have come to find naive, we seem to have lost sight of the social and cultural contexts of the civic drama. I would like to suggest some modifications in our assessments of the drama and its role within the culture. For this, I will first use the example of Chester in the early and late sixteenth century and then will turn to some of the other cities known to have had cycles of plays or elaborate ceremonial processions.

The Chester cycle of plays underwent a number of changes and considerable elaboration in the early sixteenth century at the same time that other customs were being initiated or reformed.[2] Many of these changes occurred at about the time that the city was granted its Great Charter by the king which enlarged the freedoms and liberties of the city.[3] We need to consider the possibility, therefore, that the development and maintenance of customs were not just an expression of civic pride—or that they could afford to do it—but also that the customs were signs of their free status. There is not just an economic motive here; rather there is, in addition, an assertion of political identity and of the city's concern for the welfare of its citizens.

Second, it was the elected representatives of the guilds who sat as the city council and who decided whether such plays were to be performed.

It may be simplistic, therefore, to argue that the religious plays were suppressed by Protestants who objected to the Catholic orientation or quality of the plays. The impression of the situation at Chester, given by the records there, is that in the 1560s and 1570s the struggle over whether to produce the plays was a struggle between two, perhaps more, Protestant factions, and that these groups had very firm ideas about what was and was not appropriate in the representation of religious subject matter. In addition, I think that the directives from the Archbishop of York to Chester (*REED: Chester*, 96–97) and to Wakefield (Cawley, *WP*, pp. 125–26) suggest that the issue was not simply one of Catholicism versus Protestantism as much as it was a question of the appropriateness of representing or impersonating the deity and of counterfeiting rituals.

There is evidence of civic ceremonial or dramatic performance in Chester as early as 1399, and there are sufficient records to indicate that three of the most important activities in the fifteenth century were the Christmas Watch, the Corpus Christi procession, and the Corpus Christi play.[4] At the beginning of the sixteenth century, however, a number of activities were invented, reformed, or enlarged. In 1499 the Midsummer Show was first set forth in anticipation of the Midsummer Fair (*REED: Chester*, 21–22); in 1512 the Sheriffs' Breakfast Shoot on the Roodee was begun (*REED: Chester*, 23); in about 1521 the Corpus Christi play, which had been performed at St. John's on Corpus Christi day, was shifted to Whitsunday and within a few years had been so expanded that it began to be played over a period of three days (Clopper, "History"); and in 1540 the ancient homages to the Shoemakers and Drapers were reformed to more profitable uses (*REED: Chester*, 39–42). One of the puzzling facts about this increase in costly civic activity is that much of it occurred at a time when the city was still in the grip of an economic decline that had lasted for over a hundred years (Morris, p. 459).

The city's economic fortunes can be traced through the histories of the fee farm and port activity. Chester was a fortunate city in many respects because it was a county palatine whose earl was either the king or, most often, the Prince of Wales. In 1300 Edward I honored the city of Chester with certain freedoms for which the city was to pay a fee farm of £100 (Morris, p. 490). Obviously, the fee farm was not onerous, and the city—because of its port activity and trade in Wales—was able to make payments. Chester, however, was not one of the large ports of England because, even though it did have some trade with Spain, it was not situated to profit from trade with the Low Countries or the Continent. But it was an important port of entry, one at which not only Chester but the king could tax goods (Woodward, pp. 1–7). Chester, however, does not lie on the coast: It is situated on the banks of the river Dee quite a few miles from the sea. During the fifteenth century, the river Dee silted up so much that goods were required to be ferried twelve miles from the anchored ships to the city. Trade declined, and in consequence of that and

the Welsh disorders, the fee farm was reduced to £50 (Morris, p. 511).
In 1484 the farm was reduced to £30 and in 1486 to £20 (Morris, pp.
516, 521). Although these last two reductions came in the first year of
the reigns of Richard III and Henry VII, respectively, and therefore may
be attributable in part to the new monarchs' desires to gain the support
of the city, there can be no doubt that the city had seriously declined.
In the charters that reduced the fee farm and in the Great Charter of 1506
there is recognition of the city's economic decline, of the disrepair of the
walls, and of a vastly reduced population as a consequence of the inhabitants having moved elsewhere.[5] The economic stagnation and decay continued into the sixteenth century at least until the later years of Henry
VIII's reign. Most of the new ceremonial and dramatic activity, therefore,
developed at a time of economic hardship.

Nevertheless, of all the new practices only one, the Midsummer
Show, can be described as an attempt to attract persons for economic reasons. I do not mean to suggest that there may not have been economic
incentives in the development of other practices, but many of the other
activities were strictly oriented toward the freemen of the city or, as in
the case of the plays, had other motives in addition to economic ones.
There seems to have been a Midsummer Watch in the years prior to 1499;
this Watch consisted of the local dignitaries or their representatives and
the guilds and their representatives going about the city in ceremonial
fashion and then retiring for feasting and music.[6] The Midsummer Show,
on the other hand, included at various points in its history, fantastic
beasts—elephants, dromedaries, and the like; characters from the plays—
Mary Magdalen, Judas, Simeon and the Christ Child, the Devil in his
Feathers; naked boys, the alewife with her cups, and her demonic suitor.
The Midsummer Show was held, in those years that the plays were not
presented, on the eve before the fair on the Feast of St. John the Baptist.
It was on this feast day that the minstrels of the surrounding area—and
in olden time, the whores—were summoned to the Dutton's minstrel
court to pay homage and their fees (REED: Chester, 461–66, 486–89;
Rastall). The fair itself was held over a four-day period outside the gates
of the Abbey; indeed, the fair was owned by the Abbey, although the artisans of the city participated in it (Jones, pp. 39–40). The Midsummer
Show very probably was intended to attract persons from the surrounding
countryside to the city for the fair in the hope of increasing revenues.

The other activities introduced in this period seem to be the consequence of more complex historical forces. As has been suggested earlier,
there were advantages to being a county palatine; but there were also dis-
advantages. There was an economic disadvantage insofar as tolls and
taxes at the port were higher than at nearby ports; one consequence was
that Dublin often sent ships to Liverpool first in order to avoid the payment of entry fees (Jones, p. 4). There were also some political disadvan-
tages that were compounded by the presence of the Abbey of St. Werburg

(Jones, pp. 4–5, 39–40). The second power in the city—the earl was the first—was the abbot of St. Werburg, whose monastery took up one quarter of the city, almost the whole of the northeast quadrant. The abbey had been successful in fending off the city's attempts to increase its jurisdiction throughout the fifteenth century, but in 1506 Henry VII granted the city its Great Charter containing impressive freedoms. This is the earliest charter to describe the procedures for electing the mayors, the council, the sheriffs, and other officers. It broadens the legal jurisdiction of the city in every respect. It makes the mayor an officer in the earl's administration in addition to head of the local government and grants the sheriffs all the privileges of other county sheriffs. The charter enlarged the city's freedoms so much that when the city again came into conflict with the abbey during the period 1507–1509, it was necessary to call in royal arbiters and these gave complete victory to the citizens over the claims of the abbey. The charter and the freedoms it granted seem to have shifted the balance of power to the civic governing body to such an extent that civic customs were developed as signs of corporate identity and supremacy.

The civic government's new prominence is signaled by the transference of the plays from Corpus Christi to Whitsuntide, by increased civic control over the plays, and by a lengthening of the cycle (Clopper, "History"). In about 1521 the cycle play seems to have undergone some major revisions and expansions; probably of the Old Testament and Nativity sections of the cycle; by 1531 or 1532 these had occasioned the transference of the plays to Whitsuntide and necessitated their performance over a three day period at several locations in the city. Prior to this time, the guilds had marched in procession from St. Mary's just north of the Castle to St. John's, the cathedral church, outside the walls of the city where they performed a play on Corpus Christi day (*REED: Chester*, 38–39). It is not clear why the procession started at St. Mary's except possibly that it was the preeminent parish church within the city. It is probable that the procession went to St. John's because that church was believed to have a piece of the True Cross and thus was an important local shrine (Jones, pp. 50–51). It is also the obvious center for the celebration of Corpus Christi, and, if my speculation is right that the old Corpus Christi play was primarily a Passion play, then St. John's is even more appropriate. In the Early Banns, which describe the new Whitsun play, we are told that the colleges and priests of St. John's continued to bring forth a play on Corpus Christi day (*REED: Chester*, 38)—possibly as late as Edward VI's reign. The location of the play at St. John's and the prominence of the colleges and priests suggest that the earlier Corpus Christi play may have resulted from clerical initiative and remained under their auspices despite the fact that the guilds were involved in and probably paid for the production (e.g., *REED: Chester*, 6–7; 10, l. 20; 12, l. 15; 13–15, etc.).

There are a number of differences between the Corpus Christi play and

the Whitsun plays: (1) the civic authorities and the guilds have control
of the playbook and the production of the Whitsun plays; (2) they decide
when it is to be played; (3) the play takes place over three days rather than
one and is performed in the four principal streets of the city instead of
at the cathedral church of St. John's outside the walls of the city; and
(4) some weeks before the performance of the plays there is the Riding
of the Banns which involves a procession not from one church to another
but through the principal streets of the city with stops at Northgate and
the Castle prisons for the distribution of alms to the prisoners (REED:
Chester, 77, 81). These two stops are significant because they acknowledge symbolically the two major legal jurisdictions, the city's and the
earl's.

It is possible that there were also some economic considerations involved in the move. Coventry's plays had gained a national reputation
and had succeeded in attracting royalty on several occasions.[7] The city
of Chester may have felt that a move to Whitsuntide would result in less
competition for merchants and playgoers and would increase the city's
commerce during the time of the plays. Still, noneconomic motives seem
the more important. Some of the city's noneconomic motives are revealed by the changes that Mayor Gee made in the homages to the Shoemakers and Drapers (REED: Chester, 39–42). These homages, of an uncertain but ancient date, were celebrated with a presentation of a football
and then a game and foot race. In the records these latter sound less like
Olympian contests than a general running amok. Consequently, in 1540
Mayor Gee reformed the homages to make them more useful to the city
and participants. The mayoral order as we have it is rather garbled and
the preamble, which explains the reasons for the changes, has more to
do with the Sheriffs' Breakfast Shoot than with the homages. In any
event, the preamble explains that because the shooting of the long bow
has fallen into such decay in the country, the old civic practices are to
be reformed to encourage the more profitable exercise of bowmanship.

It is significant that the civic customs should be reformed on such
grounds because Chester was a traditionalist city; that is, it was resistant
to social and political change. Its defense of the change is that as a corporate body it ought to concern itself with the welfare of the individual,
the city and the nation. The rationale that is offered in the Early and Late
Banns for the plays (REED: Chester, 27–28, 32, 240–42) also suggests a
new concept of its corporate responsibility. The Banns and the Proclamation admit that there are economic motives behind the production of the
plays, but they also claim that the plays are produced "for the Aug-
mentacion & incresse of the holy and catholyk ffaith . . . to exhort the
myndes of the comen peple to gud deuocion and holsom doctryne . . ."
(REED: Chester, 33). We could argue that this second reason is simply
a mask for the true, the economic, motives, but if I am correct in believing that the development of these plays during a period of economic

stress occurred as a consequence of the city's coming to supremacy in the local power arena, then I think that we ought to concede that the city had gained a sense of responsibility for the moral and religious welfare of the citizenry as well. The transference of religious drama from clerics to laymen is not so much an illustration of "secularization" in Chambers's sense as it is a redefinition of corporate lay responsibility.

Secular control of vernacular Biblical drama survived during the years of uncertainty when there were shifts back and forth between Catholicism and Protestantism and when there was growing sectarianism within Protestantism. It has been traditional for us to accept the late Renaissance dictum that the Chester plays were suppressed because of the superstition in them; that is, they were the victims of Protestantism. To be sure, this is to some extent true. For example, one of the chroniclers of the period said of the 1575 performance that some of the plays were left unplayed because of the superstition in them (*REED: Chester*, 110, 1. 15). But if one reads the extant texts of the Chester plays, one is hard pressed to find much that could be classified as superstition. Although there are some apocryphal elements, there are no wild-eyed stories of saints or martyrs to which the Protestants could have objected, and the representation of the Virgin by the 1560s at the latest was most circumspect given the fact that the "Purification" had been transformed into a "Presentation at the Temple" and "Christ and the Doctors," and since the "Assumption" had been deleted under Edward (Clopper, "History," pp. 226, 231–33).

Perhaps we have been too concerned with the opposition between the Catholics and Protestants and not enough with that between groups of Protestants. For example, it is puzzling that the city council thought they would be able to go ahead with a performance of the plays in 1575 (*REED: Chester*, 103–105, 112–17) when the Archbishop of York had inhibited them (or tried to do so) in 1572 (*REED: Chester*, 96–97). There was opposition to the plays even within the council when the council voted on the question of whether it would be "meet" to perform them. It was agreed that it was "meet" but it was also noted that they should be "reformed," that is, edited, by the mayor and his advisors—but not by the clergy—if they felt it "meet" and convenient. Whatever editing was done must have been relatively minor for the plays began less than four weeks after it had been agreed that they should be performed, and the cycle that year seems not to have been shortened since it took three and a half rather than three days to perform it.[8]

It is possible that the "superstition" thought to exist in these "popish plays" had much to do with their mode of presentation, for there is some evidence that there were objections to the representation of God the Father as a person and of the sacraments "in game." In addition, it is possible that some of the Protestants objected to the representation of material they regarded as fables or inventions unauthorized by scriptures, whereas other Protestants within the city felt that such representation was "meet."[9] Even though some of the opposition must have been directed at the plays because they were thought to be popish or because they were associated with persons known to be Catholic survivalists, it is a simplification to see it just as a Protestant attack on popish superstition.

We may take the reviser of the Late Banns as a contemporary witness of the concerns about the plays and as a defender of them. In the prologue the Reviser gives a history of the cycle and defends "Rondoll," the monk of Chester Abbey who was believed to have written the plays, on the grounds that he was not "monckelyke" because it had been his desire to reveal to the common man the sacred knowledge of the scriptures in the English tongue (*REED: Chester*, 240–41). He also apologizes for the inclusion of "Some thinges not warranted by anye writte" (*REED: Chester*, 240, l. 15). For example, he apologizes for the Tanners' "Fall of Lucifer," but adds that some writers warrant the matter and therefore it has been allowed to stand (*REED: Chester*, 242, ll. 9–15). He points out that the scriptures do not warrant the midwives' episode in the Nativity play (*REED: Chester*, 243, ll. 11–12), and that there are few words in the Shepherds' Play that are true because all the author had to work with was the *Gloria in excelsis* (*REED: Chester*, 243, ll. 18–20). The Shoemakers' "Entry into Jerusalem" is commended because it is a true story (*REED: Chester*, 244, ll. 21–24); the Bakers are admonished in their presentation of the Last Supper to utter the same words that Christ himself spoke (*REED: Chester*, 245, ll. 1–5). He acknowledges that it is a matter of faith that Christ descended to Hell, but reminds the audience that it is not known what occurred there; the author, he says, wrote the play "after his opynion" and the audience should credit the best learned on the subject (*REED: Chester*, 245, ll. 19–25).[10] The Banns Reviser does not simply assert that the plays do not contain superstition; rather, he at times distinguishes those plays that have scriptural authority from those that do not. But he also defends others by saying that some authorities warrant them. He seems to think that certain apocryphal or invented stories can instruct even if they are not strictly true.

If this revision of the Banns was made during Elizabeth's reign—and the evidence suggests that it was—then it might be understood not so much as a defense against the charge that the plays are Catholic doctrinally as a defense against the charge that the plays are non-scriptural and thus untrue. There is some confirmation for this interpretation in the comment made at the end of the play entry in the first edition of the Rogers *Brevary*:

> And we haue all cause to power out oure prayers before god that neither wee. nor oure posterities after us. maye neuar see the like Abomination of Desolation, with suche a Clowde of Ignorance to defile with so highe a hand. the moste sacred scriptures of god. (*REED: Chester*, 252, ll. 4–8)

If there was a concern about the accurate representation of the scriptural texts, there was also one about the propriety of representing rituals and the deity. At the end of some copies of the Late Banns is an objection both to the former mode of presentation and to the unfortunate quality of the one that the audience is soon to see:

> Of one thinge warne you now I shall
> that not possible it is these matters to be contryued
> In such sorte and cunninge & by suche players of price
> As at this daye good players & fine wittes. coulde deuise
> ffor then shoulde all those persones that as godes doe playe
> In Clowdes come downe with voyce and not be seene
> ffor noe man can proportion that godhead I saye
> To the shape of man face. nose and eyne
> But sethence the face gilte doth disfigure the man yat deme
> A Clowdye coueringe of the man. A Voyce onlye to heare
> And not god in shape or person to appeare.
>
> (*REED: Chester*, 247, ll. 8–20)

The objection to the representation of the Godhead is confirmed in the directive to the Burgesses of Wakefield in 1576: The Commissioners at York have been given to understand that the plays use many things "which tende to the Derogation of the Maiestie and glorie of god the prophanation of the Sacramentes and the mauynteynaunce of superstition and idolatrie[; therefore,] The said Commissioners Decred a lettre to be written and sent to the Balyffe Burgesses and other the inhabitantes of the said towne of Wakefeld that in the said playe no Pageant be vsed or set furthe wherein the Maiestye of god the father god the sonne or god the holie ghoste or the administration of either the Sacraments of Baptisme or of the lordes Supper be counterfeyted or represented . . ." (Cawley, *WP*, p. 125). If the Commissioners simply objected to the plays, if they thought that they were irredeemably Catholic, they could have banned the plays; instead, they objected to the mode of representing the Godhead and forbade the "counterfeiting" of certain sacraments. This directive does not seem to forbid the appearance of Christ *in his manhood*; thus, it does not constitute an attempt to halt the plays without explicitly forbidding them.

But there is the objection to the "counterfeyting" of the sacraments of Baptism and the Last Supper. Chester did not have a Baptism play, and there is no indication in the extant records that it ever had one.[11] The presentation of the Lord's Supper, on the other hand, has a rather complex history at Chester (Clopper, "History," pp. 232–33). The Bakers were responsible for performing the Last Supper, according to both the Early and Late Banns; however, they did not perform their play in 1550 and it seems temporarily to have dropped out of the cycle altogether or was abbreviated and performed by the Shoemakers that year. It is possible that the

play was excised or reduced because of objections to the counterfeiting
of the sacrament or, possibly, because the language of the presentation
was too Catholic. The language is certainly of great importance; at issue
since at least the fourteenth century in England was how one stated the
mystery of transubstantiation. The writer of the Late Banns appears to
have been conscious of both objections to the representation of the making of the sacrament and to the language used to describe transubstantiation:

> And howe Criste our sauioure at his laste supper
> Gaue his bodye and bloode for redemtion of us all
> yow Bakers see yat with the same wordes you vtter
> As Criste himselfe spake them to be a memorall.
>
> (*REED: Chester*, 245, ll. 1–4)

I do not know whether the Bakers returned to their old text when the
play was restored to them after 1550, but I would point to the fact that
the extant text lays considerable stress on the notion of "signs." It is in
this play that Christ speaks at greatest length in the Chester cycle, and
it is in this play that some of his words are non-scriptural. In the opening
section of the play, Christ explains that they must eat the Paschal Lamb
as the law commands. Then he tells them that the time has come that
"sygnes and shadowes be all donne, / Therefore, make haste, that we
maye soone / all figures cleane rejecte" for He will begin a new law (Play
XV.69–72). At that point, the play returns to a close translation of the
scriptural texts.

It might be argued that this still constitutes a counterfeiting of the
sacrament, but it seems to me that the playwright has made an effort to
historicize the event and that he has tried to imply that his representation is a "sign" of the sacrament, not the sacrament itself. It would also
appear that the Banns writer understood the scene to be a "memorall"
as long as the key words that the player uttered had scriptural authority.

Despite their inclusion of apocryphal and invented matter in the Old
Testament and Nativity plays, the Chester playwrights are often strikingly literal in their translations of some Biblical passages; indeed, at certain momentous occasions they are as literal as it is possible to be.[12] At
present, it cannot be argued that the extant plays were rewritten in the
age of Elizabeth in response to the desires of "fundamentalist" Protestants; but the Reviser's remarks in the Late Banns suggest that there was
a felt need to defend the plays at that time. It is possible that the extant
texts were put in their present form, as Professor Travis has argued (pp.
74–61), during a time (1521–1531) when such "literalizing" of the text
would be consistent with the contemporary religious sentiments, especially in the North, and that the Reviser is simply defending that text.
The primary point, however, is that the literal rendering of certain scriptural passages may suggest a Protestant re-formation of the texts and that

at the time of their demise, therefore, the texts did not contain a great deal of material that might justly be classed as popish superstition.

The discrepancy between the charge that the plays contained popish superstition and the fact that the texts show little evidence of such content brings us back to an unresolved question: Why did the governors of Chester move their play from Corpus Christi to Whitsunday? The move could not have occurred as a consequence of the banning of the feast of Corpus Christi because that did not occur until 1548 and the plays had been moved by 1531. Earlier it was suggested that the plays were moved for commercial reasons: If the plays were performed at Whitsuntide, they would not be in competition with the Coventry plays which were performed at Corpus Christi. But if the plays underwent a major revision at the time that they were shifted, and if their revision was responsive to the demands of the more "fundamentalist" citizens of Chester, then it is possible that there was some desire to move the plays away from the celebration of the eucharistic sacrament and toward the salvific words of Christ, away from the body of Christ (Corpus Christi) and toward the words of Christ—the making of the Creed, the evangelical teaching in tongues, both of which are associated with Whitsuntide, a feast that celebrates a scriptural event rather than a feast "newly" established by men.[13]

We cannot expect that the social, political, and economic forces, nor the responses to these, would have been the same in all boroughs throughout the period; yet we might try to determine why some cities and towns produced plays and why others only had processions, or whether drama had the same function in other cities that it did in Chester. A brief overview of the northern cities for which we now have sets of dramatic records or new social histories suggests that the kind of government in place had an effect on the type of drama or ceremonial that occurred in a given city or town.[14] We know that Coventry and York had cycles of plays early in their histories, and both cities document regular annual productions through the fifteenth and much of the sixteenth centuries. Both cities had strong civic governing bodies and important civic freedoms before the institution of their plays occurred in the late fourteenth century. The situation in Newcastle is similar, but the evidence suggests they never developed a complete cycle of plays. Chester and Norwich, both of which had dramatic and ceremonial activities in the fifteenth century, seem not to have created the cycles we know them to have until the sixteenth century when there were marked changes in civic governance and responsibilities. Lincoln provides the case of a city that never developed an extensive cycle of religious drama, and it is a city that had to share its power with its secular cathedral and in which the ruling classes were identical with religious guild membership.

Cycles of religious dramas, therefore, seem to have appeared in northern England in those cities that established strong governments centered in the trade guilds. In those cities and towns where civic government had to compete against powerful ecclesiastical establishments or where religious rather than trade guilds dominated, cyclic drama does not seem to appear; instead, processions, fairly unelaborate dramas and other quasi-dramatic activities seem to be the norm. The conclusion that can be tentatively drawn is that cycles of drama are to be identified with the secular or lay guild government, perhaps as an expression of civic control, civic pride, and civic concern for the religious education of the townspeople.

In addition, vernacular drama seems to be the product of and under the control of laymen. This observation may not seem very startling until one recognizes the implications: that there is no continuous development from liturgical to vernacular drama, and that the clergy seem to have been little involved in the production, presentation, or oversight of vernacular drama once it appeared.[15]

The origins of civic vernacular drama are obscured by time. We have no decrees establishing a cycle of plays; in most cases, the initial references to civic drama tend to be casual ones embedded in a guild dispute or some other record. The earliest references are from the late fourteenth and early fifteenth centuries, long after the invention of liturgical drama. Cycles of civic plays, therefore, are not likely to be earlier than the 1370s and very probably did not reach the scale suggested by the extant texts until well into the fifteenth century or, as in the cases of Chester and Norwich, until the early decades of the sixteenth.[16]

Earlier scholars of the drama believed that the cycle plays originated in the choirs and naves of churches; however, there is no direct evidence of a performance of a *cycle* in Latin or the vernacular in any English church or within any ecclesiastical precinct (i.e., the steps, close, cemetery, or the like); there is no evidence of *vernacular* plays within any church before the sixteenth century; and there is little evidence of ecclesiastical sponsorship of cycle plays at any time during their documented histories.[17] Indeed, it is only at the time of the cycles' demise that we find ecclesiastical intervention in the production and regulation of civic religious drama.

The clergy's separation of itself from the theatre has historical roots in the church's aversion to the decadent and lascivious *spectacula* of the late empire; consequently, clerical participation in the drama was hedged about with difficulties (Henshaw; Woolf, pp. 77–101; Briscoe). It is true that *ludi* had been inserted into the liturgy in England as early as the tenth century, but these celebrations were symbolic and liturgical rather than historical representations of Biblical events. It was when ecclesiastical bodies moved toward representation that involved the assumption of the identity of an historical personage or of some character (a devil, a dead man) that critics within the church raised objections against the impropriety of drama because of its impersonation and its use of costume. For others, the circumstances of production were crucial; for example, the author of the *Manuel des Péchiez* objected to false clerks disguising their faces with masks (which was forbidden); however, he permitted modest presentations of Christ's resurrection in church during divine service and cites Isidore against playing in cemeteries and streets.[18] Since canon law contained legislation against clerics associating with or being actors, one's impression is that even though the cloistered religious were permitted to participate in liturgical *ludi*, they did not act in plays and were discouraged from viewing such idleness. Without claiming that monks remained as pure as canon law would have them, I think it is significant that monastic records for payments to minstrels and royal or aristocratic players are usually to musicians rather than to actors and their companies.[19]

There is very little evidence, in fact, that clergy of any kind were involved in the creation of or participated in dramas other than those interpolated into the liturgy. Of all the cities known or thought to have had cycle plays, only Chester asserts any kind of clerkly origin for the cycle; however, there is no extant evidence to support the claims that Ranulf Higden (*REED: Chester*, 1–2, 240) or Henry Francis (*REED: Chester*, 27–28), monks of St. Werburg, wrote the Chester cycle. Both claims are probably sixteenth century fabrications (Salter, pp. 33–45; Clopper, "Arnewaye"). There is a tradition that in London, between 1378 and 1409, productions of Old and New Testament plays were performed by the parish clerks of that city (Chambers, II, 379–82; Nelson, pp. 170–78), but I suspect that these clerks, like Chaucer's Absolon, were in minor orders rather than clergy who were priests. In addition, there is some evidence that the Guild of Parish Clerks was understood to be a trade rather than a religious guild or a company of priests (Unwin, pp. 208–10). If the London clerks were only in minor orders or were simply freemen of the city, then there would be no impediment to their acting in a play, and we ought not to understand this as evidence of performance by secular clergy or members of the priesthood.[20]

In some cities the clergy seem to have maintained some distance from civic religious activities. For example, in 1419 Bishop Repington had to exhort the clergy of Lincoln to take a proper place in the citizens' procession on Corpus Christi day rather than feasting and wasting the occasion (Kahrl, *Plays and Players*, p. 29). Yet the activities of the secular cathedral and the city remained separate throughout much of the fifteenth century (Kahrl, pp. xii-xxi). The cathedral's Coronation of the Virgin alternated with the city's Corpus Christi and Pater Noster plays, the cathedral sponsoring its *visus* in years that the city play was not performed. In those years that the Corpus Christi play was performed, the clergy viewed the play and had their feast as a body separate from the lay populace.[21] They apparently made no financial contribution toward the support of the Corpus Christi play. In 1483 the Coronation and Assumption of the Virgin was integrated with the St. Anne's Day Procession, which was overseen by the religious guild of St. Anne. However, the Coronation *visus* was not displayed in the streets but in the nave of the cathedral at the conclusion of the procession (Nelson, pp. 100–104). The displaying of the *visus* at the cathedral, their continued celebrations with liturgical *ludi* at Christmas and Easter, and their lack of involvement in the Corpus Christi play suggest that for the clergy at Lincoln, at least, there was a perceived separation between city and cathedral and that the two engaged in two entirely different kinds of dramatic activity.[22]

Of monks, secular clergy, friars of the marketplace, and guild priests, the latter two seem the more likely sponsors of vernacular drama. We know that Franciscans used popular forms—lyric, for instance—to teach basic Christian concepts. Among their other devices are semidramatic sermons, creches, and plays—at least on the Continent. Undoubtedly the friars were sympathetic to drama, but the documentary evidence for their direct involvement in English drama has yet to be established. The case that they were involved has been argued by Craddock—and elaborated by Jeffrey and Sticca—however, their historical documentation is often flawed when it cannot be shown to be a bibliographical or historical ghost.[23] For example, Craddock presents evidence associated with the *N-Town* manuscript and the Coventry plays that these were performed "by" the Franciscans. The evidence consists of a flyleaf inscription made by Cotton's librarian, James, circa 1628, in which he says that the codex contains scenes of the New Testament acted "olim per monachos sive fratres mendicantes," and Dugdale's note that the plays were acted "by" the Grey Friars in Coventry. This last item is said to be confirmed by the Coventry record that Henry VII came to see the plays acted "by" the Grey Friars. As K. S. Block and Hardin Craig have pointed out, the Grey Friars in the records is *the place* where the plays were performed; it is not a reference to the actors.[24] Furthermore, the flyleaf note indicates that James did not inspect the manuscript very carefully because he does not mention the Old Testament plays, and there is no reason to suppose that his assertion they were produced by monks or friars is anything more than a guess based on the assumption that religious plays are performed by religious orders.

The production of plays by friars would not seem to be inconsistent with the aims of Franciscan spirituality but Craddock only presents one piece of evidence that might stand up under scrutiny, and there is much evidence to suggest that drama was not a part of the English Franciscan evangelical work. The lyric, "Against the Minorites," Craddock argues, documents the fact that the friars enacted a series of pageants on the life of Christ. The lyric, he says, is a Wycliffite attack on the representation of scenes from the life of St. Francis in which the speaker particularly objects to the simulation of miracles and the "Franciscanization" of the crucifixion.[25] It is quite possible that Craddock is correct in his analysis, but some scholars believe the poem refers to a pictorial rather than a dramatic cycle. In any event, it does not suggest that the friars were involved in the presentation of Biblical drama or of Christ's Passion; indeed, the very opposite seems to be the case since the speaker objects to the transformation of Christ into a winged seraph on a tree.

Other evidence implies that friars supported but were not deeply involved in the presentation of dramas, at least in the early fifteenth century. The friar, Pauper, in the *Dives and Pauper* commends plays, even if they are performed on Sundays and feast days, but he only specifically refers to Christmas and Easter dramas and cites the same canons that the writer of the *Manuel des Pechiez* did that permit the playing of Herod and the Three Kings at Christmas and other "proces of þe gospel" both then and at Easter "and in oþir tymes" as "leful and comendable" (Barnum, p. 293). The reference to performances at "oþir tymes" and to other "proces of þe gospel," of course, makes the statement rather open-ended; nevertheless, the friar only specifies one subject, one that we know to have been frequent in liturgical drama, and only the two principal feast days on which liturgical drama took place. He does not refer to the production of cycles of plays. There is a similar omission in the *Tretise of Miraclis Pleyinge* and other antimendicant tracts.[26] None of these accuses the friars of producing plays; they do not list among their purported fables, "lesynges," chronicles, and the like, the performance of plays.

Perhaps William Melton is typical of mendicant "support" for dramas; indeed, his defense of the York plays is very much like that provided by the Pauper.[27] In 1426 Melton appealed to the city of York to move its play to the day after Corpus Christi. He was sympathetic toward the play and commended it because it instructed the common people in the elements of the faith and because the viewing of it could accrue to the merit of the participants. But he also noted that its performance on Corpus Christi day sometimes led to distractions such as drinking and feasting with the result that the inhabitants of York did not attend masses and other services for which they would receive Pope Urban IV's pardons. The Melton affair suggests that the friars recognized the value of civic and lay worship in the form of plays and supported those efforts as long as they did not interfere with other more traditional forms of worship. The city's decision to ignore Melton's advice suggests perhaps that they felt the play was an appropriate kind of "secular" celebration on the feast day—so they moved the procession rather than their play.

It is likely that guild priests, either of religious or craft guilds, may have performed at least an advisory function to the participants in the cycles. There is ample evidence that until their dissolution in 1547 religious guilds, usually made up of laymen but some also including clergy, were involved in dramatic and processional activity. Thus, religious guilds may have performed plays in the choir of Louth in the sixteenth century (Kahrl, "Louth"), and they were responsible for processions at Lincoln. Those of York were responsible for the Creed and Pater Noster plays (Johnston, "Plays of the Religious Guilds"). Their guild priests, some of whom were secular clergy and others of whom were friars, may have helped organize ceremonial and dramatic activity and may even have been authors of plays, but we have no names of playwrights before the sixteenth century and those who sign their work, like Robert Croo at Coventry, are not clerics.[28]

I do not wish to argue that there were no clerical playwrights, only that there is no documentary evidence there were. Further, it should be noted that by the late fourteenth and early fifteenth centuries the materials were available that would enable laymen who were unlearned in Latin to write plays for laymen. The *Stanzaic Life of Christ*, the *Northern Passion*, the *Cursor Mundi*, the *Gospel of Nicodemus*, and the Franciscan *Meditations on the Life and Passion of Christ* were available in English and alone could supply all of the materials that playwrights would need to construct a cycle or part of a cycle of plays. These vernacular works were part of the phenomenon of northern and late medieval lay spirituality. If their existence made it possible for laymen ignorant of Latin to write Biblical dramas—and source studies suggest these vernacular pieces were often the immediate precursors of the drama—then the distance between the civic Biblical plays and the liturgy may be greater than has been assumed in the past.

The very suppression of religious drama presents a curious kind of record that the church accepted secular authority over the plays. For example, York was a center of Catholic survivalism, and one would have expected Archbishop Grindal (1570–1576) to have taken an aggressive role in confiscating play texts and putting down the plays of the city. And he did. But oddly enough it was the city that seems to have made the first overtures toward the clergy with regard to their texts (*REED: York*, 352). In 1568 the Dean of the cathedral church was asked to read the Creed play to see if it might be played. He said it ought not to be because there were some sections that deviated "from the senceritie of the gospell." The commons desired that the Corpus Christi play be performed instead, but the mayor and council ruled that the book should be perused and amended before it was played. The Corpus Christi play was performed in 1569 (*REED: York*, 355–57) but there is no record that it was performed in 1570 or 1571.

Grindal, in fact, did not act against civic plays until 1572, after a disturbance at the performance of the Pater Noster play. In April the mayor and council ordered that the text be brought to the mayor that it might be "pervsed amended and corrected" (*REED: York*, 365). The mayor, William Allyn, was a Catholic sympathizer; two of the aldermen were Protestants who were committed to ward and later disenfranchised for avoiding the performance and complaining to the Council of the North.[29] Three weeks later the two men were restored to their franchise, and two months after the performance the Archbishop asked that the book be brought to him. In 1575 the city sent a commission to require the books of the Archbishop but there is no record of a reply (*REED: York*, 377–78), and it has been assumed that he had the books destroyed (but see White, "Disappearance"). In 1579 the city agreed to perform the Corpus Christi play (*REED: York*, 390), but only after the book had been taken to the Archbishop and Dean for correction. There is no extant record that the plays were performed that year.

The Archbishop's actions in this period are not entirely consistent. It is obvious that he objected to unseemly games and ceremonials especially in or near churches (*REED: York*, 358), but he did not make any outright ban of religious plays. It is not clear why he should have attempted to stop the Whitsun plays in Chester in 1572 and not the Pater Noster play in York a week later. He may have acted against Chester because it was reported to him that the plays contained popish superstition; but he did not ask to read the text then or in the years afterwards. He must have suppressed the York Pater Noster play after the fact because he felt it was too Catholic. Yet he apparently did not act against the Wakefield play until 1576 (Ingram, "1579"; Cawley, *Medieval Drama*, p. 125). The situation remained sufficiently cloudy that York thought it might perform the Corpus Christi play in 1579, after Grindal was no longer Archbishop, and the commons even made a request for a production in 1580.

One observation that might be made is that cities like York and Chester or factions within these cities felt strongly that the plays and the jurisdiction over them lay with the city rather than with the ecclesiastical hierarchy, and the hierarchy honored that authority to some extent. For example, the mayor of Chester, who was summoned to London because he had caused the plays to be performed in 1575, was acquitted on the grounds that the city council had voted in favor of the performance, and the fact that Grindal had attempted to enjoin the performance of 1572 seems to have had little authority against the decision of the city's council in 1575 (*REED: Chester*, 112–17). Nevertheless, the Archbishop's successful suppression of the York Pater Noster play in 1572 and his action against Chester in 1575 undoubtedly was enough of an object lesson for most cities in the north, and plays gradually ceased to be performed. (But see the records of the Kendal play to 1606 in *REED: Westmoreland*.) Alternatively, the conservative factions within these cities gained dominance and made it impossible to continue the old customs.

At the present state of our studies, we lack the substantive and documentary evidence that would establish much of a clerical presence in civic Biblical drama. And we cannot, I think, attribute the absence of references to the clergy in the dramatic records solely to the loss of documents because, in those cities where records are extant, the clergy still do not seem to play a very significant role. Although it is difficult to generalize from so many different situations, the rule seems to be that the clergy were involved in initiating, and often participated in, Corpus Christi and other feast day processions in which craft guilds and other groups marched. But even in these the city usually regulated the procession, the participants, and the ordering of those groups. The clergy were also involved through religious guilds in processions, and, in some cases, the performance of plays like the Creed and Pater Noster plays. But the cycles of Old and New Testament plays seem remarkably free of ecclesiastical control and participation. These cycles are the products of the citizenry, and their composition and development often reflect the power structure of the corporation.

For many years we have imagined the growth of cycles and the drama to have been a consequence in some way of the transference of the plays to the city government and of the subsequent growth of the craft guilds which constituted the ruling body. But the precise details of these events have often been sacrificed to the evolutionary theory of the secularization of the drama; in addition, we have not been fully cognizant of the fact that cities and towns did not develop in the same way or receive equal status at the same time. It is possible, therefore, that the development of local governance and the presence of power groups other than craft guilds not only affected the elaboration of established ceremonials but also the kinds of drama and ceremonial that were created. Many of the larger cities, for example, had monasteries or cathedral churches that had been granted privileges before the secular part of the city sought incorporation. In some cases—Chester, Newcastle, and York, for example—the crown retained significant powers as a consequence of granting the city the status of county palatine. In the case of Chester, as we have seen, the abbey and the crown dominated the city until the crown aided the civic authorities in gaining dominance early in the sixteenth century. At York, on the other hand, civic authorities were able to establish a strong secular government much earlier than at Chester, and, at Coventry, the city gained dominance over its powerful Benedictine abbey almost 200 years before Chester did over its abbey.

Cities that were governed by trade guilds tended to be oligarchies centered in the oldest or most prestigious guilds. This kind of stratification is seen most obviously in York with its inner ruling body of the Twelve, from which mayors were selected, and the Twenty-four, which was made up of former sheriffs and was the pool from which members of the Twelve were selected.[30] The Twelve and the Twenty-four were drawn mainly from the trading crafts. The third governing body, the Forty-eight, was drawn from the manufacturing crafts. In 1517 it became the common council of the Forty-one made up of two members of each of the thirteen major crafts and one member of each of the fifteen minor crafts. Effective power lay with the mayor and the inner councils. Chester's guild government is more egalitarian perhaps because it did not receive full powers to govern until late in its history, after the guilds had developed independently into major companies.

But many cities were not governed by trade guilds on the simple model of Chester; nor were all ceremonial activities undertaken by the crafts. In some cities religious guilds were synonymous with the civic governing body. Thus, the Guild of St. George constituted the ruling class of Norwich, but it is not known to have engaged in any dramatic activity (Dutka, "Mystery Plays"). In Coventry, on the other hand, religious guilds combined important roles in both ceremony and governance. Charles Phythian-Adams has shown that the numerous ceremonies in Coventry helped define corporate bodies within the city at the same time that they helped designate social strata ("Ceremony"; James, "Ritual, Drama and Social Body"). Many of the processions, for example, were made up of the male freemen of the city, but this body was subdivided into craft and religious guilds. The two religious guilds constituted two ranks within the city and were tied closely to city government: The Master of Corpus Christi guild became mayor and then, upon leaving office, Master of Holy Trinity. The order of march in the Corpus Christi procession and at Midsummer also reflected a guild's status with regard to the governing body; the order was not based on economic class divisions but on occupational groupings according to the quantity and ancientness of their contribution to office-holding. The procession began with the victuallers, who, by parliamentary statute were banned from holding civic offices. These were followed by the leather and metal trades and then the wool and textile trades, the latter group of which culminated with the most prestigious Dyers, Drapers, and Mercers, in that order.

The Corpus Christi plays were regulated by the city government, as is the case elsewhere; however, individual pageants seem to have been controlled and dominated by the oldest and therefore most prestigious guilds.[31] This coterie seems to have been able to sustain its dominance, with a few exceptions, even after other guilds were forced to contribute to the costs of the play. Thus, in 1494–95 at the end of the long fifteenth century economic decline, the city ordered all guilds not contributory to the plays to become associated with them (*REED: Coventry*, 78–80). In most cases, this simply resulted in the lesser guilds paying money to the older guilds; that is, they shared the costs of the pageants but apparently were not as directly involved in the production of the play as were the older guilds. In the 1530s, during a short-term decline, guilds that had not complied with the earlier order were pressed to become contributors (*REED: Coventry*, 136), and there was a major reshuffling occasioned by the decay of the Cardmakers and the emergence of the Cappers as the largest industry in Coventry (*REED: Coventry*, 128–33). Except for the case of the Cappers, therefore, the plays were produced and controlled from their inception to their demise by the oldest and most powerful crafts in the city. I think there is little doubt that the establishment of a strong secular government in the mid-fourteenth century, a government that had gained dominance earlier over its Benedictine abbey, partially accounts for the fact that Coventry's play was controlled by the oldest guilds of the city and that the city had an almost unbroken record of annual performance of its play through the fifteenth century up until its final production in 1579. The date of the last performance is a significant indicator of the secular government's identification with its play because it suggests that this city felt it could perform the cycle despite the actions of Archbishop Grindal against Chester, York, and Wakefield.[32]

A strong guild government does not guarantee that large-scale dramatic production will develop. Newcastle-upon-Tyne seems to fit the profile of other cities that produced cycles of scriptural plays: It was a fairly prosperous trading center, had a secular government from an early period, and was made a county in 1400 (*REED: Newcastle*, ix). There was no monastery or cathedral in the town to compete for power (Knowles and Hadcock). There was a hierarchy of guilds: The highest were the Twelve, through whom the mayor was chosen; and there were fifteen second-ranked "by-guilds" as well as assorted others not named as either (*REED: Newcastle*, x). But Newcastle apparently did not create an extensive cycle of plays.[33]

There are company orders from as early as 1427 in "sustentacion of the procession And Corpus christi play" (*REED: Newcastle*, 3). Individual guilds were "yerly atte the fest of Corpus christi [to] go to gedder in procession . . . and play ther play at ther costes." With the exception of the Bricklayers, the eight guilds for which we have fifteenth century orders were from either the Twelve or the fifteen by-guilds; thus, as at Coventry, only some of the oldest and most prestigious guilds were involved in dramatic activity.

It seems unlikely that the Bricklayers were producing a play as early as the order suggests. The nineteenth-century copy of the order, internally dated 1454, calls for them to perform two plays, "The Creation of Adam" and the "Flight into Egypt" (*REED: Newcastle*, 6). There is also a 1579 order for the Slaters and Bricklayers to perform the "Abraham and Isaac" (*REED: Newcastle*, 63). Drama historians have counted all three of these plays in their estimates despite the fact that the Bricklayers are associated with two entirely different companies. There are no other company orders that make such arrangements. I suspect that the nineteenth-century summary is a conflation made by antiquarian copyists or that it is a summary of orders that had been altered over a period of time by the company to reflect their changing status. I also suspect that the rather early date for the formation of the Bricklayers' company derives from its later association with the Slaters. There is a Slaters' order, dated 1452 (*REED: Newcastle*, 6), which does not mention any relationship with the Bricklayers, yet it is the Slaters and Bricklayers who are said to be responsible for the "Abraham and Isaac" play 125 years later, whereas the Bricklayers' purported 1454 order is made with the Plasterers. The Bricklayers, therefore, may have backdated their orders to coincide with the time they understood the Slaters' company to have been formed.

The three most prestigious guilds, those which formed the Merchant Adventurers Company in 1480, were apparently little involved in the drama before the mid-sixteenth century.[34] In the orders from the time of their formation (*REED: Newcastle*, 8–9), there is no reference to any obligation toward the Corpus Christi play though they were to participate in the Corpus Christi procession. The order is most concerned with establishing the proper disposition of guilds within the procession. The Merchant Adventurers come last, as befits their ancientness and prestige.

In 1552 the Merchant Adventurers undertook the production of five plays. Their expenditure of over £31 seems an extraordinary—not a typical—one. It would appear that they were the organizers and sponsors of the production, for they collected money from a guild not associated with them, the Vintners, and they produced a play normally performed by another company not associated with them, the Hostmen, for which they taxed the city £4. It sounds as if the wealthiest and most prestigious company in the city decided to undertake sponsorship of plays under the unsettled circumstances of Edward's proclamations against the playing of plays and other activities which might be judged seditious.[35]

I suspect that Newcastle had a procession of guilds on Corpus Christi day and that some of these guilds, perhaps annually before 1550 and from time to time after 1559, performed a group of plays. There is insufficient evidence to indicate that there was ever a complete cycle of plays from the Fall to Doomsday; in any event, the evidence argues against the traditional estimate of a cycle of twenty-five plays. Nevertheless, the fact remains that a secular government was involved in the production of scriptural dramas.

Lincoln provides an example of a city in which a cycle of plays did not develop perhaps because of the importance of its religious guilds and the prominence of the cathedral. Once thought to have been the home of the *N-Town* plays, Lincoln seems to have had relatively modest dramatic and ceremonial aspirations; furthermore, the activities that they did engage in seem to have remained fairly segregated along secular and ecclesiastical lines.[36] The two important powers, at least with regard to ceremony, were the cathedral and the Guild of St. Anne (founded 1344). There was some dissociation between these two factions even in their observance of Corpus Christi and St. Anne's Day. From the records available, it appears that the city's plays, which possibly included saints' lives and a Corpus Christi and a Pater Noster play, usually were performed one year and the cathedral's Assumption and Coronation *visus* was displayed in alternate years. The St. Anne's procession was annual in the sixteenth century, but it does not seem to have included performances of plays if, as appears to be the case, the Assumption and Coronation was a mechanical device rather than a dramatic reenactment.

There is no information about the contents of the Lincoln Corpus Christi or Pater Noster plays or even who paid for them. There were guilds of Corpus Christi and of Pater Noster, and it is possible that these paid for the plays. It might be significant that in the guild return of 1389 the Corpus Christi guild said that it was composed of common and middling people (Jacob, pp. 388–89; Westlake). Consequently, the guild may not have been able to afford regular or frequent production, at least without additional help, and it may imply that these plays were fairly simple, as at least the Pater Noster plays at York and Beverley appear to have been. The Guild of St. Anne, on the other hand, seems to have been made up of the *potentiores* and remained powerful at least into the sixteenth century when the civic government, in order to aid the guild, required "euery man And woman wtin this Citie beyng Able" to become contributory (Kahrl, *Plays and Players*, 47). Kahrl suggests that this became necessary because the guild had begun to decay and was no longer able to support or command the support for the St. Anne's procession. But the civic government probably also intervened because it was identified with the Guild; thus, the ruling clique within the secular city seems to have been made up of members of the Guild of St. Anne, and, after their terms were over, the mayor and the sheriff's peers became the officers within the Guild responsible for the maintenance and collection of fees for the bringing forth of the St. Anne's procession. The order requiring everyone to contribute (Kahrl, *Plays and Players*, 55), therefore, is not entirely disinterested, and it is very much like the action of other city councils in the late fifteenth and early sixteenth centuries that required greater participation by all crafts and citizens in the city's ceremonials without always giving up the rights and privileges belonging to the original ruling clique.

York, which had a strong craft-dominated government from an early period, produced a cycle of Biblical plays, but the city also had important religious guilds, two of which were responsible for plays (see Johnston, "Plays of the Religious Guilds"). The two religious guilds represent different corporate bodies from that of the civic government; consequently, their motives for performing the plays and the conditions under which they were performed differ from those of the city's plays. The Corpus Christi guild, made up of laymen, laywomen, and priests sponsored the Creed Play, which was performed fairly regularly at ten year periods from the late fifteenth century up to the aborted performance in 1568 (*REED: York*, 352–54). The Pater Noster guild, which merged with the Guild of St. Anthony in 1446, was responsible for the production of the Pater Noster play. It too seems to have been performed on a regular, possibly a ten-year schedule until 1572 (*REED: York*, 365–68). The citizens of York, therefore, would have had occasion to see annual productions of the Corpus Christi plays as well as performances of the Creed and Pater

Noster plays at regular intervals. But the auspices of the productions were different. In the guild returns of 1389 the Pater Noster guild claimed that it had no property other than that pertaining to the play and that it existed solely for the purpose of sponsoring the play to the greater glory of God and the reproving of sins and vices (Westlake). Similarly, the purpose of the Corpus Christi guild had been to hold the properties, books, and other appurtenances of the play and to see that it was performed as the city requested. The city regulated these plays, as it would any activity that fell within its jurisdiction, but I think that, at least initially, the productions of the Pater Noster and Creed plays were acts of personal piety for the good of the commonwealth. After the dissolution, when the mayor and city were more directly involved in the production of the plays and when the craft guilds financed them, as they did in 1558 (*REED: York*, 327–28), they became more like the city's cycle of Biblical plays, a production of a corporate body for the good of that corporate body.

The situation at Norwich provides one last configuration.[37] At the end of the fourteenth century the Great Guild, composed of the city notables, was the center of political influence. As a consequence of the civic disturbances of the first half of the fifteenth century, the Great Guild disappeared, in 1452, and the Guild of St. George took over as the center of influence and wealth. There is no evidence that either the Great Guild or the Guild of St. George undertook to sponsor plays or other religious ceremonials in the city. At some point in the fifteenth century, the Guild of St. Luke, which was made up of painters, stainers, and other related crafts prominent at the time, became responsible for the production of "diuers disgisinges and pageauntes as well of the liff and marterdams of diuers and many hooly sayntes as also many other lyght and feyned figures and pictures of other persones and bestes . . ." (Davis, pp. xxvii-viii). In 1527 the Guild of St. Luke petitioned the city to request that other guilds be required to share the costs of the show. Professor Dutka has argued that their motive for making this request was not that the Guild could not pay for the show but that the city and other crafts profited from the concourse of people brought in by the ceremonies and the Whitsun fair. Most significant, Professor Dutka says, is that the fair, formerly owned by the priory, had been transferred to the city in 1524; consequently, city companies were no longer forced to pay the priory in order to sell in their own city, and, it might have been argued, those fees could be applied toward the costs of the show. In this case the development of the drama seems to have been a consequence of an improvement in the economic situation at the same time that it coincided with an increase in the city's privileges and responsibilities.

There has been considerable discussion of this change, especially about whether the craft guilds of the city simply divided up the old show after the petition had been granted. To the contrary, I think that important guilds in the city accepted the logic of the petition but decided to substitute plays for the old procession. First, there is no record of any action occurring until two years later, in 1529, when the Weavers made their pageant of the Holy Ghost, an appropriate one for the Pentecost. The Grocers copied their Paradise pageant into their records in 1533, the year, Dutka believes, that it was probably written, and the Tanners and Cordwainers agreed only in 1534 to produce "God in the Bush" and "Moses and Aaron."

Despite the fact of the lag in compliance with the city order, recent critics have not argued that the Norwich Whitsun plays began as a consequence of the 1527 petition, as I believe to be the case. Yet a simple understanding of the petition and the surviving list of pageants suggests that the plays were new inventions. It describes a typical procession, not a cycle of plays. For example, the "light" in the petition probably refers to the very common carrying of torches to be found in processions elsewhere, and the "feyned figures" seem to be three dimensional creations as opposed to "pictures of other persones and bestes." The former of these seems reminiscent of the various giants, dragons, and the like, to be found in Midsummer shows, and the latter may be nothing more than religious pictures or guild crests and symbols. The "liff and marterdams of diuers and many hooly sayntes" is certainly not represented in the list of Biblical pageants in the Old Free Book and would not describe the action of any cycle now extant. In fact, this description sounds closer to that of the procession of Lincoln that was under the direction of its religious guild or of any procession on a feast day in which groups displayed signs and figures of patron saints, symbols of one's craft or status (see Wasson, "Ipswich").

The history of the drama at Norwich has been further obscured by the assumption that the list of pageants in the Old Free Book is an incomplete record of that city's cycle of Biblical plays. The evidence suggests, however, that Norwich never intended to create a *cycle* of plays, if by that term we mean a set of plays that runs from Creation to Doomsday. First, it is clear from the Grocers' prologues that in some years the Paradise pageant was performed without the Creation pageant (Davis, p. 11). Second, the list of pageants in the Old Free Book does not describe a cycle. The first six pageants constitute a typical Old Testament sequence: Creation, Hellecarte, Paradise, Abell and Cayme, Noah, Abraham and Isaac, Moses and Pharaoh, and David and Goliath. There are Nativity, Shepherds and Magi plays, but the last three plays in the sequence depict only the Baptism of Christ, His Resurrection, and the Descent of the Holy Ghost. Davis concluded that this was an incomplete list of a cycle because it did not include the Passion or Doomsday. But Davis's logic can be accepted only if one also accepts his assumption that all sequences of Biblical plays must be complete cycles (see also Kolve on Norwich, pp. 53–54). The Norwich plays resemble the ones at Newcastle insofar as they do not achieve the complete cyclic form of those at Chester, York, and Coventry. Perhaps there are so few plays from the life of Christ, especially from His passion, because there was resistance to the "gaming" of the crucifixion and matter "unwarranted" by any script.

I think the evidence of Norwich is important for two reasons. First, if I am correct in believing that Norwich instituted its plays after it took over the fair from the priory, then Norwich provides an instance, as does Chester, of a city establishing a sequence of plays at a point in its history when it gains some kind of new dominance. Second, I think these events provide additional evidence against the evolutionary model and the assumption that the cycle drama was common. Chambers's and Craig's impression that cycle drama was widespread is a consequence of their assumptions about the evolution of drama from the church into the streets. When they found only partial evidence of a cycle—a list of stories from the Bible, for example—they concluded that the evidence proved the existence of a cycle but that the evidence for the remaining parts of the cycle was no longer extant (see also Kolve, chs. 3–4). Recent study suggests that cycle drama was rare.[38] Most smaller towns did not mount lavish dramatic productions but contented themselves with performances by traveling players, plays of single biblical episodes or saints' lives, or cooperative projects.[39] In any event, at least in the north, it would be feasible to go to larger boroughs to see cycles of plays. Most civic drama was not "cyclic" at all, if by that term we mean a series of plays from Creation to Doomsday. In some cities—Lincoln, for example—such a concept seems never to have developed. In others—Coventry, and Chester up to the sixteenth century—the cycle was probably confined to New Testament subjects. In other cases—Norwich, Newcastle—there was an incomplete cycle or one that does not fit modern conceptions of what a cycle is.

This examination of the published documentary evidence from the northern cities allows some tentative conclusions but raises many questions that require further study. The evidence suggests a divorcement between the ecclesiastical and secular establishments with regard to plays. Religious, especially monks, had their liturgical dramas within their abbey precincts; corporations had their vernacular plays within the city's precincts. This kind of separation is not so rigid in the case of processions, for there is evidence that processions were originally initiated by the clergy and that often they continued to march in them. Indeed, Corpus Christi processions, as well as those of many religious guilds, often required clerks to carry the sacrament. At Lincoln, the mayor and council ordered that a guild priest was to oversee the arrangements for the St. Anne's procession (Kahrl, *Plays and Players,* 45), and, of course, processions often ended with a mass either at the church or, in the case of religious guilds, at the church or friary where they maintained their chapel.

At some point, but possibly from the beginning, civic governments took over the management of processions insofar as they decided who could march and what the ordering was to be. It is not clear how or why civic government became involved, but it was very probably a consequence of the preponderantly lay participation; many processions were instituted, in fact, in order to encourage lay participation in the religious life. But the ultimate source of the cities' involvement may arise from their jurisdiction over the secular parts of the city. A mayor greets a visiting dignitary not only to show respect but to grant him and his entourage admission to the city. Similarly, within cities where there are competing jurisdictions, one jurisdiction must grant permission, especially if there is a body of people involved, for the other one to move through it. The secular governments may have become overseers of religious processions simply because the procession was going to move through the city's jurisdiction.

Most, if not all, of these processions remained processions; that is, once they were established, they continued as processions even if plays . later came into existence. Furthermore, plays seem to have remained distinct or separate from processions throughout their respective histories. If a play is connected with a procession, it is performed at the end or in the afternoon of the feast day. In those cities where the plays themselves were processional—performed in more than one place through the city— the religious procession usually occurred one day and the play the next.

We cannot make any simple correlations between Catholicism and Protestantism and the continuance or demise of civic religious drama. York seems to have remained a stronghold of Catholic survivalism until late in the sixteenth century and had several kinds of religious plays. Coventry seems to have housed Lollard and Protestant groups throughout our period and may have been predisposed toward the Protestant cause earlier than other cities. It may be significant, therefore, that Robert Croo revised some plays in 1534 after the breach with Rome. But it is also significant that Coventry continued to produce its cycle until 1579. Certainly much more needs to be done to ascertain whether cities that produced, put down, or kept plays were predominantly Catholic or Protestant at the time the plays were revised or put down, but it seems unlikely that we will find any simple relationship between one brand of religion and plays (see Palliser, "Popular Reactions").

It is also not clear why cycles or large sequences of plays occurred in the north or why Old Testament subjects seem to have dominated in those places where single plays were performed or even why Old Testament subjects had a preponderance in sequences that were not complete cycles. No single explanation will account for the diversity of the phenomena. Economics, no doubt, placed certain limits on dramatic extravaganzas. Some cities simply could not afford to mount large numbers of plays; indeed, the large cities that did mount them ultimately were required to force all the guilds, or a large part of the populace, to finance the city's dramatic activities. In those places where individual plays were performed, there may have been a preference for Old Testament stories because they were of limited scope in the sources, because they were particularly given to moral interpretation, and because there were some who thought that the representation of Christ's passion was inappropriate. It is more difficult to determine why cycles and sequences were established only in the north. Competition undoubtedly played some role. Once Coventry produced its cycle, Chester may have desired to imitate it. Once York created its cycle, cities in that region may have wished to rival it or at least provide the same kind of activity. Many of the largest cities are in the north and the oldest guilds in many of these are involved in the cloth trade. Perhaps the merchants' contacts with the Low Countries, where lay pious movements were even older and more intense than in northern England, encouraged an interest in the drama.

There seem to have been numerous changes made in the cycles and other ceremonials in or around the 1520s. For example, there is a reference to "new plays" at Coventry in 1518–19 (*REED: Coventry*, 114); the Louth plays seem to have begun about 1515 (Kahrl, *Plays and Players*, xxiii, 78); at Beverley in 1519 William Pyers, poet, was hired to make a "transposing" (*transposicione*) of the Corpus Christi play but the plays seem to have ceased the next year (Leach, "Some English Plays"; Nelson, 98–99). Chester made a major transformation of its cycle about 1521 and had moved it to Whitsunday by 1531; Norwich may have begun its cycle of plays shortly after 1527. Some of these alterations can be attributed to changes in the economic and governing status of some of the cities.[40] Norwich, for example, had little more than half York's tax paying population in 1377, but had the highest tax subsidy outside of London in 1523. It changed its civic ceremonies in 1527 after having got the priory fair in 1524. Its plays may have been intended to celebrate its improved economic status and its control over the fair. Coventry remained in about the same position, and there seems little change other than in the financing for the plays and some revision of the texts. Some cities dropped in rank; perhaps, as a consequence, they never initiated drama in this period as other cities did. Between 1377, when it was fifth in tax paying population, and 1523–1527, Lincoln fell to eighteenth place. In 1519 it made every man and woman in the city a member of St. Anne's Guild and thus contributors to the cost of the procession. Plays seem to have been irregular throughout the late fifteenth and early sixteenth centuries. Ipswich, on the other hand, rose from twenty-sixth place in 1377 (with one-fifth of York's population) to seventh in the sixteenth century, but there seems to have been little dramatic activity there and the play and Corpus Christi procession, which became irregular in Henry VIII's reign, were laid down forever in 1531 for reasons that are not clear (Wasson). Although Ipswich does not seem to have initiated new drama in this period, its drama and ceremonial faltered at the time that it did in a number of other cities. There seems to have been a flurry of dramatic activity in the early sixteenth century; many cities tried producing plays and then often ceased (Coldewey). We should attempt to discover the reasons for the changes in customs and ceremonials at this particular time.

There is apparently some connection between the development of lay spirituality, the growth of civic governments and the incorporation of towns, and the establishment of vernacular religious drama. Plays, especially cycles or collections of plays, tended to occur in those cities where civic government, especially by trade guilds, was strong, and often plays seem to have been introduced or elaborated when the balance of power shifted toward secular dominance. Those cities without a secular government and those that were dominated by ecclesiastical establishments or even religious guilds seem to have placed greater emphasis on procession than on drama. In Lincoln, for example, there were liturgical plays in the cathedral, the St. Anne's Day procession, overseen by the *potentiores* of the city who constituted the guild, and only occasional instances of public vernacular drama such as the Corpus Christi and Pater Noster plays. The evidence of an elaborate Corpus Christi play is lacking. The *Tobit* play, a "standing play" that may have been large-scale, was presented only after the religious guilds were put down (Kahrl, *Plays and Players*, 67–68). If my speculation about Norwich is correct, they did not institute their plays until the city gained control of the fair. Chester seems to have enlarged its cycle when the secular government gained dominance. On the other hand, York and Coventry, both of which gained important liberties early in the period that protected them against competing ecclesiastical establishments, show evidence of having had elaborate dramatic cycles throughout the fifteenth century.

The most intriguing question is why civic governments put on cycles of religious plays in the streets. They often tell us that they produced them to the honor of God and the profit of the citizenry. Without denying the existence of the profit motive, I think it equally clear that the plays were intended to educate and confirm laymen in their religion. The preacher in the *Hundred Merry Tales* says that if you wish to understand the articles of the Creed, then go to Coventry where you can see them enacted (Rastell). The Wycliffite preacher points out that you can see the articles of the Pater Noster enacted at York (Matthew, *English Works of Wyclif*, p. 429). The curious fact is not that these plays were intended to instruct but that the providers of the instruction were secular guildsmen and secular governments rather than the clergy. If the cycle plays were invented at the end of the fourteenth century or even in the fifteenth century, then they came to life during the period of the rather intense late medieval lay pious movements. I think that civic magistrates, when they gained power, recognized themselves to have a separate responsibility from the clergy for the morals and education of their people. They were expected to entertain the citizens at great personal expense, and they were expected to present a moral example to the city that involved public worship. Once the obligation to provide a moral example and to educate is recognized, there is the problem of finding the means of fulfilling it. One method, a very successful one for churches in the Middle Ages, was to provide "pictures," either paintings or statues, for those laymen who were unlettered. However, guilds and city governments did not have places suitable for large concourses of people; they had no churches or cathedrals. Consequently, they placed their "pictures" in the streets.

NOTES

1. Chambers's *Mediaeval Stage* remains a valuable source book for the drama and related phenomena and for its statement of the issues reviewed below. The Victoria County Histories, especially the more recent ones, and county and historical and archeological society publications provide important information on life and institutions in medieval and Renaissance towns and cities. There are several new social histories: Phythian-Adams's on Coventry, Palliser's on York, Gottfried's on Bury, and Tanner's on Norwich. For the drama and other ceremonial activities, perhaps one might begin with Kolve's chapters on game and earnest in drama, Travis's on Corpus Christi observations, the relevant sections of the *Revels History* (Cawley et al.) and Stevens.

2. References to Chester's dramatic documents are cited from the Records of Early English Drama series. Most citations will appear in parentheses in the text as *Reed: Chester* followed by the page number and, where necessary, the line numbers. Other volumes in the *REED* series are *REED: Coventry*, ed. Ingram; *REED: York*, ed. Johnston and Rogerson; *REED: Newcastle*, ed. Anderson; *REED: Westmoreland*, ed. Douglas; *REED: Gloucestershire*, ed. Greenfield; and *REED: Devon*, ed. Wasson. For Lincoln, see Kahrl, *Plays and Players in Lincolnshire*.

3. Because it publishes a number of documents, the standard history remains Morris's. Also valuable because it publishes documents and early antiquarian books is Ormerod's. The Great Charter was granted in 1506; see Morris, pp. 524–40, for a transcription and translation.

4. Early descriptions of these customs appear in Rogers's *Brevary*, the first edition of which was completed in 1609 (*REED: Chester*, 234ff., 320ff., 351ff., and 433ff.).

5. These conditions are cited as the rationale in several charters for the granting of the charter or the lessening of the fee farm. Morris, pp. 518, 521–22.

6. Rogers is not entirely clear on the subject of the Midsummer Watch and Show (see *Reed: Chester* 252–53, 353–54). My impression is that the Watch and the Show were two different phenomena and that the Watch is the ancient custom and the Show an addition made in 1499.

7. Royalty came to see the Coventry plays in 1485, 1487, 1493, and 1511 (*REED: Coventry*, 66, 67–68, 77, 106–07, 114). The fame of the plays is also attested by the references in Heywood's *4PP* (lines 830–32) and John Rastell's *A Hundred Merry Tales*, pp. 115–16.

8. *Reed: Chester* 116, lines 15–18. The additional half-day for the performance does not necessarily indicate that the plays were expanded. In that year they began in the afternoon rather than the morning and ran for three more days. The stanza added at V.448 suggests that only five plays were performed on the first day.

9. Bills, "'Suppression Theory.'" Bills's argument is that there was no system-

atic attempt to suppress Biblical or cycle plays during the earlier Protestant years. He cites instances in which Protestants wrote or supported Biblical plays in those years. The antagonism against cycle plays in the 1570s, he thinks, may be attributed to Puritan attacks on the stage and the mixing together of scurrilous and sacred matter.

10. The Harrowing of Hell seems to have caused difficulties for Protestants because it was a part of the Creed but not scriptural. Bills, pp. 162–63, reports that when John Bale was accused of unorthodox preaching, he responded: "He never denied that descendit ad inferna was an article of the Creed . . . [but] . . . Told them not to believe it 'as they see it set forth in the country there in a certain play.' They must not suppose that Christ fought violently with the devils for the souls of the faithful. . . ."

11. None of the lists of pageants and neither of the Banns contains a reference to a Baptism play; the records are continuous enough after ca. 1531 to be able to say that there was certainly no Baptism play after that date.

12. Compare, for example, Chester XVI.251–92 and John 19:33–38.

13. This is, I think, the basis of Travis's argument in chapter 7, especially pp. 217–22. But the revision may have occurred later in the century, in the 1560s or 1570s, in response to objections about the inappropriateness of certain kinds of representation. If this is the case, the authors may simply have taken advantage of the fact that the plays were performed in Whitsun week.

14. Two northern cities, Kendal and Beverley, seem to have had cycles but there is insufficient data about the first (see Douglas, REED: Westmoreland, 168–71, 218–19) and the new edition of the records of the second has not yet been published (see Leach for an older study).

15. O. B. Hardison, Jr., has provided the classic rebuttal to the evolutionary theory of the drama and has presented (pp. 253–83) the case for the separate development of liturgical and vernacular drama. Not all scholars have accepted the argument. For a restatement of the connection between the two dramas, see E. Catherine Dunn, "Popular Devotion," and Rosemary Woolf, English Mystery Plays, pp. 3–76.

16. Siegfried Wenzel ("An Early Reference") thought he had found an early reference, ca. 1330, to a Corpus Christi play in one of Holcot's writings. There is no other evidence for such an early date for a cycle, and Abigail Young ("Plays and Players") has shown that the comment derives from earlier commentaries on good and bad forms of ludi (recreation).

17. The Ordo repraesentationis adae or Jeu d'Adam is the one exception to the first clause, and there may have been plays in churches in the sixteenth century (see Kahrl, "Louth"; Davis, "Allusions," pp. 77, 87–90). However, some of these records may be to plays in church halls rather than churches, as is the case in a reference from Tewkesbury, 1600–1601, to performances in the abbey, formerly site of the parish church but by then the church hall (REED: Gloucester, 339–42, 429n). For the liturgical drama, see Young, Hardison, and Flanigan.

18. Cited by Chambers, I. 92–93.

19. Gibson, "Bury," has argued for monastic auspices for N-Town, but I think the logic of her argument is flawed and the case built too much on what might be "possible" rather than probable or demonstrable. Also see her essay on Wisdom.

20. There is evidence at Beverley and Chester that the clergy "bring forth" or help to bring forth plays, but I do not think this indicates that they participated or played in them; rather they sponsored (Chester) or helped pay for them (Beverley). See REED: Chester 38, lines 37–38, and Chambers II, 340–41.

21. Nelson interprets a series of references to payments for a room for a feast at Corpus Christi and for the Pater Noster play as evidence for indoor perfor-

mances of plays (p. 114), but the references seem to state that money was paid for a private room for a feast before or after, not during, the play.

22. Douglas Cowling has noted that the York clergy's procession at Corpus Christi remained separate from the city's. Similarly, at Exeter, the dean and chapter and the vicars choral emphasized processions, but there was a Corpus Christi play performed by guilds in the fifteenth century (*REED: Devon*, xvi, xxix-xxx, 82–3).

23. Jeffrey follows Craddock's format and argument except that he enlarges the section devoted to Franciscan spirituality and makes a case for the Franciscan auspices of *N-Town* and some of the morality plays. Sticca's essay provides no additional documentation; instead, he presents as fact Wickham's speculation that the friars and secular clergy were midwives to the drama (Wickham, I, 124–28).

24. Block, pp. xxxvii-xl; Craig, pp. 239–41. More recent information about the manuscript and the notes is to be found in Stephen Spector's "Provenance"; he believes the James inscription was made between 1633/34 and 1638 (pp. 30–31). Craddock, Jeffrey, and Sticca quote an inscription they believe to be in the MS ("Videntur olim coram populo sive ad instruendum sive ad placendum a Fratribus mendicantibus repraesentata"); however, the inscription is from Smith's catalogue description of 1696 and very probably derives from the James flyleaf note or Dugdale.

25. *Historical Poems*, pp. 163–64. Robbins (p. 335) thinks the poem may describe a series of paintings rather than a play.

26. The first half of the text, with valuable notes, is published in Hudson's *Selections*, pp. 97–104, 187–89. A recent edition of the entire text (with commentary) is Clifford Davidson's, but see Davis's review and analysis ("Another View").

27. *REED: York*, 42–44. For a discussion of the Melton incident, see Johnston, "Procession."

28. Although there is no evidence that he wrote plays, Master Thomas Bynham, O.P., wrote the Banns for the Beverley cycle (Chambers, II, 339). However, "writing" may not mean "composing"; it may mean "copying."

29. *REED: York*, 366–68. See Palliser's discussion of the incident (*York*, pp. 246–47). His chapter, "Religion and Reformation," pp. 226–59, is a valuable study of the religious climate in York in the sixteenth century.

30. There are several relevant essays in Stacpoole et al.; otherwise, see the introduction to *REED: York* and Palliser's *York*. On the value and importance of examining local government situations, see Kahrl, "Learning about Local Control," and Coldewey's response in the same volume.

31. The following discussion is based on the records and Ingram's essay, "To find the players."

32. One might note that Coventry was not a Catholic survivalist stronghold but had early links with Lollardy; in fact, John Careles, who had been imprisoned for his religion in 1556, asked to be released on his own recognizance for one day that he might appear in the Weavers' play with his fellows. He voluntarily returned to jail and afterwards was sent to London where he thought to die in the fire for the profession of his faith except that his martyrdom was prevented by his death in prison (*REED: Coventry*, 207–208). See also Luxton, "Reformation and Popular Culture," especially pp. 67–68.

33. Historians of the drama have concluded that there were possibly as many as twenty-five plays in the cycle at Newcastle, but I think the evidence unconvincing because it is arrived at by the simple addition of references scattered over 150 years. This method of achieving a total overlooks changes brought about by internal and external forces and fails to comment on the significance of absent

data. See Holthausen, p. 16; Chambers, II, 424; Craig, p. 305; Davis, p. xliii; and Cawley and Anderson, p. 11.

34. *REED: Newcastle*, xi. The three guilds were part of the Twelve; thus, they form an inner circle within the highest group. The Merchant Adventurers' accounts are fairly continuous through the period 1480–1568. They paid for plays in 1552. In 1561 they contributed £14 toward the plays (pp. 28–29). The only other reference to plays in their book is in 1519 when they spent 12s. 4d. "to pay for the playes" (p. 17). Perhaps this small amount was a contribution toward the general costs of the plays or for the company's entertainment at playtime.

35. On 6 August 1549 Edward VI issued a proclamation banning plays and interludes containing matter tending to sedition or condemning sundry good orders and laws. Although it did not specify scriptural plays, it seems to have had a chilling effect on ceremony of all kinds throughout England. For the proclamation, see Davis, "Allusions," p. 80.

36. The discussion is largely condensed from Kahrl's introduction to the records. Spector, pp. 26–27, summarizes the current thinking on the placement of *N-Town* in East Anglia rather than at Lincoln.

37. The discussion is based on Dutka, "Mystery Plays." I have departed from her analysis of the significance of the 1527 alterations in customs. Also see her "Lost Dramatic Cycle."

38. Johnston's argument that cycle plays were few (see her essay in this volume) is confirmed by a comment of Reginald Pecock in his *Repressor* (ca. 1449). In a passage on images he attacks the Lollard assertion that a man is a more perfect image of Christ than stock or stone. Pecock denies this on the grounds that an image of the crucified Christ fits the three conditions of a perfect image of another thing "except whanne a quyk man is sett in a pley to be hangid nakid on a cros and to be in semyng woundid and scourgid. *And this befallith ful seelde and in fewe placis and cuntrees*" (I, 221; my italics).

39. See Coldewey, "Last Rise."

40. The analysis which follows is based on Hoskins's studies of the subsidies and census of 1377 and 1523–1527. Hoskins notes that these are not entirely equivalent standards of measures and should be used with that reservation in mind. Also, some cities and counties were exempt, the most important of which for our purposes was Chester. See his appendix, "Ranking of Provincial Towns," in *Local History*; and "English Provincial Towns," pp. 68–85. On the increase in the incorporation of boroughs, see Tittler, "Incorporation of Boroughs," and Weinbaum.

WORKS CITED AND SUGGESTED READING

Anderson, J. J., ed. *Records of Early English Drama: Newcastle*. Toronto: University of Toronto Press, 1982.

Barnum, Priscilla Heath, ed. *Dives and Pauper*. Early English Text Society, o.s. 275. London: Oxford University Press, 1976.

Bills, Bing D. "The 'Suppression Theory' and the English Corpus Christi Play: A Re-Examination," *Theatre Journal* 32 (1980), 157–68.

Block, K. S., ed. *Ludus Coventriae, or The Plaie Called Corpus Christi, Cotton MS Vespasian D.VIII*. Early English Text Society, o.s. 120. London: Oxford University Press, 1922, repr. 1960.

Briscoe, Marianne. "Some Clerical Notions of Dramatic Decorum in Late Medieval England," *Comparative Drama* 19 (1985), 1–13.

Cawley, Arthur C., ed. *The Wakefield Pageants in the Towneley Cycle.* Manchester: Manchester University Press, 1958.

Cawley, Arthur C., and John Anderson. "The Newcastle Play of *Noah's Ark*," *Records of Early English Drama Newsletter,* vol. 2, no. 1 (1977), 11–17.

Cawley, Arthur C., et al. *Medieval Drama.* The Revels History of Drama in English, 1. London: Methuen, 1983.

Chambers, E. K. *The Mediaeval Stage.* 2 vols. Oxford: Clarendon Press, 1903.

Clark, Peter, and Paul Slack, eds. *Crisis and Order in English Towns 1500–1700: Essays in Urban History.* London: Routledge & Kegan Paul, 1972.

Clopper, Lawrence. "The Chester Cycle: Review Article," *Medieval and Renaissance Drama in England,* 2 (1985), 283–91 (Review of Lumiansky and Mills, *Essays*).

——. "The History and Development of the Chester Cycle," *Modern Philology,* 75 (1978), 219–46.

——. "Arnewaye, Higden and the Origin of the Chester Plays," *Records of Early English Drama Newsletter,* vol. 8, no. 2 (1983), 4–11.

——, ed. *Records of Early English Drama: Chester.* Toronto: University of Toronto Press, 1979.

Coldewey, John. "The Last Rise and Final Demise of Essex Town Drama," *Modern Language Quarterly,* 36 (1975), 239–60.

Cowling, Douglas. "The Liturgical Celebration of Corpus Christi in Medieval York," *Records of Early English Drama Newsletter,* vol. 1, no. 2 (1976), 5–9.

Craddock, Laurence G. "Franciscan Influences on Early English Drama," *Franciscan Studies,* 10 (1950), 383–417.

Craig, Hardin. *English Religious Drama of the Middle Ages.* Oxford: Clarendon Press, 1955.

Davidson, Clifford, ed. *A Middle English Treatise on the Playing of Miracles.* Washington, D.C.: University Press of America, 1981.

Davis, Nicholas. "Allusions to Medieval Drama in Britain (4): Interludes," *Medieval English Theatre,* vol. 6, no. 1 (1984), 61–91.

——. "Another View of the *Tretise of Miraclis Pleying*," *Medieval English Theatre,* vol. 4, no. 1 (1982), 48–55.

Davis, Norman, ed. *Non-Cycle Plays and Fragments.* Early English Text Society, s. s. 1. London: Oxford University Press, 1970.

Douglas, Audrey, ed. *Records of Early English Drama: Cumberland and Westmoreland.* Toronto: University of Toronto Press, 1986.

Dunn, E. Catherine. "Popular Devotion in the Vernacular Drama of Medieval England," *Medievalia et Humanistica,* n.s., 4 (1973), 55–68.

Dutka, JoAnna. "The Lost Dramatic Cycle of Norwich and the Grocers' Play of the Fall of Man," *Review of English Studies,* n.s., 35 (1984), 1–13.

——. "Mystery Plays at Norwich: Their Formation and Development," *Leeds Studies in English* 10 (1978), 107–20.

Dutka, JoAnna, ed. *Records of Early English Drama: Proceedings of the First Colloquium.* Toronto: University of Toronto Press, 1979.

Flanigan, C. Clifford. "The Liturgical Drama and Its Tradition: A Review of Scholarship 1965–1975," *Research Opportunities in Renaissance Drama,* 18 (1975), 81–102.

Foster, Frances A., ed. *The Stanzaic Life of Christ.* Early English Text Society, o.s. 166. London: Oxford University Press, 1926.

Gardiner, Harold C. *Mysteries' End: An Investigation of the Last Days of the Medieval Religious Stage.* Yale Studies in English 103. New Haven: Yale University Press, 1946; rprt. Archon Books, 1967.

Gibson, Gail. "Bury St. Edmunds, Lydgate, and the *N-Town Cycle*," *Speculum,* 56 (1981), 56–90.

————. "The Play of *Wisdom* and the Abbey of St. Edmund," *Comparative Drama*, 19 (1985–86), 117–35.

Gottfried, Robert S. *Bury St. Edmunds and the Urban Crisis*. Princeton: Princeton University Press, 1982.

Greenfield, Peter, ed. *Records of Early English Drama: Gloucestershire*. Toronto: University of Toronto Press, 1986.

Hardison, Jr., O. B. *Christian Rite and Christian Drama in the Middle Ages: Essays in the Origin and Early History of Modern Drama*. Baltimore: The Johns Hopkins University Press, 1965.

Heal, Felicity, and Rosemary O'Day, eds. *Church and Society in England: Henry VIII to James I*. Hamden, Conn.: Shoestring Press, 1977.

Henshaw, Millett. "The Attitude of the Church Toward the Stage to the End of the Middle Ages," *Medievalia et Humanistica*, 4 (1952), 3–17.

Holthausen, Ferd, ed. *Das Noahspiel von Newcastle on Tyne*. Göteborgs högskolas årsskrift 3, no. 3. Göteborg: Wald. Zachrisson, 1897.

Hoskins, W. G. "English Provincial Towns in the Early Sixteenth Century," in *Provincial England: Essays in Social and Economic History* (London: Macmillan and Co., 1963; rprt. 1965), pp. 65–85.

————. *Local History in England*. London: Longmans, 1959; 2d ed. 1972.

Hudson, Anne, ed. *Selections from English Wycliffite Writings*. Cambridge: Cambridge University Press, 1978.

Ingram, Reginald W., ed. *Records of Early English Drama: Coventry*. Toronto: University of Toronto Press, 1981.

————. "1579 and the Decline of Civic Religious Drama in Coventry," in *The Elizabethan Theatre VIII*, ed. G. B. Hibbard (Port Credit, Ont., 1982), pp. 114–28.

————. "'To find the players and all that longeth therto': Notes on the Production of Medieval Drama in Coventry," in *The Elizabethan Theatre V*, ed. G. B. Hibbard (Hamden, Conn.: Archon, 1975), pp. 17–44.

Jacob, E. J. *The Fifteenth Century, 1399–1485*. Oxford History of England 6. Oxford: Oxford University Press, 1961.

James, Mervyn. "Ritual, Drama and Social Body in the Late Medieval English Town," *Past and Present*, 98 (1983), 3–29.

Jeffrey, David L. "Franciscan Spirituality and the Rise of Early English Drama," *Mosaic*, vol. 8, no. iv (1975), 17–46.

Johnston, Alexandra. "The Plays of the Religious Guilds of York: The Creed Play and the Pater Noster Play," *Speculum*, 50 (1975), 55–90.

————. "The Procession and Play of Corpus Christi in York after 1426," *Leeds Studies in English*, 7 (1973–74), 55–62.

Johnston, Alexandra F., and Margaret Rogerson, eds. *Records of Early English Drama: York*. 2 vols. Toronto: University of Toronto Press, 1979.

Jones, Douglas. *The Church in Chester: 1300–1540*. Chetham Society, 3rd ser., 7. Manchester, 1957.

Kahrl, Stanley. "Learning about Local Control," in Dutka, *Proceedings*, pp. 101–27.

————. "Medieval Drama in Louth," *Research Opportunities in Renaissance Drama*, 10 (1967), 129–33.

Kahrl, Stanley, ed. *Records of Plays and Players in Lincolnshire 1300–1585*. Collections VIII. Oxford: The Malone Society, 1974 (for 1969).

Klausner, David. "Research in Progress," *Records of Early English Drama Newsletter*, vol. 4, no. 1 (1979), 20–24.

Knowles, David, and R. Neville Hadcock. *Medieval Religious Houses*. London: Longmans, 1953.

Kolve, V. A. *The Play Called Corpus Christi*. London: Edward Arnold, 1966.

Leach, A. F. "Some English Plays and Players," in *An English Miscellany Presented to Dr. Furnivall in Honour of His Seventy-Fifth Birthday* (Oxford, 1901), pp. 205–34.

Lumiansky, R. M., and David Mills. *The Chester Mystery Cycle: Essays and Documents.* Chapel Hill: University of North Carolina Press, 1983.

Lumiansky, R. M., and David Mills, eds. *The Chester Mystery Cycle.* 2 vols. Early English Text Society, s. s. 3 and 9 (London: Oxford University Press, 1974, 1986).

Luxton, Imogen. "The Reformation and Popular Culture," in Heal and O'Day, pp. 57–77.

Matthew, F. D., ed. *The English Works of Wyclif Hitherto Unprinted.* 2d rev. ed. Early English Text Society, o.s. 74. London: Kegan Paul, 1902; rprt. Kraus, 1978.

Morris, Rupert H. *Chester in the Plantagenet and Tudor Reigns.* Chester, n.d. (ca. 1895).

Nelson, Alan. *The Medieval English Stage: Corpus Christi Pageants and Plays.* Chicago: University of Chicago Press, 1974.

Ormerod, George. *The History of the Country Palatine and City of Chester.* 3 vols. London, 1819.

Palliser, D. M. "Popular Reactions to the Reformation during the Years of Uncertainty 1530–70," in Heal and O'Day, pp. 35–56.

———. *Tudor York.* Oxford, 1979.

Pecock, Reginald. *The Repressor of Over Much Blaming of the Clergy,* ed. Churchill Babington. Rolls Series 19. London, 1860.

Phythian-Adams, Charles. "Ceremony and the Citizen: The Communal Year at Coventry 1450–1550," in Clark and Slack, pp. 57–85.

———. *Desolation of a City: Coventry and the Urban Crisis in the Late Middle Ages.* Cambridge: Cambridge University Press, 1979.

Rastall, G. R. "The Minstrel Court in Medieval England," in *A Medieval Miscellany in honour of Professor John Le Patourel,* ed. R. L. Thomson. Proceedings of the Leeds Philosophical and Literary Society: Literary and Historical Section, vol. XVIII, part I (1982), 96–105.

Rastell, John. *A Hundred Merry Tales,* ed. P. M. Zall. Lincoln: University of Nebraska Press, 1963.

Robbins, Rossell Hope, ed. *Historical Poems of the XIVth and XVth Centuries.* New York, 1959.

Salter, Frederick M. *Mediaeval Drama in Chester.* Toronto: University of Toronto Press, 1955.

Spector, Stephen. "The Provenance of the N-Town Codex," *The Library,* 6th ser., 1 (1979), 25–33.

Stacpoole, Alberic, et al. *The Noble City of York.* York, 1972.

Stevens, Martin. *Four Middle English Mystery Cycles: Textual, Contextual, and Critical Interpretations.* Princeton: Princeton University Press, 1987.

Sticca, Sandro. "Drama and Spirituality in the Middle Ages," *Medievalia et Humanistica,* n.s., 4 (1973), 69–87.

Tanner, Norman P. *The Church in Medieval Norwich.* Studies and Texts 66. Toronto: Pontifical Institute of Mediaeval Studies, 1984.

Tittler, Robert. "The Incorporation of Boroughs, 1540–1558," *History* 62, no. 204 (1977), 24–42.

Travis, Peter W. *Dramatic Design in the Chester Cycle.* Chicago: University of Chicago Press, 1982.

Unwin, George. *The Gilds and Companies of London.* London, 1908.

Wasson, John. "Corpus Christi Plays and Pageants at Ipswich," *Research Opportunities in Renaissance Drama* 19 (1976), 99–108.

————, ed. *Records of Early English Drama: Devon*. Toronto: University of Toronto Press, 1986.

Weinbaum, Martin. *The Incorporation of Boroughs*. Manchester, 1936.

Wenzel, Siegfried. "An Early Reference to a Corpus Christi Play," *Modern Philology* 74 (1977), 390–94.

Westlake, Herbert F. *The Parish Guilds of Medieval England*. London, 1919.

White, Eileen. "The Disappearance of the York Play Texts: New Evidence for the Creed Play," *Medieval English Theatre*, vol. 5, no. 2 (1983), 103–09.

Wickham, Glynne. *Early English Stages: 1300–1600*. 2 vols. in 3 parts. London: Routledge & Kegan Paul, 1959–72.

Woodward, D. M. *The Trade of Elizabethan Chester*. Hull, 1970.

Woolf, Rosemary. *The English Mystery Plays*. Berkeley and Los Angeles: University of California Press, 1972.

Young, Abigail. "Plays and Players: The Latin Terms for Performance (Part ii)," *Records of Early English Drama Newsletter*, vol. 10, no. 1 (1985), 9–16.

Young, Karl. *The Drama of the Medieval Church*. 2 vols. Oxford: Clarendon Press, 1933.

ALAN H. NELSON

Contexts for Early English Drama

The Universities

Although the universities of Cambridge and Oxford were an integral part of medieval and Renaissance English society, they provided a social and intellectual context which resulted in idiosyncratic developments in drama and other forms of entertainment. Perhaps the most general observation which can be made from the perspective of the history of drama is that the universities were relatively catholic consumers of culture, but relatively discriminating producers. Ape wards, minstrels, parish players, and professional companies were welcomed into the colleges and in the university towns from the fourteenth century to at least the middle of the sixteenth, but the plays produced within the universities were normally in Latin, were Latinate (or at least Italianate) in style, and, though often published for and read by the outside world, were seldom if ever performed by nonuniversity players.[1]

University drama in England is essentially a postmedieval phenomenon. Apart from parish plays, disguisings, and several *ludi* at King's College, Cambridge, and Magdalen College, Oxford, college plays seem to have developed in the course of the humanist revival of the first half of the sixteenth century. Although plays continued until 1642, their heyday was the middle third of the sixteenth century. At Cambridge, for example, some sixteen college performances are recorded from the fifteenth century, approximately three hundred from the sixteenth century, and scarcely twenty-five from the seventeenth century.[2] Accordingly, the focus of the present discussion will be on the period from approximately 1450 to 1564. This focus is further justified by the fact that recent discoveries have shed considerable new light on the earlier years.

The foundation of Oxford is traditionally dated 1133 (or 1163), that of Cambridge, 1209.[3] In their early years both universities were small and occasionally disorderly collections of lodging houses and hostels, or "halls." During the thirteenth century the first colleges were founded to ensure a more orderly and productive academic environment.

Both universities were situated in towns of middling size, and the academic institutions came to dominate their towns. Cambridge and Oxford had mayors and aldermen like many other towns, but the universities, most conspicuously in the person of the vice-chancellor, maintained judicial authority over university members and other "privileged persons." In the interest of maintaining a proper moral climate for the scholars, the universities eventually won and jealously guarded the right of supervision over the movement and conduct of strangers within five miles of the university—in effect, over the entire town and all its suburbs. Town challenged gown on numerous occasions, but appeals to higher authorities usually guaranteed victory to the gown.

The colleges were not only houses of academic instruction, but social assemblies with the distinct character of "households." The master, senior fellows, junior fellows, scholars, choristers, and some servants might all dwell together within the college walls. The total population of a college might vary from twenty or thirty to more than a hundred. Rank, determined by academic degree and by seniority, was everywhere observed, and was particularly evident when the college gathered in the hall for meals. Mealtime was the occasion for the reception of guests, and, at appropriate times, for entertainment. The most common form of entertainment was music played by waits, who might receive both a meal and a fee (Smith, "Academic," 150–51; Alton).[4] Visiting actors occasionally performed in the hall, and college plays, acted by students, were normally performed in the hall as well.

The university was governed by the heads of colleges, one of whom served as vice-chancellor. The university sponsored and supervised communal events such as royal entries, and exercised jurisdiction over strangers and over university members charged with misbehavior. The town government consisted of a mayor and aldermen who had jurisdiction over the town waits (or minstrels), and over the town hall, where plays were sometimes performed (Cooper, 1530–31, 1547–48, 1567–68, 1569–70).[5] Beginning in the latter half of the sixteenth century, the universities frequently took steps to exclude visiting professional players; the towns, however, continued to support visiting players. Thus, plays themselves became a source of friction between town and gown.

Of all these institutions, the colleges were by far the most important for the development and support of dramatic activity. In a negative sense, their own activities, together with the influence of the university over the town, probably inhibited the development of large-scale guild activities and "Corpus Christi" or biblical plays. It is true that a "Ludus filiorum Israel" was sponsored by the Cambridge guild of Corpus Christi in 1353; the more important fact may be that this is virtually the only record suggesting the existence of liturgical drama in Cambridge (Bateson, 51). In Oxford, liturgical drama was apparently performed in the late fifteenth and early sixteenth century by Magdalen College (Alton, 43–47), but the town of Oxford is not known to have had a cycle of plays.

As households, the colleges played host to parish players from nearby towns or counties, to minstrel companies sponsored by other towns or by royalty and nobility, and to itinerant musicians and entertainers of every description. As both households and cultivators of the intellect, the colleges eventually became wholesale producers of dramá, establishing a reputation for excellence that reached to London, to the court, and even to the Continent.

Evidence for dramatic activities in the colleges, as well as in the universities and the town, is abundant, indeed overwhelming (Smith, "Academic"; Alton; Chambers, 213; Billington).[6] Colleges maintained scrupulous and closely audited accounts of all expenditures down to the most trifling, and these have survived in considerable number. Members of colleges, as advocates and practitioners of literacy, put on plays, published or otherwise preserved the texts, and recorded their reactions in letters, controversial tracts, autobiographical reflections, and diaries. The vice-chancellor conducted extensive inquiries into civic and collegiate disorders and into questions of moral and legal conduct: records of these inquiries survive in great numbers in the university archives. The town treasurers also maintained detailed accounts which yield information about town waits and visiting minstrels, jugglers, and players. Further civic information is contained in council minute books and in parish churchwardens' account books.[7]

Though the very earliest accounts for any given college are often lost, two Cambridge foundations preserve extensive accounts covering most of their history: these are King's Hall, whose accounts run in an occasionally defective but numerous and essentially representative series from 1337 to 1546; and King's College, whose accounts run with few lacunae from 1447 (in the decade of its foundation) to the present.[8]

Payments to *histriones* and *lusores* abound in fourteenth-century King's Hall records, with as many as twenty-two payments in 1362–63 to perhaps fifty performers (King's Hall Accounts Vol. II, fols. 71v–79v). These performers doubtless included the Cambridge waits, who visited the college regularly on major college feast days. The performers were probably musicians who perhaps occasionally exercised other talents including some form of mimetic display.

The earliest King's College accounts reveal similar payments, and indeed such payments persist through the sixteenth and into the seventeenth century in most colleges. At King's College, however, the members themselves put on "disguisings" for their own benefit and for the benefit of guests, including the mayor and aldermen. King's College produced disguisings regularly from 1456–57 to 1489–90; records of plays (*ludi*) occur somewhat less regularly, beginning in 1465–66 but continuing to 1614–15.[9]

Although we know nothing of the subject matter of the pre-1500 disguisings and plays, they apparently involved music, costumes, painted sets, and written texts. In this respect, King's College probably imitated conventions and standards set by the royal household and by noble households throughout England. The best insight into the nature of the King's College disguisings and plays may perhaps be gained from a reading of *Fulgens and Lucres* and *Nature*, both by Henry Medwall, who attended King's College from 1480 to 1483, and who certainly witnessed Christmas disguisings (Nelson, Introduction). King's College also maintained the tradition of the Boy Bishop, another quasi-dramatic ceremony, connected more with the chapel than with the hall (Chambers, *Medieval* I, 336–71).

At Oxford, only Magdalen College is known to have produced plays in the fifteenth century: records of these performances date from 1485–86, and answer generally to King's College records from Cambridge. Magdalen College also supported a Boy Bishop, and was host to many visiting performers (Alton, 40–62).

The period of the King's College disguisings coincides with a period of visiting interlude players from Cambridge or nearby towns. These include players from (Saffron) Walden in 1467–68, along with unnamed players "from the country" (*de Patria*); players from Ramsey, Walden, and Bury (St. Edmunds) in 1468–69; players (or perhaps minstrels) from London in 1472–73, along with players of interludes from Fulborn; various players in 1488–89, in particular players of the Cambridge parishes of St. Clement's and Little St. Mary's (outside Trumpington Gates); players from Madingley in 1489–90; and players from Great St. Mary's, the "university" church, in 1499–1500 and 1500–1501 (*Liber* accounts; *Mundum Books*). Such performances at the end of the fifteenth century are worth noting in part because they seem characteristic of that half-century but of no other time; aside from visits by parishioners at Hock-tide (Cobban, 229–30), such visits are rare after 1500.

Possibly King's College was unique in Cambridge for performing so many of its own plays in the decades before 1500, but during the first half of the sixteenth century plays came to be performed in almost all colleges. King's Hall apparently put on plays in 1503–1504, 1507–1508, and 1508–1509; in 1510–11 the college performed a comedy of Terence, the first recorded play by a classical author in either university; in 1516–17, master Thrope of King's Hall received payment for a play of Terence performed by the boys under his tutelage (Cobban, 227–28). In 1522–23 a comedy of Plautus was given at Queens'—possibly this was *Miles Gloriosus*, the performance of which was subsequently remembered with extraordinary fondness by John Leland, and also by Stephen Gardiner, who played the part of Periplectomenus (Bradner).

Records only recently discovered suggest that the habit of performing plays in the colleges on a regular basis was fully established as early as the 1520s, when the humanist revival was beginning to dominate the universities. In Cambridge, St. John's College was known to be at the forefront of this revival. In 1521 John Smyth, a priest who seems to have been in charge of the day-to-day operations of the college in the absence of the master, John Metcalfe, and the founder, John Fisher, wrote to Metcalfe: "And owr compeny myght haue the play that my lorde made thei wolde prouyde to play yt"; "the compeny wolde gladly haue my lordes play" (St. John's Archives, MSS D.105.47, 49). The expression "my lord" in this context almost certainly refers to John Fisher, then bishop of Rochester. Perhaps Bishop Fisher may be regarded as the first recorded college playwright.

In 1524 St. John's paid for four players' gowns, incuding a woman's gown. The records up to 1538 are spotty, but plays were certainly performed in 1527, and again in 1535:

```
. . .
Item settynge vp removynge & takyng downe ye stage     ij s    (i)iiij d
. . .
               Item to Mr Wade for a comedie vt patet billam iij s
               Item to sir hatcher for a dialoge patet billam xxiij d
               Item to Mr cheke for therence patet billam x s iiij d
               Item to Mr redmayne for dyuerse playes v s
. . .
```

John Cheke and John Redman were at the forefront of the classical revival. In 1538 the bursar's accounts record a payment for "vij comedes and one Greek dialogue" (St. John's Archives, MSS D106.11–13).[10] No other entry testifies to so many performances in a single college in a single year.

By 1545 play-acting had become such an established part of college life at Cambridge that it was institutionalized in the revised statutes of St. John's, followed by Queens' (1559) and by Trinity (1560). The motive expressed in the various statutes is essentially pedagogical: the performance of plays aided the scholars in learning and pronouncing Latin and Greek (Boas, *University*, 8–9, 16–17).

The pedagogical intention alone, however, can scarcely account for the enormous burgeoning of dramatic performances by the colleges. From the 1540s, St. John's College at Cambridge often produced three plays each year, perhaps one in Greek, and two in Latin. Trinity College, founded in 1546 from the disbanded King's Hall, produced five plays each year during the 1550s. King's College also produced plays, as did Corpus Christi, Queens', Christ's, and Jesus. Even tiny Peterhouse is known to have produced plays on at least four occasions (Smith, "Academic"; Peterhouse Bursar's Rolls 1562–63, 1571–73, 1575–76).

At Oxford, Magdalen College may have been producing nonliturgical plays by 1502–1503; evidence for plays at New College, Christchurch, and St. John's does not antedate 1550, but doubtless some of these colleges were active earlier (Alton).

Most of the earlier college plays were classical in origin, but some were the work of contemporary playwrights. Some of these plays came from the Continent (Kirchmayer's *Pammachius* of 1545); others were of native origin (Nicholas Udall's *Ezechias* of 1564). Some were plays in English by members of the colleges (*Gammer Gurton's Needle* at Christ's College, ca. 1553, apparently by William Stevenson), and a few were in Greek (John Christopherson's *Iephthe*, ca. 1544). The vast majority were in Latin. In all, nearly a hundred University authors and some hundred and fifty extant Anglo-Latin plays have been identified, the majority probably written at and for the colleges. Other plays have not survived. Judging from this evidence, it is not too much to say that Cambridge and Oxford rivaled the professional companies of London in dramatic output.

Dramatic performances in the colleges were tied closely to the liturgical and to the academic calendars (in many respects these were one and the same calendar). Colleges tended to sponsor plays during the period of festivity between Christmas day and Twelfth Night, that is to say, from December 25 to January 6. Plays were also scheduled for the bachelors' commencement, which occurred in January, February, or March. Individual colleges sponsored various forms of entertainment on patronal feast days—thus, for example, King's College, devoted to St. Mary and St. Nicholas, regularly held the ceremony of the boy bishop on St. Nicholas day, December 6, and invited the town waits to perform on the feast of the Purification of the Virgin, February 2. Sometime before 1588, St. John's College established a tradition of performing a comedy on the coronation day of Queen Elizabeth, November 17 (Cambridge University Archives MS CUR 6.1, Art. 35, f 2r [ca. 1588]).[11] Plays were prepared long in advance, and attracted visits from other academics, from university officers, from townsmen and townswomen, and occasionally from nobility and even royalty.

Visiting players might perform during practically any period of the year, with the possible exception of Lent, so that in addition to the scheduled and virtually predictable records of performances in the accounts, bursar's books indicate the appearance of entertainers on fairly random occasions.

College plays were usually performed in the college halls. By way of exception, they might also be played in a courtyard, in the chapel, or in the master's lodgings (Moore Smith, *College Plays*, 23–24). A full understanding of staging practices at Cambridge requires us to start with an inventory drawn up in 1640 of the Queens' College stage (Moore Smith, "Academic Drama," 199–204). The Queens' College stage was a demountable theater or scaffolding erected in the hall for the annual performances of the college plays. College bursar's records make it probable that the demountable stage was originally constructed in the 1540s, the chief work being accomplished 1546–49 (*Magnum* II 1546–47, 1547–48, 1548–49). With due consideration for the changes which doubtless occurred with the passage of time, the 1640 inventory will allow us, with some degree of probability, to reconstruct a theater which antedated the London professional theaters by a quarter of a century.

   The main floor of Queens' College hall is about 44 feet long by 27 feet wide. The stage proper was a raised, apparently bare platform approximately 15 feet wide by 9 feet deep. Perhaps the most challenging fact about this stage, for modern scholarship, is its position: it was set not against the screens, where the doors might serve as entrances and exits for actors, and where the screen itself might serve as a scenic backdrop; rather, it was set against the far or "upper" end of the hall, near the dais. Additional evidence from both Cambridge and Oxford suggests that college plays were normally staged at the upper end of the hall, away from the screens.[12]

   The word "stage," as it is used in the inventory, covers not only the platform, but the spectator galleries erected around the perimeter of the hall. A triple gallery, with raked seating, was set up behind the stage; double galleries were erected along the East and West walls; another gallery was apparently set against the screens. On either side of the stage were three-storied tiring houses, called the East Tyring House and the West Tyring House. Leslie Hotson has published both a ground plan and a perspective drawing of the Queens' College theater (169–72). The arrangement of the scaffolds and stage platform in his drawings is generally accurate and deserves further study: the reader should be cautioned, however, that Queens' College hall is small as college halls go, whereas Hotson's perspective drawing makes it look as large as Westminster Hall in London.

   Other colleges had demountable stages similar to that of Queens'; in general, a team of two to six carpenters spent two to five days erecting the stage in each college. As at Queens', the full stage entailed the stage platform, the surrounding galleries for seating, and "houses" representing playing locales, sometimes serving also as tiring houses for the actors. In 1550–51, a mechanical contraption called a "heavens" was perhaps suspended from the ceiling of Queens' College hall; this was not the first device of its kind, however, for John Dee constructed a lifting apparatus in Trinity College several years earlier, to the delight and astonishment of the spectators (Moore-Smith, "Academic Drama," 188; Dee, 5–6).

   Costuming for the plays was highly elaborate. Each college kept a stock of costumes which served year after year. So valuable were the costumes that they were kept in chests in the Master's living quarters, or kept locked in the college tower along with the college plate, where they were checked out and checked back in. Players' gear figures importantly in inventories of college properties: the archives of St. John's, Trinity, and Queens' colleges in Cambridge all contain such inventories, some of which run on for half a dozen pages, detailing women's gowns, beards, wigs, armor, and props (Billington, 1–10; Moore Smith, "Academic," 195–98, 230; Trinity College Archives Box 29.136 [unpublished]). On special occasions college officials requested costumes from the office of the robes in London.[13]

Texts of plays written for performance in college halls convey much
information concerning production techniques. Thomas Legge's two
plays, *Richardus Tertius* and *The Destruction of Jerusalem* (?1579 and
?1581), contain numerous stage directions (in English) which give a sense
of the action which might occur in any play, for example:

> After they have thus declared what everything signifieth let the singers sing
> being placed on the toppe of some of the houses in the mean season let such
> ceremonyes be used for the coronation as the chronicle declareth and after
> let them departe....

Legge's plays include "mutes," or extras, guns and trumpets, curtains, a
sacred bull, rain, thunder, and lightning. A particularly gory scene requires a woman in a siege episode to display "the head, an arme, one legg,
And som part else (of her child) roasted" (Lordi, 534–39).[14] In 1552–53
King's College used thunder barrels and a brace of live hunting dogs "for
Hippolytus" (*Mundum* [12.5]); live hunting dogs were also used at Peterhouse in 1572–73. Finally, the town waits were often hired to provide
music (Moore Smith, *College Plays*, 32).

The pedagogical nature of the dramatic enterprise in the colleges logi-
cally implies that the scholars and fellows were the principal actors in
the plays, and so they were. More than a dozen lists of the original actors
survive in manuscripts or printed copies of the Cambridge plays (Boas,
University, 390–401; Moore Smith, *College*, 74–88), so that more can ultimately be known about the individual participants in the university
drama than in almost any other dramatic activity in England of this time.
The names of senior fellows who were responsible for producing the plays
also survive in abundance.

Most of the writers of plays at Cambridge were amateurs in the true
sense of the word, but a few took up careers in the professional theater.
Best known of these is the Cambridge graduate Christopher Marlowe;
other Elizabethan dramatists include Robert Greene and Thomas Nashe
of Cambridge, and George Peele and John Lyly of Oxford. Probably half
of the known English playwrights up to 1642 were university men who
were presumably influenced in some way or other by university plays.[15]

On many occasions, either the playwrights or their admirers made it
a point to preserve the texts of the plays, whether in manuscript or in
print. Many of the texts were apparently prepared as "presentation copies," while others were recorded in student commonplace books along
with witty, sentimental, or bawdy verse. Several play manuscripts contain marginal notations which suggest that they were used in an actual
production.[16]

Although the plays were sponsored and even required by the colleges,
condoned or positively supported by the university, and attended by resi-
dents of the town, by nobility, and even by royalty, certain members of
the colleges and certain authorities objected to the plays on political or

religious grounds. Matthew Parker incurred the wrath of Archbishop Stephen Gardiner for having the temerity to condone a production of Kirchmayer's *Pammachius* in 1545 (Muller, 129–35). Gardiner found this play too violently anticlerical and anti-Catholic. More objections came from the stern Puritans, who were probably responsible for the cessation of all dramatic activity at Christ's College (home of *Gammer Gurton's Needle*) from 1567–68.[17]

Whatever the objections of the Puritans, when Queen Elizabeth chose to visit Cambridge in 1564, college plays became a principal focus of her sojourn. Elizabeth spent six days at Cambridge, arriving on August 5. During her visit she was to have seen four plays.[18]

Initially the university officials planned to have the plays performed in the colleges, but when the Queen's surveyors inspected the stage erected in King's College hall, they declared that it was not sufficient. Certainly it was too small to accommodate the Queen and her retainers as well as the appropriate University officials and college fellows, and probably it was too fragile to accommodate the press of the crowd without risk to the Queen. The royal surveyors therefore erected, at their own expense, a huge stage in King's College chapel. The stage spanned the entire width of the building, the side chapels serving as "houses" for the actors. Most of the audience sat in front of the stage, while the Queen sat on the stage itself, with her back to the south wall.

On Sunday, August 6, Elizabeth witnessed Plautus's *Aulularia*. On Monday the 7th, she saw *Dido*, written by Edward Haliwell, a former member of the college. On Tuesday the 8th, she saw Udall's *Ezechias* (now lost). On Wednesday the 9th, she was to have seen *Ajax Flagellifer*, a Latin version of Sophocles' *Ajax*, but she declared herself too weary, much to the disappointment of all concerned. On Thursday the 10th, she left Cambridge for Hinchinbrook, a private estate near Huntingdon.

An account by the Spanish ambassador Guzman de Silva provides information concerning still another performance:

When the Queen was at Cambridge they represented comedies and held scientific disputations, and an argument on religion, in which the man who defended Catholicism was attacked by those who presided, in order to avoid having to give him the prize. The Queen made a speech praising the acts and exercises, and they wished to give her another representation which she refused, in order to be no longer delayed. Those who were so anxious for her to hear it, followed her to her first stopping-place, and so importuned her that at last she consented.

The actors came in dressed as some of the imprisoned Bishops. First came the bishop of London carrying a lamb in his hands as if he were eating it as he walked along, and then others with different devices, one being in the figure of a dog with the Host in his mouth. They write that the Queen was so angry that she at once entered her chamber using strong language, and the men who held the torches, it being night, left them in the dark, and so ended the thoughtless and scandalous representation. (Boas, *University Drama*, 382–85)

The events of 1564 may be taken as a fair representation of the general tenor of drama in the university context to that date. The plays included a play in Latin by an admired classical author (Plautus), an original play by a member of the university written in imitation of a classical model (*Dido*), a play in English (Udall's *Ezechias*), a Latin translation of a Greek play (*Ajax Flagellifer*), and finally a raucous maske in English, perhaps a late representative of the oldstyle "disguising." Oxford sent a delegation to observe the visit, including the plays, to prepare for a similar reception, which occurred in 1566.

Elizabeth's visits to Cambridge in 1564 and to Oxford in 1566 set a royal seal of approval on college drama. News of the dramatic tradition spread across England and even across Europe. Thus on the verso of the Braun and Hogenberg map of Cambridge (ca. 1575), in the Latin, German, and French editions, William Sone, former Regius Professor of Civil Law, proclaimed:

> In the months of January, February, and March, to beguile the long evenings, they amuse themselves with exhibiting public plays, which they perform with so much elegance, such graceful action, and such command of voice, countenance, and gesture, that if Plautus, Terence, or Seneca were to come to life again, they would admire their own pieces, and be better pleased with them than when they were performed before the people of Rome; and Euripides, Sophocles, and Aristophanes, would be disgusted at the performances of their own citizens. (Cooper, *Annals* iii, 329)

Even discounting the hyperbole of this advertisement, it is clear that the English academic drama achieved its maturity and a wide reputation well before the drama of the professional theaters in London.

Although the academic theatre will repay study in its own right, the student of drama will not rest satisfied until the question of the relationship between the academic and the professional theater has been deliberated. Materials for exploring this question are being prepared on two distinct fronts. On the one hand, archival records of the colleges, universities, towns, and counties of Cambridge and Oxford are being gathered systematically under the auspices of Records of Early English Drama. On the other hand, the texts of college plays are being edited in photographic facsimile and with individual introductions under the auspices of a project entitled Renaissance Latin Drama in England.[19] Scholarly editions of academic plays are being published in a less systematic manner, but at a discernible pace (Harbage, Part 2). Until these current projects are completed, patience and caution should be the watchword. Nevertheless, enough evidence is already available in print to keep a student of the drama busy until the promised volumes make their appearance.

NOTES

1. The standard study of this subject is Boas, *University Drama in the Tudor Age*; this is supplemented for the post-Tudor period by Stratman, "Dramatic Performances at Oxford and Cambridge 1603–1642." An earlier study which remains useful is Frederick S. Boas, "Univesity Plays," *CHEL*, Vol. 5, Chap. 12. Chambers, *The Elizabethan Stage*, takes frequent note of academic performances (see especially Appendix K), as does Bentley, *Jacobean and Caroline Stage*. Records are transcribed in Moore Smith, "The Academic Drama at Cambridge"; and in Alton, "The Academic Drama in Oxford." Much information is gathered in Harbage and Schoenbaum, *Annals of English Drama*. The most recent bibliography is the *New CBEL*, Vol. I., cols. 1761–80; an important article published recently is J. W. Binns, "Seneca and Neo-Latin Tragedy." An important study for Cambridge is Smith, *College Plays*.

2. Compiled from records currently being assembled for the *Cambridge* collection of Records of Early English Drama. (See Moore Smith, *College Plays*, 50–72, for a less complete list.) The bias for Cambridge in this essay reflects the author's current editorship of the REED *Cambridge* collection. The author wishes to express his gratitude for assistance to John Elliott, editor of the REED *University of Oxford* collection.

3. Historical information on the towns and their colleges and universities is drawn from the relevant volumes of the Victoria County History series: *History of the County of Cambridge* and *History of the County of Oxford*. These volumes should be consulted for bibliographical references to other historical studies.

4. See also Cobban, 222–27.

5. Cambridge University Archives MS Comm. Court II/13, f 128v, contains evidence of a dispute over the hall as late as 1606.

6. I estimate that only sixty percent of the relevant Cambridge material has been published; Professor Elliott estimates about ninety percent for Oxford.

7. Treasurers' records and other town documents from Cambridge are transcribed in Cooper.

8. The King's Hall accounts, bound in 26 volumes, are kept among the Trinity College archives; they are described by Cobban, xii, 321. The King's College archives include two principal series, the *Liber communarum* and the *Mundum Books*: no list of the volumes in these two series has been published. Excerpts from both accounts are printed by Moore Smith, "Academic Drama," 150–51, 214–19.

9. References to disguisings for these years are scattered through the *Liber communarum* accounts and the *Mundum Books*. References to women as guests occur in the *Liber communarum* (7.3), fifth week after Christmas; and (9.1), ninth week after Michaelmas. Some information is transcribed by Moore Smith, "Academic Drama," 214–19.

10. For the careers of Cheke and Redman, see Stevens.

11. "The master hath inhibited all manner of playes euen yat comedy which was vsually and yearly played to celebrate the Queenes day."

12. Southern argues that virtually all pre-Shakespearean plays were played before hall screens. Wickham, 355–59, argues that the plays were staged against the lower end of Christ Church Hall, Oxford, in 1566. The same arrangement is proposed by Manning. The crux of the matter is a confusing contemporary statement translated by Wickham as "in the upper part of [the Hall], which looks back on the West" (I, 358). I feel that the reference to the upper part of the hall excludes the possibility of playing against the screens.

13. British Library, Lansdowne MS 78, fol. 34r, transcribed in Chambers, "Dramatic Records," 213.

14. The recently discovered text of Legge's *Destruction of Jerusalem* is Cambridge University Library MS 7958, fols. 12r-84r. Stage directions are from fols. 26v-27r, 41v, 46r, 69r, 71v.

15. Playwrights are listed by Chambers, *Elizabethan Drama*, and Bentley, *Jacobean and Caroline Stage*. See also Harbage, *Annals of English Drama*, Part 4.

16. Play manuscripts are listed in Harbage and Schoenbaum, *Annals of English Drama*, Appendix.

17. See, for example, the objections of John Smith, 1586, noted by Cooper, *Annals* ii, 415–16.

18. Information concerning Elizabeth's visit is preserved in "Stokys's Book," Cambridge University Archives MS Misc. Collect. 4, fols. 63r-79v; Cambridge University Library MS. Ff.5.14, fols. 87v-94r: Abraham Hartwell, *Regina Literata* (London, 1565); and Folger MS V.a.176 (the Nicholas Robinson account—not foliated). Much of this material is printed in Nichols, *Progresses*. Robinson's transcription is not included in the 1823 reprint.

19. Marvin Spevack and J. W. Binns, general editors, published by Georg Olms Verlag, Hildesheim, West Germany.

WORKS CITED AND SUGGESTED READING
MANUSCRIPT SOURCES

King's Hall Accounts, Vol. II, fols 71v-79v.
King's College *Liberi communarum* and *Mundum Books*
Peterhouse Bursar's Rolls
Queens' College *Magnum Journals*

PRINTED SOURCES

Alton, R. E. "The Academic Drama in Oxford: Extracts from the Records of Four Colleges." Malone Society *Collections*, Vol. V. Oxford, 1959, pp. 29–95.
Bateson, Mary, ed. *Cambridge Guild Records*. Cambridge Antiquarian Society Publications, 39 (1903).
Bentley, Gerald Eades. *The Jacobean and Caroline Stage*. 7 vols. Oxford, 1941–68.
Billington, Sandra. "Sixteenth-Century Drama in St. John's College, Cambridge." *Review of English Studies*. N.S. 29 (1978).
Binns. "Seneca and New-Latin Tragedy in England." In *Seneca*, ed. C. D. N. Costa. London, 1975.
Boas, Frederick S. *University Drama in the Tudor Age*. London: 1914.
———. "University Plays." *Cambridge History of English Literature*. Vol. 5, Chap. 12. Cambridge, 1910.
Bradner, Leicester. "The First Cambridge Production of *Miles Gloriosus*." *Modern Language Notes* 70 (1955): 100–103.
Chambers, E. K. *The Medieval Stage*. Oxford, 1903.
Chambers, E. K., and W. W. Greg. "Dramatic Records from the Lansdowne Mauscripts." Malone Society *Collections*, Vol. I, Part II. Oxford, 1908.
Christopherson, John. *Iephthe* (ca. 1544).
Cobban, Alan B. *The King's Hall within the University of Cambridge in the Later Middle Ages*. London, 1969.
Cooper, Charles Henry. *Annals of Cambridge*. Cambridge, 1842–1908.
Dee, John. "The Compendious Rehearsal." *Chetham Society* 24 (1851): 5–6.
Harbage, Alfred. *Annals of English Drama, 975–1700*, ed. Samuel Schoenbaum. London, 1964.

Hartwell, Abraham. *Regina Literata*. London, 1565.

History of the County of Cambridge and the Isle of Ely, Vol. III (Town and University). Oxford, 1938– .

History of the County of Oxford. Vols. III (University) and IV (Town). Oxford, 1907– .

Hotson, Leslie. *Shakespeare's Wooden O*. New York, 1960.

Legge, Thomas. *Destruction of Jerusalem*. Cambridge University Library MS 7958, fols. 12r-84r.

Lordi, Robert J., ed. *Thomas Legge's 'Richardus Tertius': A Critical Edition with a Translation*. New York, 1979.

McKenzie, D. F. "A Cambridge Playhouse of 1638." *Renaissance Drama* (1970): 263–72.

Manning, Thomas John. "The Staging of Plays at Christ Church, Oxford, 1582–1592." Ph.D. dissertation, University of Michigan, 1972.

Muller, James Arthur, ed. *The Letters of Stephen Gardiner*. Cambridge, 1933.

Nelson, Alan H., ed. *The Plays of Henry Medwall*. Woodbridge, Suffolk, 1980.

New Cambridge Bibliography of English Literature. Vol. I. Cambridge, 1974, cols. 1761–80.

Nichols, John. *The Progresses and Public Processions of Queen Elizabeth*. 3 vols. London, 1788, 1805.

Smith, G. C. Moore. "The Academic Drama at Cambridge: Extracts from College Records" in Malone Society *Collections*, Vol. II, Part 2. Oxford, 1923, pp. 150–230.

———. *College Plays Performed in the University of Cambridge*. Cambridge, 1923.

Southern, Richard. *The Staging of Plays before Shakespeare*. London, 1973.

Stevens, Leslie, ed. *The Dictionary of National Biography*. 22 Vols. London, 1908–1909.

Stevenson, William(?). *Gammer Gurtan's Needle*. London, 1575.

Stratman, Carl S. "Dramatic Performances at Oxford and Cambridge 1603–1642." Ph.D. dissertation, University of Illinois, 1947.

Wickham, Glynne. *Early English Stages: 1300–1600*. 2 vols. in 3 pts. London, 1959–1972, 1980, 1981.

MARIANNE G. BRISCOE

Preaching and Medieval English Drama

Drama historians and critics often claim that preaching was an important influence on medieval English drama. In the 1930s Gerald R. Owst even suggested that the perspectives, if not the identities, of the playwright and preacher were virtually equivalent:

> In scene after scene of the plays . . . it [is] possible to trace each dominant idea in the preacher's mind, his view of the world as well as of religion, his little mannerisms and tricks of speech, his own tears and laughter, the peculiar inflection of his voice over some favourite tragedy or comedy of the *Ars Praedicandi*. (Owst, *Literature*, 547)

More recently Eleanor Prosser has proposed that the organization of the English cycle plays was much like that of a sermon:

> . . . the cycles present an argument: the necessity of Redemption. Thus we may conceive of a typical Corpus Christi cycle as one vast sermon on repentance; a sermon complete with *exempla*, meditations, and exhortations; a sermon utilizing all the techniques in which the medieval preacher was trained—from comic castigation of folly to impassioned prophecy of doom. (Prosser, 24–25)

Glynne Wickham regards the preaching tradition as a "vast storehouse of biographical and incidental narrative" joined to "a convenient formula for applying any item in it to moralistic ends. . . . It is inconceivable that play-makers of the fifteenth century should not already have been well schooled in narrative techniques, and should not have found the application of *exempla* indispensable to the verbal aspect of their art" (Wickham, vol. 2, pt. 2, 131).

Many of these critics work from sound intuition based on wide reading in Middle English drama and devotional materials. But their proposition, perhaps because of its simple, nearly self-evident nature, has scarcely been examined. For several decades, G. R. Owst's extensive work in sermons and preaching manuals has been our principal source on the subject. Yet A. G. Little and Leonard E. Boyle have serious reservations about Owst's work. Owst's reading and use of evidence are highly selective and his views are often patronizing; his preaching surveys are difficult to use, and he provides no bibliographies. Instead, he strings his references through pages of footnotes. And with a casual attitude toward dates, Owst brings centuries of background matter to bear uncritically on the period 1350–1450. He even created, with his own hand, the "woodcuts" that illustrate his book *Preaching in Medieval England*. Despite this, Owst remains the drama specialist's principal resource on medieval preaching. Other sources, like Woodburn O. Ross's introduction to his edition of the sermons in BL MS Roy 18 B.xxiii, offer helpful, if slender, background on late medieval English preaching. But on the whole, the standard works in sermon studies provide only sketchy and not entirely accurate guides to the field.

Despite these handicaps to research, the relationship between medieval preaching and drama does seem obvious. Sermons and plays share the same matter: the moralized lives of saints, exhortations to repentance and good living, and the salvation history of the Old and New Testaments. Furthermore, most critics now agree that the plays have instruction in faith and morals as a primary end. And so do the sermons. Indeed, about 1190, the Parisian master of theology, Alain of Lille, inaugurated the preaching handbook tradition (the *artes praedicandi*) with this very definition: "Preaching is open and public instruction in faith and morals" (col. 110). With these shared goals, preaching and plays serve one another as technical and artistic resources.

Historians of drama have long suggested that the clergy were often the playwrights, performers, directors, producers, and censors for medieval drama. So medieval audiences would have seen confessors, preachers, and celebrants creating the plays; and, conversely, these men would have brought to the plays many of the goals and attitudes that governed their work at catechism, pulpit, or altar (Wickham, vol. 2, pt. 2, 233n). Evidence further suggests that particular clerical orders and religious factions, e.g., the Franciscans and the Lollards, held categorical views on the merits of drama in religious observance. All of this is fertile ground, indeed, for history, criticism, and interpretation of medieval English drama. But it begs for better substantiation.

How justifiable are claims that English religious drama shares not only the matter, but also the manner and technique of the popular sermon? Or that the plays are rhetorical constructs that draw on preaching for much of their surprisingly uniform dramatic method? These are complex questions that are difficult to answer because little useful evidence has been collected. Historical and literary sources are not very explicit, especially in the fifteenth century and earlier, about authorship or about the formal relationship between worship and drama. Abundant evidence does not begin until the English Reformation, about 1540. But this is information from a significantly different religious climate and it must be applied to the study of medieval drama with great care. Recognizing these difficulties, this essay does not attempt a definitive description of the relationship between preaching and drama in medieval England. Instead, it surveys the range of historical evidence now available on the subject, suggests some evidence of sermon influence to be found in the play texts themselves, and finally points out some areas in need of further study.

First, let us consider the extent and nature of clerical auspices for the plays. If we knew the identities or even the occupations of medieval playwrights we could better understand the plays' source traditions and theoretical frameworks. If we could say that preachers wrote the plays, then the case for sermon influence would have a solid historical foundation. For the most part, however, we cannot do this. Not only do we not know who wrote the medieval plays, we are not even sure why, where, or even when most were written (or rewritten). This is in spite of considerable circumstantial evidence about the playwrights.

Much of this evidence suggests that the clergy did write late medieval religious drama. But each case must be examined carefully. For instance, in 1244 Bishop Robert Grosseteste complained of clergy who "make" miracle and May plays (317). But Grosseteste's term "play," or "ludus," most probably means "game" and does not refer to drama at all. We are on somewhat surer ground when a Wycliffite writer remarks, ca. 1378, "herfore freris han tau3t in englond þe paternoster in engli3sch tunge, as men seyen in þe pley of 3ork" (Wycliffe, 429). But even if this does mean that the friars wrote the Paternoster play, we have gained little. No Paternoster or Creed plays survive.

Such instances of religious men writing plays are fairly plentiful. But not all religious men were preachers. For example, John Lydgate, a Benedictine monk, wrote several mummings and pageants for London companies in the early fifteenth century. He also wrote speeches for a Corpus Christi procession. But Benedictines, in fact, did not often preach to the laity and no evidence survives that Lydgate ever preached at all. Preachers had to be ordained and, with the (disputed) exception of the mendicants, had also to be licensed to preach in England. So when we find evidence of a clerk who was possibly a preacher "writing" a play, as we sometimes do in town and parish account books, we must still proceed with caution. Such medieval clerks were often merely clerks in the modern sense, that is, literate copyists rather than creative writers. They were not in most cases preachers.

In searching for true examples of preacher-playwrights, we must also heed the cautionary tale about Ranulph Higden's authorship of the Chester Plays. Higden was the fourteenth century Benedictine author of the *Polychronicon* and of *Ars componendi sermones*, a preaching manual. The late Chester banns and the accounts of sixteenth and seventeenth century antiquarians assert that the plays were "the deuise of one Rondoll Moncke of Chester Abbaye" (Clopper, 240, 511). But most scholars now agree that the Higden association was fabricated to lend the Chester plays authority and venerability in the face of censorship and rising production costs. It is noteworthy, nonetheless, that the apologists wanted their playwright to be a monk with demonstrated competence in preaching.

Despite these doubtful and spurious attributions, there are some certain cases of preachers who wrote plays or parts of plays. For example, Friar Thomas Bynham was paid for "composing" the banns of Beverley's Corpus Christi play in 1423.[1] Such mendicant friars almost always preached and, among the laity at least, they were thought to be quite good at it. For the early Tudor period there are many more examples of preacher-playwrights. John Bale (1495–1563) and Thomas Watson (ca. 1557–92) practiced both professions. And there is one preacher-playwright who memorably illustrated a fate of less accomplished writers. In a 1537 letter to Thomas Cromwell he wrote:

> The Lord make you the instrument of my help, Lord Cromwell, that I may have free liberty to preach the truth. . . . The most part of the priests of Suffolk will not receive me into their churches to preach, but have disdained me ever since I made a play against the Pope's counselors, Error, Colle Clogger of Conscience, and Incredulity. . . . Aid me for Christ's sake, that I may preach Christ. Thomas Wylley of Yoxforthe, vicar, fatherless and forsaken. (*Calendar* 12, pt. 1:244)

At best, the evidence indicates that some preachers wrote some plays in medieval England. We cannot say that preachers or even clerks were the principal authors of the cycle plays, saints' plays, or the early morality plays.

What the evidence does suggest is that English plays were sometimes produced, directed, and performed by the clergy, some of whom were probably preachers. The early Chester banns (1539–40), for example, speak of "a play sett forth by the clergye / in honour of the fest" of Corpus Christi (Clopper, 240, 979; see also 3–4, 31ff., 435–36). John of Malvern's continuation of the *Polychronicon* records clerical productions in London in 1384 and 1391 (Higden, 47, 257). And A. G. Little and R. C. Easterling found documents concerning a fifteenth century Dominican production in Exeter (9). Clerks also probably helped when parish guilds produced plays because these confraternities often had clerical as well as lay members and all had chaplains. In fifteenth and sixteenth century Lincoln, for example, the St. Anne's Guild chaplain, who very probably preached, was paid to produce their pageants (Kahrl, 33ff.). And it is likely that the Beverley guild sponsored a 1467 performance where clerks shared the production of a "viciouse" pageant in a Paternoster play (Leach 142–43). But the fact that clergy may have participated regularly in the production of late medieval religious drama casts little light on the actual relationship between medieval English preaching and plays. At best it suggests that men who may have been preachers helped to stage plays whose authors' occupations and backgrounds are not, in general, known to us.

We must, then, be cautious about concluding that preaching influenced the drama. In view of our limited knowledge about the relationship between preachers, sermons, and plays we should be reluctant to declare that the plays were written by preachers. Furthermore, we should be quite certain about our historical assumptions when asserting that preaching technique influenced playwriting. Nevertheless, one can be too circumspect; for sermons were a dominant element in medieval literature and culture, and their content and style could readily be employed by men who were never licensed to preach.

Why, then, would medieval playwrights—especially those who did not regularly preach and for whom "sermonic" expression would not, presumably, be an accustomed style of discourse—why would such men employ sermon elements in their plays? Some early twentieth century critics who held much medieval drama in low esteem regarded dramatized preaching as inelegant, heavy-handed didacticism and dismissed such sermonizing as bad judgment on the playwright's part (see, for example, Rossiter, 89, and Browne, 8). Yet what we know of the role of sermons in English social life suggests this was not the view in the later Middle Ages. It appears instead that Tudor England, at least, regarded preaching much like the drama, as popular entertainment. Our appreciation of this fact is clouded because preaching historians like G. R. Owst emphasize reports of rowdy, misbehaving sermon audiences (*Preaching*, 167–221, *et passim*). But in truth most of this evidence dates from the seventeenth century and is often based on churchwardens' presentments, that is, on documents which are merely accusations, not proven facts or findings.

To balance such disdainful views we should note that the Elizabethan John Mannyngham kept a diary in which he faithfully recorded and evaluated the sermons he attended, as many as two a day. His contemporary, Lady Margaret Hoby traveled from Yorkshire to London just to hear Stephen Edgerton preach (Herr, 21). And in 1543 a large crowd gathered in the rain in Greyfriars churchyard, Exeter, to hear Bishop Latimer preach—even though he suffered from a nosebleed (Little and Easterling, 27). Some sixteenth century evidence, at least, argues that the English loved to hear sermons.

We also know that sermons were considered appropriate for ceremonial observances and civic entertainment. Latin sermons for the clergy and English sermons for the laity were regularly given at episcopal visitations and general convocations. An early fourteenth century account of a Palm Sunday procession at Wells Cathedral tells us that the ceremony stopped at midpoint to hear a sermon (C. Brown, 105–10, 116–17). And fifteenth and sixteenth century civic records at York show that a commissioned sermon regularly climaxed their festive Corpus Christi observances (Johnston and Rogerson, vol. 1: 102, 188, 203, 207, 259, 265, 279; these entries are for the years 1468, 1501, 1505, 1507, 1535, 1538, 1542).

Sermons could also accompany dramatic performances or other entertainment. Boy Bishop ceremonies usually included a comic sermon. (Erasmus, for example, wrote one: "A Sermon for the Chylde Jesus," 1536.) Royal progresses, where tilts, masques, and interludes were common fare, frequently included sermons as well. And an entry in the diary of Henry Machyn for 1562 describes a guild entertainment that combined preaching and playing:

> the x day of August was Barbur-surgyons' fest, and they captd ther communion at sant Alphes at Crepull-gatt, and master Recherdsun dyd pryche, the Skott; ther was good syngyng; and after to ther halle to dener, and after dener a play. (Machyn, 290)

More work must be done to determine whether this view of preaching as a natural and suitable dimension of royal and civic entertainment prevailed before, as well as after, the English Reformation. But the available evidence suggests that in Tudor times, at least, preaching was not the intrusive, sobering element that modern historians sometimes imagine. Indeed, this rather enthusiastic attitude toward preaching suggests that recognizable sermon elements would not conflict with and might in some cases actually enhance the recreational or festive motives, as well as the didactic goals, of late medieval dramatic entertainment.

Lacking solid historical justification, and also wary of making unfounded assumptions, we must resort to the play texts and the preaching materials themselves to learn more about how sermons influenced the plays. The first premise to examine must be the frequent claim that popular preaching lent medieval drama themes and topics already familiar to audiences. Pursuing this line of argument, Sister Mary Philippa Coogan found that the vernacular sermon collection, *Jacobs Well*, was a major source for *Mankind*. But, as she notes in passing, these sermons in turn rest on earlier traditions that include devotional literature, penitential manuals, and the thirteenth century sermon collection, *Legenda Aurea*. (See Brandeis's edition of *Jacob's Well*, ix, on the sources of the work.) A sources and analogues approach like Sr. Philippa's places too much emphasis on single sermon texts and does not sufficiently acknowledge the cumulative and largely "unoriginal" nature of most medieval sermons.

The medieval preacher rarely set out to compose an "original" sermon.[2] Instead he worked within a unique medieval convention, known as the university or thematic sermon, which was well defined by the fourteenth century. The preacher began with a "theme," usually a short scriptural passage from the day's lection or liturgy, which served as the topic of his sermon. After stating the theme he sometimes introduced a "protheme" or short moralizing digression related to the sermon's topic. Then he prayed, usually seeking divine aid in his preaching. Then he "divided" his theme, most often into three parts. Each part or division was then "proven" or "dilated." This proof made up the bulk of a sermon, and sermon manual (*ars praedicandi*) writers went to great length to define and codify the methods available for proving divisions. One of the most popular was the citation of confirming "authorities," usually short passages taken from scripture, the Fathers, or classical authors. Authorities, like all other sorts of sermon proof, were the means through which the preacher made his instructive points. A brief passage from a fifteenth century sermon manual, spuriously attributed to Thomas Aquinas, demonstrates their approach:

> . . . the theme is the prelocution, made for the proof of the terms of preaching present in the theme, through authoritative passages of the Bible and learned men, and by bringing in the authorities of philosophy through some simile, moral point, proverb, or natural truth. (Pseudo-Aquinas, 74)

Most preachers, then, like the author of *Jacob's Well*, methodically and unabashedly assembled sermons from available component parts. This does not mean that preaching was a slavish, workmanlike undertaking; on the contrary, it required much rhetorical creativity. But given what we know of sermon theory and practice, a hunt for drama sources and analogues in the matter of sermons is frequently simply an interesting route to a different literary destination.

Preaching is better thought of as "sacred oratory." Preachers took the received truth of Scripture and the Fathers and delivered it to congregations in effective, helpful ways. Sermons were far less important to medieval culture as sources of literary invention or topoi than as transmitters and preservers of traditional scriptural truths and exegetical interpretations. Sermons were foremost instructional and hortative rhetoric and this point was constantly reiterated by the manual writers. In the fifteenth century, Martin of Cordova summarized their view:

> a sermon is an instructive speech, uttered by a preacher, which tells the faithful what they should believe, do, avoid, fear, and hope for. (Martin de Cordova, 330)

When we look at the ways in which medieval drama is also instructional and hortative, we can begin to understand the real influence of medieval preaching. This is what Wickham and Prosser are suggesting in the quotations that opened this essay. The difficulty has been that few critics have tried to document these insights or pursue them to meaningful conclusions.

Instruction appears to have been a conscious motive of the cycle playwrights. Nothing written by these unknown authors survives to confirm their views, but the late fourteenth century Paternoster Guild in York resolved to produce their Creed Play in part because it was edifying:

> First, as to the cause of the founding of said fraternity, it should be known that after a certain play on the usefulness of the Lord's Prayer was composed,

in which play, indeed, many vices and sins are reproved and virtues commended, and was played in the city of York, it had such and so great an appeal
that very many said: "Would that this play were established in this city for
the salvation of souls and the solace of the citizens and neighbours." Where-
fore, the whole and complete cause of the foundation and association of the
brothers of the same fraternity was that that play be managed at future times
for the health and reformation of the souls, both of those in charge of that
play and of those hearing it. And thus, the principal work of the said fraternity is that the play should be managed to the greater glory of God, the de-
viser of the said prayer, and for the reproving of sins and vices. . . . (Johnston
and Rogerson, vol. 2: 693)

Others agreed that the plays offered valuable lessons. The Franciscan William Melton, while preaching in York in 1426, also praised the educational and devotional value of the Corpus Christi plays; though he urged
the city to reschedule the performances so that fewer playgoers missed
Corpus Christi mass (Johnston and Rogerson, vol. 2: 728–29).

But simple instructive motives would not require the playwrights to
borrow preaching or even argumentative techniques. Medieval picture
books, wall paintings, and much devotional literature accomplished didactic ends without resorting to the persuasive, demonstrative devices
found in sermons. So, if we are to speak of preaching influence, we need
to identify instances in the plays where preaching or preaching methods are actually employed to carry the dramatic action or to persuade an
audience.

Such examples are quite easy to find. Sometimes it is clear that the
playwrights have preaching so much in mind that they put sermons into
the mouths of their characters. Sometimes characters have qualities that
identify them as preachers. Of all the medieval plays, *Mankind* is probably the best known example of a play that shows preaching influence. The
play opens with a long audience address by Mercy, who acts much like
a preacher. The speech is written in a fulsome, aureate style that suggests
high oratorical seriousness and that contrasts vividly with the plain style
of the devils and much of Mankind's speech. Myscheffe interrupts at line
45 with some deadly mimicry of both the style and its content and offers
assurance that Mercy is preaching to the audience:

> I beseche yow hertyly, leue yowr calcacyon.
> Leue yowr chaffe, leue yowr corn, leue yowr dalyacyon.
> Yowr wytt ys lytyll, yowr hede ys mekyll, ye are
> full of predycacyon.
>
> (Eccles, 155; ll. 45–47)

Some earlier critics concluded that such effective and repeated mockery
at the hands of Myscheffe meant the playwright set little store by the theology of priests like Mercy (Adams, 304 n1; Smart, 308–309). But this po-

sition cannot easily be justified. The message of the play is surely exactly
what Mercy tells us it is:

> O Ye souerens þat sytt and ye brothern þat stonde ryght
> wppe,
> Pryke not yowr felycytes in thyngys transytorye.
> Beholde not þe erth, but lyfte yowr ey wppe.
> (Eccles, 155; ll. 29–31)

And whatever parody we may enjoy at Mercy's expense, he nonetheless
remains the serious and essential center of the play. He is the preacher/
priest who lectures the audience and who is mocked by Myscheffe and
his fellows; and he is also the personified "daughter" of God who enables
Man's salvation. He explains this in his opening speech to the audience:

> Mercy ys my name, þat mornyth for yowr offence.
> . . . .
> I prey Gode at yowr most nede þat mercy be yowr defendawnte.
> (Eccles, 154; ll. 18, 24)

Not even Mercy's well-satirized aureate style is really dismissed as silly.
Mankind uses it with great seriousness when he is looking to his salvation:

> O Mercy, my suavius solas and synguler recreatory,
>   My predilecte spesyall, ye are worthy to hawe my lowe;
> For wythowte deserte and menys supplicatorie
>   Ye be compacient to my inexcusabyll reprowe.
> (Eccles, 183; ll. 871–74)

And Mercy concludes the play with several stanzas of triumphant aurea-
tion, for example:

> Mankend ys wrechyd, he hath sufficyent prowe.
>   Therefore God grant yow all per suam misericordiam
> þat ye may be pleyferys wyth þe angellys abowe
>   And hawe to your porcyon vitam eternam. Amen!
> (Eccles, 184; ll. 911–14)

   This is a boisterous and rich play, both in diction and in characterization, and it is doubtful that many effective fifteenth century preachers
really sounded or acted just like Mercy. Still, within the dramatic hyperbole there is a readily recognizable preacher, one who draws overzeal-
ously on some verbal tools of his trade. We know he is a preacher because,
despite the aureate polysyllables, he talks like one. Compare the opening
passage from John Fisher's early sixteenth century Good Friday sermon
to the speech with which Mercy begins Mankind. Fisher begins:

> The Prophet Ezechyell telleth that hee sawe a booke spread before him, the
> which was written both within and without, & there was written also in it,

Lamentationes, Carmen, et vae, that is to say, lamentation, songe, and woe. . . . this booke to our purpose may bee taken vnto vs, the Crucifixe, the which doubtlesse is a merueylous booke, as wee sall shewe heereafter. In the which if wee doe exercise our admiration, wee shall come to wonderfull knowledge. (Fisher, 388)

Mercy's speech in *Mankind* is filled with similar preaching devices. First there is the clear establishment of rapport with the audience: line 1 uses the second person plural pronoun "owr" and it is repeated often throughout the passage. Much like Fisher's second paragraph above, Mercy next gives the burden of his instruction (and the play's): to live well and to look to one's salvation. Mercy quotes scripture, "Se how þe hede þe members dayly do mangyfye" (Eccles, 155; l. 32; quoting Corinthians 12. 27 and Colossians 1. 18) and immediately explicates the passage:

> Who ys þe hede forsoth I xall yow certyfye:
> I mene Owr Sauyowr, þat was lykynnyde to a lambe;
> Ande hys sayntys be þe members þat dayly he doth satysfye.
> (Eccles, 155; ll. 33–35)

The only missing elements are a thematic division with proof (which Fisher develops at length later in his sermon) and a Latin quotation that is subsequently "Englished." Myscheffe knows this, too, and supplies comic versions in a rowdy interruption:

> Ande ye sayde þe corn xulde be sauyde and þe chaff xulde
>   be feryde,
> ˴ Ande he prouyth nay, as yt schewth be þis werse:
>   "Corn seruit bredibus, chaffe horsibus, straw
>   fyrybusque."
> Thys ys as moche to say, to yowr leude wndyrstondynge,
> As þe corn xall serue to brede at þe nexte bakynge.
> (Eccles, 155; ll. 55–59)

Although Mercy has a dramatic role in *Mankind*, every appearance also introduces a preacherly presence. The character is not a relentless didact; he is applying the moral of the story for Mankind and for the audience in ways that a preacher would use.[3]

Other medieval moralities are not so subtle in the use of preachers or sermon devices; but most do employ them. For example, during the battle in *Castle of Perseverance* each virtue methodically confirms her speech with a scriptural or liturgical authority. Part of Paciencia's speech demonstrates the method:

> Fro þi dowte Crist me schelde
>   þis iche day, and al mankynde!
> þou wrecchyd Wrethe, wood and wylde,
>   Pacyens schal þe schende.

> Quia ira viri justicam Dei non operatur. [James 1.20]
> For Marys sone, meke and mylde,
>   Rent þe up, rote and rynde,
> Whanne he stod meker þanne a chylde
>   And lete boyes hum betyn and bynde,
> þerfor, wrecche, be stylle.
>   [Eccles, 66; II. 2121-2129]

Many examples of sermon influence in the plays, like the one in *Castle* just cited, actually interrupt the flow of dramatic action. The authors, it seems, will not allow the stories to play themselves out. Instead, they have characters stop to explain the moral import of events or even to prove or confirm points through the citation of proverbs or of scriptural or patristic authorities, just as "Pseudo-Aquinas" and Martin of Cordova have instructed preachers to do.

While the methods used in the plays to point out morals are often those of sermons, it is more significant that the very motivation to control characterization and flow of action also stems from preaching theory and practice. Several *artes praedicandi* describe how preachers controlled narrative to point out morals. Their techniques are familiar to modern literary critics; what is important to understand is that in the Middle Ages *only* the *artes praedicandi*, the preaching handbooks, articulated and justified these methods. Later medieval playwrights who used them thus found both the theory and practice of the methods well developed in the preaching tradition. Here are three examples of the handbooks' instructions on controlling narrative flow for instructive, sermonic purposes.

The fifteenth-century East Anglian sermon handbook author Simon Alcock instructed preachers to set forth the purpose or end of their sermon stories before and during their telling:

> But for the most part, when a story, either long or short, or a scriptural authority, is used in preaching, make certain that some prayer or conclusion precedes which is confirmed, illustrated, or proven in the story or authority that follows. (Alcock, 212)

Dealing with narrative exposition, the thirteenth-century manual writer William of Auvergne cautioned that preachers should carefully balance tales of vice with examples of virtuous conduct:

> It is necessary that contraries be considered when preaching the word of God. . . . You have begun to speak of pride. In consequence humility, its opposite, ought to be discussed. And so, in turn, should be the opposite of the other vices that follow, as, for example, if you preach about jealousy and hate you ought not omit speaking of the virtue of charity which is the contrary of jealousy. . . . because contraries when juxtaposed shine forth more beautifully. (William of Auvergne, 198)

The fifteenth-century "Pseudo-Aquinas" emphasized the importance of voice modulation to convey moral points:

> If the sermon delivered is from some authority of the Bible or the Saints, he must preach vigorously in order that his utterance may leave his mouth vigorously and abide in the listener's heart. Hence the preacher must sometimes try to speak with wonder, as at the passage: "I was not in safety, neither had I rest." . . . At times with irony and derision, as at: "Dost thou still retain thine integrity? Curse God and die." . . . At times with impatience and indignation, as at: "Let us make a captain." . . . Often with hate and turning away of the face, as at: "Depart from me, ye cursed". . . .
>
> (Pseudo-Aquinas, 73–74)

Preachers who followed such advice would frame and then freely interrupt their narratives with instructive tones or with "proofs" and explanations about their lessons—just as Patience and her sister virtues do in the siege of the Castle of Perseverance.

But the modulation of the preacher's tone of voice described in the passage from "Pseudo-Aquinas" cited above was much more difficult for the playwright to replicate than was the interplay between narrative and moral application discussed in Simon Alcock and William of Auvergne. Standing in the pulpit or preaching cross in full view of his audience, the preacher could reinforce the instructive effect of his words through tones of irony, censure, and praise. A playwright who desired to instruct could rarely speak in his own voice for he had no access to pulpit gesture or voice modulation and only occasionally, generally between episodes, could he put his own persona on the stage in the form of an expositor. So the playwrights found another means to make their interpretive voices heard: they occasionally interjected a preacher's "sermonic" voice in the speeches of their characters. Sometimes, as in Paciencia's and the other virtues' lines in *Castle*, the preacher's voice is well suited to the character and situation. But at other times, when carrying the message of the sermonic voice, the characters actually moralize against their own best interests and out of keeping with their natures. Thus *Castle*'s Bad Angel, having won Man's soul, begins his victory speech to Anima not with rejoicing, as the occasion requires, but with a lament:

> Za, why woldyst þou be coueytous
> And drawe þe agayn to synne?
> (*Castle*, Eccles ed., ll. 3073–74)

And later in this speech Bad Angel actually admits that "þi Good Aungyl tawth þe . . . Alwey to þe beste" (*Castle*, Eccles ed., ll. 3103–7).

Thus we see that medieval morality playwrights worked under some different constraints and assumptions than did classical or modern dramatists. Generally, the larger outlines of medieval English dramatic plots and characterizations were fixed by tradition, scripture, and patristic commentary: they showed the fall, repentance, and salvation of man who is accosted by the temptations of wholly evil vices and villains. To these conventions of plot and characterization the morality playwrights added a further constraint, one they shared with preachers who followed the instructions of handbook authors like Alcock, William of Auvergne, and "Pseudo-Aquinas." They took steps to avoid having the vices or man in sin address their audiences in uncensored and uncensured voices. Rather than the direct dramatic discourse typical of modern and classical dramas, the evil morality characters speak and act in a form of "indirect discourse" that is referenced, sometimes subjectively and other times overtly, to the authors' instructive, demonstrative or hortative objectives. It is the same device, used with the same motive, that preaching manuals from the twelfth to the sixteenth centuries instructed preachers to use in their stories and exempla.

Of all the medieval English religious dramas, the moralities seem the most sermonic in style and use of materials. They take as a common theme the topic of penitence; and, albeit within a narrow allegorical convention, they freely invent or borrow plot and incident to motivate their audience to good living and repentance. In contrast, the English cycle plays gave less latitude in shaping their plots. Indeed, their very purpose was to portray a set of events that was fixed by scripture and patristic commentary.

Despite this important conceptual difference, there are still many similarities between the technique of the medieval sermon and that of the cycle plays. Surely the expositors, doctors, and other characters who tell the audience what they are about to see and what they can expect to learn have instructive and hortative ends in mind. Sometimes characters, like Christ on the Cross in the York Passion play (Smith, 357, 363, 365), actually preach, or at least invoke the audience's attention and then cite, confirm,and prove scripture to make a moral point. The cycle plays are also lengthy, complex dramas made up of many linked shorter plays. So there may be much to learn about the relationship between sermons and drama if we look for resemblances between the play cycles and collections of *sermones temporale*, that is, sermon cycles that were keyed to the liturgical year. There is a great deal of untilled land here; but I wish at this time to focus instead on a simpler, more essential sermon technique: the use of rhetorical, argumentative structure at the expense of logical consistency in some late medieval sermons and cycle plays. That is, I want to consider several instances where both medieval playwrights and preachers focus on their instructive goals and in so doing use methods that distort characterization and flow of argument or plot to achieve their instructive, sermonic ends.

The cycle playwright's plot and moral application were sufficiently prescribed by scripture and tradition that it can be difficult to identify his handiwork beyond the level of diction and versification. When we find characterizations or stories, such as Noah's comically shrewish wife or the tale of Mak the shepherd, which are not dictated by sources and traditions, modern critics give them an enormous amount of critical attention, seizing a rare glimpse of the free hand of the playwright. I, too, will consider a "sourceless" incident, though it is a less studied one, that occurs in several of the Passion plays and that shows an important rhetorical aspect of cycle play technique. The incident is a variation on the *stabat mater* theme and consists simply of Mary's rebuke of Christ at the Crucifixion. In the sermons we will observe anomalous voices and attitudes which fulfill sermonic, instructive ends reaching well beyond the particular Passion scene. In the contemporary plays we can see the same devices used for similar instructive objectives.

There is no scriptural authority for any speech by Mary at the Crucifixion. Indeed, of the Evangelists, only John notes that Mary was even there (John 19. 25–27). This silence so impressed one fifteenth century English writer, the author of the *Southern Passion*, that he tells us, "We ne ffyndeþ nouȝt ywrite þ . at oure lady in al hure sore/spak out" (Brown, 55, ll. 1515–16). Nevertheless, commentators and devotional writers developed a considerable tradition about Mary at Calvary and by the thirteenth century the *planctus mariae* was firmly established in liturgy, liturgical drama, and lyric. Most Marian laments suggest that the Virgin was overcome with grief at Calvary, that the dimension of her grief increased Christ's own suffering, that she prayed to die, and that her grief was a fulfillment of Simeon's prophecy, "Yea, a sword shall pierce through thy own soul also . . ." (Luke 2.35). Many of these motifs appear in medieval sermons and English Passion plays. A few, notably the N-Town and Towneley plays, also show Mary reproaching Jesus. Here is the rebuke of the N-Town Mary:

> O my sone my sone • my derlyng dere
> what haue I defendyd þe
> þou hast spoke to alle þo • þat ben here
> and not o word þou spekyst to me.
>
> To þe jewys þou art ful kende
> þou has for-gove al here mysdede
> and þe thef • thou hast in mende
> for onys haskyng mercy • hefne is his mede.
>
> A my sovereyn lord why whylt þou not speke
> to me þat am þi modyr • in peyn for þi wrong
> . . . .   (Block, 300)

While these Marys never descend to coarse insults, neither are they the paragons of humility and compliance that we expect to find at the Crucifixion. The rhetorical function of this characterization in two sermons contemporary to the cycle plays may help to explain the playwrights' motives for including this unusual Marian attitude.

A fifteenth-century Passion sermon in Bodley MS 806 takes the scripture "Christus passus est pro nobis peccatis" as its theme. The quotation is explained,

> these words of peter accorden for this day & been thus muche
> for to seye Christ hath suffurd for us / the ungilti for
> the gilti the lord for his seruaunt / the loomb for the
> flook / the kynge for is rewme the spouse for is wyif. . . .
>
> (fol. 51ᵛ)

The theme is then divided:

> & therefore my bretheren the thingis in this mater we
>   schulde take heede unto
> Oon is the cause of is suffrynge . the manere of is suffrynges
>   & the wourdes that weren wrou3t in his suffrynges
>
> (fol. 51ᵛ)

In the second division, concerning the "manner" of Christ's suffering, the preacher offers a synoptic account of the Passion with frequent stops for moral application. At the end of this division he narrates Christ's seven words and the account of Mary's rebuke occurs here:

> [Christ said] "Behold, woman, thy son": a how sorowful was this to owre lady
> to his seruaunte to be here kepere insted of here derwothe sone, the suget
> instede of the lorde, that louely loom wit ou3ten synne, what wonder was
> 3if here sorowe was grette, seyinge so dispituesly the flowre of hir virginite
> so hithe hange on a cros. . . . (fol. 54)

This sermon intends an affective account of Christ's agony, and since the focus is sorrow and suffering, Mary's own grief gets considerable attention. But when the preacher considers Mary's role at the Crucifixion he seems to have put aside the usual commentaries and sources. He also seems to find Christ's words to Mary, "Behold woman thy son," very puzzling. While others might believe Christ refers to himself, the Bodley 806 preacher interprets the words differently. He believes they refer to John who, he knows, is not Mary's son. So he decides this is the very point: Christ's words, factually in error, redoubled Mary's grief and fulfilled Simeon's prophecy. Mary's anguish further increased because John, once a servant, is to take Christ's place as Mary's master. And this, for the Bodley 806 preacher, demonstrates or "proves" the expanded theme with which he began the sermon: "the ungilti for the gilti the lord for his seruant." In short, the preacher did not want to tell us simply that Mary was grieved at Calvary, he also wanted to use Mary's grief to "prove" the efficacy and relevance of his interpretation of the sermon's theme. While the relevance of this theme to Christ's sacrifice may be apparent, the application to Mary and John is less felicitous. Nonetheless, it is clear that the preacher's unusual interpretation of Christ's words and his use of Mary's rebuke derived from hortative and demonstrative sermonic motives. That is, he used the situation, especially Mary's rebuke, to make his point.

The fifteenth century preacher Hugo Legat is more subtle in his portrayal of Mary's rebuke at the cross; but, in fact, she is more reproachful:

> Swete child, quod sche, "knowe þi modur & ha ruthe & compassiun vpon hire, & here hure preyer; for hite besemith," sche seith, "a lovinge child to knowe & to comford is modur, þat is desolat & for-sakin". . . ."3e, alas!" sche seith, "where is þat ilke ioye bi-come þat i hadde whanne I lullid þe in þi cradil, whanne i fedde þe with mi pappis, whanne i hocklid þe on mi kne & kissid þi lippus & ti mouth as a kinde modur schulde? Al þis is a-goon & i am laft alone as a woful womman & a modur for-sakyn." (Grisdale, 12)

Legat's treatment is surprising since he actually employs this Crucifixion narrative to establish Mary's meekness in suffering and her consequent fitness as an intercessor with Christ. That she was brought to the remonstrations, for Legat, helps prove his point about her compliant suffering at the Crucifixion. He portrays Mary as a good, compelling example of his Passion sermon theme, "accipiant repromissionem vocati" (Heb. 9.15).

The Towneley playwright had similar demonstrative and hortative motives in his portrayal of Mary at the Cross, for this "Crucifixion" uses the motif of reproach as an organizing theme. Pilate opens the pageant reproaching the audience for its restlessness (England, pp. 258–59, ll. 1–28). The deliberate, cruel, slow scene with the torturers and a silent Christ provokes in the spectators an obvious mood of reproach toward the torturers (England, pp. 265–67, ll. 233–94). A lengthy following speech by Mary begins with an affective account of Christ's wounds, continues with a descriptive lament and itself evolves into a reproach:

> A son, thynk on my wo!
> whi will thou fare me fro?
> On mold is noman mo
> That may my myrthes amende.
>   (p. 269, ll. 369–72)

These lines set forth what is to become a repeated rebuke, "Whi will thou fare me fro?" ("How can you leave me?"), as a virtual refrain for the rest of Mary's complaint (see p. 270, l. 391; p. 271, ll. 413, 424). John interrupts Mary four times but then abandons his effort to console her (p. 271, ll. 416–17). Finally, after all her laments, Christ begins stanza 70 with a rebuke of his own, "My moder mylde, thou chaunge thi chere! / Sease of thi sorow and sighyng sere . . . " (p. 272, ll. 447–48). And in the next stanza he assumes an instructive voice, "the fyrst cause, moder, of my

commyng / Was for mankynde myscarying . . . " (p. 272, ll. 458–59).
These lines contain the fullest rebuke of all, in effect, "stop grieving,
Mary, I was born to you to save mankind, not to comfort you." The last
line in Christ's speech, "Now thryst I, wonder sore" (p. 273, l. 479) re-
turns the play to the rapid enactment of the well-known events in the
Passion.

While the Towneley playwright set no scriptural theme to "prove,"
as a preacher would have, his concentration on reproaches at the Passion
suggests that he had a rhetorical, argumentative design in mind. The rich,
poetic, and very popular affective tradition of late medieval Passion meditations encouraged lingering on Christ's physical suffering. However,
the playwright portrayed much of the agony not through Christ's speech
or action, but by provoking audience reaction to the tormenters. He effectively vented this pent-up anger and gave good expression to the poetic
tradition through Mary's lengthy, inconsolable grieving. Earlier, however, Jesus opened the scene exhorting us, the audience, not to grieve for
him but to lament instead for our own sins and for the fact that we are
so sinful that we need redeeming; in the end He rebukes Mary (and us)
for her empathy and finally us, once again, for our sins. Thus Mary serves
as the exemplar of horrified, affective fascination with the Crucifixion
and also as the rhetorical pivot of the play's argument. By giving her grief
full play and then rebuking it, the playwright uses Mary to focus instruc-
tively on the larger issue, the salvation history, that is the overriding
theme of the whole cycle. This is not adaptation of sources or analogues;
nor is it doctrinal exposition. Mary's rebuke is a strategy allowing the
Towneley playwright to communicate the redemptive message of the
Passion while at the same time offering the traditional, affective sequence
of events and emotions. It is the same practical, demonstrative function,
albeit with different ends, that Hugo Legat and the Bodley 806 preacher
found for their Marian rebukes.

Each author has written what would conventionally be seen as anomalous speeches for the Virgin Mary at the Crucifixion because both
preachers and playwright wanted to focus hearers' attention on bigger
points, if you will, on the "themes" of their works. The Towneley playwright stresses our salvation; Legat focuses on Mary's compliance despite her suffering at the Crucifixion ("accipiant repromissionem vocati");
the Bodley preacher fixes on the tragic irony of the Lord's sacrifice for
his servant. The technique is firmly grounded in preaching theory and
practice, where, as we have seen in a passage cited earlier, "Pseudo-
Aquinas" explains "the theme is the prelocution, made for the proof of
the terms of preaching present in the theme . . . through some simile,
moral point, proverb, or natural truth" (74).

This brief analysis of Mary's speeches at the Cross explores just one
of the many ways that sermon design and technique can be seen in the
English plays. It should, however, demonstrate that understanding more

about the incidence of rhetorical strategy, sermonic voice, preacherly personifications, and other dimensions of popular medieval sermons can greatly enhance our understanding of medieval English drama.

But just as we have seen that the historical evidence about preachers and their putative identities as playwrights is vexed with too many easily drawn inferences and far too little hard data, so the study of sermons as models for the plays rather than as graveyards for sources and analogues is in need of much serious supporting research.

First, the practice of medieval preaching needs more study. Who were the preachers and what was their background? What was the preaching like that audiences of medieval drama commonly heard and would therefore respond to when its methods and commonplaces were employed in the plays? Sound answers to these questions will require much study because most surviving sermon texts are either anonymous or have fanciful, disputed, or multiple authors assigned to them. So, for the most part, we have to study the preachers and their texts as a general class of authors, who, much like the dramatists, are unknown to us in most of their particulars.

We also know very little about what medieval popular preaching was like. Few helpful critiques or eyewitness accounts have been found. And the plentiful works on preaching theory, the *artes praedicandi*, where we might expect to find insights into the practice of the art, are difficult to relate to the sermon texts themselves. In recent discussions, some scholars have suggested that the *artes* preserve a learned style that was never actually employed in popular sermons. They argue that surviving handbooks show that, in the later Middle Ages, neither the old manuals nor the newer, derivative ones delivered easy solutions to the preacher's perennial need for ready sermon material. Instead *florilegia* and sermon collections provided the inspiration, or the actual sermon, for the less accomplished preacher. This may have been true; but there are also many fifteenth century sermons, seemingly written for popular audiences, that follow the organization of the thematic sermon as put forth in the *artes praedicandi*. In some, perhaps not yet understood manner, the *artes* must have aided in the translation of the university sermon style to the late medieval popular pulpit.

We should also keep in mind that the *artes* may tell us more about medieval preaching than their somewhat unpromising appearance first suggests. The manuals are remarkably uniform in their organization, vocabulary, and in the general concepts about sermon writing that they purvey. Clearly, by the later Middle Ages a sermon handbook writer worked in a rigid framework. However, some, like the late fifteenth century German Johann Ulrich Surgant, wrote on "modern" topics such as how to preach to the laity in the vernacular (ff. Mvii-viii). Others, like Simon Alcock in his relentless march through no fewer than fifty ways to expand a sermon theme, buried insights into medieval narrative technique like the passage on *historia* cited above. Finally, because the manuals were so formulaic, we would do well to read them with constant reference to contemporary sermons and also to look at them for what they *assume* about preaching, as well as for what they actually say on the subject. It is probable that a medieval preacher did not need to have some concepts (for example, explanations about acceptable demonstration and proof within the confines of Christian sacred oratory) articulated in ways that are now necessary for modern readers.

Drama historians and critics who wish to work on ideas related to preaching will discover that little work has been done on preaching. Not only has Owst long been regarded as the authority on the relationship between sermons and plays, his other book, *Preaching in Medieval England*, has served just as long as the definitive work on English preaching. And it is no easier to use than *Literature and Pulpit*. Interest in sermons is growing and it is to be hoped that the regular scheduling of a biennial conference on sermon studies at Oxford University (begun in 1976) will foster better progress in the work of establishing a reliable and representative corpus of printed preaching texts.

Meanwhile, those wishing to work with available editions or with the manuscripts themselves should take a few, perhaps obvious, precautions. First, the language in which a late medieval sermon of English provenance is recorded often bears no relationship to the language in which it was preached. Popular sermons preserved in Latin, sometimes with a few English interpolations, were probably preached in English. The Latin version may have been prepared as a prompt text by a cleric who preferred to write in Latin and who included the English passages because the exact vernacular words were essential to his argument or to his sermon's "poetry." Regardless of the text's language, if the sermon audience is clearly made up of laymen, by the fifteenth century it is almost certain that the preacher spoke in English. This means that all sermons of English provenance, regardless of language, ought to be considered by drama critics interested in sermon influence.

Furthermore, full, seemingly "live" sermon texts in any language are probably the result of transcriptions and include revisions and embellishments made by the preacher, secretary, or follower after the sermon was preached. It is unlikely that a preacher preparing his Sunday sermon would choose to read a polished text rather than an outline. Other complete sermons may never have been preached by their authors at all. For example, the fifteenth century author of the *Speculum Sacerdotale* "wrote" his sermon collection ("I have here disposyd and writen") to help fellow preachers (Weatherly, 3); he gives no evidence that he used the sermons himself and the text contains many expository "bridges" between sermons. We thus find ourselves in the discomfiting position of having to assume, when confronted with a complete sermon text, that it was probably never preached as we possess it. This means that "close readings" of sermon texts can be risky. Students of medieval preaching learn to live with this paradox as, increasingly, do medieval drama scholars working with play texts. In both cases, we should heed the paradox and be careful when drawing inferences based on textual evidence.

Care should also be taken that the sermons under study are addressed to an appropriate audience on an appropriate occasion. Unless a playwright seems to have had a clerical audience clearly in mind, synodal sermons or others prepared for audiences of religious may be of limited use in studying transfers of sermon technique to popular plays. Medieval preachers also consciously classified their works according to occasion and time in the liturgical year. No harm may be done when a marriage sermon, a funeral sermon, or a St. Clement's Day sermon is used to help understand the use of sermon technique in a play about the Nativity; but preaching materials, and probably methods, considered suitable for one occasion may not be clearly applicable to another. We are on surer ground when, for example, we compare Good Friday or Passion Week sermons to plays about the Crucifixion.

In a similarly cautious manner, sermons of English provenance that are roughly contemporary to the plays should be used for comparison. The later Middle Ages was a time of complex religious controversy and the sermon was an adaptive pastoral tool. Thirteenth century sermons simply do not assume the same audience or the same instructive and rhetorical responsibilities as those from the fifteenth century. Fifteenth-century drama texts may warrant comparison with the *Speculum Sacerdotale* or *Jacobs Well*. The late Chester texts dating into the seventeenth century may not. The same caveat holds against using late medieval continental sermons to elucidate English plays. Although, conversely, some sermon collections, manuals, and aids from earlier eras and from other European cultures were frequently copied or printed in England in later periods. Such documents should be studied for they are important traditional sources; but they must always be interpreted with contemporary, indigenous materials close to hand.

With all these rules and warnings to observe, it is clear that sermon/drama study requires a challenging combination of literary critic and textual scholar. But the field is an important one; for if we seek a true literary context for the medieval English plays, it is incumbent on us to look at contemporary sermons. During the two or more centuries in which this drama flourished, scores of sermons were probably preached each day in England. By the thirteenth century the mendicant friars had established the idea that every crossroad was a suitable pulpit. Preaching was ubiquitous and, unlike poetry or patristic works, it was freely available to all. While books were very expensive and many people could not read, popular sermons cost nothing to hear and were delivered in the vernacular. And a great many were written expressly for the same working and merchant classes that patronized the medieval drama. Sermons shared subject matter and audiences with the English plays; and they were the most practiced form of literary expression in the Middle Ages. It appears that some preachers were involved in the composition and production of plays and in some cases, at least, they have common persuasive objectives. Sermons were a vital part of the literary milieu of the medieval plays. But an understanding of the precise nature of their influence will require much more study in historical sources, in the preaching manuals, and in the sermon and play texts themselves.

NOTES

1. "Master Thomas Bynham, Friar Preacher, for making and composing the banns ('les banes') before the Corpus Christi play proclaimed through the whole town, 4 May, 6s. 8d." (Leach, 160).
2. For excellent, concise descriptions of medieval sermon form and practice see Batillon, the introduction to Ross, and Murphy. The best study of medieval sermon handbooks remains Charland.
3. For more on this subject see Neuss, 41–68.

WORKS CITED AND SUGGESTED READING

Adams, J. Q., ed. *Chief Pre-Shakespearean Dramas*. Cambridge: Houghton Mifflin Company, 1924.
Alain de Lille. *Summa de arte praedicatoria*. J. P. Migne, ed. *Patrologia Latina*, Vol. 210. Paris: J. Vrin, 1855, cols. 110–98.
Alcock, Simon. *De modo dividendi thema pro materia sermonis dilatanda*. Mary F. Boynton, ed. "Simon Alcock on Expanding the Sermon," *Harvard Theological Review* 34 (1941), 201–16.
Batillon, Louis J. "Approaches to the Study of Medieval Sermons." *Leeds Studies in English* 11 (1980), 19–50 and 111–116.
Boyle, Leonard E. Review of *Literature and Pulpit*, by G. R. Owst. *Medium Aevum* 33 (1964), 228–30.
Brandeis, A., ed. *Jacob's Well*. Early English Text Society, O.S. 115. London: Kegan Paul, Trench, Trübner & Co., 1900.
Brown, Beatrice Daw, ed. *The Southern Passion*. Early English Text Society, O.S. 169. London: Kegan Paul, Trench, Trübner & Co. , 1927.
Brown, Carleton. "Caiphas as a Palm Sunday Prophet" in *Anniversary Papers [for] George Lyman Kittredge*. Boston: Ginn & Co., 1913.
Browne, E. Martin. "Producing the Mystery Plays for Modern Audiences," *Drama Survey* 3 (1963), 5–15.
Calendar of the Letters and Papers of King Henry VIII, vol. 12, part 1. James Gairdner, cataloguer. London: H. M. Stationery Office, 1890.
Charland, Thomas-Marie. *Artes Praedicandi: Contribution à la histoire de la rhétorique au moyen âge*. Paris and Ottawa: J. Vrin, 1936.
Clopper, Lawrence M., ed. *Records of Early English Drama: Chester*. Toronto: University of Toronto Press, 1979.
Coogan, Sister Mary Philippa. *An Interpretation of the Moral Play "Mankind"*. Washington, D.C.: Catholic University of America Press, 1947.

Eccles, Mark, ed. *The Macro Plays.* Early English Text Society, O.S. 262. Oxford: Kegan Paul, Trench, Trübner & Co., 1969.

England, George, and A. W. Pollard, eds. *The Towneley Plays.* Early English Text Society, E.S. 71. London: Kegan Paul, Trench, Trübner & Co., 1897.

Fisher, John. *The English Works of John Fisher.* John E. B. Mayor, ed. Early English Text Society, E.S. 27. London: Kegan Paul, Trench, Trübner & Co., 1876.

Grisdale, Dorothy, ed. *Three Middle English Sermons from the Worcester Chapter Manuscript F.10.* Leeds Texts and Monographs. Leeds: Leeds University Press, 1936, p. 12.

Grosseteste, Robert. *Roberti Grossetesti; Epistolae.* Henry Richards Luard, ed. Rolls Series, Vol. 25. London: Longman, Green, Longman and Roberts, 1861.

Herr, Alan Fager. *The Elizabethan Sermon.* Philadelphia: n.p., 1940.

Higden, Ranulph. *Polychronicon.* Josseph R. Lumby, ed. Rolls Series No. 41, vol. 9. London, 1866; rpt. Kraus, New York, 1964.

Johnston, Alexandra F., and Margaret D. Rogerson, eds. *Records of Early English Drama: York.* Toronto: University of Toronto Press, 1979.

Kahrl, Stanley J. *Records of Plays and Players of Lincolnshire, 1300–1585.* Malone Society *Collections* Vol. 8. Oxford: Oxford University Press, 1974.

Leach, A. F., ed. *Report on the Manuscripts of the Corporation of Beverley.* Historical Manuscripts Commission, Vol. 54. London: Mackie & Co., Ltd., 1900.

Little, A. G. Review of *Literature and Pulpit,* by G. R. Owst. *English Historical Review,* 49 (1964), 115–16.

Little, A. G., and R. C. Easterling. *The Franciscans and Dominicans of Exeter.* History of Exeter Research Group Monograph 3. Exeter, 1927.

Lydgate, John. *Lydgate's Minor Poems; Part I, Religious Poems.* H. N. MacCracken, ed. Early English Text Society, E.S. 107. London: Oxford University Press, 1911.

Machyn, Henry. *Diary of Henry Machyn.* John G. Nichols, ed. Camden Society, no. 42. London: J. B. Nichols and Son, 1848.

Mannyngham, John. *The Diary of John Mannyngham.* John Bruce, ed. Westminster: Camden Society, No. 99. London: J. B. Nichols and Son, 1868.

Martin de Cordoba. "'Ars Praedicandi' de Fray Martin de Cordoba." Fernando Rubio, ed. *La Ciudad de Dios,* 172 (1959), 327–48.

Medieval Sermon Studies Symposium, 1982. Proceedings of the Third Medieval Sermon Studies Symposium. 7–9 July 1982. Oxford: Linacre College, Oxford University, 1982.

Murphy, James J., ed. *Medieval Eloquence: Studies in the Theory and Practice of Medieval Rhetoric.* Berkeley: University of California Press, 1978.

———. *Medieval Rhetoric: A Select Bibliography.* Toronto, University of Toronto Press, 1971.

———. *Rhetoric in the Middle Ages: A History of Rhetorical Theory from St. Augustine to the Renaissance.* Berkeley: University of California Press, 1974.

———, ed. *Three Medieval Rhetorical Arts.* Berkeley: University of California Press, 1971.

Neuss, Paula. "Active and Idle Language: Dramatic Images in *Mankind.*" *Medieval Drama.* Neville Denny, ed. Stratford upon Avon Studies 16. London: Edward Arnold, 1973, pp. 41–68.

Owst, Gerald R. *Literature and Pulpit in Medieval England; A Neglected Chapter in the History of English Letters & of the English People.* Oxford: Basil Blackwell, 1933, rev. 1961.

———. *Preaching in Medieval England; An Introduction to Sermon Manuscripts of the Period.* Cambridge: Cambridge University Press, 1926.

Prosser, Eleanor. *Drama and Religion in the English Mystery Plays.* Stanford: Stanford University Press, 1961.

Pseudo-Aquinas. *A Brief Religious Tract on the Art and True Method of Preaching.* Harry Caplan., trans. "A Late Medieval Tractate on Preaching" in *Studies in Rhetoric and Public Speaking in Honor of J. A. Winans.* A. M. Drummond, ed. New York: Century Co., 1925.

Ross, Woodburn O., ed. *Middle English Sermons from MS. Roy. 18 B. xxiii.* Early English Text Society, O.S. 209. Oxford: Oxford University Press, 1938.

Rossiter, A. P. *English Drama from Early Times to the Elizabethans; Its Background, Origins, and Developments.* London: Hutchinson's Universal Library, 1950.

Smart, W. K. "Some Notes on Mankind." *Modern Philology,* 14 (1916), 308–309.

Smith, Lucy Toulmin, ed. *York Plays.* Oxford: Clarendon Press, 1885.

Surgant, Johan Ulrich. *Manuale Curatorum; Liber Secundum: De practica artis predicatione iuxta vulgare theutonicum.* Argentinae: Johan Prüs, 1506.

Weatherly, Edward H., ed. *Speculum Sacerdotale.* Early English Text Society, O.S. 200. London: Kegan Paul, Trench, Trübner & Co., 1936.

Wickham, Glynne. *Early English Stages 1300 to 1600.* 2 vols. London: Routledge and Kegan Paul, 1959–1972.

William of Auvergne. *De facibus mundi.* A. de Poorter, ed. "Un Manuel de prédication médiévale." *Revue Néoscholastique de Philosophie* 25 (1923), 92–209.

Wycliffe, William. *English Works of Wycliffe; Hitherto Unprinted.* F. D. Matthew, ed. Early English Text Society, O.S. 74. London: Oxford University Press, 1880.

PAMELA SHEINGORN

The Visual Language of Drama

Principles of Composition

The fundamentally visual nature of Middle English drama, so apparent
to its medieval audience, often escapes the attention of modern scholars.
The lines drawn between disciplines hinder easy access to methods that
would enable readers to pass from a text to a visual reconstruction of it.
Nonetheless, the readers of dramatic texts need to visualize stage properties, costumes, and sets, and, when appropriate, to see beyond their literal
meaning to their symbolic import. Further, readers must see gesture,
placement, and interrelationship of actors, and understand how these
visual elements contribute to the content of a play.[1]

Scholars of medieval drama have long been aware of the resources
available to them in the pictorial arts for the study of symbolic meaning,
the area of art history called iconography.[2] Iconographers investigate the
meanings of visual signs, including gestures, and compile them in lexi-
cons of iconography. But, perhaps because art historians themselves have
tended to accept a binary division of their subject, drama scholars have
shown relatively little interest in exploring the applicability to drama of
the other major field of art history, the study of forms or style, which
art historians usually see as historically based and divided into a sequence of period styles, each recognizable as a set of distinctive and characteristic ways of giving form to objects and scenes. This essay reflects
the views of art historians who are dissatisfied with the extent to which
the discipline has tolerated the separation of form and content; it seeks
a universal, integrative approach in ways of seeing. I thus begin with the
premise that these ways of seeing, as codified in perception theory, make
a valid point of departure for visual analysis precisely because perception
theory demonstrates that form and content are integrally related. Some
general principles of visual composition that can be derived from perception theory are here applied to the visual arts of the Middle Ages. Arguing
for the integrity of the Middle Ages as one historical period, I present a
theoretical framework from art history to account for changes in artistic
values within that period, and I define principles of composition in the
late medieval visual arts that successfully control the organization of dis-
parate kinds of material. The underlying assumption is that the princi-

ples of composition governing the medieval pictorial arts also govern stage picture in the medieval drama.Thus, this chapter offers the means for increased study of the visual aspects of medieval drama through analytic methods taken from the discipline of art history and applied to visual composition in the drama.

Visual analysis of any text, including medieval drama, requires reading that text visually, finding the visual in the verbal. For the student of medieval drama, visual reading requires familiarity with the pictorial arts of the Middle Ages, keeping in mind D. W. Robertson, Jr.'s observation that "much evidence from the visual arts has been destroyed by religious or rationalist zeal, or simply the ravages of time. We are thus often forced to adduce traditions rather than sources, but in any event it is necessary to exercise extreme care to become familiar with available primary sources and to avoid speculation as much as possible" (14). An important route of access to primary sources is through the publications of the Early Drama, Art, and Music project, which aims to collect references to the pictorial arts from the regions to which play texts can be localized.

In order to make the best use of the pictorial arts of the Middle Ages, the student of drama must have some understanding of medieval methods of composition because visual composition, the ordering of individual visual units, shapes content and contributes to meaning. Principles of visual composition arise from the decisions artists make in giving form to desired content by organizing the elements necessary to the subject matter to create a coherent and visually legible composition. The visually literate viewer can deduce or read the results of the artist's decisions in the work of art. In an analogy between organizational principles in language and those in the visual arts, Donis A. Dondis refers to principles of composition as visual syntax: "There is visual syntax. There are guidelines for constructing compositions. There are basic elements that can be learned and understood by all students of the visual media, artists and nonartists alike, and that, along with manipulative techniques, can be used to create clear visual messages. Knowledge of all these factors can lead to clearer comprehension of visual messages" (11).

Along with Dondis, and in accordance with the findings of Gestalt psychology, I assume the existence of "a basic, perceptual visual system, one that all human beings have in common" (12).[3] Principles of composition based in this universal visual system ought, therefore, to apply to the visual arts of the Middle Ages and to be the most basic route of access to an understanding of those arts. However, these principles derive from perception theory based on experimental psychology, which works with living subjects. Further, most applications of perception theory to the pictorial arts choose illustrative examples from post-Renaissance Western art. No comparable experiments can be done to derive principles by which medieval people perceived works of medieval art. Thus, in applying perception theory to the medieval visual arts we step into new territory. Our goal is to determine specific ways in which the Middle Ages applied general compositional principles and to demonstrate that these applications reflect what we know of the medieval world view.

Underlying this approach is the assumption that it is useful for some purposes to view the Middle Ages as a whole. Justification for that assumption can be found in a theoretical framework that describes the process of change in the pictorial arts and applies to the visual aspects of drama as well. This framework looks at art history in terms of conventions. A convention might be thought of as a solution to a recurrent visual problem; for example, how to render a subject like the human form, or part of a subject like the ear, so that it can easily be drawn and recognized (one convention for the portrayal of an ear is as a letter C with a dot in the center). A convention arises, David Summers suggests, because the first solution to a recurrent visual problem defines a new concept. "A formulation once arrived at may have almost perfect authority simply because it is identified with the thing that it is. . . ." (119).

For change to occur in the pictorial arts, conventions must change. Ernst Gombrich's influential theory as to the kinds of stylistic change in the pictorial arts posits the existence of schemata (*Art and Illusion*), the schema being, according to David Novitz (*Pictures and Their Use*), "a method or formula for arranging lines and colors in a way which results in a picture of a particular object or kind of object" (47). Since a schema roughly equals a convention, I use the latter term here. Gombrich describes change in art as taking place through a process of making and matching—the artist creates an image, compares that image to the original model, and adjusts the conventions (schema) to resemble the model more closely. When the original model arises in nature, as Gombrich assumes, then imitation of nature is the central goal of art. However, if the spiritual or visionary holds a central place in the culture, as in the Middle Ages, then matching may mean interpreting more accurately the language of visionary literature like that in the Apocalypse or in visions of saints like Hildegard of Bingen or Bridget of Sweden.

A useful modification of Gombrich's theory has been proposed by David Novitz, who sees two kinds of conventions operating in the pictorial arts; in addition to the simple convention (schema), he describes the "umbrella" convention, in which the artist follows "certain rule-governed methods or procedures when attempting to produce a picture of an object" (45). An example of an umbrella convention is the primary commitment of Egyptian art to providing for the eye as much information as possible rather than restricting the viewer to any one vantage point. When rendering the human form the Egyptian artist thus combined points of view and created a composite whole—profile head with full-front eye, full-front torso with profile legs. For Novitz changes in simple conventions are incremental; they take place *within* a pictorial style and thus within an umbrella convention: the Egyptian artist could change the way he formed the pupil of the eye while still placing a full-front eye in a profile head. Such changes in simple conventions do not, to Novitz, explain radical changes, which are changes in umbrella conventions that he calls "pictorial revolutions."[4]

To apply this theory to the Middle Ages means to assert that one umbrella convention governs the period ca. 500 to ca. 1500. Although she does not use the term "umbrella convention," the "medieval image style" that Annemarie Mahler sees as defined in the writing of St. Augustine fits Novitz's definition. Mahler points specifically to Augustine's theory of threefold vision, corporeal, spiritual, and intellectual, in which the highest level, the intellectual, having received an image via corporeal and spiritual vision, evaluates that image against "immutable number." For Augustine the artist plays a crucial role in this process: "The artificers of all corporeal forms work by number and regulate their operations thereby. In working they move their hands and tools until that which is fashioned in the outer world, being referred to the inward light of number, receives such perfection as is possible, and being reported on by the senses, pleases the internal judge who beholds the supernal ideal numbers" (*De Libero Arbitrio* II, xvi, 42; cited in Mahler, p. 285). Thus the medieval artist does not attempt to reproduce what he sees, but, aiding the process of intellectual vision, creates forms that reveal their origin in number—proportion, geometric shape, symmetry. Since the goal of intellectual vision is to gain knowledge of divine wisdom, rather than of the mutable world, the medieval artist correctly refuses to focus on nature as a model or to accept the limitations of physical sight.

A key aspect of the medieval umbrella convention is, then, its use of form as a vehicle for content. It emphasizes clarity of content—communicability of the spiritual sense of that content—over fidelity to visual experience. As Gerhart B. Ladner comments with regard to the Lindisfarne Gospels, "It was the purpose of the illuminator of the Lindisfarne Gospels to make the physical appearance of man a mere function of spiritual meaning and didactic purpose" (24). The medieval umbrella convention places certain limitations on innovation. Kurt Weitzmann observes that ". . . a methodical treatment of medieval works of art has to take into account the artist's primary concern with the iconographically accurate rendering of the content, which looms larger in his mind than formalistic problems, and furthermore his adherence to an established, sanctified tradition of rendering certain themes which goes hand in hand with self-imposed limitations on his invention of new subject matter" (151). I am convinced that the medieval umbrella convention governs medieval religious drama as well, for it also demonstrates more concern for the clear communication of spiritual truth than for imitation of the visible world and renders crucial themes in accordance with established tradition.

Scenes that present subject matter governed by traditional means of presentation in the medieval visual arts reflect specific ways of using the principles of visual composition based in perception theory, the most basic of which is the concept of balance. When first examining a work of art, we look for a balancing center that imposes stability on a composition and we are uncomfortable with the sort of ambiguity in which visual elements fail to organize themselves about such a center. Experiments in perception demonstrate that we seek balance by positing a main vertical axis and a subsidiary horizontal axis as referents, and then by "weighing" the visual elements on opposite sides of these axes. Various factors affect visual weight, including size, shape, color, and placement in relation to other elements and the entire field. When a large and important figure coincides with the vertical axis of the composition and the eye finds that figure to be the balancing center, a strong sense of stability results. Such is the case in medieval art and drama when the figure of God, Christ, or a saint occupies the vertical axis of the composition. The "immobility of the central position" (Arnheim, *Power*, 73), expresses in visual language both God's eternal existence and his position as lord of creation. In the Chester Creation play, usurpation of the central position belonging to God and marked by his throne states in visual terms the overweening pride that Lucifer's speech reveals: "Above greate God I will me guyde / and set myselfe here; as I wene,/ I ame pearlesse and prince of pride, / for God hymselfe shines not so sheene" (ll. 182–85).

Other qualities that surface in the medieval visual arts because of the identification of the center with God include symmetry and hierarchy. Symmetry arises from the most direct kind of balance, the repetition of visual elements on either side of the center. It reflects God's power by expressing the order he imposed on the creation. Thus the angels appear in ordered rows, symmetrically placed about God's throne. Conversely, chaos adds to the expressive content of scenes set in hell, as, for example, Lucifer's fall. As more figures are added to scenes balanced about the central figure of God, clarity of relationships can be further underscored through hierarchy. This convention places each figure with regard to its relative importance as measured against the central figure ("Nyen ordres of aungels full clere" [York 1. 23]). It may also assign size according to the same relationship. Thus the size and placement of God, orders of angels, saints, and human beings directly state the hieratic relationships among them.

The simple balance created by absolute symmetry and hierarchic ordering about a strong balancing center characterizes the heavens or the prelapsarian creation, not the world of fallible humans. On a more pragmatic level, if the eye immediately fathoms the structure of a work of art, which it does in the case of a simply balanced composition, it feels no need to examine the work further. Therefore, in many compositions, balance is supplied not by absolute symmetry, which creates repetitive pattern, but by stress, or the imbalance of individual elements or clusters of elements, which creates tensions that are resolved in the work as a whole. Both the Last Judgment plays in the Corpus Christi cycles and representations of the Last Judgment in late Gothic art demonstrate the use of stress about the balancing center by the introduction of non-symmetrical vertical movement in the two groups of the saved and the damned arranged symmetrically at the right and left hands of Christ. The stress created by these conflicting vertical motions effectively reminds viewers of the stressful choice between good and evil behavior that confronts them (Bevington et al.).

Even if no figure coincides with the balancing center, an axis may be "felt," as in a dialogue between two figures like Mary and the angel in Annunciation pictures and plays. Here the empty center reflects the gulf between human and divine across which, to the great surprise of Mary, direct communication takes place. Of all the dialogues in medieval art and drama, this one must unfailingly be composed about a balancing center in order to communicate its full message.

A second element of perception theory asserts that the human eye, after seeking a balancing center, displays a marked tendency to scan the lower left portion of the visual field. The balancing center exerts a certain "pull" on all objects in the field, but that pull is lessened in the lower left because of the tendency to scan from left to right. Therefore weightier objects can occupy the lower left rather than lower right, where weight accrues to objects because of the tension required to maintain their positions away from the balancing center. Dondis comments on this problem:

> The favoring of the left part of the visual field could be influenced by the Western print formation and the fact that there is strong conditioning in the way we learn to read from left to right. There is little research and a great deal to be learned about why we are predominantly right-handed organisms and specialize our left-to-right reading and writing competencies to the left hemisphere of the brain. Oddly, right-handedness extends to cultures that have written from top to bottom and presently write from right to left. We also favor the left field of vision. If we do not know for sure why, it may be sufficient to know that the fact does prove out in practice. Watch the eyes of an audience scan a stage on which there is no action when the curtain goes up in a theater. (29)

The medieval stage exploits the possibility of placing weighty forms on the left by making this Satan's side. Certainly the tendency to read from left to right influences the composition of scenes involving journeys, such as the Flight into Egypt or the Entry into Jerusalem. Interestingly, each of these scenes suggests that travel continues beyond the frame at the right edge of the image. Entry from the right, on the other hand, suggests arrival at the intended goal, as, for example, in the adoration of the Magi. The left frame of the image seems to create an impenetrable barrier, whereas that of the right allows the viewer to imagine motion continuing through it.

Another aspect of perception theory seems more problematic when applied to the Middle Ages. Perception theory asserts that the visual arts are anisotropic, that is, that they reflect a universal perception of gravity and the resulting asymmetry of gravitational space, so that "an element in the upper part of a pattern carries more visual weight than one in the lower part and therefore should be smaller if it is to counterbalance a corresponding element below" (Arnheim, *Power*, 18). Anisotropism does not depend on an understanding of gravity, but it does suggest that the world of the work of art reflects that of the world of the artist's experience. Thus the rejection of anisotropism in medieval art would coincide with its rejection of any interest in the physical world for its own sake. Arnheim observes that "as long as art wishes to reflect the experience of living with the constraints on human existence, it is likely to display the anisotropy of space, the coping with weight" (*Power*, 145). It certainly seems likely that anisotropism was neglected when staging plays such as the creation of the angels and the fall of Lucifer, where the "weight" is on an upper stage representing heaven. This is also true of the representation of visions, such as illustrations of the Apocalypse in the pictorial arts. Often the Middle Ages seems indifferent to "the constraints on human existence," or at least prefers to focus on a world where they did not exist. Thus, anisotropism as an aspect of human perception may be more culture bound than the balancing center and the tendency to read from left to right.

In spite of an acknowledged conservatism in the introduction of new subjects, no one would claim that art in the Middle Ages was without change. Indeed, art historians divide the era into a number of periods, each characterized by a "period style." Not only are these periods not always the same as those of the literary historian, a fact that can cause confusion in interdisciplinary study, but further, as Eugene Kleinbauer notes, "When art historians speak of art as being of this or that century, generation, or decade, they are using interpretative, evaluative terms, not merely chronological ones" ("Determinants," 15).[5] Often these terms emphasize the differences between periods, rather than the thread of continuity running from one period to the next. "In practice—in art history texts, for example—periodization implies radical difference. . . . Thus two periods that share much in common are treated as if they were unrelated traditions. Since art history has been mostly concerned with the Western tradition, this habit of periodization has made the Western tradition itself seem much less unified than it actually is" (Summers, 115). This observation by David Summers applies especially well to the distinction between

Romanesque and Gothic, the periods from about 950–1150 and 1200–1500 in northern Europe, often described in terms of opposites rather than as sub-periods of the Middle Ages.

Similarly, those studying medieval drama posit two "periods," that of liturgical drama, and that of the cycle plays, and derive two sets of implicitly antithetical characteristics. Thus, starting from the point of view of the late Middle Ages, the qualities that characterize Romanesque art and liturgical drama seem "old," whereas gothic art and cycle plays are "new": representation is old—illusionism is new; traditional iconography is old—literalism is new; symbolic staging is old—environmental realism is new; the narrative is old—devotional subjects, especially those dealing with the Passion, are new. By implication, such drastic changes must bring with them a new period, a new umbrella convention.

In both art and drama the hypothetical point of division falls in the twelfth century, suggesting that the "renaissance of the twelfth century" mounts a significant attack on the medieval umbrella convention. One of the most important aspects of this "renaissance" is that it justifies study of the physical world: If the creation partakes of the glory of God then his presence can be seen in man and nature. This shift affects style in the pictorial arts by validating observation of nature, although, in fact, such observation tends not to focus on actual objects, but on those objects as rendered by the art of the Greco-Roman period. Renewed interest in nature affects content by surfacing the realization that Biblical characters are human and that their actions can be portrayed in terms of motives that other human beings can understand. Composition is affected in that there is diminished emphasis on the centricity of God; if he is omnipresent in his creation, he need not always occupy the center of a composition. Thus, with the concomitant growth of narrative in the pictorial arts, there is a higher proportion of scenes that do not exhibit features of centricity, symmetry, and hierarchy to such a marked degree as in earlier art. Another aspect of the twelfth-century renaissance, the emphasis on the human nature of Christ, also reduces the formality of many scenes and tends, at some moments, to integrate the figure of Christ into a composition as one human form among others, a new view of Christ which appears strikingly clear in the *Greater Passion Play* from the Carmina Burana manuscript. But, as I will demonstrate below, these changes are made selectively, always taking into consideration the content to be conveyed. Although increased emphasis on the experience of the natural world leads artists and writers of drama to increase the number of changes in simple conventions, incorporating their perceptions of their own world into their art so that it becomes more realistic and illusionistic, the medieval umbrella convention holds so long as they continue to view the sensory world as the *signatura rerum*, the visible evidence of invisible truth, rather than finding it worthy of study for its own sake. Its failure to break the medieval umbrella convention leads Erwin

Panofsky to call the twelfth century a period of "renascence," not "renaissance."

In spite of the impact of the twelfth-century renaissance, the visual arts of the late Middle Ages may usefully be viewed as configurations of individual qualities that represent steps in the adjustment of simple conventions within the medieval umbrella convention. For example, if the contents of the cycles are seen as a continuum from the completely supernatural—God in heaven with his creatures and no mortals about—to the earthly—the conversations of shepherds, soldiers, or torturers among themselves, then it seems—generally speaking—that the more otherworldly a play is, the more traditional elements—liturgical language, Latin, traditional iconography, symbolic staging—it contains: relatively few simple conventions have been adjusted. The "old" elements do not survive because these are "old" plays, but rather because they are the best conveyers of supernatural content. Thus when the Wakefield Master rewrote the very traditional, symmetrically ordered York Judgment play, he did not disrupt its balancing about the central figure, Christ the judge, of those who performed the seven acts of mercy against those that did not. Yet he wove into the traditional structure many "new" elements, notably the character of the demon, Tutivillus (Stevens, "Language"). Another reviser, the York Realist, rewrote most of the Passion sequence in that cycle, filling it with the devotional imagery and psychological realism suited to its content. The same writer rewrote the Creation, but here, in presenting God's perfect world he refrained from making changes in its symbolic staging, traditional iconography, and formal language (Davidson).[6] A play's resistance to change bears no relationship to its antiquity, for the Creation play has no ancestry to compare with the Shepherds' plays, which were substantively altered. The *Officium Pastorum* may be among the earliest of liturgical plays, yet the writers of the cycles felt free to introduce a great deal of environmental and psychological realism into their treatment of this subject. It is a subject suitable for transplant to the pastures and villages of England in a way that the Creation is not.

In making use of traditional iconography, artists often adjust their simple conventions in the direction of literalism as they move into the late Gothic period. However, the kind of literalism that operates in the drama and art of the late Middle Ages does not destroy traditional iconography and even, in some cases, creates new symbols. Rudolph Arnheim argues that reading a painting accurately requires grasping the level of abstraction intended by the artist ("Aesthetic Fact"). Late medieval literalism lowers the level of abstraction but does not discard abstraction altogether. For example, the use of an actual chalice in the scene of Christ's agony in the garden to illustrate the words, "let this cup pass me by," cited as an example of literalism, actually makes visible a verbal metaphor and lowers the level of abstraction, but does not destroy the metaphor. Rather it creates a new symbol, enriching the repertoire of Christian iconography. It also adds a level of interpretation, for the angel who "descendyth of jhesus and bryngyth to hym A chaly with An host þer in" in the N-Town cycle explains to Jesus, "þis chalys ye þi blood þis bred is þi body" (l. 953).

Further, what first appears to be naive literalism may be instead the end product of a long tradition. For example, the Chester records list a *mappa mundi* as a stage property in the Creation play. This use of a map, which God presumably displays as he describes his creation, might be satisfactorily explained as a practical solution to the need for visual interest during God's long introductory speeches, if we did not know that the creation and the map had already been combined in visual exegesis. A page from a thirteenth-century English psalter shows God making the syndesmos gesture, i.e., standing frontally with arms outstretched; flanked by angels, he holds a *mappa mundi* (reproduced in Esmeijer, fig. 81a). If we assume that in the Chester Creation God also used this gesture, "the all-embracing gesture with hands outspread, by which harmony is established. . . . the cosmogenic gesture of creation" (Esmeijer, 97), then the figure of God displaying a *mappa mundi* refers to a well-established tradition based in antique school schemata.

The disguised symbol, as described by Erwin Panofsky, is another late medieval way of introducing the literal without abandoning the symbol. Symbols are assimilated to the picture and take their place in it as genre elements. On one level they are phenomena of the real world—a glass window and a ray of light—and on another level they have symbolic meaning—the light passes through the glass without breaking it as Christ into his mother's womb without disturbing her virginity. The ways the late medieval visual arts alter traditional iconography reveal an impressive degree of flexibility. Level of abstraction can be lowered without compressing range of meaning.

The dichotomy between old and new may seem less pronounced if the two can be seen to have similar underlying goals. In the case of representation and illusionism, each urges identification between audience and actors by use of familiar costume and setting. The reading for Easter Matins taken from a homily of Gregory the Great first counsels imitation of the Marys at the tomb and then, Gregory says, the identification that results from imitation will follow: "If we—believing in him who has died and filled with the sweet scent of virtues, and bearing the reputation of good works—seek out the Lord, then indeed do we come to his monument with aromatic spices." The audience listening to this reading saw, at the end of the same service, the *Visitatio* play in which members of their own community, dressed in familiar liturgical garments, singing the familiar melodies of the plainchant, and moving through the space that they themselves used every day, play the roles of the Holy Women, as if in a literal reading of Gregory's metaphor. A similar motivation activates the cycle plays. Stage characters place themselves firmly in the world of their late medieval audience by the rhetorical level of their language and its references to local geography, by their occupations and concerns. The urban setting is to the secular audience as the sacred setting is to the monks (Stevens, *Mystery Cycles*). Certainly the late medieval theater uses a larger number of illusionistic devices, but the relationship between play and audience remains, in many scenes of the plays, similar to that relationship in early medieval drama.

Similarly the goals of realism in the late medieval theater resemble the goals of more symbolic modes of presentation. Bacon's views on the purpose of accuracy of representation in the pictorial arts apply equally well to the drama. He says that by greater knowledge and application of geometry the good Christian artist could create a better likeness; the "literal sense" of the depicted object would then give better comprehension of its true "spiritual sense" (see Edgerton, "Renaissance Picture-Making"). Thus, in the drama, psychological realism successfully rationalizes the behavior of human characters; the portrayal of Eve's psychology may be troublesome to a modern audience, but faithfully and vividly illustrates the contemporary view of the susceptibility of the female to flattery and pseudological persuasion. However, Scripture contains an element of the transcendent that defies rational understanding and that often lies at the center of crucial narrative. Both God's motives and his mercy lie beyond our grasp, even if he is sometimes represented with environmental realism as a kind of superpope. When Christ's character was rationalized, as in some of the late medieval German passion plays, he became abusive and angry, undoubtedly just as the playwright imagined he himself would in the same situation.[7] Psychological realism fails to rationalize the superhuman forbearance of Christ, and it was surely this realization that restricted the Wakefield Master to writing a mere four lines for Christ out of the approximately 3,000 lines that he supplied for the cycle (Stevens, "Language"). Nor could environmental realism cope with all the content of the cycles. It supplies elaborate costumes and familiar stage properties, but avoids altering the traditional iconography of God's throne and hellmouth for scenes that take place literally outside of the environment.

Although the medieval umbrella convention governed the adjustments of simple conventions that resulted in the introduction of "new" qualities alongside traditional qualities in the late medieval pictorial arts, the convention alone does not supply the means of ordering this highly varied material so as to create aesthetic unity. New principles of composition modulate transitions from scenes of static hierarchy to those of motion and emotion, weaving new scenes of visual variety and complexity into the doctrinal sequence of those firmly composed about a balancing center. These new principles, juxtaposition, recapitulation, and framing, mediate between older and newer simple conventions to create, in the cycle plays and in late medieval art, a synthesis of form and content.

Juxtaposition, the first of the new principles, means the placing of images next to one another so as to create disjuncture in moving from one to the next. At its most basic level juxtaposition pairs opposites like Church and Synagogue, Virtues and Vices, deadly sins and acts of mercy, pairings that both summarize narrative content effectively and make antithetical relationships immediately clear. For this reason morality plays tend to employ a structure of paired opposites, and the cycle plays use such pairings most obviously in the visual juxtapositions of paradise and hell, and the elect and the damned in the judgment plays. A more sophisticated type of juxtaposition is typological, as in the presentation of Abel as a Christ figure, which requires the audience to read a play or picture on two levels at once, with a resulting disjuncture in linear narrative.

Reading such juxtapositions is a fundamental habit of mind in the Middle Ages. We see juxtaposition in the way medieval builders couple a new choir with an old nave, or place a new altarpiece in an old chapel, and again when playwrights like the Wakefield Master and the York Realist rewrite individual plays of a cycle or even insert one or more stanzas into an existing play. Apparently in none of these cases is there a sense of disjuncture. As Meyer Schapiro observes with regard to the varied architectural styles of Chartres Cathedral, "the fact that mediaeval art is full of such incongruities, accidental and designed, and can tolerate the unfinished and the partial, points to a conception of the beautiful in art fundamentally different from the ancient" ("Aesthetic Attitude," 23–24). Some medieval juxtapositions were, of course, matters of economic necessity, of halted building campaigns, or plans not carried out. Nonetheless, as a mode, juxtaposition is so pervasive in the Middle Ages that it can scarcely have been viewed negatively.

Especially applicable to the drama is a type of juxtaposition characteristic of the late Middle Ages, as exemplified in a French manuscript of the early fifteenth century, the De Buz Book of Hours. The mode of presentation in this book juxtaposes standard Christian iconography with scenes of disguised symbolism, environmental realism, or devotional import. The artists composed the illustrated pages as groupings of three scenes: one is larger and the other two clearly subordinate to it. The larger scenes present traditional subjects in a formal way whereas the smaller scenes add "modern" material. For example the Annunciation, a scene composed with a clear balancing center, governs a page that also illustrates the scene of the Virgin at her loom, a genre scene of environmental realism, also, of course, to be read on the level of disguised symbolism (fol. 20r, reproduced in Hindman, pl. 54). A Pieta Madonna that emphasizes the divine nature and mission of Christ, and is composed so that the Madonna's form coincides with the vertical axis and the body of Christ with the subordinate horizontal axis, is juxtaposed to two images, each less rigidly composed (fol. 155r, reproduced in Hindman, pl. 55). In one of these Christ steps falteringly toward his mother, a frankly human child learning to walk. It is not accidental that his halo is minimized in this scene. The other image, a purely devotional scene in which Mary adores the child, is based on the visions of St. Bridget of Sweden. Sandra Hindman concludes that "these genre-like scenes probably suggested to the viewer of the book that the activities of holy personages were not so far removed from the humble pursuits of mortal man" (97–98).

Juxtaposition in late medieval drama uses similar means to achieve similar effects. All of the realistic events in the Second Shepherds' play, culminating in the scene of Mak's "child" in its cradle, take on a new meaning when the play ends with the birth of Christ. This "old" scene, composed about the balancing center of the madonna and child ("Lady / so fare to beholde, with thy childe on thi kne!" [Wakefield, ll. 746–47]) is surely staged so that false and true nativities are visually juxtaposed. The play thus resolves the dissention in the world of the shepherds in a profoundly moving moment that bridges the gulf between sacred and profane and at the same time, through juxtaposition, resolves the conflict between "old" and "new" modes.

In another method of synthesizing the old and the new, both art and drama of the later Middle Ages juxtapose dramatic action with the stationary moment. In the production (The Cloisters, New York, March 1982) of the *Greater Passion Play* from the Carmina Burana manuscript, a staging derived from twelfth-century art, actors assumed positions familiar in the pictorial arts and held them, often for the duration of a musical passage (Coletti et al., "Carmina"). These groupings frequently resulted in symmetrical compositions around the figure of Christ as the balancing center. Movement to a new position involved entrances and exits and in general a high level of activity. Although in late medieval drama the balance may have shifted toward greater action with fewer static scenes, such scenes still form the centerpieces of many individual pageants. Compositions such as the court of heaven before the fall of Lucifer, the adoration of the shepherds and of the Magi, the Crucifixion and the Ascension, fit Otto Pächt's description of the Descent from the Cross in the Albani Psalter: "Out of action a stationary moment has been gained; a scene, cut out as it were from the flow of events, held up to the beholder 'like a picture,' hereby subliminating a passing episode into a ceremonial display of lasting significance" (31). Pächt calls this a "frontal appeal to the spectator, who cannot but feel directly addressed." Such moments of frontal appeal, "cut out from the flow of events," occur throughout the plays, and provide the audience with memorable and familiar images accompanied either by direct address, as when Christ speaks from the cross (With bittirfull bale haue I bought, / þus, man, all þi misse for to mende," ll. 183–84, York), or by music, as in the resurrection plays when the angels sing a liturgical antiphon to the resurrected Christ ("Tunc cantabunt angeli 'Christus resurgens,'" Wakefield) (Sheingorn, "Moment").

Along with juxtaposition, a second principle, long familiar to the pictorial arts, also informs individual figures, episodes, and pageants in the cycles. As the content of the narrative becomes more complex, recapitulatory symbols, gestures, and figures and locations serve to stress its underlying unity. The cruciform halo is a recapitulatory symbol, for its presence refers to the entire Passion. If placed about the head of the Creator it refers to the Christ-Logos, and, in a cycle, would have been especially effective if only one actor played God throughout, as is likely at least at York, where the judgment play refers interchangeably to Deus and Jesus. In the Passion, the cruciform halo takes on a foreboding quality as the inevitability of the Crucifixion approaches, and in the judgment the cruciform halo, along with the Instruments of the Passion and the bloody shirt Christ wears, recapitulate God's actions on earth.

The syndesmos posture provides recapitulation by means of gesture, for the frontal figure of God with outstretched arms in the Creation recurs in the Crucifixion, where it refers to Christ's divine nature at his most human moment of physical suffering. When the judging Christ assumes the syndesmos posture he not only separates the blessed from the damned but also summarizes the entire history of the created universe and definitively states that he has brought that history to an end.

Reuse of individual figures and locales recapitulates preceding action and urges the audience to see connections. Adam functions as a recapitulatory figure when he reappears in the Harrowing of Hell: "Mee thou madest, lord, of claye, / and gave me paradyce in to playe; / but through me synne, the soothe to saye, / depryved I was therefroe, (Chester, ll. 9–12); his questioning of Enoch and Elias in the same play elicits the first mention in the cycle of Antichrist ("but here ordaynt we are to bee / tyll Antechriste come with hise," ll. 247–48); thus the recapitulatory figure of Adam serves to tie together widely separated episodes in the cycle. Similarly, in the Lucerne play, the place used for Eden, where man was successfully tempted, is reused on the second day of the play as the Mount of Olives, where Christ at his most human resists the temptation to avoid the Crucifixion.[8]

The principle of framing resembles that of juxtaposition, though its effects differ somewhat. The practice of introducing elaborate borders for book pages began early in the Middle Ages. These patterned frames evolved to include naturalistic foliage and genre vignettes, becoming more and more illusionistic. Sandra Hindman suggests that the use of such frames "created a subjective transition between the viewer's space and the picture space facilitating identification with the imagery . . . " (92). In the drama narrators such as Contemplacio in the N-Town cycle form one kind of frame. In the Annunciation play of the Wakefield cycle, comic scenes featuring the wholly earthbound character of Joseph, who consistently fails to perceive the intervention of the divine, frame the traditional scene between Gabriel and Mary that is composed about a balancing center. In the Chester cycle, the soldiers at the tomb, braggarts before the Resurrection ("Yf that he ryse, we shall found / to beate him adowne," ll. 144–45), awakens quivering cowards ("Wytt me wantes withowten were, / for fearder I never was," ll. 196–97). In each case these frames, which at first seem incongruous, provide the audience with mediators between the human and the divine that facilitate interpretation of the central, doctrinally significant scene.

Framing also serves to control the relationships between scenes by defining their cosmic significance. In many medieval English churches the Rood, a life-sized crucifix flanked by figures of the Virgin and John, gains immeasurably in impact because its frame, the chancel arch, is painted with a large Doomsday, an ever-present contextual frame through which both the Rood and the high altar must be seen. The human suffering of Christ and, by implication, the salvation of mankind that Christ purchased through his suffering gain in impact on the worshipper who must recognize the need for salvation in the face of imminent and final judgment. In the cycle plays, as in the pictorial arts, principles of composition control structure and enhance meaning. The deep grief of the Passion is framed most closely by the joyous moments of Nativity and Resurrection to create a complete cycle of the life of Christ. Framing this are the historical events of the Old Testament and of the church on earth from the apostles through Antichrist. And embracing all is the cosmic frame of Creation and Doomsday, holding the cycles within the frame of two plays built entirely about balancing centers. Music further reinforces the perception of this outer frame, for the singing of the *Te Deum* by the blessed souls in heaven at the end of the Judgment play ("Make we all myrth and louyng / With te deum laudamus," Towneley, ll. 619–20) reminds the audience that the universe has been restored to the harmony of the opening of the cycle when the newly created angels praised God with the same song. In both art and drama, such frames differ fundamentally from the delimiting frame—a physical boundary—that began to appear in the fifteenth century. In medieval wall painting, as in the medieval theater, there is no firm division between viewer and field of vision. The audience is in the work of art (Arnheim, *Power*, 52). Framing as a principle of visual composition imposes meaningful order by supplying the appropriate context.

With these principles of composition, juxtaposition, recapitulation, and framing, late medieval artists and playwrights forged unity out of their diverse materials. It is a unity capable of encompassing great variety, from stasis to action and from hieratic formality to emotive humanity. It is based in communicating, by a variety of means, the spiritual sense of its content that lies at the heart of the medieval umbrella convention and that creates the sense of decorum governing the adjustment of simple conventions. Newer conventions are used with a sense of propriety, where appropriate to the content and to underscore the impact of that content on its audience. Most modifications of simple conventions arise from the principle of increased observation of nature, including human nature. Thus psychological realism is observation applied to the drawing of character; environmental realism is observation applied to the setting. There is a great deal of adaptation of individual qualities, but not of the raison d'être of drama.

This essay asserts that the visual nature of medieval drama has received inadequate attention and that study of that visual nature will result in fuller understanding of medieval drama. Understanding of principles of visual composition, based in perception theory, provides new insights into the meaning of medieval drama for its medieval audience by helping us to see what they saw. Although much of the concern here has been with form, the separation of the visual from the verbal and of form from content must lead ultimately to a reintegration that underscores the unique nature of drama, and that demonstrates the contribution art history can make to the study of medieval drama.[9]

NOTES

1. For an excellent introduction to the discipline of art history, see Kleinbauer (*Modern Perspectives*). For principles of composition and perception theory, see Arnheim (*Art and Visual Perception*), (*Power of the Center*), (*Visual Thinking*); Dondis (*A Primer of Visual Literacy*); Gombrich (*Art and Illusion*); Nodine et al. (*Perception and Pictorial Representation*); Novitz (*Pictures and Their Use in Communication*). For discussions of the concept of style, see Ackerman ("A Theory of Style"); Gombrich ("Style"); Lang (*The Concept of Style*); Schapiro ("Style"). For a discussion of basic reference works in iconography, see Sheingorn ("Drama and the Visual Arts"). On gesture, see Barasch (*Gestures of Despair*); Garnier (*Le Langage de L'Image au Moyen Age*); Gombrich ("Ritualized Gesture and Expression in Art"); Roeder (*Die Gebarde im Drama des Mittelalters*). For medieval art, see relevant articles with extensive bibliographies in *The Encyclopedia of World Art*, especially Dynes ("Medieval Art") in vol. 16 (supplement volume); Coldstream ("Art and Architecture in the late Middle Ages"); the basic tool for further research is *RILA:International Repertory of the Literature of Art*, a bibliographic service that includes abstracts. For medieval art and drama, see Davidson, *Drama and Art* and subsequent volumes in the EDAM Monograph and Research Series as well as the EDAM Newsletter; see also Sheingorn ("Drama and the Visual Arts").

2. See, for example, the excellent work of Gibson ("'Porta haec clausa erit'"), and Coletti ("Spirituality and Devotional Images").

3. Both Ernst Gombrich and Rudolph Arnheim have made use of Gestalt psychology in developing their ideas about perception in the pictorial arts.

4. Novitz suggests, but does not press, an analogy to Kuhn's theory of progress in science that posits a revolution in which one paradigm is replaced by another.

5. On what periodization means in art history and how it differs from periodization in literary history, see also Janson.

6. I am grateful to Professor Davidson for allowing me to see his book in typescript.

7. For example in the Frankfort Passion Christ says, "ach du vil dorechte Judischeit, / mit der lantzen hastu eyn himelschen durchstochen: / das werde ich nit lassen ungerochen!" ll. 3672–74, in *Das Drama des Mittelalters*, Richard Froning, ed. (Darmstadt: Wissenschaftliche Buchgesellschaft, 1964). I am grateful to Vincent Marsicano for providing this example.

8. See plans for the first and second days of the 1583 production reproduced in Nagler (30, 31).

9. I gratefully acknowledge the special debt I owe to Martin Stevens for reading two different drafts of this paper and making many helpful suggestions. I also thank others who read this paper and discussed it with me: Mary Weitzel Gibbons, Richard Wengenroth, the Medieval History Group of the Institute for Research in History, and Clifford Davidson, who served as commentator at the session of the Medieval Academy where a draft of this paper was presented.

WORKS CITED AND SUGGESTED READING

Ackerman, J. S. "A Theory of Style." *Journal of Aesthetics and Art Criticism* 20, 1962, pp. 227–37.

Arnheim, Rudolph. *Art and Visual Perception.* Berkeley: University of California Press, 1954.

——. *The Power of the Center: A Study of Composition in the Visual Arts.* Berkeley: University of California Press, 1982.

——. *Visual Thinking.* Berkeley: University of California Press, 1969.

——. "What Is an Aesthetic Fact?" *Studies in Art History.* Proceedings of the Middle Atlantic Symposium in the History of Art. College Park: University of Maryland, 1976, pp. 43–51.

Barasch, Moshe. *Gestures of Despair in Medieval and Early Renaissance Art.* New York: New York University Press, 1976.

Bevington, David, and Pamela Sheingorn, "'All This Was Token Domysday to Drede': Visual Signs of Last Judgment in the Corpus Christi Cycles and in Late Gothic Art," in *Homo, Memento Finis: The Iconography of Just Judgment in Medieval Art and Drama,* ed. David Bevington. Kalamazoo: Medieval Institute, 1985.

Coletti, Theresa. "Spirituality and Devotional Images: The Staging of the Hegge Cycle," Ph.D. dissertation, University of Rochester, 1975.

Coletti, Theresa, and Pamela Sheingorn. "The Carmina Burana *Greater Passion Play* at the Cloisters," *RORD* 25, 1982, pp. 139–44.

Coldstream, Nicola. "Art and Architecture in the late Middle Ages," in *The Later Middle Ages,* ed. Stephen Medcalf, 1981, pp. 172–224.

Davidson, Clifford. *Drama and Art.* Kalamazoo: Medieval Institute, 1977.

——. *From Creation to Doom: The York Cycle of Mystery Plays.* New York: AMS Plays, 1984.

Dondis, Donis A. *A Primer of Visual Literacy* Cambridge, Mass., and London: MIT Press, 1973.

Das Drama des Mittelalters, ed. Richard Froning. Darmstadt: Wissenschaftliche Buchgesellschaft, 1964.

Edgerton, Jr., Samuel Y. "The Art of Renaissance Picture-Making and the Great Western Age of Discovery," in *Essays Presented to Myron P. Gilmore,* ed.

Sergio Berelli and Gloria Remakus. Florence: La Nuova Italia Editrice, 1978, vol. 2, pp. 132–53.

Esmeijer, Anna C. *Divina Quaternitas: A Preliminary Study in the Method and Application of Visual Exegesis*. Assen: Van Gorcum, 1978.

The Encyclopedia of World Art. New York: Crown Publishers, 1969.

Garnier, François. *Le Langage de L'Image au Moyen Age: Signification et Symbolique*. Paris: Le Leopard d'Or, 1982.

Gibson, Gail McMurray. "'Porta haec clausa erit': comedy, conception, and Ezekial's closed door in the *Ludus Coventriae* play of 'Joseph's Return,'" *Journal of Medieval and Renaissance Studies* 8, 1978, pp. 137–56.

Gombrich, Ernst. *Art and Illusion: A Study in the Psychology of Pictorial Representation*. Princeton, N.J.: Princeton University Press, 1961 (1972).

———. "Ritualized Gesture and Expression in Art," *Philosophical Transactions of the Royal Society of London*, Series B. Biological Sciences, no. 772, vol. 251, 1966, pp. 393–401.

———. "Style," *International Encyclopedia of the Social Sciences*. vol 15, 1968, pp. 352–61.

Hindman, Sandra. *Text and Image in Fifteenth-Century Illustrated Dutch Bibles*. Leiden: E. J. Brill, 1977.

Janson, H. W. "Criteria of Periodization in the History of European Art," *New Literary History* 1, 1970, pp. 115–22.

Kleinbauer, W. Eugene, ed. *Modern Perspectives in Western Art History: An Anthology of 20th-century Writings on the Visual Arts*. New York: Holt, Rinehart and Winston, 1971.

Ladner, Gerhart B. *Ad Imaginem Dei. The Image of Man in Medieval Art*. Latrobe, Pa.: The Archabbey Press, 1965.

Lang, Berel, ed. *The Concept of Style*. Philadelphia: University of Pennsylvania Press, 1979, pp. 95–117.

Mahler, Annemarie. "Medieval Image Style and Saint Augustine's Theory of Threefold Vision," *Mediaevalia* 4, 1978, pp. 278–313.

Nagler, A. M. *The Medieval Religious Stage: Shapes and Phantoms*. New Haven: Yale University Press, 1976.

Nodine, Calvin F., and Dennis F. Fisher, eds. *Perception and Pictorial Representation*. New York: Praeger, 1979.

Novitz, David. *Pictures and Their Use in Communication. A Philosophical Essay*. The Hague: M. Nijhoff, 1977.

Pächt, Otto. *The Rise of Pictorial Narrative in Twelfth-Century England*. Oxford: Clarendon Press, 1962.

Panofsky, Erwin. *Early Netherlandish Painting. Its Origins and Character*. 2 vols. Cambridge, Mass.: Harvard University Press, 1960.

———. *Renaissance and Renascences in Western Art*. Stockholm: 1960; 2nd rev. ed., Uppsala, 1965; New York: Harper Torchbook, 1969.

RILA, *International Repertory of the Literature of Art*.

Robertson, Jr., D. W. "Simple Signs from Everyday Life in Chaucer," in *Signs and Symbols in Chaucer's Poetry*, ed. John P. Hermann and John J. Burke, Jr. Tuscaloosa: University of Alabama Press, 1981.

Roeder, Anke. *Die Gebarde im Drama des Mittelalters*. Münchener Texte und Untersuchungen zur deutschen Literatur des Mittelalters, 49. Munich: C. H. Beck, 1974.

Schapiro, Meyer. "On the Aesthetic Attitude in Romanesque Art," in *Art and Thought: Issued in Honor of Dr. Ananda K. Coomaraswamy on the Occasion of His 70th Birthday*, ed. K. Bharatha Iyer. London: Luzac and Co., 1947; reprinted in Meyer Schapiro, *Selected Papers: I Romanesque Art*. New York: Braziller, 1977.

———. "Style," in *Aesthetics Today*, ed. Morris Philipson. Cleveland: World Publishing Co., 1961; originally in *Anthropology Today*, ed. A. L. Kroeber. Chicago: University of Chicago Press, 1953.

Sheingorn, Pamela. "Drama and the Visual Arts: An Introductory Methodology," *RORD* 22, 1980, pp. 101–109.

———. "The Moment of Resurrection in the Corpus Christi Plays," *Mediaevalia et Humanistica* n.s. 11, 1982, pp. 111–29.

Summers, David. "Conventions in the History of Art," *New Literary History* 13, 1981.

Stevens, Martin. *Four Middle English Mystery Cycles*. Princeton: Princeton University Press, 1987.

———. "Language as Theme in the Wakefield Plays," *Speculum* 52, 1977, pp. 100–17.

Weitzmann, Kurt. "The Narrative and Liturgical Gospel Illustrations," in *New Testament Manuscript Studies*, ed. M. Parvis and A. P. Wickgren. Chicago: University of Chicago Press, 1950.

RICHARD RASTALL

Music in the Cycle Plays

I

At the First Colloquium on Records of Early English Drama in 1978, Reginald Ingram described Thomas Sharp as "the first man of REED: our patron scholar if we should seek one, who concentrated his attention on the dramatic activities of one place" (Dutka, 60–61). Sharp's work was certainly crucial in the study of early English drama, not least because he used guild records and other accounts that were the focus of the REED colloquium (Sharp). In music, too, Sharp set an excellent scholarly precedent by including in the *Dissertation* (1825) a quasi-facsimile engraving of the music prepared by his illustrator, David Jee. How accurately Jee did his work we shall never know, for the manuscript was destroyed in 1879, but the indications are that in copying a decidedly corrupt musical text Jee made some secondary errors.

Sharp's precedent was an initiative worth following, and it is not surprising that Lucy Toulmin Smith included the written music in her edition of the York plays (Smith). Unfortunately, however, the music was not well served, for the musicologist involved, W. H. Cummings, did not understand the notation. Consequently he edited only the simpler pieces, the rest being presented in a monochrome photographic reproduction.[1] The inaccuracy of Cummings's edition, and the uselessness of monochrome presentation of a notation in which red ink is musically significant, were probably enough to prevent the York music from being known for another century; but in addition, Toulmin Smith herself made adverse comments on the aesthetic value of the music, a judgment that we can now see (or rather, hear) to be mistaken (Smith, 524f.). In other respects, of course, Toulmin Smith's edition dealt more successfully with matters vital to the study of music in the plays. She faced the question of liturgical music, for instance (a matter that had not concerned Sharp because the two Coventry songs are vernacular and secular), and tried to find the texts of the York 45 pieces in the York liturgy and elsewhere, besides giving basic necessary information on the stage directions, including those that mention music.

It was known in 1960 or so that John Stevens was preparing the York music for Arthur Brown's edition of that cycle, but the edition has not yet appeared; Stevens's work was transferred to the edition by Richard

Beadle (1982; in Beadle's edition the Assumption play is no. 45; in Toulmin Smith's, no. 46). The first of the six pieces appeared in Stevens's *New Grove* article "Medieval drama" (1980), while this and one other piece were performed during his 1958 paper to the Royal Musical Association; but the rest of his edition was unknown until the publication of Beadle's work. The York pieces waited until 1971 for complete publication in an edition by Ruth Steiner attached to Carolyn Wall's paper "York Pageant 46 and its Music" (700–12). They have also appeared in a complete edition by Rastall (*Six Songs*).

In his 1958 paper Stevens also presented a performance of the first Coventry piece, which had by then been published in an edition by John P. Cutts (1957). Both Coventry pieces were later edited by Thurston Dart (1962) and Rastall (1973). Stevens also mentioned in 1958 the "snatch of plainsong in the Chester Cycle," which he later published (in his *New Grove* article) as "a simple measured monophonic *Gloria in excelsis deo.*" The Chester fragment is also presented in my 1983 essay on the music of that cycle (149). Finally, JoAnna Dutka included editions of all the York, Coventry, and Chester music in her doctoral thesis (1972) and subsequent book (1980).

Despite these various editions, the music surviving from the cycles is not well known. Indeed, most of the editions, attached as they are to scholarly discussions, have the air of appendices. Only those of the Coventry and York music by Dart and Rastall have appeared as commercial publications in their own right.[2]

It is hardly surprising that such work has been subsidiary to literary studies of the drama, however, for the surviving written music is only a fraction of that actually required in performance. One effect of this has been that work on music has concentrated on trying to understand the functions of music in the plays—to place the music in its dramatic context and thus to explain satisfactorily why the plays should contain music at all.[3] Two pieces of work have provided vital keys to our understanding. First, Stevens's 1958 paper developed the idea of music as *representation*, a consequence of the Boethian universe in which angelic music signified Divine Order and was therefore heard at times when God intervened in human affairs. From this, Stevens explained the singing of souls and of chosen mortals as representing their in-tuneness with God's Will. Second, JoAnna Dutka's exposition of the dramatic functions of music in the cycles explained how music was used to cover movement about the acting area, a change of focus from one location to another, exits and entrances, the passage of time, and so on (1980, 6–9).[4]

These two concepts were worked out on the basis of inter-cycle comparison (i.e., what the cycles have in common), however, and so are subject to the limitations inherent in the comparative method.

First, Stevens's work did not adequately explain the use of music by *bad* characters such as Herod and the Chester gossips. Second, Dutka's dramatic functions cannot always be used to elucidate the dramatic action because often we do not have the knowledge necessary to define it; for instance, the question of whether music functions to cover an entrance or only a change of focus may depend on whether the actor has been out of the audience's sight or not, and therefore on the type of staging that was used (which may be unknown). And third, inter-cycle comparison becomes positively misleading once the basic work is done. For example, it fails to take time and place into account, and there is every reason to suppose that sixteenth-century Coventry did not do things the same way as fifteenth-century York did. Just as important, it makes assumptions about what plays are comparable; while we easily recognize that the stage directions in a morality play may not tell us much about the use of music in a cycle, it is harder to define reasons for our unease when Stevens uses the famous musical stage direction from the Bodley *Resurrection* in his discussion of music in the cycle plays ("Music," 90; for the play text see Baker, 190).

The second of these problems is outside the scope of the present paper, but I shall return to the first and third. In order to do so, I shall first consider four traditions that form the philosophical and social background to the subject. They concern the place of music in the universe at large and in earthly society, and the making of music in liturgy and in minstrelsy.

II

Almost throughout the Middle Ages the teachings of Boethius (ca. 480–ca. 525) about the place of music in the universe were standard. According to this view the universe, divinely created, was founded on the simple mathematical proportions, as were the consonant musical intervals. Such was the relationship between the mathematical and the acoustical properties of music that music became a *speculum* for Divine Order. But music was not simply an analogy for Divine Order; the Creation itself produced music, the harmonious sound made by the rotating crystal spheres to which the heavenly bodies were thought to be attached. The Music of the Spheres, or *musica mundana*, was potentially audible, though the sinful ears of mankind were incapable of hearing it (Chadwick, 78–81, 86; Irwin, 189). This teaching, which Boethius transmitted to the Middle Ages from Pythagoras and Plato, not only identifies music as a vital ingredient in the standard cosmology, but allows it also to be a human representation of Divine Order. Thus music in the plays, both visible and audible, is an appropriate representation of God's Will, not only in angelic music but in the music of those mortals whom God chooses to be his instruments on earth. As Stevens pointed out, the angels—the first created beings—praise God in song as soon as they are created, there is heavenly music when God intervenes in human affairs, and the most musical mortal characters are those who are closest to God ("Music," 82–87). (I shall return to the apparent exceptions.)

Boethius's classification continued with *musica humana*. Like the Music of the Spheres, this was thought to be an aural reality inaudible to sinful man; it concerned the harmonious proportions of the smaller-scale universe, including the relationship of man's body to his soul. This, too, explains why it is usually the godly characters who sing. It is in them that the body and soul are most harmoniously related, and sin most nearly overcome, with consequent benefit to the state of the soul. A third category, *musica instrumentalis*, covered all audible human-made music, both vocal and instrumental. Since the music of angels is audible to man when God wishes it to be so, *musica instrumentalis* was potentially a means of praising God in imitation of the angels.[5]

This tradition explains the great majority of musical items in the cycle plays. But it is directly opposed by the performance of minstrelsy for Herod (Chester 8/144+SD; N-Town 18/19–20, 20/53, 20/231–32 and SD following) and the singing of Mrs. Noah's gossips (Chester 3/225–36).[6] Whatever the philosophical explanation of this problem, it is clear that the contradiction must tell us something important about the type of music performed on these occasions, and the kind of performance it received. That is, there cannot have been any aural confusion between the music of Divine Order and the music of such as Herod. (*Visual* distinction is of course a matter for the producer.)

Stevens postulated realism to explain those musical items that were not obviously governed, directly or indirectly, by Boethian cosmology. Remarking that it is not difficult to see "how music, from being a naturalistic detail . . . becomes through its association with the more seductive courtly pursuits . . . itself a symbol of seduction," he cited the morality plays in support of his argument ("Music," 88f.). This is an attractive idea, and Dutka is among those that have subscribed to it (*Music*, 6). But I believe that it is untenable, and in addition that it prevents our clearer understanding of music in medieval drama generally, not just in the cycles. First, the chronology of the cycles and moralities does not allow any progression in the use of music to be traced from one to the other. If there is a similarity in the use of music between the cycles and the moralities (principally *The Castle of Perseverance, Mankind,* and *Wisdom*) we ought to assume rather that the same tradition informs both, and attempt to identify it. Second, music as a symbol of seduction is much older than the cycles and moralities, so that such a tradition clearly did already exist. Third, the existence of such another tradition makes it possible for Stevens's own idea of *representation* to cover all of the relevant examples, while the resort to naturalism or realism brings to bear something of a quite different nature from that of *musica mundana*.

Before discussing this second tradition and its relationship to the first, let us consider some examples of musical "realism," starting with the music for Herod's entry in Chester 8/144+SD. The scene here is a royal audience chamber, which Herod enters to interview the Magi. Although the music of actual royal audiences may inform the use of music in this scene, few of the play's spectators would have attended a royal audience and thus know by experience that it was "real." Rather, the music is part of the representation of Herod's character as an earthly king, informed by the bystanders' common knowledge that when nobility or royalty entered their city (for example) they did so with the ceremonial music of shawms and trumpet. This distinction between reality and representation in Herod's music may seem a fine one, but it is vital. Its importance can be seen if we consider the Entry into Jerusalem, another event that Stevens saw as essentially realistic, calling to the spectator's mind the various royal entries that he would have seen. Here the argument of non-experience does not apply; most spectators probably *had* seen an entry and would recognize such an event in a play modeled on it. But if royal entries are indeed the model for the Entry plays, where are the loud ceremonial music, the fountains running wine, and the singing virgins dressed as angels? There is good reason to omit the last of these in a drama where actors represent angels, for the spectacle of actors playing the part of people dressed as angels would be unacceptably confusing in plays that require characters and their functions in the drama to be clearly defined. But there is a much more important reason—namely, that Christ is not an earthly king and deliberately did not enter Jerusalem as one. The audience is not allowed to confuse Christ's heavenly kingship with the rule of such as Herod, and indeed any confusion of this sort would be a theological blunder.

To claim royal entries as the model for the Entry plays, moreover, turns the whole question on its head. For, as any late medieval dramatist knew, the royal entry was itself modeled on Christ's entry into Jerusalem. The singing of "Benedictus qui venit in nomine Domini" at Henry V's triumphal return to London after the Agincourt campaign of 1415 is a good instance of this fact; and it is not the blasphemy that we might think it, but the proper expression of the role that the British have always expected their monarchs to play.[7] It is surely inconceivable that a cycle dramatist should confuse exemplar and copy when writing an Entry play. Clifford Davidson offers the much more likely explanation that the Entry plays follow the Procession of Palms, the procession immediately before High Mass on Palm Sunday (89f.).

Nor is realism on safer ground when it is proposed for the drinking song performed by the Chester gossips. This is not a real drinking song, although it should no doubt be performed like one. Again, though the incidental realism must be such as to identify the gossips for what they are, the primary function of the music is as a *representation* of their character.

How is this non-Divine Order music to be explained? The answer lies

in Boethius's third category, *musica instrumentalis*, or rather in its practitioners. Boethius, like all of his educated contemporaries, considered
the real musician to be not the performer but the thinker, interested in
the speculative side of music as a science. This places *musica instrumentalis* on a lower plane than either of the other categories, and this,
together with the low social status of the performers, was responsible for
a general disparagement of music as entertainment by Boethius and the
intelligentsia of his time.

Throughout the Middle Ages this caused much thinking and writing
about the ethics of musical performance. On the one hand, *musica
instrumentalis* had a clear and acceptable place in the cosmology, at the
bottom end, as it were, of the vertical line from Heaven to earth; and
as such it could sensibly be seen ideally as a *speculum* of Divine Order.
On the other, the observable fact was that some minstrels were the vicious and despicable dregs of society. A unanimous opinion on the recon-
ciliation of cosmological theory and social fact could not be expected, and
the picture of medieval attitudes to music is indeed a complex one
(Rastall, "Minstrelsy," *passim*).

To avoid confusion, it is best to separate the theological and social aspects of the problem. Church dignitaries often justified their employment
of a private minstrel by reference to traditions ultimately derived from
the medieval view of *musica mundana* and *musica humana*, while at the
same time they forbade religious houses to take in itinerant minstrels and
other casual entertainers. This separation of philosophical theory and social fact is nothing if not realistic; but because it also requires a distinction to be made between respectable minstrels (such as the bishop's
harper) and the vicious members of the profession, it was necessary to
classify performers in some way. The best-known attempt to do this is
probably that of Thomas de Chabham (fl. 1214–1230), who defined those
minstrels whose art made them damnable and those who could be saved
(Chambers, I, 59–62, II, 262 f; Tydeman translates the passage, 187f.). Not
everyone took quite as liberal a view of the matter as Thomas did, however, and an opposing body of opinion saw only music's undoubted connection with prostitution, petty theft, and so on, and classified all secular
music accordingly. Insofar as this became a tradition parallel to that
based on the consequences of *musica mundana*, it is the attitude informing the use of music in the moralities, where music is associated with
the vices; and it is also the basis for the second representational use of
music in the cycles, where there are considerable morality-type elements
(Woolf, 111, 239f.).[8] While these two representational uses of music may
seem to us to be mutually exclusive, the Middle Ages clearly did not find
their coexistence confusing. We shall return to the question of what this
must imply in terms of the style and type of performance.

The third tradition concerns vocal music. Plays used vocal music in
ways related closely, rather distantly, or not at all to the everyday busi-

ness of those singing. The difference can be important, not only to the provision of music for a modern performance but for our understanding of the play in question. To take one extreme, liturgical drama—that is, Latin drama entirely sung—was possible only because the performers worked in the circumstances, and with the techniques, of their normal everyday liturgical activity. They used their special knowledge of liturgical singing, ceremonial, and gesture; their costume was largely liturgical; they normally played the drama in the building in which they spent their professional lives; and even their audience was largely the usual congregation. (This is a simplification, for the congregation might be augmented and non-liturgical costume and gesture might be used, but the point made is basically correct.)

These circumstances could obtain in secular, as well as monastic, establishments. As Susan Rankin has shown, the three fragmentary plays now at Shrewsbury, which despite their vernacular texts are closer to liturgical drama than to the cycles, belong to the corpus of processional music performed at Lichfield Cathedral.[9] Like most English processional polyphony of the period, the music is written in conductus style in three parts (alto, tenor, and bass). The Shrewsbury shepherds sing polyphony, then, because they are a part of the liturgical ceremony of a secular cathedral, the actors being members of the cathedral's musical establishment, and it would be a serious methodological error to use this music as evidence that the shepherds sang polyphony in the civic cycles. One might argue that the Coventry play of the Nativity supports a general use of polyphony by mortal characters in the civic plays, there being polyphony for the shepherds and the Mothers of the Innocents; but in the hundred years or so that separate the two plays much happened to change the musical scene in England. We should not regard the Coventry music as general evidence for the cycles, but rather treat it as an isolated case to be assessed on its own merits.

It is worth considering whether any other vernacular drama can be identified as belonging to a context similar to that of the Shrewsbury plays. It is difficult to make positive identifications, in view of an apparent lack of documentary evidence or clear internal references, but we may guess that the Bodley plays of the Burial and Resurrection are of this type (Woolf, 331–35).[10] The special interest of this lies in a stage direction near the end of the *Resurrection*, prescribing the polyphonic or at least antiphonal performance of *Victimae paschali laudes*. This direction, then, should not be assumed to indicate the normal resources for that piece when it is sung by mortals in a *civic* resurrection play (Baker, 190, 229f.).

For the music in civic cycles was performed in very different circumstances. Here, the organizers and actors alike were non-musicians whose business was never liturgy, and the plays were performed away from any liturgical setting. The evidence suggests that the dramatists, civic authority, and producers had little to do with the music chosen or its method of performance. While a particular liturgical piece may some-times have been specified by the dramatist or producer, some stage direc-tions that name Latin pieces seem to have been marginal directions origi-nally, written probably as a record of what had been sung rather than as a directive of what should be (Meredith, esp. 259; Mills, "Stage," esp. 50). The men in charge of the plays were not, of course, in any sense experi-enced in liturgy and music; and it is likely that when singers were pro-cured from the local cathedral the organizers were only too pleased to tell them what was required and then leave them to provide it in their own way. No doubt the singing-man in charge elected to provide singers and (if necessary) books, and to rehearse the singers sufficiently; and it seems to me quite possible that the producer did not always know, until the actors and singers first rehearsed together, what pieces had been chosen. Nor were the available forces as large as would be the case when a church put on a play in its own building. A cathedral choir had its own daily du-ties to perform, and if it was not to be too depleted and overworked in fulfilling its obligations, only a few boys and one or two clerks could be made available to the cycle in any one year. Thus, in Chester the Smiths hired a group of singers—specified as five boys in 1561—for their Purifi-cation play in 1554 and 1561; but in 1567 and 1568 no boys were hired, and the Smiths paid two clerks instead. In the latter years the Painters had probably hired boys for their Nativity play, and we may guess that they stole a march on the Smiths by hiring boys first, making their offer before the Smiths could do so. If this is a correct reading of the very in-complete records, it means that the cathedral was unable to supply two such groups of boys simultaneously (Rastall, "[Chester] Cycle," 135).

One consequence of this situation is that the play texts do not always specify what piece is to be sung; another is that the plays may have in-cluded heavenly music at places where there is no indication of it. It is not always easy to distinguish when the Latin incipits occurring as stage directions or otherwise really do indicate the use of liturgical pieces in the cycles. After all, the biblical narrative includes a number of set pieces that could properly be sung—such as the Magnificat in St. Luke 1.46–55—without the need for a liturgical tune. To this there are two answers; first, that the Scriptures do not say that such pieces were sung, so that—Boethian cosmology notwithstanding—only the liturgy, as a normally sung series of texts, would invariably suggest sung performance; second, that in those cases where the Vulgate and liturgical versions differ (such as the angelic Gloria at the Nativity) it is the liturgical version that is used.[11] This is what one would expect; the cathedral singers had a regular repertory which was suitable to the purpose, and it would be natural for them to use it even if they could not transfer the ceremonial and trap-pings that normally accompanied it.

The last tradition is that of minstrelsy. No title is given for any piece of instrumental music in the cycle plays, and we can assume, I think, that the producer of the play did not need to specify what piece should be played. Indeed, it is likely, given the absence of text, that he did not need to know, either in advance of the performance or later. The minstrel tradition was an aural tradition, which impinged very little on the tradition of written, composed music until the sixteenth century. The implications of this need to be borne in mind; in England, at least, it is virtually unthinkable that these two traditions should be brought together. Certainly until the sixteenth century, when minstrels began to play from written music, it is most unlikely that minstrels and church singers could work together. Although iconographical sources show minstrels and singers together—in depictions of such subjects as the Coronation of the Virgin, for instance—we cannot accept this as evidence of such performance. The pictures do, of course, have their own very strong symbolism of the type already discussed. In fact, the records seem to show that in the sixteenth century singers in the plays were accompanied by a small organ played by a church organist (Clopper, 78; Ingram, *passim*, esp. 208, 216, 256),[12] a much more austere musical force than iconography would suggest. Altogether, it seems that the minstrels worked independently on their part in the plays until such time as it became necessary to coordinate music and action in the rehearsals and performances.

These traditions seem to inform the use of music, then, in vernacular English drama—biblical plays (civic and ecclesiastical), saints' plays, and moralities—and they help us to solve the problems facing us. At the same time, not all the evidence supports the strictest interpretations of the traditions. One reason for this is that the traditions themselves were weakened with time and in the face of practical considerations; another, that the evidence itself is incomplete and often difficult to interpret.

III

I have discussed elsewhere the main types of evidence in general terms, and some of it in detail, as it bears on the provision of music (Rastall, "All hefne" and "Some Myrth"), but one type, the surviving written music itself, has yet to be examined as closely as it deserves. Music survives in the play texts of the York, Coventry, and Chester cycles. I have found no concordances[13] for any of this music, which strengthens the supposition that music copied into the play manuscripts in full was probably composed specially for the play. It may also indicate that the music could not be used in any other context by the professional singers who performed it and the establishment for which they normally worked.

The oldest of these cycle manuscripts is the York register, kept by the Common Clerk of the city. Beadle and Meredith have assigned its main compilation to the period 1463–1477 ("Further Evidence," 55). Play XLV, *The Assumption of the Virgin*, belongs to this main compilation. At three points in the play there is angelic singing, the music itself, two-part polyphony in score, being copied into spaces accurately left for it by the main text-scribe. The music hand is a professional one. The music would seem to have been copied immediately after the main text of the play (Rastall, "The [York] Music"). The style of the music, however, suggests a rather earlier date, and it is possible that the music was composed some twenty or thirty years before this copy was made (Rastall, "Vocal Range").

At the end of the play are three more musical items, settings of the same three texts copied by the same scribe. Close examination shows that these settings (which Ruth Steiner has called the "B" versions) and those in the body of the play (the "A" versions) were all composed by the same man. One difference between the A and B settings is immediately apparent, for the B settings are rhythmically more complex than the A settings, and are written in separate parts, not in score; and they are also longer than the A settings. Another difference is that the B settings use a wider and higher vocal range, suggesting that they were composed for boy trebles while the A settings were for altos or countertenors.

Investigation into the use of pitches in the two groups of settings, however, shows that both were written for treble voices. The significance of the alternative settings is, therefore, one of difficulty; the A versions are relatively easy pieces, while the B versions could probably be sung only by the most able choristers. Alternatively, the A versions would be suitable for performance in the open air, while the B versions would probably have to be sung in more helpful acoustic conditions than outdoor performance usually allows. It is significant that the B settings, which are more hurriedly copied, are also seriously defective in the texts of two pieces out of the three. It is impossible to know what effect this had on performances. If the omissions were due to hasty copying of the music into the Register, then the exemplar from which that copy was made was presumably a good one; indeed it is hard to see why the Register copy was made unless there was a possibility of performing the B versions at some time. We can safely assume also that the exemplar was in the care of a professional musician—probably a singing-man at the Minster or other church—and not in the hands of the Weavers. Possibly the music scribe of the Register was in charge of the music for the play, and he himself kept the performing material. In that case the music could be performed without reference to the Register copy until the performing copies disintegrated. Thereafter, it seems doubtful that a director of music could reconstruct the B settings from the defective reference copies in the Register, or would trouble to do so.

Carolyn Wall has noted that the version of the Assumption legend followed in this play seems to come from Prato, and she has suggested a wool-trade link between York and the area around Florence ("Apocryphal"; "York," 691 n. 13). This version differs in important respects from that given in *The Golden Legend*, and the texts given there, too, are not exactly those of the York pieces, although very close (see Smith, 25–27; Hoffman, 236–39; Wall, "York," 685–87; Dutka, *Music*, 38, 44, 47). "Surge proxima mea" and "Veni de Libano sponsa" probably derive ultimately from the *Canticum Canticorum* (II/10, 13–14, and IV/8, respectively), and there are some liturgical items closely related to them. The second part of "Veni electa mea" is from Psalm 44, verse 12a—not the Vulgate version, but that used in the tract "Audi filia"—while the full text appears several times in the liturgy, though sometimes with slightly altered wording. Since the precise wording appears (among other places) in a Matins responsory for the feast of the Assumption, it would seem that the York dramatist went at least partly to the liturgy for his texts (Lawley II, col. 481, also cols. 63, 77, 476, 489, 490, and 547; Henderson II, 155).

Of the three texts, then, only the last had its own musical setting in the plainsong of the York liturgy. However the other two texts were composed, they seem to be based on those found in *The Golden Legend*, but adapted by reference to other related texts. There is, however, no question of any of the York settings being based on plainsong. It is true that the absence of plainsong in late medieval polyphony is impossible to prove (Sparks, 2), but even "Veni electa mea" seems to bear no musical relation to the possible plainsong tunes. This means that none of these six pieces could have been used liturgically; hence, also, that the music must have been composed specially for this or a similar purpose; and that copies were likely to have been made only for use by those singing in the play. Bearing in mind that performing copies of the B versions probably could not be replaced by reference to the Register copy, and that all performing copies surviving into the mid-sixteenth century would become useless when the Marian plays were suppressed, it is hardly surprising that no other copies of this music seem to have survived.

The York pieces are the most substantial body of music surviving from the plays, and it is a pity that they are not well known. In turning to the music in the Coventry plays we encounter one piece—the famous "Coventry Carol"—known to almost everyone.[14] The two plays surviving from the Coventry cycle were both edited by Thomas Sharp (1825 and 1836) from manuscripts that were apparently the guilds' own copies of the plays; but only one of these manuscripts—that of the Weavers' Purification pageant—is still extant. It has the texts of two songs, but no music (Craig, 70f.). The other manuscript was that of the Shearmen's and Tailors' pageant dealing with the Nativity and Massacre of the Innocents. This, however, was destroyed by fire at the Birmingham Free Library in 1879, so that Sharp's 1825 edition is now the unique source both for the play itself and for the music that it contains.

The copy of the play from which Sharp worked, dated 14 March 1534, was a revised version made by Robert Croo; but the songs, which are added at the end of the play, were copied by Thomas Mawdyke on 13 May 1591. The question arises whether the songs were included in the text that Croo produced, or were added some time between then and Mawdyke's work. The style of the music is compatible with a date in the 1530s. The shepherds' song, "As I out rode this enderes night," has the simple imitative entries that one might expect from a piece of that date, with the chordal start that allows a confident beginning to the performance. Moreover, the play text gives a stage direction naming this piece after the shepherds have decided to visit the child at Bethlehem; "There the Schepperdis syngis ASE I OWT RODDE & Josoff seyth. . . ." It might not be the same setting, of course, but no other is known.

The second verse of this song, "Down from Heaven," is copied separately from the first, the lullaby coming between them. Craig assumed that the separate copying was due to the two verses being sung on different occasions, and he referred to "Down from Heaven" in a footnote to the stage direction "There the schepperdis syngith ageyne and goth forthe of the place . . . " (after line 331) following the shepherds' adoration of the Child. In this interpretation Craig was followed by Stevens and Dutka (Craig, 12; Stevens, "Music," 91; Dutka, *Music*, 7). It cannot be correct, however, for the prophets who discuss the events in the next scene state (a) that the shepherds went away from the stable praising God, and (b) that they are now admitted to Heaven, where they sing "Nowell" (Craig, 16). Only (a) concerns us here, and "Down from Heaven" does not fulfill these conditions for the shepherds' second song. Clearly the shepherds' whole lives are altered by their visit to the Christ-Child (as is the case in other cycles, too), and it would be inadequate simply to revert to singing about the angelic vision (which indeed is logical enough on their way *to* the Child). Moreover, the use of the two verses to frame the adoration scene does not fully explain the problem of their separation in the copy of the music at the end of the play text. Since the lullaby comes between them, any solution must account for the wrong ordering of the music.

I conclude that the shepherds sang the whole of "As I out rode," including the second verse, on their way to Bethlehem; that they sang a song of praise to God at the end of the adoration scene; that this second song was omitted from the play text either by oversight, because the music was not available to the copyist, or perhaps because it was a preexistent song of which copies were available elsewhere; and that the music copyist overlooked the second verse of "As I out rode" when he copied the first, adding it only when he discovered his mistake after copying the lullaby. Alternatively it may be that the copyist became confused and really thought that "Down from Heaven" was a separate song. In any case we must suppose that "Down from Heaven" was originally written on a separate piece of paper, but there are so many unknowns of this sort that we are unlikely now to find a completely satisfactory explanation of the music copying.

R. L. Greene included the Coventry texts in *The Early English Carols* (42, 59f.). However, neither is a carol—that is, they do not have the late medieval carol form, in which the verses alternate with a formally independent burden—but a strophic song with refrain, the refrain being part of the overall structure that includes the verse. Greene regarded the shepherds' song as a carol now lacking its burden; certainly its three-line aaa-rhymed verse is typical of the carol structure, and a number of carol texts are clearly related to it. He also treated the lullaby as a carol with a possibly preexistent burden.

The lullaby text does look like that of a carol, mainly because the opening lines, of 4, 3, 2, and 3 feet, do not match the other verses, which have 4, 3, 4, and 3 feet. But these lines are not a carol burden, for the musical setting is the same as that for the other sections (Ex. 1). The only difference is the loss of four syllables from the second half of the verse, together with the relevant notes. Thus the would-be burden, which we must recognize as the first verse, is slightly shorter than the other verses, and its structure is asymmetrical in consequence. It is tempting to restore the "missing" notes and adjust the text accordingly, but, as a matter of fact, it is hard to see how one might add to the text, and even harder to imagine by what process those few notes could have been omitted at some stage in all three parts. Unsatisfactory as it seems, I believe that the lullaby has to be left as it is.

The two Coventry pieces are sung by, respectively, the three shepherds and the three mothers of the Innocents. Both songs are for the "three-men's" texture of alto, tenor, and bass, but the singers impersonate men in one case and women in the other. For this reason the composer has made the textures very different.[15] In the lullaby the whole texture seems lighter and higher, as befits the impersonation of women. Reference to the vocal ranges shows that the higher-sounding texture of the lullaby is not caused by higher overall vocal ranges, but comparative examination of the use of pitches reveals that a concentration of higher notes in the upper voices results in a separation of those voices from the bass, the tenor, and the alto being in a fairly constant relationship.[16]

Considering the relative rarity of, and financial reward demanded by, such a group of singers, it would be surprising if the Shearmen and Tailors did not double the roles of the shepherds and the mothers of the Innocents. I calculate that some twenty-five minutes elapse between the final exit of the shepherds and the entrance of the mothers with the Innocents—more than enough time for the necessary costume change.

Like the York B versions, these two songs stand at the end of the play text. In both cases the immediate source for the play text as it survives is almost certainly a working text belonging to the guild concerned. The music appears in the text, presumably, because it was included in the guild's own material for the play, either incorporated into the text or (more likely, perhaps) associated with it as a separate copy. As with the York pieces, the lack of concordances for the Coventry "carols" seems to suggest that the music was composed specially for the play and used only during its performance.

The latest and smallest of the musical items in the cycle texts appears in one of the Chester manuscripts, H, which is dated 1607. In this source only, the angelic *Gloria* sung to the shepherds in the Painters' and Glaziers' pageant (Play 7) is written out (facs. Mills, *Chester*, f. 42; eds. Dutka, *Music*, 29; and Rastall, "[Chester] Cycle," 149). The text set is "Gloria in excelsis deo," but this is not the complete piece; the stage direction after line 357 gives also the next line of text, "et in terra pax hominibus bone voluntatis," and the shepherds' discussion following this confirms the longer text.

William Mahrt has suggested that, as the repetitions of the word "deo" bring the syllables of the underlaid text to the same number as those of the next (unwritten) line, "et . . . voluntatis," the second line of text may have been intended to be sung to the same music. (Ex. 2)[17] This solution was used in the performances at Leeds and Chester in May and June 1983, the tune being decorated by the singer on the repetition ("et . . . voluntatis"). Although this was an effective way of solving the difficulty, stylistic considerations suggest that it is not the correct solution. This music looks to me like the incipit of a voice from a mid-sixteenth-century polyphonic setting, and in preparing music for the 1983 performances I did construct a four-part setting using the given music as a tenor part, to be sung as a solo accompanied by a regals playing the whole texture. This piece would of course have been incomplete; from "et in terra" onwards one would have to construct a new section based on the relevant plainsong tune ("[Chester] Cycle," 147; "Some Myrth," 84f.).[18]

The musical fragment in MS H seems not to be a piece specially composed for the play, then, as in the York and Coventry cases, but an incipit identifying for the producer or musical director of the play a polyphonic setting available in the normal music books used by the singers in the liturgy. If the musical setting indicated was indeed used in mid-century performances, the musical fragment was presumably part of the material from which H was copied. However, we must also bear in mind the possibility that the setting was included in MS H for antiquarian reasons, and was never in fact performed as part of the play. The main scribe of H, James Miller, was a minor canon and precentor of Chester Cathedral, and so would have access to any pre-Reformation music books remaining there (Mills, *Chester Cycle*, viii-ix).[19] Against this, we should note that by 1600 or so a specific pre-Reformation piece chosen for such a purpose would more likely be copied complete; and on the whole it seems probable that the setting identified was used in performances toward the end

Ex. 1   Coventry lullaby, vv. 1 and 2: top voice only

1. Lul - ly, lul - -lay, thou lit-tell tyne child,

2. O sis - ters two, how may we do

By, by, lul - ly, lul - lay: Thou lit-tell tyne child,

For to pre -serve this day Oure pore yong - ling For

By, by, lul - ly, lul - lay.

whom we do singe   By, by, lul - ly, lul - lay.

Ex. 2   Chester Gloria

Glo - - ri - a   in ex-cel-sis de - -o, de -
et   in ter - ra pax ho - mi - ni - -bus bo -

o, de - o,   de - o.
nae vo - lun - ta - tis.

of the cycle's life. It is unfortunate that no music from this period survives at Chester Cathedral. As it is, the search for the *Gloria* setting concerned has so far been unsuccessful.

I V

In this essay I have tried to keep sight of my ultimate aim, the inclusion of music in performances of the cycle plays. As soon as one begins to work on a production a host of questions present themselves, and the answers are not all easy to find. Indeed, it may be that there are no firm answers, and that some narrowing down of possibilities into probabilities is the best that we can hope for. Nevertheless, we should be optimistic about our chances of arriving at sensible solutions eventually. Much useful work has been done, and we shall gain much from the information being unearthed by the REED editors and others. What we need to go with this, I think, is a slightly different approach, a new way of asking the same questions (though it is also true that the full range of questions has not yet been posed). It is possible to ask a number of questions about, for example, angelic music in the cycles: Was it plainsong, improvised polyphony, or composed polyphony? Was it accompanied by instruments? If it was improvised polyphony, what sort of improvisation was used? If it was composed polyphony, how many angels sang it, and in how many parts? And so on.

In a sense these are the right questions, the specific questions to which we ultimately want the answers. Put like this, however, they are too theoretical, and the framework of a particular type of music makes inter-cycle comparison almost irresistible. We now need to pose the questions differently by placing them in a framework of thought that allows us from the start to treat each cycle as an individual unit—and indeed each play within the cycle if necessary.

The musical problems of the individual cycle might best be considered in relation to four main areas:

1. *Technical.* The eventual aim in this area will be to answer the questions about the use of plainsong, polyphony, etc., for each cycle. First, however, we should look at the evidence in each cycle concerning the technical abilities of the musicians. In the Nativity plays where the shepherds make it clear that the *Gloria*-singing angel has an exceptionally good voice (e.g., Chester, 7/406–407: "He had a mych better voyce then I have, / as in heaven all other have soe"), it would be unreasonable not to have the *Gloria* performed by a singer possessing a trained voice of professional quality. On the other hand, we cannot assume that "as in heaven all other have soe" necessarily applies to other cycles or even to other plays in the same cycle. Other items of angelic music do not have the same special performance traditions in the liturgy, do not make such a special appearance in the banns (though the Chester banns do mention

Christ's Last Judgment item "Venite benedicti"), and do not receive the same acclaim in the play texts. For the Chester Flight into Egypt, for instance, the angel need not have a stunning voice and the singing need not be of a virtuoso character (Chester 10/498); a pleasant and accurate good amateur voice is all that is required. In other places it would actually be harmful to have a professional singing angel who would outshine another singer. In the York Annunciation, for example (York 12/145–240+SD), Mary's Magnificat at the end of the play should not be notably inferior musically to the angel's singing earlier in the play. Indeed, this would be a serious production defect.

The answer may be that Mary and the angel were both played by professional singers—the relevant guild accounts do not survive at York. I doubt if there is a single answer to this, however, for the plays' musical requirements of characters such as Mary and Simeon are very varied. If the Chester Smiths did indeed hire Robert White in 1568 to take the part of Simeon when they had difficulty in filling the role (Rastall, "[Chester] Cycle," 135), this may have been a special solution for that year; but it does not necessarily mean that the actor playing Simeon was usually of an amateur standard as a singer. Besides, "amateur" and "professional" are not precise qualitative terms, and the border between them, then as now, was a vague one. There is no reason why the average professional singer from the main church in the area should necessarily have outshone an amateur with a good voice and a quick ear. The main difference between them is likely to have been that the former read music and the latter learned his music by ear. This is why I think it important to consider the existence of "show-piece" items (such as the *Gloria*, the only undoubted contender so far) in the plays, and to identify the precise liturgical items sung so that we can assess their difficulty (see Rastall, "[Chester] Cycle," 142–61).

2. *Stylistic.* This area concerns the style of musical performance; it is closely related to the first area, and even depends upon it insofar as the style will relate to the musical repertory involved and the technical details of the music.

We must consider first whether there is likely to be any stylistic difference between the singing of angels and that of such mortals as Mary and Simeon. On this matter we have no direct evidence, although some of the arguments presented under (1), above, probably apply. Leaving aside the *Gloria* (which in the Towneley shepherds' plays, in addition to the argument already put forward, requires a virtuosity that marks out the angel as a highly skilled performer), we know that angelic singing in general may be matched fairly closely by that of Mary and Simeon (the latter is, after all, a priest in most of the Purification plays). Musically, there will probably be two differences: a lack of virtuosity in the mortals' singing (Magnificat and Nunc Dimittis being canticles) that may be present in the angels'; and the possibility of instrumental accompaniment for angels, never accorded to mortals' singing. Otherwise, the differences are likely to be nonmusical; a clear visual differentiation due to costuming; and the fact that the angels belong to the heavenly location, even though they sometimes descend to other parts of the acting area.

The shepherds present a more complex problem. In the Towneley plays there must certainly be a qualitative difference between them and the angels (see Carpenter), the most likely solution being that the shepherds (who can nevertheless sing in tune) have no formal musical training. The same should be true in Chester play 7, but here there are chronological considerations. Let us suppose that at the end of the fifteenth century the text already included the previously quoted remark "[the angel] had a mych better voyce then I have" (Chester 7/406). As already stated, we ought to take this at face value; the angel was probably a highly competent professional singer, while the shepherds could simply be musical amateurs. However, the Chester direction for the shepherds' singing of "Trolly lolly lolly lo" (Chester 7/447+SD) must surely have started life as a marginal direction,[20] so that it does not necessarily match up with the intentions of the text concerning the shepherds' abilities. Insofar as it is clearly a secular song, and in English, we may guess that the repertory makes up for the shepherds' amateur status as singers—that is, that the entertainment value of their song offsets their lack of technical expertise as sigers. This *may* also be true in the Towneley plays (and of the York play, too, although that includes no indication of the angel's superiority), where no text is specified for the shepherds' songs. Only in the N-Town cycle is a Latin piece specified for the shepherds (Block, *Ludus*, 148); this is in keeping with the more liturgical feeling of that cycle, although we cannot dismiss the possibility of Latin texts in the York and Towneley cycles. Since the performance of plainsong (as opposed to the chanting of psalms and canticles) does require considerable training, it seems likely that the N-Town shepherds would have been played by professional singers. This might explain the use of instrumental accompaniment for angelic singing in that cycle, for that would provide a very clear differentiation between angelic and mortal singing.

To return to the Chester shepherds. While "Trolly lolly lolly lo" might well fit with the fifteenth-century text, there is also the possibility that it was sung to a polyphonic setting. The Coventry Shearmen's and Tailors' pageant required polyphony apparently as early as 1534, and this certainly means that the actors playing the shepherds and the mothers of the Innocents were professional musicians. We know that polyphony was used also in the Norwich cycle for mortal singing, so that the possibility for sixteenth-century Chester cannot be dismissed.[21]

Extension of the various arguments just presented should enable us to define at least some of the qualities of the singing of Noah's family, the souls of the prophets in Limbo, the Apostles at Pentecost, and the

Saved Souls at the Last Judgment; and also of Christ's singing in the Chester Ascension and Judgment plays.

The final problem of vocal performance style comes with the use of music by bad characters—Mak in the Towneley Second Shepherds' Play and the gossips in the Chester Noah. In the Towneley case there is no doubt that Mak gives a highly unmusical performance; the First Shepherd says that he sings out of tune (Towneley 13/477). This suggests that Mak is tone deaf, but in any case the result is that his singing distinguishes him very clearly from the musical shepherds and other mortals chosen by God to work his Will. The singing of the Chester gossips need not be so bad, since the words themselves are enough to characterize this song as ungodly (Chester 3/225–36); but the words must be clearly audible, or the point of the song is lost. This requires some competence, because the gossips must not sound either refined or godly; their song is presumably appropriate to a rather rowdy drinking session. In stylistic terms, these conditions may indicate a degree of out-of-tuneness (much less than Mak's, however), a moderately raucous delivery, and possibly some "pub" harmony (or at least its sixteenth-century equivalent, which might reasonably include some use of parallel 4ths or 5ths). It is not easy to guess whether this would have required professional singers in the sixteenth century; I feel that it need not have done so.

Finally under this heading I want to consider the possible playing styles of the instrumentalists concerned. The N-Town and Chester cycles both require *bas* (soft) minstrelsy for heaven as well as *haut* (loud) minstrelsy for King Herod. How were these two types—one heavenly and the other vicious—differentiated other than by the instruments used? We must in fairness say that they may not have been differentiated further; *haut* and *bas* music make quite different sounds that would not be confused by medieval and sixteenth-century audiences, and their representational functions would be well understood. While we should not overestimate the sweetness of the sound made by *bas* instruments,[22] we can say with certainty that the loud consort of shawms and trumpet, the standard loud outdoor band surely used to announce Herod, is not only very loud by comparison with *bas* consorts but also very raucous. In this respect we have the same difference as between godly characters and the Chester gossips, but there is an important difference, in that *haut* and *bas* minstrels alike would certainly be skilled professionals.

The only other differentiation possible, I think, is one of repertory. Here one can say nothing definite, however, because no item of minstrelsy in the plays is named. It would no doubt be suitable for the angelic minstrelsy to be improvised over a plainsong tune, or at least over a nonliturgical religious song-tune (such as "Angelus ad Virginem," if required for an Annunciation play); similarly, it would seem suitable for Herod's *haut* minstrels to improvise over a courtly tune such as a *basse dance*.

A medieval audience would certainly recognize the style of such tunes, and in many cases the tunes themselves. But this is pure speculation. We have nothing to guide us other than the negative proposition reversing this argument; namely, that a medieval audience would recognize the *unsuitability* of angels playing a *basse dance* (or *would* this be so unsuitable?) or of Herod's *haut* minstrels improvising over a plainsong tune. These two types, plus the nonliturgical religious song, do not exhaust the available repertory, of course; but they account for a large part of it and are obvious choices for a twentieth-century producer.

3. *Symbolic.* A similar problem arises over the symbolism of individual instruments. The *bas* instruments are closely identified with angelic minstrelsy in late medieval iconography. The portative organ, a secular rather than an ecclesiastical instrument, is included in many depictions of heavenly music, and we can assume that a cycle play audience would accept it as part of the representation of heaven; and regals similarly, no doubt. Of other *bas* instruments we need be concerned only with the harp, which is specified in a direction in the N-Town Assumption play; "hic discendet angelus ludentibus citharis" ("Here the angel will descend to the playing of harps"; Block, *Ludus*, 358). The harp was commonly understood to symbolize Christ on the Cross, the sinews of his body (the strings) being stretched over a wooden frame (Brunne I, 158; see also Bowles, 76f.).

The difficulties arise over those instruments that have a dual or manifold symbolism attached to them; those concerned in the plays are the trumpet and the bagpipe.

The trumpet took three forms at the time of the plays. The long straight ceremonial *buisine*, often depicted in scenes of the Last Judgment, is the obvious instrument for use in the Doomsday plays; second, there is the rather longer-tubed S-shaped instrument; and third, the trumpet with a slide in the manner of a trombone, known (with many spelling variants) as a *sacqueboute*, or sackbut (see Downey). For our present purpose no distinction is needed between the S-shaped trumpet and the slightly later sackbut; both were musically superior to the *buisine* and were used in shawm and trumpet bands. The sackbut appeared also in various sixteenth-century consort-groupings. I have already said that I think the shawm and trumpet band most suitable for Herod, and one of my reasons for this is the symbolism of the *buisine*. A medieval king was entitled to trumpets as part of the trappings of his kingship, and this might include (depending on the date) any of the types of trumpet just described (Rastall, "Some English Consort-Groupings," 187–92). From the point of view of realism, then, Herod could have a fanfare from a group of *buisines* or from a mixed consort of *buisines* and S-trumpets or sackbuts. I reject these latter, however, because of the commonly understood symbolism of the *buisine* for judgment, of which its iconographical connection with the Last Judgment is the major part. Thus the *buisine* as a royal instrument is symbolic of the king as judge. That is one reason why I think it unsuitable for Herod, who is not a wise, God-fearing ruler.[23] Even more important, *any* use of trumpets that might preempt the Last Trump in the plays would seem to be a mistake.

The problem of the bagpipe is similar to that of the use of music itself in the cycles and moralities. The proper musical instrument for a medieval shepherd was the pastoral bagpipe, the instrument shown in many depictions of the angelic announcement to the shepherds. One reason for the appearance of the instrument is probably that it had connections with pilgrims, and the shepherds are the first Christian pilgrims when they go to see the Christ-Child. But bagpipes also had a very strong symbolic association with the Vices, notably with gluttony and lechery (Block, "Chaucer's Millers"). The problem may be posed in this way; if a bagpipe were to appear in a shepherds' play, would the dramatic context be strong enough (as that of a book of hours, for instance, clearly was) to abolish the symbolic association with vice for the occasion? The evidence suggests that the answer to this should be "yes," and therefore that the "pipe" among the gifts made to the Christ-Child in the Coventry and Chester shepherds' plays could be a bagpipe (Rastall, "Some Myrth," 86–89). The possibility may have been limited practically by the difficulties of finding an actor who could play the instrument, however, and this is something to watch for as the *REED* series progresses.

4. *Of staging.* Under this final heading I wish to discuss matters affected directly by the production. These are largely concerned with the visibility and audibility of the musicians.

It is possible that in a pageant production, where space was limited, singers and instrumentalists might have performed out of sight behind the wagon. However, this does not seem very likely, and the evidence of the accounts contained in *REED* volumes so far published points in the opposite direction. It follows that all angelic music was visible to the audience and contained in the heavenly location (except when an angel was sent elsewhere); that singers were costumed and on stage; and that we are right in assuming that the speaking angelic roles were also the singing roles. The limitations of space on a wagon may partly explain why there is so little evidence of instruments other than the regals being used in processional cycles, although the directions for "minstrelles" in Chester play 2 indicate at least two *bas* minstrels. All the same, the use of harps in the N-Town Assumption may well point to less restrictive heavenly quarters in a fixed-stage production.

Another reason why regals may have been preferable to minstrels' instruments in the processional cycles is that of all instruments regals would be one of the least vulnerable to climatic conditions. Unlike costumes (in relation to which one thinks of wet weather as being inimical) musical instruments can be damaged as much by sunshine as by damp, so that the matter is of some importance. The whole question of weather conditions and the care of properties, instruments, etc., is an interesting one on which we have almost no information; one wonders if the wagons were not more solidly walled in at the back (and perhaps the sides, too) than we sometimes assume. At least we may guess that the heaven on a fixed stage was as weatherproof as sightlines would allow.

The question of shelter raises that of audibility. Another reason for the use of regals in processional plays must surely be that they are more audible than a portative pipe organ or any *bas* minstrels' instrument. In a narrow medieval street, such as Stonegate in York, the buildings act as a soundboard in front and behind, but it is unlikely that *bas* instruments could make much effect outside the Abbey gates at Chester, for instance—there is simply not enough support from nearby buildings. In either place, too, the noise of an audience and passersby significantly affects the audibility of singing and *bas* minstrelsy. Again, I wonder if heaven did not have a solid back and roofing that would focus the sound forward. With fixed staging, where the audience is larger, the same problem must have obtained; the harps in the N-Town Assumption would need some help from the set if they were to make much impact.

It is true that much of the importance of heavenly minstrelsy lay in the visual side of it; the audience expected to *see* Divine Order in action in the plays, just as they did in pictures and roof corbels. Nevertheless, minstrelsy was surely too expensive not to be heard, and in any case medieval audiences were used to minstrelsy as an aural phenomenon. I find it hard to believe that any music was allowed to be inaudible.

In this essay I have been selective in the topics chosen for discussion and in the evidence presented. If this makes some areas—section four, especially—seem rather speculative, that is by no means misleading. To a large extent, informed guesswork is the only way forward in this subject at present, although the word "informed" is one that needs to be stressed.

In the first section of this paper I briefly reviewed scholarly work on my subject. I noted that its position as a minor part of literary studies tended to result in various types of inadequacy, at least in the sense that such work should be influential both in informing subsequent scholarly activity and, ultimately, in making it possible to perform the plays with suitable musical items. In section two the commonly accepted views of music history were drawn on to define four traditions necessary to an understanding of the plays; and this was followed in section three by a specifically musicological study of the surviving music. In the final section I attempted to redefine the questions to be asked, and then to combine the viewpoints of the musicologist, the music historian, and the student of early drama in suggesting methods and ways of thinking that might be useful in answering such questions.

Although my subject is a long-standing one—it dates back at least to Thomas Sharp's *Dissertation* (1825), with which I began—it has for various reasons never quite "taken off." Now that performances of complete, or nearly complete, cycles are taking place relatively frequently, it is increasingly important to see the music, like the plays themselves, as a living art that flourished against the background of living traditions. That, at least, is what I understand by the "context" of music in early drama.

NOTES

1. One should perhaps not be too hard on Cummings's ignorance. The principles of fifteenth-century notation were not then widely known, and the York pieces are still puzzling and problematic to an editor. The three settings in the body of the text were edited (Smith, 517–21); facsimiles were presented of the third of these (frontispiece) and of the three pieces at the end of the play (plates 2 and 3, following p. 528).

2. See Dart (*Two Coventry Carols*) and Rastall (*Six Songs*). The Coventry lullaby is in a sense an exception to this, for it is a standard item in hymn books and carol collections; but it appears in such publications in a four-part version with altered rhythms. See n. 14, below.

3. See the survey of previous work in Dutka (*Music* 1, 130). Understandably, such work has generally taken stage directions, not music, as its starting point.

4. The representational and structural functions of music in the plays are further discussed in Rastall ("[Chester] Cycle," 114–23). The most important of the structural functions, using music to mark scene divisions, had been mentioned in Carpenter (esp. 213), but she did not follow up her lead.

5. The audibility of angelic music is discussed by Irwin (189–92). On the earthly imitation of heavenly minstrelsy, see Rastall ("Minstrelsy Church and Clergy," esp. 84–88).

6. Citations of play texts refer to the standard editions listed in the Bibliography: references are to play/line(s), with "+SD" referring where necessary to the stage direction following the line cited. On the problems of the Chester gossips' song, see Rastall ("[Chester] Cycle," 156ff).

7. On royal entries generally, see Withington (I, ch. 3); on music in entries, Rastall ("Music for a Royal Entry, 1474," 463–66); on the 1415 entry, Bent (23). Gordon Kipling has discussed the relations between the royal entry and Christ's entry into Jerusalem.

8. It is significant that the most obvious of these, the appearance of Death in N-Town play 20, coincides with Herod's minstrel-accompanied feasting: Block, *Ludus* (174–76).

9. See also Davis, especially Frank Llewellyn Harrison's reconstruction of the music on pp. 124–33. The vernacular dialogue is spoken, but the sung polyphony is to Latin texts. Such spoken plays are not strictly "liturgical," and in any case that term is useful for sung Latin drama, but they might be called "ecclesiastical," perhaps.

10. I am grateful to Peter Meredith for discussions on this point.

11. The Vulgate gives "Gloria in altissimis Deo" (St. Luke 2.14), whereas all liturgical versions read "Gloria in excelsis Deo," as do all the play texts that I have seen. I do not forget that Latin versions other than the Vulgate and the liturgical texts were available, but these two were certainly the commonly used sources.

12. For regals, see n. 22, below. The *organa* of the N-Town stage direction "Et hic assendent in celum cantantibus organis" ("And here they will go up to Heaven

with the music of *organa*," Block, *Ludus,* 373) should probably be translated as "organs" (i.e., a single keyboard instrument comprising many pipes) rather than the alternative "instruments." See also Davis (xxxii).

13. I use "concordance" and "source" here with specifically musicological meanings: the former is "another copy of the same music," the latter "manuscript or print in which the music is found." In the second of these, late scholarly editions are excluded unless (as is the case with the Coventry music) no original or early source survives.

14. This is best known, however, in Martin Shaw's four-part version with altered rhythms, which appears with an edition of the original version in Dearmer. Shaw's version, with its simpler rhythms and regular SATB texture, is suitable for amateur church choir use, and as such is popular. Besides the alterations just noted, Shaw truncated verse 1 to form a two-line burden of 4+3 feet.

15. I assume a single composer here, but it is impossible to adduce the kind of evidence available in the York pieces (Rastall, "Vocal Range").

16. In connection with the discussion of texture here, it is worth noting that Thurston Dart decided that these songs were originally in four parts. It is significant that in the shepherds' song he chose to add a part between alto and tenor, whereas in the lullaby the added voice comes between tenor and bass.

17. Mahrt was responding to an early version of this paper in session 151 of the 17th International Congress on Medieval Studies at Kalamazoo, 8 May 1982.

18. Although it seems that the "Gloria" in the plays can safely be identified with the verse of the first respond at Christmas Matins, *Hodie nobis celorum rex,* there is a parallel use of the Benedictus antiphon, which appears in a picture, by Jacob van Oostzaaien, of the Nativity, now in the Museo di Capodimonte, Naples. I am grateful to Dr. Geoffrey Chew for a transcription of the music.

19. Play 7, including the music, was copied by the unidentified Scribe A, but this does not invalidate the suggestion, since an overall scheme for the manuscript can be discerned involving all three scribes. "Pre-Reformation" in the present context must include settings of Latin texts copied or composed during Mary's reign (1553–58).

20. The marginal nature of this direction can be seen in the facsimiles of the MS Bodley 175 (Leeds Texts and Monographs, vol. I, 1973: see f. 57v) and Huntington Library MS 2 (Medieval Drama Facsimiles, vol. VI, 1980: see f. 46v); but not in that of MS Harley 2124 (Medieval Drama Facsimiles, vol. VIII, 1984: see f. 43r), which has a different, Latin, direction. On the identity of "Trolly lolly lolly lo," see Stevens (*Music and Poetry,* 243, 401), and Rastall ("[Chester] Cycle," 160f).

21. The Norwich music was certainly polyphonic in the sixteenth century, and probably before the middle of that century: see Davis (xxxii, 11, and 18). The case for polyphony in Chester is not based only on reference to Coventry and Norwich. Conditions of music-making changed considerably in the first half of the sixteenth century. Until about 1500 the liturgy (and especially the performance of polyphony) was the province of highly trained and musically literate singers, while instrumental music was performed by minstrels working in an aural tradition. In the sixteenth century a new type of musician grew up—the professional and musically literate instrumentalist-singer. The Coventry town waits were of this latter type in the sixteenth century (see Ingram, *REED: Coventry, passim*), for they were church singers as well as instrumentalists. Simpler musical notational styles were among the many factors involved in this change.

22. For instance, the regals known to have been used at Chester and Coventry would have made quite a loud penetrating sound, even though the instrument is technically a *bas* instrument. The regals is an organ sounding by free reeds. See n. 12, above.

23. The trumpets specified in the Coventry Shearmen's and Tailors' pageant amongst the instruments playing to Herod must be treated as a special case. It is by no means certain that the speech should be taken at face value, and it is also difficult to see how this list of musical entertainments conformed to late medieval ideas (Craig, 19).

WORKS CITED AND SUGGESTED READING

Baker, Donald C., John L. Murphy, and Louis B. Hall, Jr., eds. *The Late Medieval Religious Plays of Bodleian MSS Digby 133 and E Museo 160.* Early English Text Society, o.s. 283. Oxford: Oxford University Press, 1982.

Beadle, Richard, ed. *The York Plays.* London: Edward Arnold, 1982.

Beadle, Richard, and Peter Meredith. "Further External Evidence for Dating the York Register (BL Additional MS 35290)." *Leeds Studies in English.* n.s. 11 (1980), 51–58.

Bent, Margaret. "Sources of the Old Hall Music." *Proceedings of the Royal Musical Association* 94 (1968), 19–35.

Block, Edward A. "Chaucer's Millers and their Bagpipes." *Speculum* 29 (1954), 239–43.

Block, K. S., ed. *Ludus Coventriae, or The Plaie Called Corpus Christi.* Early English Text Society, e.s. 120. London: Oxford University Press, 1922.

Bowles, E. A. "The Role of Musical Instruments in Medieval Sacred Drama." *Musical Quarterly* 45 (1959), 67–84.

Brunne, Robert Mannyng de. *Handlyng Synne.* ed. F. J. Furnivall. Early English Text Society. London: Oxford University Press, 1901 and 1903.

Carpenter, Nan Cooke. "Music in the *Secunda Pastorum.*" *Speculum,* 26 (1951), 696–700. Rpt. in Jerome Taylor and Alan H. Nelson, eds. *Medieval English Drama: Essays Critical and Contextual.* Chicago: University of Chicago Press, 1972, 212–17.

Chadwick, Henry. *Boethius.* Oxford: Clarendon Press, 1981.

Chambers, E. K. *The Mediaeval Stage.* 2 vols. Oxford: Oxford University Press, 1903.

Clopper, Lawrence M., ed. *Records of Early English Drama: Chester.* Toronto: University of Toronto Press, 1979.

Craig, Hardin, ed. *Two Coventry Corpus Christi Plays.* Early English Text Society, e.s. 87. London: Oxford University Press, 1902. 2d ed. 1957.

Cutts, John P. "The Second Coventry Carol." *Renaissance News* 10 (1957), 3–8.

Dart, Thurston. *Two Coventry Carols.* London: Stainer and Bell, 1962.

Davidson, Clifford. *From Creation to Doom: The York Cycle of Mystery Plays.* New York: AMS Press, 1984.

Davis, Norman, ed. *Non-Cycle Plays and Fragments.* Early English Text Society, s.s. 1. London: Oxford University Press, 1970.

Dearmer, Percy, ed. *The Oxford Book of Carols.* London: Oxford University Press, 1928.

Downey, Peter. "The Renaissance slide trumpet: Fact or fiction?" *Early Music* 12/1 (February 1984), 26–33.

Dutka, JoAnna, ed. *Records of Early English Drama: Proceedings of the First Colloquium at Erindale College.* Toronto: University of Toronto Press, 1979.

———. *The Use of Music in the English Mystery Plays.* Ph.D. dissertation, University of Toronto, 1972.

———. *Music in the English Mystery Plays*. Early Drama, Art, and Music, Reference Series, 2. Kalamazoo, Mich.: The Medieval Institute, 1980.

Greene, R. L. *The Early English Carols*. Oxford: Oxford University Press, 1935. 2d ed., 1977.

Henderson, W. G., ed. *Missale ad Usum Insignis Ecclesie Eboracensis*. Durham: Surtees Society 59 and 60, 1874.

Hoffman, C. Fenno, Jr. "The Source of the Words to the Music in York 46." *Modern Language Notes* (1950), 236–39.

Ingram, Reginald W., ed. *Records of Early English Drama: Coventry*. Toronto: University of Toronto Press, 1981.

Irwin, Joyce L. "The mystical music of Jean Gerson." *Early Music History*, 1 (1981), 187–201.

Kipling, Gordon. "The Idea of the Civic Triumph: Drama, Liturgy and the Royal Entry in the Low Countries." *Dutch Crossing* 22 (April 1984), 60–83.

Lawley, S. W., ed. *Breviarium ad Usum Insignis Ecclesie Eboracensis*. Durham: Surtees Society 71 and 75, 1879 and 1883.

Meredith, Peter. "John Clerke's Hand in the York Register." *Leeds Studies in English*. n.s. 12 (1981), 245–71.

Mills, David. "The Stage Directions in the Manuscripts of the Chester Mystery Cycle." *Medieval English Theatre* 3:1 (1981), 45–51.

———. *The Chester Mystery Cycle: A Facsimile of British Library MS Harley 2124*. Leeds Texts and Monographs: Medieval Drama Facsimiles, vol. VIII. Leeds: University of Leeds, 1984.

Rankin, Susan. "Shrewsbury School, Manuscript VI: a Medieval Part Book?" *Proceedings of the Royal Musical Association*, 102 (1976), 129–44.

Rastall, Richard. "Minstrelsy, Church and Clergy in Medieval England." *Proceedings of the Royal Musical Association* 97 (1971), 83–98.

———. *Two Coventry Carols*. Newton Abbot: Antico Edition, 1973.

———. "Alle hefne makyth melody." Paula Neuss, ed. *Aspects of Early English Drama*. Totowa, N.J.: Barnes and Noble, 1983, 1–12.

———. "Music in the [Chester] Cycle." R. M. Lumiansky and David Mills, eds. *The Chester Mystery Cycle: Essays and Documents*. Chapel Hill, N.C.: University of North Carolina Press, 1983, 111–64.

———. "Music for a Royal Entry, 1474." *Musical Times*, 1612 (June 1977), 463–66.

———. "The [York] Music." Richard Beadle and Peter Meredith, eds. *The York Play (BL MS Add. 35290)*. Leeds Texts and Monographs: Medieval Drama Facsimiles vol. VII Leeds: University of Leeds, 1983, xli-xlv.

———. "Some English Consort-Groupings of the Late Middle Ages." *Music and Letters* 55/2 (April 1974), 179–202.

———. "Some Mirth to his Majestee: Music in the Chester Cycle." David Mills, ed. *Staging the Chester Cycle*. Leeds Studies in English (1985), 77–99.

———. "Vocal Range and Tessitura in Music from York Play 45." *Music Analysis* 3/2 (1984), 181–99.

———. *Six Songs from the York Mystery Play "The Assumption of the Virgin."* Newton Abbot: Antico Edition, 1985.

Sharp, Thomas. *A Dissertation on the Pageants . . . at Coventry*. Coventry, 1825. Rpt. Wakefield: EP Publications, 1973.

———. *The Presentation in the Temple*. Edinburgh, 1836.

Smith, Lucy Toulmin, ed. *York Plays*. Oxford, 1885. Rpt. New York: Russell and Russell, 1963.

Sparks, Edgar H. *Cantus Firmus in Mass and Motet 1420–1520*. Berkeley: University of California Press, 1963. Rpt. New York: Da Capo Press, 1975.

Stevens, John. "Music in Mediaeval Drama." *Proceedings of the Royal Musical Association* 84 (1958), 81–95.

———. *Music and Poetry in the Early Tudor Court.* London: Methuen, 1961.

———. "Medieval drama" in Stanley Sadie, ed. *The New Grove (Grove's Dictionary of Music and Musicians,* 6th ed.), Vol. 12. London: Macmillan, 1980, 21–58.

Tydeman, William. *The Theatre in the Middle Ages: Western European Stage Conditions, c. 800–1576.* Cambridge: Cambridge University Press, 1978.

Wall, Carolyn. "York Pageant XLVI and its Music." *Speculum* 46 (1971), 689–712.

———. "The Apocryphal and Historical Background of 'The Appearance of Our Lady to Thomas' (Play XLVI of the York Cycle)," *Medieval Studies* 32 (1970), 172–92.

Withington, Robert. *English Pageantry.* Cambridge, Mass., 1918. Rpt. New York: Benjamin Blom, 1963.

Woolf, Rosemary. *The English Mystery Plays.* Berkeley: University of California Press, 1972.

STANLEY J. KAHRL

Medieval Staging and Performance

The plays comprising the meager stock of surviving medieval English dramatic texts were all composed no earlier than the mid-fifteenth century. These texts demonstrate that their playwrights had a firm sense of the theatrical possibilities of the spaces commonly employed at that period in the history of English drama. The playwrights wrote, that is to say, for spaces they knew well, and understood. For example, when, during the first Passion sequence in the N-Town Passion, the playwright includes the stage direction "Here crist enteryth in-to ye hous (of Simon the Leper) with his disciplis and et ye paschal lomb and in ye mene tyme ye cownsel hous beforn-seyd xal sodeynly onclose . . . ," he clearly has a space in mind inhabited by two separate groups of actors, seen as visual contrasts by the audience. This and similar space relationships we must recover if we are to share the experience the playwrights wished to convey. To see the plays as they were once performed we must understand the essential qualities of medieval theatrical spaces which give this period's plays its own special dynamics.[1]

When the playwrights constructing civic religious drama in the Middle Ages came to build their cycles, what form of staging did they choose? To answer that question, one is led, sooner or later, to the original records of dramatic activity. Because E. K. Chambers appeared to have done just that, his description of the manner in which medieval plays were performed has long remained persuasive. According to Chambers,

> The characteristic English type of play was the long cycle given annually under the superintendence of the corporation or governing body of an important city and divided into a number of distinct scenes or "pageants," each of which was the special charge of one or more of the local "crafts," "arts," or "occupations." (*Mediaeval Stage*, II, 113)

These scenes were typically performed on wagon stages, referred to as "pageant wagons," which the individual guildsmen pulled from station to station, there to be performed, seriatim (*Mediaeval Stage*, II, 133–34). More recently, Arnold Williams stated that "presentation on pageants and seriatim performance of successive plays in the same station . . . was

followed in such major cities as York, Coventry, and Norwich, and presumably also at Beverley and Wakefield" (*Drama*, 96–97). The plays in
the manuscript now catalogued in the British Museum as Cotton Vespasian D.viii, referred to most often nowadays as the "N-Town" plays (from
a line in the introductory banns stating that the plays will be performed
"at vj of the belle . . . in N. towne"), Williams listed as the sole exception
among the great cycles. Also, "the passion plays of the South of England,
the Cornish plays, and probably the Digby plays were done in a quite different manner" (*Drama*, 97).

The idea that the English civic religious plays were mostly performed
on pageant wagons pulled from station to station undoubtedly stems not
just from Chambers's own formulation of medieval stage history. More
importantly, this concept derives from the nature of a particular group
of early records that dominated the thinking of scholars studying the original conditions of performance for medieval English drama. David
Rogers's antiquarian accounts of the pageant wagons in Chester, written
down between 1609 and 1637, were based on records collected by his father, Archdeacon Robert Rogers, near the time of the final performances
of medieval drama in that city. Containing the sole account even re-
motely contemporary with the plays themselves, this description naturally has been reproduced by generations of scholars (see Clopper, "The
Rogers' Description").

Thomas Sharp's *Dissertation*, published in 1825, also provided much
original matter illustrating the use of pageant wagons by trade guilds in
one of the leading medieval cities of England. Because of Coventry's prox-
imity to Kenilworth Castle, royalty often came to see the Coventry plays.
Coventry civic religious plays were seen by Richard III at Whitsuntide,
the normal time of their playing, a few short months before his death in
1485. An apparently unusual performance of the plays was staged for
Richard's successor, Henry VII, on St. Peter's Day, 14 June 1487, but he
and his queen saw them at the regular time, Whitsun, in 1492. No doubt
as a result of this expressed interest, Henry VII and his queen were made
honorary members of the Corpus Christi and Trinity guilds in 1500. Pageants, apparently scenes from the annual play, were performed during the
royal entry of Henry VIII in 1511 and of Mary Tudor in 1526. Elizabeth
I saw the plays in 1567. Of greatest interest to theatre historians, however, has been the visit of Queen Margaret of Anjou in 1457 when she
"Wold not be met but came preuely to se the play there on the Morowe
(of Corpus Christi Day) and She sygh then alle the Pagentes pleyde saue
domes day which myght not be pleyde for lak of day . . . " (Ingram, *Coventry*, 37). This detail, an important confirmation of the difficulty of performing an entire cycle in one day, regularly appears in theatre histories.
Most important of all, these royal visits helped to establish the Coventry
plays in the minds of many as the national norm.[2]

The influence of these accounts of medieval staging practices in two major English cities was enhanced by the accidents of text survival for the plays themselves. The plays of Chester, the sole body of civic religious plays to survive in more than one manuscript, have long been considered important because an early tradition dated their first performance around 1325. This date, had it been correct, would have made the Chester plays the earliest by far to have survived.[3] The first edition of the Chester plays, by Thomas Wright, was published by the Shakespeare Society in 1843, not long after Sharp's *Dissertation* appeared. This was succeeded by the edition prepared for the Early English Text Society by Hermann Deimling and Dr. Matthews, the first volume of which, containing the text, appeared in 1892 (see Lumiansky and Mills, xliii). As for Coventry, Sharp had included an edition of the pageant belonging to the Shearmen and Taylors in his *Dissertation*. This play, together with the other surviving Coventry pageant, was edited by Hardin Craig in 1902 in an edition (*Two Coventry Corpus Christi Plays*) including matter which illustrated the staging practices in Coventry.

Even more influential than Wright's or Sharp's texts, however, in forming a general conception of staging practices in medieval England was the edition of the Ashburnham manuscript of the *York Plays* prepared by Lucy Toulmin Smith in 1885. Miss Smith had been much influenced by the work of her father, Toulmin Smith, who edited many English trade guild records. In editing the records, he necessarily came across a number of references to the performance of plays both by city-wide religious guilds, such as the guild of Corpus Christi or the Trinity guilds which were widespread in the British Isles, and by individual craft guilds. Lucy Toulmin Smith was drawn to the Ashburnham manuscript undoubtedly because she knew that in the voluminous medieval records of York lay a treasure house of information about the production of medieval plays. Much of this information she excerpted herself in her lengthy introduction to the plays.

Thus by the time that Chambers came to write his history of the medieval stage, the pattern had already long been set, both by the nature of the town records best known to the nineteenth-century scholars and editors, and by the nature of the earliest edited texts. The plays of Chester, Coventry, and York all were presented on movable pageant wagon stages. And if they, why not assume the same for the others? Not only the texts of the plays which survived from Coventry, Chester, and York seemed to scholars like Chambers to support the idea of pageant wagon staging as the norm for medieval English drama, however. A fourth surviving major collection of plays, in the possession of the Towneley family, owners of Towneley Hall, Lancashire, also seemed to support the same pattern. The Towneley family allowed their plays to be edited first for the Surtees Society in 1836 (Raine et al., *The Towneley Mysteries*). Raine and Gordon, the editors of that edition, identified the town of Wakefield as a probable location for the original performances of the plays in the Towneley manuscript. Pollard supported this localization in his own introduction for the Early English Text Society's edition of the plays, prepared for publication by George England in 1897. More important to our purposes was Pollard's recognition of the fact, first noted by Lucy Toulmin Smith (York, xlvi), that "The publication of (the York) cycle revealed the fact that five of the York Plays were based, in whole or in part, on the same originals as five of the Towneley" (England, Towneley). Pollard himself was interested only in comparing metric patterns as a path toward the identification of sources.[4] His introduction contains not a word about the staging of the cycle. However, the close identification he established between parts of the York cycle and parts of the Towneley family manuscript in all the three stages of revision he identified has meant that all subsequent discussion of that cycle, until well into the second half of the present century, has assumed that the cycle supposedly performed in Wakefield borrowed both text and staging techniques from the most prestigious city of the North (England, Towneley, xvi-xxviii).

Just as the plays in the Towneley family manuscript had been drawn into the orbit of a better known cycle, the remaining manuscript containing a full cycle of plays came, too, to be thought of as one of the cycles performed on wagon stages. The error which created this impression began early in the seventeenth century, and persists to this day. The play manuscript in the Cotton Library catalogued as Cotton Vespasian D.viii, referred to earlier, was apparently acquired for that collection by Sir Robert Bruce Cotton's first librarian, Richard James, around the year 1629. On the flyleaf of the manuscript James wrote the following note: "Elenchus contentorum in hoc codice (vespasian D.viii)" and under it "Contenta novi testamenti scenice expressa et actita olim per monachos sive fratres mendicantes vulgo dicitur hic liber Ludus Coventriae sive ludus corporis Christi scribitur metris Anglicanis" ("Title of the contents of this codex: Scenes of the New Testament shown and acted formerly by monks or mendicant friars. This book is called 'The Play of Coventry' or 'The Play of Corpus Christi'; it is written in English meters" [Meredith and Kahrl, N-Town Plays, xxvi]).

Much of what James stated about the contents of the manuscript is wrong. The plays contain scenes from both the Old and New Testaments. No evidence suggests that either friars or monks commonly acted in any civic religious plays.[5] However, the plays are written in "metris Anglicanis," and it is quite possible that by the second quarter of the seventeenth century in the public mind the terms "ludus Corporis Christi" and "ludus Coventriae" were synonymous. In any case, the title Ludus Coventriae has stuck until this day, despite the fact that there is not a shred of evidence connecting the plays in this manuscript to the city of Coventry.[6] Furthermore the surviving Coventry plays we do have, already alluded to above, bear no resemblance to the plays on the same subjects in Cotton Vespasian D.viii. Because an alternative geographical location has not been firmly established for this cycle, it is now current practice to refer to it as the N-Town cycle.[7]

In any case, James's erroneous title stuck, and led quite soon to a much more specific statement that the plays in Cotton Vespasian D.viii were not only performed in Coventry, but that they were performed there on pageant wagons, as were all the plays known to have been performed in that city. William Dugdale, in his *Antiquities of Warwickshire Illustrated*, published in 1656, while describing the Grey Friars of Coventry stated that

> Before the suppression of the Monasteries their City [i.e., Coventry] was very famous for the pageants being acted with mighty state and reverance by the friars of this house [i.e., the Grey Friars] had Theaters for several scenes, very large and high, placed upon wheels and drawn to all the eminent parts of the City for the better advantage of Spectators; And contain'd the story of the New Testament, composed into old English Rithme, as appeareth by an antient MS. intituled Ludus Corporis Christi or Ludus Coventriae [here a note in the margin adds the specific reference: In bibl. Cotton sub effigie Vesp. D.9 (apparently a slip for viii)]. I have been told by some old people who in their younger days were eye-witnesses of these pageants so acted that the yearly confluence of people to see that show was extraordinarily great. (Block, *Ludus Coventriae*, xxxviii-xxxix)

Dugdale's error arose initially from misreading an entry in the local Coventry annals which stated that in the mayoralty of Thomas Churchman, "king Henry 7. came to see the Plays acted by the Grey Friers, and much commended them" (Ingram, *Coventry*, 77). In this entry it is now clear that "by" means "near." But Sharp, trusting Dugdale's scholarship, accepted all the statement quoted above, thus giving it currency down to the end of the nineteenth century and beyond.[8] Twentieth-century scholars, particularly Hardin Craig, who made himself familiar with the Coventry material in his edition of the two surviving pageants, increasingly recognized that the plays in Cotton Vespasian D.viii used a very different kind of staging than was found in Coventry. Craig particularly argued for Lincoln as an alternative site, and against any further association of the manuscript with the city of Coventry. Yet when she edited the plays for the Early English Text Society in 1922, K. S. Block still kept the old erroneous title, with all the possibilities of misassociation, because by then the title was so familiar. When Arnold Williams used it in 1959, it was still the best known title, and remains in circulation even today.

Small wonder, then, that Chambers saw pageant wagons moving through most of the streets of the British Isles, serving as stages for the bulk of the civic religious drama. By the close of the nineteenth century, every major surviving text had been identified with cities where local records spoke of wagon stages. There was an additional reason why Chambers saw wagons more often than they appeared. In preparing to write *The Mediaeval Stage*, Chambers read voluminously in the main reading room of the British Museum. The state of our knowledge would never be what it now is had he not done so. But it is essential that we also understand the limitation built into his sources. One has only to look closely at the sources he cites to realize that "he did not read the records, he read published excerpts of the records. One need only work through a few pages of Appendix W, 'Representations of Medieval Plays,' to realize that every reference is to a published text" (Kahrl, "What We Do Not Find"). When one turns to the actual texts that Chambers used, now themselves often rare books, available only in major libraries, one discovers why Chambers needed to have a simplified concept of medieval staging practice if he were to make sense of what he saw before him. For the most part he read either volumes of the Historical Manuscripts Commission, where the searchers' assigned task was merely to suggest the nature of the entries in the surviving records (but not to transcribe them fully), or local histories prepared by Trollopian parsons during the nineteenth century. These writers, as I have suggested before,

> were interested in "the juicy bits," the local activities that would be most interesting. If there were medieval plays, they would simply say that they were a part of the medieval scene, give an entry that held (for the historians) the most interest, and pass on. (Kahrl, "What We Do Not Find")

If one goes behind the work of the antiquarian historians, with their penchant for excerpting only the most unusual items of interest, one finds that the pattern Chambers established does not hold up. Pageant wagons there were, to be sure, but used in many different ways. At the peak of its civic religious dramatic activity, York had forty-eight plays, each one an individual scene, performed on a single wagon, each short play mounted and sponsored by a different craft guild. These scenes were indeed performed seriatim at a number of stations, the number varying mostly between twelve and sixteen. The effect was to create a cycle within which there were a great many short scenes, a cycle that was, in fact, unlike any other that we know of in England! At Coventry, on the other hand, the practice developed of joint guild sponsorship. The surviving Shearmen and Taylor's pageant includes the following scenes: a prologue prophecy, the Annunciation, Joseph's Trouble with Mary, the Shepherds sandwiched between the Nativity sequence (Journey to Bethlehem, the Nativity, two prophets, Herod and the Magi), and the Massacre of the Innocents. In the introduction to his meticulous edition of the Coventry records, Ingram remarks that "Coventry's cycle is unique in that it consisted of ten plays only, each of which would have provided individual matter for three or four individual plays in York or Chester" (*Coventry,* xvii). We must then think of each city's plays, each town's performance as unique. The more one studies the local records in detail, the more one finds local and religious variation.

At Lincoln, for example, the Cordwainers, or Shoemakers, did have a wagon stage upon which actors represented the Nativity.[9] But this stage was apparently pulled to the Cathedral in the Corpus Christi procession, where the plays of that city were performed (Kahrl, *Collections VIII*, 35–38). In such a setting, the wagon stage would function as a set piece. The same practice was followed at other towns, such as Louth, in Lincolnshire, or Bishop's (now King's) Lynn, in Norfolk (Kahrl, *Collections VIII*, 75–84; Wasson and Galloway, *Collections XI*, 47–52). At Lynn the plays were performed not only in the market, but in the local hall of Lord Scales (Kahrl, "Learning"). The recently published records of Norfolk and Suffolk list a number of towns where pageant wagons rolled on Corpus Christi day in the procession that was an invariable part of that feast, but where no other evidence of even semidramatic activity survives. Indeed, unless there is concrete evidence that plays were performed in conjunction with the setting forth of pageants, where pageants appear alone in a set of town records we may have only a series of *tableaux vivants* (Wasson and Galloway, *Collections XI*, xi).

But the variation goes much further than simply a varying use of wagon stages. Martial Rose, the first director to stage the Wakefield cycle, found in practice that much of that cycle had been adapted for performance at a fixed location (Rose, "Staging"). Typically plays performed in a single large open area employed a number of raised platforms, now most often referred to as scaffolds. Much of the action in such performances used the open area between the scaffolds extensively. This area was known as the *platea*, from Latin stage directions referring to that acting area by that term. The English translation, also much in use, was 'place.' Hence this type of staging is most often referred to as "place-and-scaffold staging."[10] Rose has argued, as have others since, that the older plays preserved in this cycle, written originally for performance on wagon stages, had been adapted to place-and-scaffold staging in the period when the manuscript we have was being copied, from a revised text (Rose, *Wakefield*, 30–42). Plays in the N-Town cycle, especially those presenting the Passion of Christ, have long been recognized as written primarily for place-and-scaffold staging. But so was the *Castle of Perseverance*, and so was the life of Mary Magdalen, contained in the Digby MS. Scholars have searched for the possible homes for these plays in East Anglia and Lincolnshire because the dialects of the scribes copying down those plays are closest to the dialect of the East Midlands.[11] As they have done so, it becomes clear that the staging employed in the East of England was primarily place-and-scaffold staging. This also was the form of staging employed in and around London and the South. The citizens of Norwich processed on Whitsunday to a field outside of town, there to watch their play (Galloway, *Norwich*). The citizens of Louth and Lynn both used their large open markets. John Coldewey ("That Enterprising Property Player") has found examples of similar performance practices at Maldon and Chelmsford. Further south, across the Thames, the same theatrical practice was followed at Lydd and New Romney (Dawson, *Collections VII*, 199–200, 202–11).

But locations other than the village square, or a green on the outskirts of town, also were used for the large productions located in a single space. In Cornwall evidence suggests that the ancient rounds were used for performances of the cycle plays, of which two manuscripts still survive (Southern, *Round*; Hoseley). Alan Somerset, after examining the records of Shrewsbury for evidences of local civic religious drama, has concluded that the stage on a "frame of timber that stood in the quarell (i.e., quarry) behind the walles" which was ordered dismantled and delivered to Mr. Ashton, the schoolmaster, for his use in the mid-sixteenth century, had been the continuous permanent site for dramatic productions since at least 1445–46.[12] The more one looks, the greater the diversity. Indeed, as the evidence for diversity mounts, one is forced more and more to agree with Glynne Wickham's most recent conclusion:

> All this information, and much more, tells us that the drama of Christ Crucified was as popular as it was widespread in England, but it does not help the historian to provide a short and concise account of how it was organized, financed and stage-managed; the very diversity of the evidence prohibits simplification and generalization. (*Medieval Theatre*, 69)

So the focus must narrow, the attempt to describe medieval drama in the British Isles must no longer consist of a panoramic view of a single line of development. Instead we must focus on single centers to see what happened in each, recognizing wide local differences. But even that task is not easy. For example, much is known about the locations of the different stations on the pageant route in York. The locations used generally offered small audience areas. It is probable that at any given station not more than 250–300 people would have been present. Knowing this, we can understand better why the York cycle contains so many small scenes, almost all written as though for a close audience able to appreciate small nuances of character (Kahrl, *Traditions*, 53–55).

Naturally, in determining the nature of the playing areas used in a city like Coventry, where wagons were also used for the staging, one would like to know where the plays were performed as well. A search of the records, however, proves to be an exercise in frustration. The Leet Book, the primary source of our knowledge of the regulations enacted by the mayor and council for the governance of Coventry, includes no order stating specifically where the pageant wagon stages were to stand during performances of the scenes they carried (Ingram, *Coventry*, xvi). In the introduction to his edition of the two Coventry plays, Hardin Craig once argued that since there were ten plays in the Coventry cycle, then there must have been ten playing places, one for each of the ten wards of the city (*Two Coventry Plays*, xii-xiv). To arrive at this number, he included any location used for any kind of dramatic or semidramatic performance, including the speeches read from fountains and street corners during royal entries (Wickham, *Stages*, i, 51–111). Toward the end of his career, however, he changed his mind. Writing in the early fifties, in *English Religious Drama*, Craig stated: "As to stations, or customary playing places, in the city of Coventry, there is some uncertainty" (*Religious Drama*, 294). There is, indeed; so much so that Ingram nowhere in his edition of the Coventry records states either how many stations there were, or where they might have been located!

Craig's uncertainty stemmed, as he himself admitted, from the recurrent entries in the Drapers' (admittedly late) accounts for 3s 8d for "iij worlds." Annually, apparently, the Drapers bought three "worlds" for their pageant of the Last Judgment, and then paid a man 16d "for kepyng hell mouth and settyng *ye* worlde on fyre & blackyng *ye* facys (of the damned souls)" (Ingram, *Coventry*, 257). Three worlds to set on fire each year suggest performances at only three stations. But where were even those three? Several entries state that the pageant wagons lined up initially in Gosforth Street (Ingram, *Coventry*, 23, 41, 79). Thus we know where the plays originated. In 1457, the year of Queen Margaret's celebrated visit, the Leet Book entry tells us that "She was loged at Richard Wodes the Grocer where Richard Sharp somme tyme dwelled and there all the pleys were furst pleyde . . ." (Ingram, *Coventry*, 37). Ingram notes that "Richard Wode lived in Earl Street, a continuation of Gosforth Street at the further end of which the pageant wagons gathered before beginning the procession and performance of the plays. His house was at, or very close to, the traditional first acting place of the plays, *I believe*." (Italics mine.) As evidence for this "belief," he cites the fact that "In 1471 the players drank ale at Wode's Door" (Ingram, *Coventry*, 549). If even Professor Ingram, a native of Coventry, who knows its streets at firsthand, and who has made the study of its records a lifelong work, can still not be certain that this was the first station, what certainty can the rest of us find? And what of the other stations in Coventry, supposing that the three worlds do mean that there were three separate playing places? One attractive list of locations appears from the royal entry of Queen Elizabeth in 1566. Elizabeth I entered the city at Bishop's Gate, the opposite end of the city from Gosforth Gate (the normal point of entry if royalty were coming from Kenilworth). The annals noting the event state both that three and that four pageants were presented on the occasion. The discrepancy is irreconcilable, but all do seem to agree that the first location was at Cross Cheaping, a natural location often used for royal entries. Sharp, quoting from annals now lost, stated that the Drapers' pageant was the one located at the Cross. It is interesting to note that in 1570 and 1573 the Drapers paid for ale for their players at another of the locations named in the 1566 list, "the Swan door." The only problem here is that the Swan's location is unknown (Ingram, *Coventry*, 573). There was a Swan tavern in Smithford Street in the mid-eighteenth century, but Ingram is reluctant to posit that as the location for a station used two hundred years earlier. And so it goes. A house in Bayley Lane is referred to as "ouer agynst the procession way" in 1552 (Ingram, *Coventry*, 193). This is interesting as both Much Park, which debouches into Gosforth Street near Wode's house, and Bayley Lane enter Gosforth Lane near each other. But finally, once the search is over, the best we can say is that there may have been three stations in Coventry, at which apparently as many as ten different longish plays were performed, and that one of them was probably located near the point in Gosforth Lane where it passes Much Park and Bayley Lane to become Earl Street. We may guess that this space was somewhat larger than those used in York. But we cannot be sure.

The problem of locating an actual route for a Corpus Christi procession is not unique to Coventry. At Lincoln, too, where references in local annals and payments for dramatic activities speak of a long tradition of both a Corpus Christi procession and plays, as well as an Assumption play on St. Anne's day (26 July), a Pater Noster play, and dramatizations of several saints' lives, it is impossible to state with certainty where the plays were performed, or which route the citizens of Lincoln took when they processed from the lower town to the cathedral at the top of the hill.[13] The ancient Roman road, Ermine Street, passes between the castle and the cathedral at the top of the hill in Lincoln, and then descends precipitously through the ancient walled city to the valley below. As it was the original main road, it must have been used by people and wagons regularly. But anyone climbing that portion of the old road known today as Steep Hill would certainly wonder whether men or horses would ever have pulled any dramatic set mounted on a wagon up that hill if the alternate route, known as Potter Gate, swinging to the east in a more gradual curve and entering the cathedral grounds from the rear, were in use for processions in the fifteenth century.[14] The best we can say is that the guild of Cordwainers, or Shoemakers, required its members annually to "goo in precession / Wt the Graceman Brether & Susters of this Fraternite / From the chappell of Saint thomas of ye hy brige in Lincoln / Vnto the cathedrall churche of Lincoln." The wardens, or officers of the guild, further swore at their installation "to dresse & redresse ye pageaunt of Bethlehem at Saint Anne tyd and to goo in precession in Saint anne guild Wt master graceman [the head officer] from ye place accustomed to ye moder churche in Lincoln & so doun a gan" (Kahrl, *Collections VIII*, 96). That is to say, on St. Anne's day at least one guild took one pageant wagon from the bridge chapel of St. Thomas, located on the High Bridge, just outside the Stonebow (the main gate into the city on the lower, or southern, side), up the hill to the Cathedral of St. Mary. After the procession had been completed, the wagon was brought back down the hill again, presumably to be housed for the rest of the year in a pageant house somewhere along High Street in the suburb of Wigford. But how the wagon went from the bridge to the cathedral we cannot say.

In using local records, we must remember the limitations built into them by their very nature. The acts of governing bodies, town councils and the like, display an interest in seeing that things run smoothly, and that major events in the town's life are properly financed. Thus the records of the governing bodies of York, Coventry, or Lincoln are full of entries describing fines for poor performance, or failure to produce a pageant on time, on the appointed day, or regulations assigning different pageants to newly prosperous guilds as the older trades died out. The town and city records, in other words, tell us that a dramatic event took place, when it took place, and how the event was managed. Those records will not tell us much about things that everyone knew about, however, if they were things that "have always been done that way." No one needed to be told how to process to St. Mary's Cathedral in Lincoln each year because there was always someone to head the procession who had been there the year before.

Thus we are always grateful when we find a record specifically indicating where a dramatic performance took place, for such records are rare. At Lynn in 1446–47 the townsfolk presented a Corpus Christi play in their spacious town square. Among those present to see the performance were Lord Oxford and Thomas, Lord Scales. The Nativity play from this cycle had been taken to Middleton, the home of Lord Scales, the year before for a performance at Christmas (Kahrl, "Learning"; Wasson and Galloway, *Collections XI*, 47–49). One can imagine Thomas de Scales inviting his friend John de Vere specifically to see the full cycle after having enjoyed a portion in his own hall as part of the celebration of the twelve days of Christmas the year before. The fact that a carter had to be hired to transport the costumes and scenery to Middleton suggests that the Nativity play performed there and in the town square was part of a large place-and-scaffold production in which pageant wagons were not a part. The town square in Lynn is still exactly the same as it was in the mid-fifteenth century, enclosed by its ranges of house fronts, many of them displaying marked similarities to houses across the Channel in the Lowlands. We can thus visualize, at least for that locale, the physical surroundings for that one cycle of civic religious drama. It is a locale similar to those described so fully in the French records discussed below by Professor Muir, a fact which should remind us how much more we need to study connections between England's medieval drama as it was performed in East Anglia, and the drama of the Lowlands and Northern France. But where we want most to find the same sort of information, in towns with known play texts, such information is almost never easy to find.

In attempting to recreate the original conditions of production, there is another, even greater gap in our knowledge, until now apparently unrecognized, that the surviving local records do almost nothing to fill. Where were the members of the audience when medieval civic religious plays were being performed? No one seems certain. When Queen Margaret came to Coventry in 1457 "preuely to se the play," she did not come alone. With her were "the duke of bukkyngham & my lady his Wyff & all their Children the lord Reuers and my lady his Wyf the lady of Shrowesbury the Elder and the lady of Shrowesbury the yonger with mony moo lordes and ladyes" (Ingram, *Coventry*, 37). Coming "privily" seems to have meant merely that the mayor and council were not required to make a formal greeting in full regalia, nor to set up a processional entry as was the apparent custom when royalty came to pay a visit to the city.[15] Did lodging at Richard Wode's house mean that the queen stayed there for the night? Since the Last Judgment play was omitted "for lak of day," that seems a fair possibility. But it could also mean that the royal party watched the play from upper windows in Wode's house. Alan Nelson has viewed such points of vantage with a sceptical eye, particularly in his discussion of the mayor and council's use of Thomas Bewyk's room to view the plays in York (*Medieval Stage*, 65ff.). However, the alternative he proposes, that such plays as the York cycle or the Lincoln cycle were performed once only, in private chambers, for the mayor and council and their friends only, has found no favor. Just as the mayor and council watched the York plays from an elevated station, the windows of Thomas Bewyk's chamber, and the canons of St. Mary's Cathedral watched the Corpus Christi play performed in the close before the Cathedral's west front from the windows of John Sharpe's chamber, so Queen Margaret and her train must have watched the Coventry plays from the window of Richard Wode.[16]

What is striking about these bits and pieces of evidence is the absence of nearly all mention of scaffolds erected to provide seating for ordinary spectators. Anyone designing a theater today will know how much time is spent in arranging for proper seating. Alfred Harbage, in *Shakespeare and His Audience*, could deduce much about the audience for Shakespeare's plays from the prices charged for entry to the various levels of the Globe. Professor Muir's French accounts are full of information about special box seats, as well as the costs for erecting general scaffold seating, built in order to charge good prices to recover the costs of producing the grandiose plays common to France in the sixteenth century. But when we search the records for local productions in England, such evidence is slim indeed. At Coventry a single entry notes that a Mr. Packwood was paid 14d by the Weavers in 1568 for "makyng of trestles & mendyng ye pagent" (Ingram, *Coventry*, 245). However, the sum involved is too small to cover any major seating as well as repairs to the wagon itself.

The dearth of evidence for special seating in Coventry may be explained by a few scattered references to scaffold seating in York. In the full, important act of the mayor and council for 1417, which lists, among other things, a series of stations at which the individual plays in the York cycle were to be performed, appears the following additional order:

... the mayor, the honourable men, and the whole said commons, by their unanimous consent and assent, order (that) all those who receive money for scaffolds which they may build in the aforesaid places before their doors on public property at the aforesaid sites from those sitting on them shall pay the third penny of the money so received to the chamberlains of the city to be applied to the use of the same commons. And if they have refused to pay or agree upon a third penny of this kind or other (monies) with the chamber decently, that then the play be transferred to other places at the will and disposition of the mayor holding office at the time and of the council of the Chamber of the city. No one spoke against this kind of ordinance except only a few holders of scaffolds in Micklegate. (Johnston and Rogerson, *REED, York*, I, 29; II, 714)

The act goes on to state that banners will be set up a day before the performance advertising where one can go to see the play. Because of this one entry, we may confidently surmise that the numerous recurring entries listing income received from those privileged to have stations before their homes offer good evidence for the existence of seating for spectators in York.[17] But note that the seats for spectators in York were entirely a matter of free enterprise. Suppose that the governing body in York had not chosen to take a cut of the income received for seats at the different stations? We would not have a shred of evidence in the records that any seating had been erected in York. Even more to the point, note that only the single entry for 1417 records the fact that the scaffolds were erected at the different stations. The subsequent lists of income received from the stations would only tell us that people paid to have the plays before their homes. From that fact alone we might infer that some sort of income was being derived from the privilege of having a station before one's home, but how that income was derived we could not say.

In using the surviving records, one must be always aware of what they can and cannot tell us. We have already noted that town governing bodies are usually most concerned to ensure that the plays took place at a set date, that they were done properly, and that those responsible for producing them did so with a minimum of fuss. Unless a town council was actually the producer of a play, as in New Romney (Dawson, *Collections VII*, 202–11), the actual lists of expenses for producing plays will turn up in the accounts of city-wide religious guilds, such as the guilds of Corpus Christi, Trinity, or St. Anne found in all the villages and towns of medieval England. They will also appear in the accounts of the craft guilds (Kahrl, "Learning"). Here we will find the property lists so dear to the hearts of earlier generations of theatre historians. Here are the devil masks, the beards, the red cloth for the Red Sea, a noose for Judas, barrels for earthquakes, and, of course, the three worlds to set on fire. But because the guilds were concerned primarily with financing and mounting the part of the dramatic spectacle which was their own special responsibility, their records say nothing about accommodations for spectators. If it were a general practice for enterprising individuals to erect scaffold seating in towns other than York, unless the town chose to make money by leasing those rights, no records of such activity are likely to come to light.

Given the happy accident that we can confidently add some scaffold seats to our picture of the physical environment in which the plays were staged in York, can we then extrapolate that evidence and say that the same must have been true elsewhere? Probably not. York's annual event was extraordinarily well organized. Nowhere else do we find such careful attention to detail. We cannot generalize practices at York to any other center of dramatic activity, unless we find good reason to do so. As far as the surviving evidence is concerned, nothing suggests that other cities encouraged the erection of scaffold seats at the performance of plays. David Rogers says nothing of such structures in Chester. As we have seen, no mention of such structures is found in Coventry. In the towns of Lincolnshire and East Anglia the same is true. In New Romney, where a fragmentary set of late records lists many, many interesting details about the place-and-scaffold play performed in that town in the mid-sixteenth century, possibly in the same form that had been used there since 1428, the only stages referred to are those for the players (Dawson, *Collections VII,* 189, 202–11). The seating for which the audience paid so much at, say, Valenciennes is not part of the expenses even of such lavish productions as those staged in Essex in the late sixteenth century. It is indeed only with the construction of playhouses in London that the separation of actor and audience to which Ann Righter points does, in fact, occur in England. But even there it is well to study closely the new model of the first Globe in Harvard's Theatre Collection. Whatever one may feel about specific details of the reconstructed facade, one cannot help but be struck by the short distance from stage to seat, of the apparent concern to keep the old standing audience close to the stage, and be impressed by the attempt to retain overall as close as possible relations between actors and audience.

Studying the records of dramatic performance which survive from the medieval and Renaissance periods enables us both to visualize the original conditions of performance, and to produce modern performances which are true to the strengths of those original productions. Further study of the increased body of evidence offered by the volumes of REED will teach us how much differing local conditions led to different local or regional practices. Patterns of local activity are still to be developed and compared on the basis of the new evidence. Rather than creating a theoretical history of staging and performance in the British Isles based on isolated local references collected into a pattern of activity supposedly true for the nation as a whole, we must learn more and more to see each locale as adapting the fundamental norms of staging and performance into the constraints of local conditions. Where texts can be associated with the newly defined local conditions of production, our understanding of the dynamics of those texts will improve as well.

A further caution must be entered as to the limitations built into the records currently being edited for REED, however. Because the surviving documents are so often the records of treasurers of various sorts, or of those concerned with public order and the keeping of laws, few details of the acual performance survive. Uncovering an indenture listing a full set of properties for the climactic York Mercers' pageant of the Last Judgment was a major discovery because we have so few of the details Henslowe so painstakingly recorded for the theatres of Elizabeth's reign (Johnston and Rogerson, "York Mercers"). Efforts to borrow costumes, as in Lincoln, or to rent them out, as in Essex, tell us some of the colors, and some of the quality of the costumes used (Kahrl, *Collections VIII*, 43 and xix-xx; Coldewey, "Last Rise"). Stage directions in the texts themselves, however, such as the description of the vice figure who opens the N-Town Passion play, still provide us with our most conclusive evidence that the plays were to be costumed to appear as those scenes appeared in contemporary manuscript illuminations of the same subjects. Old property lists may from time to time appear, but we cannot count on the records for much help here, either, as the lists will not spare many words to describe the objects listed. Again, manuscript illuminations will here serve us better. Finally, as those who have struggled to recreate Shakespeare's stage know all too well, accurate descriptions of early stage structures themselves are and will remain sparse. Glynne Wickham's study of the stages used for semidramatic occasions happily corrected the old idea of early English stages as crude, simple affairs, but one must be cautious when applying the descriptions of the stages erected for royal entries to the scaffolds erected annually for provincial civic drama in England and the rest of the British Isles. Alan Somerset may have found a permanent stage in a quarry outside Shrewsbury, but the norm seems more likely to have been to use staging that could be taken apart and stored, or hauled off and stored in a special building till needed the following year. In such settings we must look for richness in the stage furniture rather than in the stages themselves. Special structures, like Noah's ship, or Mary's cloud machine, appear in the records because they had to be taken care of from year to year. But their shapes are not revealed.

What the records will tell us in greater and greater detail as we study them in the years to come are the details of life surrounding the performance and staging of the plays, the nature of the people who strove to put them on, and the reasons they had for continuous involvement in dramatic production. Here, too, another caution is needed. One can collect every record one can find, and publish each record as carefully as possible, as the REED editors are now doing, but one must always recognize that the records so amassed are still not the whole story of dramatic activity in any single area. Gail Gibson, in searching for the home of the N-Town cycle, painstakingly researched all manner of material to build a case for Bury St. Edmunds. If one turns to the entries for Bury St. Edmunds included in the Malone Society volume, *Collections XI*, edited by John Wasson, one would hardly suspect how rich a picture one could develop of the conditions of performance in Bury (Gibson, "Bury St. Edmunds"; *Collections XI*, 147–48). Professor Gibson could build so interesting a case because she has gone well beyond the sort of records edited for REED. Both kinds of research will need to continue in the future if we are to gain as full a picture as possible of the conditions of production of medieval drama. Editors of REED, searching for the relevant records of a single county, cannot possibly undertake the sort of study in depth of a single town pursued by Professor Gibson. But only when such research is also undertaken will we be fully able to bring the past to life. The REED volumes already enable us to rebuild our history of medieval staging and performance, but they are not an end in themselves. Rather they are a beginning, an opportunity for us all to build a better understanding of the manner in which medieval plays were performed, descriptions which will increasingly help us to bring the past to life in all its strength and richness of vision.

NOTES

1. For recent discussions of these conventions, see the chapters on "The Major Theatrical Traditions," and "Dramatic Possibilities" in Kahrl, *Traditions,* and, for the European perspective, Tydeman, *Theatre in the Middle Ages.*

2. For sixteenth century references to the plays at Coventry, see Ingram, *REED: Coventry,* p. xvii.

3. For a full discussion of the date of the Chester cycle, placing it at the end, not the beginning of the fourteenth century, see F. M. Salter, *Chester,* 37–42.

4. For a fuller discussion of the reasons early editors had for editing medieval plays, see Kahrl, "Editing Texts for Dramatic Performance."

5. However, for a recent discussion of this point, indicating somewhat greater monastic involvement, at least in the dramatic life of Bury St. Edmunds, see Gibson, "Monks and Mysteries."

6. Martial Rose's modernized version of the N-Town cycle, used for the performance at Grantham in England in 1966, was initially commissioned by the city of Coventry, who believed the cycle was "theirs."

7. A close fit between dramatic events in medieval Lincoln and the contents of the manuscript caused Hardin Craig to propose Lincoln as the home of this cycle. See Craig, *Religious Drama,* pp. 265–80. For further evidence supporting this ascription, see Kahrl, *Collections VIII,* xii-xxi. Because the language of the main scribe more closely approximates that of Norfolk, alternative locations in that county have been proposed. For a recent full discussion of the alternatives,

and an extended argument for Bury St. Edmunds as an alternative location, see Gibson, "Bury St. Edmunds, Lydgate, and the *N-Town Cycle.*"

8. For a complete discussion of how Dugdale's error influenced Sharp, see Ingram, *REED: Coventry*, 558, n. 77. In conclusion Ingram reports that "the force of Dugdale's words has not fully abated. . . . Roy Palmer, in *The Folklore of Warwickshire* (London, 1976), writes: "The Grey Friars, part of whose church still remains, were celebrated for their performances of the Corpus Christi cycle, named after the day on which it was given. The subject was announced in a prologue by the Vexillator, who carried a flag with the subject printed on it" (702–703). Lucy Toulmin Smith listed the N-Town Cycle as the Coventry cycle in her "Comparative Table of English Cycles of Religious Plays," Appendix I, lxii–lxiii.

9. *Collections VIII*, 54–65, presents the relevant entries from the Cordwainers' accounts. For their regulations, see Appendix A, 96.

10. For a good brief recent description of the major forms of outdoor theatre in medieval England, with illustrations, see Hosley, "Outdoor Theatre." For dramatic readings of selected plays using these theatrical settings, see William Tydeman, *English Medieval Theatre 1400–1500*.

11. For the dialect of the *Castle*, see Eccles, *Macro Plays*, x-xv; for the possible origin of the Digby Plays, see D. C. Baker and J. L. Murphy, "The Late Medieval Plays," 153–66.

12. Paper delivered at the Seventeenth International Congress on Medieval Studies, The Medieval Institute, Western Michigan University, 6–9 May 1983, p. 3.

13. See *Collections VIII*, xvi-xvii, for a list of dramatic productions in Lincoln known to have occurred between 1410 and 1496.

14. For a map of Lincoln, ca. 1300, see Sir Francis Hill, *Medieval Lincoln*, fig. 17, p. 244.

15. See, for example, Ingram, *REED: Coventry*, 21–23, 35–36, 107, 125, 204, 243. The Mayor and Council still took the precaution of sending gifts however. See entry on p. 37.

16. See particularly Ingram's discussion of this point in "Pleyng geire," 79–82, including (p. 81) a Venetian envoy's eyewitness account of "London's festive streets" seen from just such a window.

17. Since the act of council originally stated that the council was to get one-third of the income generated, i.e., one penny per head, it ought theoretically to be possible to estimate the number of people paying to see the plays at each station. However, when the entries listing income from the stations begin to appear, in 1462 (see 2:768; 1:93) the income is described as payments for licenses for the plays to be held at specific spots. Given the medieval habit of first setting a basis for a rent, and then agreeing to farm out that rent at a discount once the usual rate of return had been established, these license fees are only likely to give us a minimum figure for the number of people paying for seats at given stations. In 1462, at least 160 people paid for seats at station 1, 80 at station 2, 132 at 3, 164 at 4, 120 at 5, 84 at 6, 120 at 7, 78 at 8, 28 at 9, and 24 at 10. The sixteenth century figures are much lower.

WORKS CITED AND SUGGESTED READING

Baker, D. C., and J. L. Murphy. "The Late Medieval Plays of MS Digby 133: Scribes, Dates and Early History." *RORD* 10 (1967), 153–66.

Block, K. Ludus Coventriae. Oxford, 1922.

Coldewey, John. "The Last Rise and Final Demise of Essex Town Drama." *MLQ* 36 (1975), 239–60.

———. "That Enterprising Property Player: Semi-Professional Drama in Sixteenth-Century England." *Theatre Notebook* 31 (1977), 5–12.

Clopper, Lawrence. "The Rogers' Description of the Chester Plays." *Leeds Studies in English* 7 (1974), 63–94.

Craig, Hardin. *English Religious Drama in the Middle Ages*. Oxford, 1955.

Dawson, Giles. *Plays and Players in Kent*. Malone Society *Collections VII*. Oxford, 1965.

Eccles, Mark. *The Macro Plays*. London, 1969.

England, G. *The Towneley Plays*. London, 1897.

Galloway, David. *Records of Early English Drama: Norwich, 1540–1642*. Toronto, 1984.

Gibson, Gail M. "Bury St. Edmunds, Lydgate, and the *N-Town Cycle*." *Speculum* 56 (1981), 56–90.

———. The Play of *Wisdom* and the Abbey of St. Edmund," in *The Wisdom Symposium: Papers from The Trinity College Medieval Festival*. New York: AMS, 1986, 39–66.

Hill, Sir Francis. *Medieval Lincoln*. Cambridge, 1965.

Hosley, Richard. "Three Kinds of Outdoor Theatre before Shakespeare." *American Journal of Theatre History* 12 (1971), 1–33.

Ingram, Reginald. *Records of Early English Drama: Coventry*. Toronto, 1981.

———. "Pleying geire accustumed belonging and necessarie: guild records and pageant production at Coventry" in *REED: Proceedings of the First Colloquium*, ed. JoAnna Dutka. Toronto, 1979.

Johnston, Alexandra, and Margaret Dorrell. "The York Mercers and Their Pageant of Doomsday, 1433–1526." *Leeds Studies in English*, N.S. 6 (1972), 11–36.

Johnston, Alexandra, and Margaret Rogerson. *Records of Early English Drama: York*, 2 Vols. Toronto, 1979.

Kahrl, Stanley J. *Plays and Players of Lincolnshire*, Malone Society *Collections VIII*. Oxford, 1969 [1974].

———. "Editing Texts for Dramatic Performance," in *The Drama of Medieval Europe*: Proceedings of the Colloquium held at the University of Leeds, 10–13 September, 1974, 39–52. Leeds, 1975.

———. "Learning about Local Control" in *REED: Proceedings of the First Colloquium*, ed. JoAnna Dutka, 101–27. Toronto, 1979.

———. "What We Do Not Find in Chambers." *Southern Theatre* 22 (1979), 11–18.

———. *Traditions of Medieval English Drama*. London, 1974.

Lumiansky, Robert, and David Mills. *The Chester Mystery Cycle*. London, 1974.

Palmer, Roy. *The Folklore of Warwickshire*. London, 1976.

Raine, James, and James Gordon, eds. *The Towneley Mysteries*. London, 1836.

Rose, Martial. "The Staging of the Hegge Plays," in *Medieval Drama*, ed. Neville Denny. *Stratford-upon-Avon Studies 16*. London: Edward Arnold, 1973.

———, ed. *The Wakefield Mystery Plays*. London, 1961.

Salter, F. M. *Medieval Drama at Chester*. Toronto, 1955.

Sharp, Thomas. *Dissertation on the Pageants or Dramatic Mysteries.* . . . Facsimile ed. (with foreword by A. C. Cawley). Totowa, N.J., 1973.

Smith, Lucy Toulmin. *York Plays*. London, 1885.

Smith, Toulmin, ed. *English Gilds*. EETS, vol. 40. Oxford, 1870.

Somerset, Alan. Paper delivered at the Seventeenth International Congress on Medieval Studies. Western Michigan University, May 1983.

Southern, Richard. *Medieval Theatre in the Round*. New York, 1975.

Tydeman, William. *The Theatre in the Middle Ages.* Cambridge, 1978.
———. *English Medieval Theatre 1400–1500.* London, 1986.
Wasson, John, and David Galloway. *Plays and Players in Norfolk and Suffolk,* Malone Society *Collections XI,* 1080–81.
Wickham, Glynne. *Early English Stages,* 1300–1660. Vol. I, 1300–1576. London, 1963.

JOHN R. ELLIOTT, JR.

Medieval Acting

There is no substantial body of commentary on medieval acting such as has grown up around the acting of the Elizabethan era. "Acting" is not even listed as a category in the index to E. K. Chambers's *Mediaeval Stage*, though Chambers furnishes many materials on which such a commentary might be based. Since Chambers, the subject has elicited only scattered comments in general studies of medieval drama and two specialized articles, one of which warns us that the purposes and conditions of medieval dramatic performances were so varied that "no single pattern" can be drawn from them (Bevington, "Discontinuity").

The prospective student of medieval acting thus faces a very different problem from the one facing the student of the acting of Shakespeare's time. Where the latter must first find his way among the many dozens of competing, highly opinionated interpretations of a limited body of evidence surviving from a relatively short period—interpretations that include some book-length studies—the student of medieval acting stands at the edge of a scholarly wilderness. Before entering this tract he must define his chronological and geographical boundaries: Is he to lump together twelfth century liturgical plays and sixteenth century moralities under the same heading of "medieval"? Are acting practices in Spain and Italy relevant to those of England and France? He must identify the types of evidence available: What of stage directions? dialogue? eye-witness accounts? records of recruitment and payment, or non-payment, to actors? literary references to actors? references to them in theological or rhetorical treatises? And he must determine the questions he wishes to ask of this evidence: Where did medieval actors come from and how were they trained? were they amateurs, or professionals, or both? what style, or styles, of acting did they use? how good, or bad, were they? If liturgical plays are to be included, then the vexing question first raised by Chambers and Karl Young—is the actor really acting?—may need to be considered too.

When we turn to the existing body of scholarship on the Elizabethan period for guidance, we find few models worthy of emulation. Most studies of acting in this period have centered on arguments for or against the existence of either a "formal" or a "natural" style of acting, without meaningful definition of either term or adequate consideration of what the object of either style might have been. Moreover, the preoccupation of scholars with the professional stage in London has led them to overlook almost totally the many other forms of traditional theatrical activity in the rest of England, of the sort that the medieval historian is most interested in. The recent volume of *The Revels History of Drama in English* dealing with the period from 1576–1613 (London, 1975), for instance, does not so much as mention the continuing existence of civic and folk drama, or of school and university plays during this period, thus giving the erroneous impression to the unwary reader that all Elizabethan and Stuart dramatic activity was of a professional nature.

The assumption that, because it was professional, the acting of Shakespeare's day must inevitably have been superior in quality to that of preceding centuries is prevalent in discussions of both Elizabethan and medieval acting. Although William Tydeman has cautioned that "very little can now be gleaned about the quality of performances," since "hardly any direct accounts of it have come down to us" (Tydeman, p. 213), commentators have, nevertheless, felt quite free to speculate on the quality of medieval acting, and their conclusions have usually been based, consciously or unconsciously, on an implicit comparison between the crudities of medieval performances and the glories of the Globe. The very scarcity of evidence about acting style during the Middle Ages, for example, led Hardin Craig to his often-quoted conclusion that

> [medieval] religious drama had no dramatic technique or dramatic purpose, and no artistic self-consciousness. . . . This drama had no theory, aimed consciously at no dramatic effects, and when it succeeded, its success came from the import of its message or from the moving quality of some particular story it had to tell. (Craig, pp. 4–5)

How a story told on the stage could have been "moving" on its own merits, irrespective of its interpretation by actors, is a question that seems not to have occurred to Craig. Instead he appears to have believed that medieval plays were written in such a way as to make the difference between the talents of a Bottom the Weaver and the talents of a Richard Burbage undetectable.

Few subsequent commentators have held such a low opinion of the artistry of medieval plays as Craig did, but most have assumed, when it comes to the question of acting styles and abilities, that there were a good many more Bottoms than Burbages on the medieval stage. Allardyce Nicoll, in his *World Drama*, states that "although there may have been a sincerity in the presentation of the parts [in the mystery cycles], we must assume that in many instances the interpretation was naive and ludicrously inadequate" (p. 151). J. W. Robinson, in the most extensive study of the subject to date, which he based on selected stage directions in plays from the twelfth through the sixteenth centuries, concludes that all the plays he examined, including those few which occasionally "gave the players an opportunity to introduce some human, naturalistic touches into their dogmatic expositions of the faith," could be characterized as requiring a "formal and stylised presentation." Robinson finds only slight traces of difference between the acting styles of the earliest and latest of these plays. The actors in the Latin liturgical dramas, he feels, must have employed "gestures and elocution [that were] highly stylized and demonstrative, formal rather than naturalistic" while the actors of mystery plays, even as late as the end of the sixteenth century, were still employing a "ritual" approach to their plays which deliberately "sacrificed dramatic effectiveness for a literal adherence to the action recorded in the gospels." This "formal and ostentatious style of acting" Robinson takes to be the norm of medieval playing, notwithstanding "the quite large number of directions . . . that should probably be interpreted as instructions for naturalistic acting" and that may therefore indicate the existence of a more "mixed style of presentation" (Robinson, "Medieval English Acting," 83–88).

The terminology used by Nicoll and Robinson to describe medieval acting has reappeared in virtually every discussion of the subject since the 1950s, despite the altered perspective which the revival of the mystery cycles in England in that decade brought to the evaluation of medieval drama as a whole. Rosemary Woolf, for example, in her study of the English mystery plays has argued that "pictorial" qualities must have dominated over "dramatic" ones, and that authors and actors alike must have shared "an indifference to . . . inwardness of characterization," since "there are no rounded characters in the mystery plays" (Woolf, Mystery Plays, 98–101). Even Tydeman, despite his complaint about the scarcity of evidence on the subject, agrees that "we may assume that psychological realism was neither expected nor sought after, [and that] it is unlikely that the technique of acting [in the mystery cycles] differed greatly from those employed in the Latin church-drama." Tydeman concludes that "one must assume that convention and tradition governed much of what was seen on the medieval stage, although there were no doubt individuals who stood out for their willingness to play a part to tear a cat in, or for their incompetence" (Tydeman, 213, 215).

There could be no clearer proof than this last remark of the extent to which Peter Quince's rude mechanicals still color our modern image of the medieval actor. If, however, we approach the evidence that does survive with no preconceptions in mind, Shakespearean or otherwise, we may with equal plausibility reach some rather different conclusions than those which have prevailed in the literature until now. I can, perhaps, illustrate this proposition most dramatically by putting one after another the following eyewitness testimonies, deliberately reversing their chronology.

1. 1610 (Oxford)

In the last few days the King's players have been here. They acted to enormous applause to full houses ... and they had tragedies, which they acted with skill and decorum, in which some things, not only speeches but actions too, brought forth tears. ... Moreover, when that famous Desdemona was killed before us by her husband, although she always acted her whole part extremely well, yet when she was killed she was even more moving, for when she fell back upon the bed she implored the pity of the spectators by the very look on her face.[1]

2. 1592 (London)

How would it have joyed brave Talbot, the terror of the French, to think that after he had lien two hundred years in his tomb he should triumph again on the stage, and have his bones new-embalmed with the tears of ten thousand spectators ... who in the tragedian that represents his person imagine they behold him fresh bleeding. (Nashe, *Pierce Penilesse*, 64–65).

3. 1536 (Bourges)

[The performers in the *Acts of the Apostles*] were sage men, who knew so well how to feign through signs and gestures the characters they were representing that most of the audience thought the whole thing was real and not feigned.[2]

4. 1485 (Metz)

A young barber named Lyonard was a very beautiful boy, resembling a beautiful young girl, and he played the part of Saint Barbara so discreetly and devoutly that many spectators wept with compassion.[3]

5. 1468 (Metz)

The part of St. Catherine was performed by a young girl, about 18 years old, who was the daughter of Dediet the glazier, and she played her part very well indeed, to the pleasure and delight of all the audience. Though this girl had 2300 lines in her role, she never stumbled, and she spoke her lines in so lively a manner and so pitifully that she made many people cry.[4]

6. 1420 (Paris)

In the Rue de la Calandre in front of the Palace there was a very touching representation of the Passion of our Lord, done by live actors ... and no man could see this representation without his heart being moved to compassion.[5]

The similarity between these descriptions, originating from five different cities in two different countries over a course of nearly two hundred years, is striking. None of the witnesses could have known the comments of the others, yet they all picked out precisely the same things to remark on in the acting performances they admired, and they used almost the same words to describe them. The audience for *Othello* in Oxford (quotation 1) wept real tears (*lachrymas*) as their tribute to the power of the King's Men's performance, and some of these tears may have been responses to the actual tears on the face of the boy-actor who played Desdemona, since the word used to describe his expression at the moment of Desdemona's death is "imploraret," meaning literally in Latin "to call upon with tears." Nashe's explanation of the "tears" provoked by Shakespeare's *Henry VI, Part One* (quotation 2) is that the actor who played Talbot (probably Richard Burbage[6]) performed the part in so lifelike a manner that the audience was able to imagine that he really was the character he played.

That this attitude toward acting was not a Renaissance discovery is borne out by the praise of a fifteenth-century spectator (quotation 3) for the Bourges actors' ability to persuade their audience into thinking that in their roles in the *Apostles* play they were the "real thing" rather than merely players (*jugeaient la chose estre vraie et no feinte*). The same attitude toward acting is implicit in the Metz chronicler's admiration for the lifelikeness (*vivement*[7]) with which the remarkable teenage St. Catherine so impressed her audience (quotation 5). It evidently made little difference, in either the fifteenth or the sixteenth centuries, whether such a part was played by a boy or a girl, so long as the actor or actress was skilled enough, since the Metz commentator gives equally high marks to the apprentice barber (quotation 4) and to the glazier's daughter (quotation 5), although the young man seems to have excelled at projecting sanctity (*prudement et devotement*) and the young girl at pathos (*piteusement*). Both are given credit for the same ability to move an audience that was displayed a century and a half later by Shakespeare's Desdemona.

Going hand in hand with the emphasis on dramatic realism in these accounts is the consistency with which they dwell on the real-life reactions of the audience. It is, in fact, only by the visible responses of the spectators that these writers are able to authenticate the skills of the actors. Passion plays, saints' lives, and domestic tragedies, whether medieval or Renaissance, all appear to have aimed alike at moving the spectators' emotions, and in particular at making them cry. (We may suppose that if we had similar accounts describing farces and comedies we would find an equivalent emphasis on visible smiles and audible laughter.) Public weeping was much more frequent and socially acceptable, even desirable, in the Middle Ages than it is now. The fourteenth-century *Treatise Against Miracle-Playing*, though antitheatrical in purpose, acknowledges that "ofte sythis by siche myraclis pleying men and wymmen, seynge the passioun of Crist and of hise seyntis, ben mouyd to compassion and deuocion, wepynge bitere teris" (Hudson, 100). And Huizinga has described a fifteenth-century priest who "shed so many tears every time he consecrated the Host that the whole congregation also wept, insomuch that a general wailing was heard as if in the house of one dead" (Huizinga, 174). The role of plays in stimulating such emotions was endorsed in 1449 by Reginald Pecock when he declared that no carved or painted im-

ages of the crucifixion could be as effective as "Whanne a quyk man is
sett in a pley to be hangid nakid on a cros and to be in semyng woundid
and scourgid" (Pecock, I, 221). The wording of the eyewitness accounts
above makes it clear that the tears of the spectators on such occasions
were not generated simply by the "moving quality of the story itself,"
as Craig believed, but by the actors' vivid impersonations of the characters, with whom the audience identified themselves. They *pleuraient de
compassion*" for Saint Barbara when she was acted by Lyonard the barber
in Paris (quotation 4), and their hearts filled with the same emotion for
the unnamed Jesus in Paris (*"n'estoit homme qui veist le mistere a qui
le cueur n'apiteast"*). Only the last description (quotation 6) might be
taken as a tribute to the playwright, or to the story in general, rather than
to the actors, since the play itself is called *"ung moult piteaux mystère
de la passion."* But it is just as likely that the author intended his praise,
like that given to the Bourges *Acts of the Apostles* a century later, as a
compliment to an unusually (or perhaps usually) well-rounded cast,
rather than as a tribute to a single ravishing star.

Then as now, we may note, women's roles, no matter who played
them, seem to have had a better shot at drawing rave reviews from male
critics than men's roles. Indeed, some medieval reports, like many modern reviews, tell us little more about dramatic interpretation than the
fact that the reviewer was smitten by the actress, as in an account written
in 1535 in Grenoble which declares that:

> Françoise Buatier, who played the part of the mother of Christ, through her
> gestures, her voice, her diction, and her delivery succeeded in charming the
> whole audience to the point of exciting a general admiration; she also added
> grace and beauty to her eloquence. (Petit de Julleville, I, 370. My translation)

We may feel equally at home when we discover that the glazier's daughter
who played St. Catherine in Metz worked her charms so successfully that
a young nobleman in the audience named Henri de Latour proposed marriage to her, a proposal which she accepted, thus setting, as Rosamond
Gilder has observed, "a precedent that has been followed ever since"
(Gilder, 84).

It is possible to conclude, then, that descriptions of medieval acting
which rely on such terms as "stylized," "formal," and "ostentatious,"
not to mention "naive" or "incompetent," may be missing an important
point. The point is that however much the medieval actor's methods of
creating character may have differed from those of later theatrical practice, and however old-fashioned they might seem to us today, the goal
of the medieval actor—at least in "serious" roles—was identical to the
goal of every actor at all times: namely, to make it possible for his audience to imagine that he really *was* the character he was playing and to
move the audience's emotions accordingly. The consistency with which
this goal was striven for, and occasionally achieved, is clear from the de-

scriptions quoted above. The goal itself was articulated in the abstract with equal consistency by theoreticians of the arts of oratory and acting from at least the time of Cicero down to that of Shakespeare, in terms which continually stress clarity, naturalness, and appropriateness of imitation:

Cicero: *De Oratore*, 55 B.C.:

> Who is ignorant that the highest power of an orator consists of exciting the minds of men to anger, or to hatred, or to grief, or in recalling them from these more violent emotions to gentleness and compassion. . . . The orator should be moderate in imitation, that the audience may conceive more than they can see represented by him; he ought also to . . . avoid everything offensive or unbecoming in word or act . . . for by action the body talks, so that it is all the more necessary to make it agree with the thought. (Cicero, II, 179)

Le Jeu d'Adam, ca. 1150:

> Adam shall be well trained not to answer too quickly nor too slowly when he has to answer. Not only Adam but all the actors shall be instructed to control their speech and to make their actions appropriate to the matter they speak of. . . . [8]

Shakespeare, *Hamlet*, 1604[?]:

> Suit the action to the word, the word to the action, with this special observance, that you o'erstep not the modesty of nature; for anything so o'erdone is from the purpose of playing, whose end, both at the first and now, was and is, to hold as 'twere the mirror up to nature. (III.ii.17–19)

There is therefore no reason to think that Hamlet was the first stage director to realize that it was only "by the very cunning of the scene" that guilty creatures sitting at a play could be "struck to the soul" (II.-ii.589–91), or that Shakespeare was the first playwright to expect emotionally realistic effects from his players. Nor, for that matter, was he the first to refer to their mastery of this ability as a "cunning," i.e., a "craft" or an "art" (*O.E.D.*, "cunning," sb. 4). The word was, in fact, commonly applied to acting throughout the fifteenth and sixteenth centuries in England. In 1528 an experienced actor, suing an apprentice for trying to start his own company, accused him of falsely claiming to be "skilled in the feat and cunning of playing."[9] And in 1476 the York City Council ordered four of the "most cunning, discrete and able players within the city" to search out candidates for parts in the Corpus Christi Play, to take on "all such as they shall find sufficient in person and cunning," but to discharge "insufficient persons either in cunning, voice, or person" (*REED: York*, I, 109).[10] The data presented so far by the first volumes of the Records of Early English Drama series suggests that payments to such "cunning" performers may have been the rule rather than the exception, and that the leading parts in the civic mystery cycles were staffed, not by Bottom the Weavers, but by experienced players who were at least part-time professionals (see *York*, pp. 69–70, 72, 323; *Coventry*, pp. 59, 61, 292).

Against this cumulative evidence that acting in the Middle Ages was regarded as an art requiring both talent and training, that its principal aim was to move the emotions of an audience, and that it boasted its share of expert practitioners, I can find only two pieces of testimony to the contrary, though both have been made much of by modern commentators. The first, quoted by Grace Frank in *The Medieval French Drama*, is a petition presented to King Richard II in 1378 by the choristers of St. Paul's in London, asking him to "prohibit some *inexpert people* from presenting the history of the Old and New Testament, to the great prejudice of the clergy, who had been at great expense, in order to represent it publicly at Christmas" (Frank, 167; my italics). This undoubtedly refers to the lavish outdoor summer productions performed in Clerkenwell Fields during the latter decades of the fourteenth century, and represents, as Frank notes, a rivalry between the regular clergy and the parish clerks, and probably lay persons as well, over the question of who should have the right to perform religious drama in London. To conclude, however, as Frank does, that most actors in plays which were performed outside the church, in France as well as in England, must have been "inexpert people," is to ignore the motives of envy and rivalry implicit in the document, as well as the fact that, notwithstanding the choristers' petition, the Clerkenwell productions continued to be staged and praised as "highly sumptuous" ("valde sumptuosum") throughout at least the next three decades. In 1390 they even received a gift of £10 toward their expenses from Richard II himself.[11]

The second document, quoted in part by Nicoll as the basis for his conclusion that medieval acting must often have been "ludicrously inadequate," is a denunciation, by the Procurator General of the Parliament of Paris in 1542, of a performance of *The Acts of the Apostles* in the previous year. In that performance, the Procurator claimed, both the production staff (*les entrepreneurs*) and the actors were "an ignorant set of men, artisans and mechanics, who didn't know an A from a B, untrained and inexperienced in playing such pieces before the public." "Their voices," he said, "were poor, their language unfitting, and their pronunciation wretched; they had no idea what they were saying; they put pauses in the middle of sentences, made exclamations out of questions, and made gestures contrary to the meaning of what they said, producing derision in the audience, so that what was intended as edification became a scandal instead" (Petit de Julleville, I, 423; my translation).

Here indeed is the very quintessence of Peter Quince. What Nicoll omits to tell us, however, is that the author of this diatribe was an aristocrat who scorned popular religious entertainment of any kind, one of those whose views eventually prevailed in the parliamentary prohibition of mystery play performances in Paris in 1548. Like the later Puritan opponents of the theatre in England, he accused all such entertainments of diverting the common people—"a half-witted, ignorant lot"—from proper religious observances; of mixing apocryphal stories and lascivious farces with sacred matters; and even of encouraging "adultery and fornication." His immediate purpose in denouncing *The Acts of the Apostles* was to persuade the Parliament to ban a proposed performance for the following year of the *Mystery of the Old Testament*, because he believed the audience to be so stupid ("a faute d'intelligence") that they might be converted to Judaism by it. Such a spokesman was unlikely to have praised even the most artful of mystery play performances. Even if we were to grant his report some degree of truth, we would still have to balance it against the account of the same play's powerful impact on its audience in Bourges six years earlier.

There seems, then, no more reason to weight our estimation of the *quality* of medieval acting in favor of its detractors than there is reason to credit its admirers with total accuracy in their enthusiastic accounts. The same may be said of the *kind* of performance that medieval playwrights and actors strove for. When we look, in the light of the eyewitness testimonies quoted above, at the stage directions on which J. W. Robinson based his study of acting style, we may wonder whether they do not point to a more realistic style than he deduces from them. The direction in the *Jeu d'Adam*, for example, that "whenever anyone shall speak of Paradise he shall look towards it and point it out with his hand," Robinson describes as a call for a "highly stylized and demonstrative" type of acting, one that relied entirely on "simple, direct gestures" (83). Yet when we read this direction in the context of the other rubrics in the play, it becomes apparent that what the playwright is asking for is the expression of the exiled Adam and Eve's feelings of grief, guilt, and loss whenever they speak of their former home, emotions which involve much more than simple, direct gestures:

> Then simulating the greatest possible grief he [the actor playing Adam] shall begin his lament." (*Medieval French Plays*, 24)

> They shall look back often towards Paradise, striking their breasts. . . they shall be seized with violent grief and prostrate themselves on the ground and sitting there they shall beat their breasts and thighs, showing their grief in their actions." (*Medieval French Plays*, 33)

This last rubric is similar to one in the Cornish *Play of the Creation* (1610)—"Eve is sorrowful, teareth her hair, & falleth down upon Adam"—which Robinson refers to as an invitation to the actor to "tear a passion to tatters." No doubt he (or she) may have done so, but it is difficult to believe that any playwright would deliberately invite a style of acting that would make a mockery of his subject, unless he were writing a sophisticated parody like *A Midsummer Night's Dream*. Nor is there any evidence to suggest that medieval or Elizabethan audiences found breast-beating, hair-tearing, or prostration to be anything other than time-tested methods for "simulating the greatest possible grief." These are things that people actually do in real life, and they became mimetic devices by which playwrights like the author of the *Jeu d'Adam* believed that actors could convincingly "show their grief in their actions."

The *Jeu d'Adam*, a vernacular Biblical play dating from the early twelfth century, is often regarded as an anomaly in a period dominated by Latin liturgical drama. Virtually all historians of the liturgical drama have posited a nonnaturalistic acting style for these plays, and some, like Karl Young, have even refused to regard them as plays at all. John Stevens has recently endorsed this verdict by declaring that "it is a safe conjecture that the style of acting was generally restrained and formal even in the larger plays."[12] Yet examples abound in rubrics and descriptions which suggest the opposite. In the *Benediktbeuern Passion Play*, for instance, dating from the early thirteenth century, the actor, or possibly actress, who sang the role of the Virgin Mary is directed to "cry out to the weeping women with every sort of lamentation, bewailing greatly and complaining vehemently" (Bevington, *Medieval Drama*, 220). A "restrained" effect would hardly seem appropriate here. Of a somewhat later *Marienklage* (or *Planctus*) from Bordesholm we hear that "when it is done by good and sincere men, it truly arouses the bystanders to genuine tears and compassion," this despite the fact that its scribe insists that "this complaint is not a stage play (*ludus*) nor a sport (*ludibrium*) but indeed a complaint and a lamentation." Like the Benediktbeuren play, the Bordesholm *Planctus* combined liturgical chant with vernacular melodies, and was performed "in the choir on a slightly raised platform, or outside the church if the weather is good" (Stevens, "Medieval Drama," 40–41). The inclusion of an at least partly lay audience may, in these and other instances, have increased the emotional tone of the performing style. Though it is generally assumed that only men took part in the casts, exceptions did occur, as in a fourteenth-century *Visitatio* in Essen which included both canons, who played the angels, and canonesses, who played the Marys. In this particular case the expertise of the performers may be in some doubt, since they were allowed a book to sing from "if they do not have it by heart and if there is light to read by" (Stevens, "Medieval Drama," 41). Generalizations about the stage effects aimed at in the liturgical drama are difficult to arrive at. A fresh study of the large body of surviving texts might, however, reveal that they are less monochromatic than was once supposed.

The conclusions about the style and quality of medieval acting that I have suggested here are, of course, more applicable to the performers of human parts than to those of divine and diabolic figures. A certain distancing from the audience must have occurred in the performance of the latter, particularly when we keep in mind the use of masks and body-paint, which recent research has indicated may have been far more extensive than previously supposed (Twycross and Carpenter, "Masks"). The actions these figures perform are mythic and larger than life, and the mirror they hold up to the audience reflects not only nature but the supernatural as well. Tyrants and torturers may fall into this category also. Herod raging on the pageant and in the street too is hardly a model of classical decorum. Yet his raging is "in character" as that character was understood by playwrights and audiences: Herod, after all, was in the business of out-tyranting other tyrants, and there is only one way to play such a character. Hamlet's remark about him in his speech to the players is often taken as a jab against medieval acting in general, but its specific target is the bad actor's habit of transferring the traits of one character (an easy one) to other roles for which they are inappropriate. There is no reason to think that this happened any more or less frequently in the medieval theatre than it did in Shakespeare's. A competent actor of Herod or Satan must have sought to terrify his audience, just as a competent actor of Jesus or Mary sought to move them to pity, and a competent actor of Peter or Thomas sought to move them to self-examination and contrition. Medieval plays contain a variety of extreme emotions, and the actor's primary job was to generate that emotion in his audience which most centrally motivated his character.

In the history of Western theatre, the goal of the actor appears always to have been the same, namely, to enable the audience to see, in Bertram Joseph's pithy phrase, "the very character embodied on the stage" (Joseph, 397). When we read histories of acting, we find that every actor claims to be more "natural" or more "lifelike" than his predecessor, and it soon becomes apparent that what he is claiming is not a different goal but a superior technique or a superior talent. Brecht, with his doctrine of "alienating" or "distancing" the audience, must be seen as an exception to this rule, yet the widespread misinterpretation of Brecht's own plays by actors and audiences alike[13] may make us wonder whether actors, so long as they are human beings, can ever be made to abandon the mimetic instincts which Aristotle thought to be such an ingrained part of human nature. We have, perhaps, been misled by some of the apparently Brechtian elements in medieval playscripts[14] into thinking that the ultimate effect of medieval plays upon their audiences was fundamentally different from that of great plays at any time. If that is so, then we should possibly throw away the notion that the goals of medieval acting were necessarily different in kind, or more limited, than those of other periods, and get on with the study of how these goals were taught, executed, and appreciated by their audiences.

NOTES

1. "Postremis his diebus adfuerunt Regis Actores Scenici. Egerunt cum applausu maximo, pleno theatro . . . Habuerunt et Tragoedias, quas decore et apte agebant. In quibus non solum dicendo sed etiam faciendo quaedam lachrymas movebant. At vero Desdemona illa apud nos a marito occisa quanquam optime semper causam egit interfecta tamen magis movebat; cum in lecto decumbens spectantium misericordiam ipso vultu imploraret." From a letter by Henry Jackson, dated September 1610, in Corpus Christi College, Oxford, MS. 304, fols. 83–84. My translation. This letter is quoted by Gamiani Salgado, *Eyewitnesses of Shakespeare* (London, 1975), 30.

2. ". . . hommes graves qui savoient si bien feindre, par signes et gestes, les personnages qu'ils représentaient, que la plupart des assistants jugeaient la chose estre vraie et non feinte." L. Petit de Julleville, *Les Mysteres* (Paris, 1880), II, 133. My translation.

3. "Un jeune fils barbier nomme Lyonard, etait un tres beau fils et ressemblait une belle jeune fille; il fit le personnage de sainte Barbe si prudement et devotement, que plusieurs personnes pleuraient de compassion." Petit de Julleville, I, 370. My translation.

4. "Le role de la sainte fut rempli par une jeune fillette, agée d'environ dix-huit ans, qui recita sans broncher deux mille trois cents vers et parla si vivement et si piteusement qu'elle provoque plusieurs gens a pleurer." Petit de Julleville, I, 370. Translation adapted from Rosamond Gilder, *Enter the Actress* (London, 1931).

5. "Et fut fait en la rue de la Kalende devant le Palais, ung moult piteaux mystère de la passion de Nostre Seigneur au vif . . . et n'estoit homme qui veist le mistere a qui le cueur n'apiteast." *Journal d'un bourgeois de Paris 1405–1449*, ed. by A. Tuety (Paris, 1881), p. 144; translation by Janet Shirley, *A Parisian Journal 1405–1449* (Oxford, 1968).

6. See *The Riverside Shakespeare*, ed. G. B. Evans (Boston, 1974), p. 1837. Quotations from Shakespeare in this essay are from this edition.

7. Randle Cotgrave's *Dictionarie of the French and English Tongues* (London, 1611) gives "Livelily" as the first definition for *"vivement"* (facsimile reprint, Columbia, S.C., 1950, n.p.).

8. *Medieval French Plays*, trans. Richard Axton and John Stevens (Oxford, 1971), p. 7.

9. See Alan S. Downer, "The Tudor Actor: A Taste of His Quality," *Theatre Notebook* 5 (1951), 76–81.

10. A similar formula was used by the Durham Weavers' Guild in 1450: see J. J. Anderson, "The Durham Corpus Christi Play," *REED Newsletter* 2 (1981), 1–3.

11. See Tydeman, *Theatre in the Middle Ages*, p. 198; Stanley J. Kahrl, *Traditions of Medieval Drama* (London, 1974), pp. 48–49.

12. John Stevens, "Medieval Drama," in *The New Grove Dictionary of Music and Musicians*, ed. Stanley Sadie (London, 1980), XII, 21–58. See also Stevens's comments on the nondramatic nature of the music of these plays in "Music in Some Early Medieval Plays," *Studies in the Arts: Proceedings of the St. Peter's College Literary Society*, ed. Francis Warner (Oxford, 1968), pp. 21–40.

13. See Martin Esslin, *Brecht: The Man and His Work* (New York, 1974), pp. 226–30.

14. On these similarities, see Martin Stevens, "Illusion and Reality in the Medieval Drama," *College English* 32 (1970), 448–64.

WORKS CITED AND SUGGESTED READING

Manuscript Sources

Letter by Henry Jackson in Corpus Christi College, Oxford, MS. 304, fols. 83–84.

Printed Works

Anderson, J. J. "The Durham Corpus Christi Play," *REED Newsletter* 2 (1981), 1–3.

Axton, Richard, and Stevens, John, trans. *Medieval French Plays*. Oxford, 1971.

Bevington, David. "Discontinuity in Medieval Acting Tradition," in *The Elizabethan Theatre V*, ed. G. R. Hibbard. Hamden, Conn., 1975, 1–16.

———, ed. *Medieval Drama*. Boston: Houghton Mifflin, 1975.

Carpenter, Sarah. "Morality-Play Characters," *Medieval English Theatre*, 5 (1983), 53–57.

Cicero. *De Oratore*, ed. H. Rackham, Loeb Classical Library (Cambridge, Mass., 1942), II, 179.

Cotgrave, Randle. *Dictionarie of the French and English Tongues*. London, 1611. Facsimile reprint, Columbia, S.C., 1950, n.p.

Craig, Hardin. *English Religious Drama*. Oxford University Press, 1955.

Davidson, Clifford. "Gesture in Medieval Drama with Special Reference to the Doomsday Plays in the Middle English Cycles," *EDAM Newsletter*, 6 (1983), 8–17.

de Julleville, L. Petit. *Les Mystères*, 2 Vols. Paris, 1880.

Downer, Alan S. "The Tudor Actor: A Taste of His Quality," *Theatre Notebook*, 5 (1951), 76–81.

Esslin, Martin. *Brecht: The Man and His Work*. New York, 1974.

Frank, Grace. *The Medieval French Drama*. Oxford, 1954.

Hudson, Anne, ed. *Selections from English Wycliffite Writings*. Cambridge, 1978.

Huizinga, J. *The Waning of the Middle Ages*, trans. by F. Hopman. London, 1924.

Joseph, Bertram. *The Tragic Actor*. London, 1959.

Journal d'un bourgeois de Paris 1405–1449, ed. by A. Tuety. Paris, 1881.

Kahrl, Stanley J. *Traditions of Medieval Drama*. London, 1974.

Mills, David. "Characterization in the English Mystery Cycles," *Medieval English Theatre*, 5 (1983), 5–17.

Nashe, Thomas. *Pierce Penilesse His Supplication to the Devil* (London, 1592), ed. Stanley Wells, *Thomas Nashe: Selected Writings*. Cambridge, Mass., 1965.

Nicoll, Allardyce. *World Drama*. London, 1950.

Pecock, Reginald. *The Repressor of Over Much Blaming of the Clergy*, ed. Churchill Babington. London, 1860.

The Riverside Shakespeare, ed. G. B. Evans. Boston: Houghton Mifflin, 1974.

Robinson, J. W. "Medieval English Acting," *Theatre Notebook*, 13 (1959), 83–88.

Salgado, Gamini. *Eyewitnesses of Shakespeare*. London, 1975.

Shirley, Janet, ed. *A Parisian Journal 1405–1449*. Oxford, 1968.

Stevens, John. "Medieval Drama," in *The New Grove Dictionary of Music and Musicians*, ed. Stanley Sadie, London, 1980. XII, 21–58.

———. "Music in Some Early Medieval Plays," *Studies in the Arts: Proceedings of the St. Peter's College Literary Society*, ed. Francis Warner. Oxford, 1968, 21–40.

Stevens, Martin. "Illusion and Reality in the Medieval Drama," *College English*, 32 (1970), 448–64.

Twycross, Meg, and Carpenter, Sarah. "Masks in Medieval English Theatre," *Medieval English Theatre*, III (1981), 7–44, 69–113.
Tydeman, William. *The Theatre in the Middle Ages*. Cambridge University Press, 1978.
Woolf, Rosemary. *The English Mystery Plays*. Berkeley and Los Angeles, 1972.

Contributors

DONALD C. BAKER is Professor of English Emeritus at the University of Colorado, Boulder, and Professor of English at the University of Wuhan Wuhan, Hubei, People's Republic of China. He served recently as Fulbright lecturer at the Faculté des Lettres et Sciences Humaines at Kairouan, Tunisia. He has published widely on medieval drama and Chaucer, and, along with John L. Murphy and Louis B. Hall, is editor of *The Digby Plays* for The Early English Text Society.

MARIANNE G. BRISCOE is Director of Corporate Relations at The University of Chicago. She is preparing the Oxford City and Oxfordshire volumes for the Records of Early English Drama and the volume on *artes praedicandi* for Catholic University of Louvain's series *Typologie des sources du moyen âge occidental*.

LAWRENCE M. CLOPPER is Professor of English at Indiana University. He has edited the Chester records for Records of Early English Drama and published articles on the medieval drama in *Modern Philology, Modern Language Quarterly, Chaucer Review,* and *Theatre Notebook.* He is completing a book entitled *The Search for William Langland.*

JOHN C. COLDEWEY is Associate Professor of English at the University of Washington. His publications include articles on medieval drama, neo-Latin drama, and Shakespeare; with Brian P. Copenhaver he has edited and translated William Mewe's *Pseudomagia* and two volumes in the *Renaissance Latin Drama in England* series. He is REED editor of Nottingham and of Essex, and editor of *Modern Language Quarterly.*

JOHN R. ELLIOTT, JR., is Professor of English at Syracuse University. He is author of *Playing God: Medieval Mysteries on the Modern Stage* and is editor of REED: Oxford University.

ALEXANDRA F. JOHNSTON is Professor of English at the University of Toronto and Principal of Victoria College. She is the General Editor of Records of Early English Drama. She edited the first collection of records for the series, the York Records, with Dr. Margaret Rogerson and is now completing editions of the records of Berkshire and Buckinghamshire for REED.

STANLEY J. KAHRL is Professor of English at the Ohio State University, where from 1969–78 he served as Director of the Center for Medieval and Renaissance Studies. He is author of *Traditions of Medieval English Drama* and editor of a Renaissance jest-book, a collection of articles on Old English, and *Collections VIII* for the Malone Society. He has also served as editor for the Medieval Supplement to *Research Opportunities in Renaissance Drama* (RORD) and the *Old English Newsletter.*

LYNETTE MUIR was formerly Reader in French and Director of the Centre for Medieval Studies in the University of Leeds, England. Now retired, she continues to work in comparative medieval studies, especially drama. Besides many articles and translations her publications include *Liturgy and Drama in the Anglo-Norman Adam* and *Literature and Society in Medieval France.*

ALAN H. NELSON is Professor of English Literature at the University of California, Berkeley. He is coeditor (with Jerome Taylor) of *Medieval English Drama: Essays Critical and Contextual;* author of *The Medieval English Stage: Corpus Christi Pageants and Plays [Fulgens and Lucres* and *Nature];* and editor of *Cambridge* for *Records of Early English Drama.*

ROBERT POTTER is Professor of Dramatic Art at the University of California, Santa Barbara, and the author of *The English Morality Play*. He is an active playwright, and author of fourteen original plays and stage adaptations produced at various professional and university theatres in the United States, Canada, and England.

RICHARD RASTALL is Senior Lecturer in Music and a member of the Centre for Medieval Studies at the University of Leeds. He is the author of *The Notation of Western Music* and articles on minstrelsy and on music in the English biblical plays.

PAMELA SHEINGORN is Professor of Art and Chair of the Art Department at Baruch College of the City University of New York. She has published articles on art and drama in the Middle Ages, as well as reviews of modern productions of medieval drama. She is the author of *The Easter Sepulchre in England*.

Index

Acting: in *Acts of the Apostles*, 245, 246; characteristics of, 238–39, 240–43, 244, 245, 247–48; in Corpus Christi plays, 244; in cycle plays, 239, 240, 244–45; in liturgical plays, 240, 247; in passion plays, 242; in *planctus*, 247; in *Play of the Creation*, 246–47; and Records of Early English Drama, 244–45; in religious plays, 239; in saints' plays, 242; in *Visitatio*, 247. *See also* Traveling players

Acts of the Apostles, The: acting in, 245, 246; staging of, 67

Adam, 57

Allyn, William, 116

Ashmole fragment, 60–61

Bale, John, 153

Baptism plays, 109, 130n.11

Benediktbeuern Passion Play, 247

Beverley plays, 130nn. 14, 20, 219–20

Biblical plays (English), 9; characteristics of, 56; evidence for, 6; financing of, 69; and French biblical plays, 56, 62; language of, 57–61; and laypersons, 107; music in, 200; organization of, 69; staging of, 67, 68; subject matter of, 61–62, 63, 64–66; types of, 6, 10–11; in York, 122. *See also specific plays*

Biblical plays (French): characteristics of, 56; and English biblical plays, 56, 62; financing of, 68–70, 71; organization of, 68–72; staging of, 67–68, 73n.17; subject matter of, 62–64, 65–66. *See also specific plays*

Bilingual plays, 58. *See also specific plays*

Black Death, 79, 80, 97n.3

Blessed Apple Tree, The, 48–49

Blomefylde, Myles, 21, 24, 25, 32

Bodleian manuscript e Museo 160 plays. *See specific plays*

Boethius, Anicius Manlius Severinus, and music, 193, 194, 195, 196–97

Burial and Resurrection of Christ, The: history of, 35–36; influences on, 35, 36, 37; style of, 36, 37; textual problems in, 35, 36–37, 38n.5

Bynham, Thomas, 131n.28, 153, 170n.1

Cambridge Prologue, The, 58, 59, 60, 61

Castle of Perseverance: and sermons, 159–60, 161; staging of, 8–9, 43, 67, 225

Cercle magique, Le (Rey-Flaud), 43

Cheke, John, 141

Chester: and economic conditions, 103–5, 106–7, 129n.5; Great Charter of, 102, 105,

129n.3. *See also specific headings*

Chester plays: changes in, 102, 105, 107, 128, 129n.8; characteristics of, 11, 45, 61; and clergy, 113, 130n.20; editions of, 221; evidence for, 103; history of, 111, 112; influences on, 64; language of, 60; music in, 193, 195–96, 200, 205–7, 208, 209, 210, 212, 215nn. 18, 19, 21; staging of, 220, 221, 232; "superstition" in, 107–11, 129n.9, 130n.10. *See also* Cycle plays

Chief Pre-Shakespearean Dramas (Adams), 41–42

Christmas Watch, 103

Civic plays: and clergy, 114, 116–18; and economic conditions, 106–7; evidence for, 103; history of, 112; and laypersons, 107; in Norwich, 127; and parish plays, 8; staging of, 220

Clergy, 151; and Chester plays, 113, 130n.20; and civic plays, 114, 116–18; and Corpus Christi plays, 117–18, 131n.22; and creed plays, 118; and cycle plays, 118; and Pater Noster plays, 118; and processions, 113, 118, 125, 128. *See also specific members of the clergy*

College plays. *See* University plays

Community plays: characteristics of, 12; evidence for, 6; types of, 6, 9. *See also specific types of community plays*

Confrérie de la Passion, 68–69

Conversion of St. Paul, The: history of, 25; and *Killing of the Children*, 28; language of, 24–25; and *Play of the Sacrament*, 34; staging of, 21, 23–24, 25, 28; textual problems in, 21–25, 34

Cornish plays: characteristics of, 45, 64, 73n.13; staging of, 67, 220, 226

Corpus Christi plays: acting in, 244; characteristics of, 12, 46; in Chester, 103; and clergy, 117–18, 131n.22; and craft guilds, 86–87, 89, 105; evidence for, 11, 86; in Exeter, 131n.22; as generic term, 11, 45; in Ipswich, 127; and laypersons, 119; in Lincoln, 113–14, 121, 122, 128, 130n.21; and passion plays, 46; and religious guilds, 122; types of, 11–12; and Whitsun plays, 105–6, 111, 130n.13; in York, 244. *See also specific plays*

Coventry plays: characteristics of, 11; and craft guilds, 120; editions of, 221; evidence for, 111; and Franciscans, 114; history of, 128; and laypersons, 119–20; music in, 193, 200, 202–5, 209, 212, 214n.2, 215nn. 14, 15, 16, 21, 216n.23;